# THE IRISH REVOLUTION

**GLUCKSMAN**
**IRISH DIASPORA**

# The Irish Revolution

*A Global History*

*Edited by*

Patrick Mannion *and* Fearghal McGarry

❧

NEW YORK UNIVERSITY PRESS
New York

NEW YORK UNIVERSITY PRESS
New York
www.nyupress.org

References to Internet websites (URLs) were accurate at the time of writing. Neither the author nor New York University Press is responsible for URLs that may have expired or changed since the manuscript was prepared.

Library of Congress Cataloging-in-Publication Data
Names: Mannion, Patrick, editor. | McGarry, Fearghal, editor.
Title: The Irish Revolution : a global history /
[edited by] Patrick Mannion and Fearghal McGarry.
Description: New York : New York University Press, [2022] |
Series: The Glucksman Irish diaspora series | Collection of essays by Martyn Frampton
and 11 others. | Includes bibliographical references and index.
Identifiers: LCCN 2021036241 | ISBN 9781479808892 (hardback) | ISBN 9781479835256
(paperback) |ISBN 9781479808915 (ebook) | ISBN 9781479808908 (ebook other)
Subjects: LCSH: Ireland—History—War of Independence, 1919–1921—Influence. |
Ireland—Foreign public opinion—History—20th century. | Ireland—History—Easter Rising,
1916—Influence. | Ireland—History—Civil War, 1922–1923—Influence. |
Anti-imperialist movements—History—20th century. | Nationalism—Ireland—
History—20th century. | Irish question.
Classification: LCC DA962 .I78 2022 | DDC 941.5082/1—dc23/eng/20220118
LC record available at https://lccn.loc.gov/2021036241

New York University Press books are printed on acid-free paper, and their binding materials are chosen for strength and durability. We strive to use environmentally responsible suppliers and materials to the greatest extent possible in publishing our books.

Manufactured in the United States of America

10 9 8 7 6 5 4 3

Also available as an ebook

# CONTENTS

# Introduction

PATRICK MANNION AND FEARGHAL McGARRY

Our dream is a world-wide organisation pledged and controlled from Home working in concert and with single purpose along clearly defined lines with a plan of campaign whereby we can meet the enemy not alone in Ireland but all over the globe. Thus only can Britain be shewn the power of Ireland. . . . To Australia, Canada, South Africa, India, Egypt, and Moscow our men must go to make common cause against our common foe.
—Harry Boland, revolutionary, to Joe McGarrity, 3 August 1920[1]

When I went to Ireland, I went not only to investigate the facts but to interpret them. I saw the situation very like the situation in Finland that we have long been familiar with; like the situation in Bohemia, the Jugo-Slav situation, the Schleswig situation, the Armenian situation, the Alsace-Lorraine situation—the situation of a people that had long been imperialized struggling to get for themselves conditions of self-development that they could not get without a new constitution—a new constitution that they could only get by securing independence.
—Francis Hackett, journalist, "Evidence on Conditions in Ireland," 1921[2]

Harry Boland's grandiose plans for a global revolutionary movement were not achieved, but the efforts of Irish republicans to internationalize their struggle met with considerable success, as Francis Hackett's testimony indicates, tilting the scales of an otherwise one-sided fight. How important were international factors in shaping the revolution that took place in Ireland between 1916 and 1923? What impact did the conflict have beyond Irish shores? What role did Ireland's global diaspora play in determining its outcome? Why did the War of Independence attract the attention of radicals, journalists, policemen, and many others with no direct connection to Ireland, across much of the world? What legacy resulted from the fleeting prominence of the Irish question as one of the most debated political issues of the day? These questions lie at the heart of *The Irish Revolution: A Global History*.

How does a global history differ from conventional approaches? Although historians are aware of the role of outside events in shaping the War of Independence, most narratives of that conflict are confined within Irish (or British) borders. Accounts of the Irish Revolution chart a series of events centering on Ireland: the Easter Rising of 1916, the 1918 general election, the formation of Dáil Éireann, the guerrilla war against the British state, efforts to establish an Irish counter-state, and the partition of the island, culminating in the creation of a self-governing southern state in 1922. The end result is a War of Independence narrated "in a claustrophobic Anglo-Irish setting, with the global war a mere backdrop to the drama in Ireland."[3] County studies—the predominant framework for studies of the revolution—reconstruct in rich detail how the shift from popular support for Home Rule to militant republicanism played out. But describing how historical processes unfolded within a particular area is not necessarily the same thing as analyzing the causes of that change. Few studies of the Irish Revolution devote much attention to the impact in Ireland of factors such as the postwar collapse of Europe's empires, the redrawing of national boundaries to accommodate new republics, the strengthening of ethnic nationalism by mass suffrage, the Russian Revolution, and a wider British imperial crisis spanning Egypt to India.

The focus on IRA violence in popular and scholarly accounts, a perspective reinforced by the release of valuable archival material from the Military Service Pensions collection and Bureau of Military History, has reinforced public understanding of the struggle for independence as a primarily military conflict.[4] By foregrounding the impact of small-scale events—ambushes and the burning of empty barracks—over popular mobilization, elections, strikes, and other protests, this approach marginalizes the importance of nonviolent forms of resistance. Political and state commemoration in Ireland during the current Decade of Centenaries has also tended to focus on the "raids and rallies" that preoccupied nationalist accounts in the years after independence. In contrast, studies that move beyond narrating such events provide greater insight into overlooked aspects such as the roles played by women and the importance of political thought in the making of the Irish Revolution.[5]

Whereas the centenary of the Easter Rising saw much emphasis placed on its international context, not only by foregrounding the importance of the First World War and support from America, but also through global participation in its remembrance, the War of Independence continues to be remembered in more insular terms. Although the historians on the Expert Advisory Group on Centenary Commemorations (EAG), whose advice shaped the Irish government's commemorative program, identified two global events as bookending the "Significant Historical Events and Themes" of 1918–1923 (the end of the First World War and Irish membership in the League of Nations), each of the eight intervening events suggested for commemoration occurred within Ireland. Moreover, the eleven events identified to mark the Independence Struggle 1919–1921 occurred within Ireland (or Britain).[6] These include the convening of Dáil Éireann; Éamon de Valera's election as president; the death of hunger striker Terence MacSwiney; Bloody Sunday; the burning of Cork; the Government of Ireland Act, which partitioned Ireland; and the Truce of July 1921.

This commemorative program highlights the difficulty of narrating the Irish Revolution in a way that makes visible the role of global forces. In reality, these events were intimately bound up with external pressures, most obviously the destabilizing impact of the First World War. Called immediately after the armistice, the 1918 general election that provided Dáil Éireann's mandate was a wartime event, its results delayed until late December to allow soldiers' ballots to be counted. The expansion of the UK electorate, from which Sinn Féin benefited, was a consequence of the war, as was the issue most responsible for Sinn Féin's emergence as a mass movement: its leadership of a popular campaign against conscription in April 1918. Central to Sinn Féin's election manifesto was an appeal for a mandate to secure a place for Ireland at the Paris Peace Conference. The iconic documents proclaimed at Dáil Éireann's first meeting (the Declaration of Independence, Message to the Free Nations of the World, and Democratic Programme) were calibrated to appeal to international as much as domestic opinion. De Valera spent most of his term as president in the United States. But he was not, as stated by the EAG, elected president of Ireland on

1 April 1919, but rather was chosen as president of the Dáil ministry. His more impressive title was invented, for propagandistic purposes, by Irish American supporters to add luster to his American tour, which succeeded in raising vast funds, focusing international attention on Ireland, and packing stadiums across the country.

While Terence MacSwiney's death was felt keenly in Ireland, it was the "worldwide sympathy for Sinn Féin" resulting from international press coverage of his seventy-four-day hunger strike that proved "a pivotal moment in the War of Independence."[7] MacSwiney is described as "a forgotten hero" in some Irish accounts, and his remarkable stature as a global icon of the Irish struggle overshadowed that of better-known republicans at home.[8] Reprisals such as Bloody Sunday and the burning of Cork by Black and Tans and Auxiliaries were utterly counterproductive for their international as much as their domestic consequences, provoking global condemnation of Britain's conduct of the war. The IRA's campaign, which inflicted comparatively few casualties on Crown forces, was less successful militarily than as a propaganda war: it provoked responses—from internment to reprisals—that many people in England, Scotland, and Wales found repugnant, while international press coverage had a devastating impact on Britain's global reputation. For many British politicians, "the most discomfiting feature of events in Ireland was that tactics of imperial repression usually concealed were now being documented and described in the daily press."[9] The condemnation of reprisals by conservative as well as liberal newspapers in Britain (and America) prompted concerns about both the morality and the efficacy of David Lloyd George's Irish policy, undermining his government's resolve to sustain its counterinsurrectionary campaign despite increasing military successes in the final months of the conflict.[10]

An awareness that it was losing the propaganda war, particularly in the United States, explains the British government's humiliating decision to negotiate with a movement it had only recently condemned as a "murder gang." The settlement that emerged was shaped by international pressures and imperial calculations. The fateful decision to devolve powers to a Unionist-controlled Northern Ireland (rather than merely excluding Ulster from the new southern Irish state) resulted, in part, from a concern to present the settlement as conforming to the gospel of self-determination, while pressure from the United States and the British Empire contributed to London's decision to concede an Irish dominion, a form of statehood defined in the treaty's first article of agreement as having "the same constitutional status" as Canada, Australia, New Zealand, and South Africa. Explaining the necessity for this unpopular concession at Westminster, Winston Churchill noted how Britain's "great interests . . . in India and in Egypt," the Dominions, and the United States had been damaged "by the loud insistent outcry raised by the Irish race all over the world."[11] The "settlement" in Ireland, moreover, was one of several initiatives, ranging from Egypt to Palestine, intended to restore stability to a troubled empire. The primary rationale behind these new forms of statehood devised by London in the aftermath of the First World War was to contain nationalist demands within a reconfigured imperial framework rather than to satisfy local democratic aspirations.[12]

Foregrounding the significance of these global contexts, this volume argues not that what Irish nationalists did in Ireland was not crucial to achieving independence, but rather that much of the importance of their actions—and those of the British—stemmed from their impact abroad. As Michael Collins advised the Dáil's representative in Rome, "Real progress is much more to be estimated by what is thought abroad than by what is thought at home."[13] Irish republicans demonstrated ingenuity and agency in their sophisticated efforts to project their conflict on the global stage. The most innovative aspect of their strategy lay not in the development of guerrilla war (used by the Boers against the British in the early twentieth century) but in the combination of this largely symbolic violence, intended to focus global opinion on Ireland, with an audacious claim to sovereignty symbolized by the establishment of a revolutionary government whose most successful components were its outward-facing departments of Propaganda and Foreign Affairs.[14] As the commander-in-chief in Ireland, General Nevil Macready, acknowledged, "This propaganda business is the strongest weapon [Sinn Féin] has."[15]

## Writing Ireland's Global Revolution

What methodologies have we drawn on to explore how the interplay of local, national, and international factors shaped revolutionary change?

"Playing with scales," by applying comparative, transnational, and global approaches, provides a range of perspectives and time frames to enable us to see how, and when, power was contested across a variety of political and geographic spaces.[16]

Enabling the Irish case to be considered alongside analogous conflicts, comparative approaches are useful in assessing how deep-rooted structural forces effected political change. The postwar experiences of the Irish part of the United Kingdom bear comparison with other "shatter zones" of empire in central and eastern Europe where the armistice, rather than leading to peace, generated new forms of paramilitary, communal, and ethno-nationalist violence that blurred conventional distinctions between combatants and civilians.[17] Points of difference can also prove illuminating. The formation of postwar republics across central and eastern Europe, carved from the territory of defeated empires with the support of the Allies, provides an obvious frame of reference for considering not only the timing but also the more limited outcome of Irish efforts to achieve self-determination. Ireland's position within an empire that emerged victorious from the First World War prompts comparisons with contemporaneous anticolonial movements, comparisons that were often overlooked both by "revisionist" historians wary of applying colonial perspectives to Ireland (given its formal integration within the UK state) and by historians of empire and anticolonialism who generally excluded Ireland from their analyses.[18] Regardless of their accuracy, such parallels, as our contributors explore, loomed larger in the consciousness of Irish and other contemporary revolutionaries than historians later recognized.

Comparative approaches also facilitate analysis of emotive issues such as violence. The low level of fatalities in revolutionary Ireland reminds us how potentially more lethal conflict, notably between Catholics and Protestants, was averted. While extensive historiographical debate has focused on several notorious incidents, notably the killing of Protestants by republicans in west Cork, the question of why much greater levels of violence did not occur has received little attention. Geopolitical factors, for example, mitigated the level of destabilization that led to the mass violence and forced population transfers that accompanied partition in the Ottoman Empire or, later, India. Comparative research, including recent work on gendered violence, suggests the need to better understand the importance of restraints on violence, including culturally determined influences that often transcended national boundaries.[19] As Tim Wilson's study of the role of language and religion in structuring communal conflict in Ulster and Silesia suggests, such wide-lensed research may shed more light on revolutionary violence than further forensic reconstructions of atypical acts of sectarian conflict.[20]

Transnational approaches provide an effective means of gauging the significance of contemporary connections. The contention that historical processes are not merely "made in different places but constructed in the movement between places, sites and regions" is a thread running through the essays collected here.[21] By making visible transnational interactions between people, networks, and movements, the biographical approach adopted by several contributors provides a useful model for interpreting connections and parallels "throughout the globe as part of a synchronous anti-imperial moment."[22] It also highlights how specific postwar sites, such as London, Paris, and New York, acted as global hubs of anti-imperialism, promoting social, intellectual, and political interchange between revolutionaries from diverse backgrounds.[23]

Heeding D. H. Akenson's call to decenter Irish history, contributors to this collection have adopted a variety of spatial frameworks to analyze where revolution occurred and to assess the impact of transnational activism on Irish (and other) nationalisms and identities. The "Irish world"—places of diasporic settlement across the globe and, above all, the United States—provides the most important of these spaces. The "British world" offers another vital context for analyzing Ireland's global revolution. As Akenson observed, "The spread and evolution of Irish nationalism as a global system was largely dependent upon the existence of two expansive empires: that of the United Kingdom and that of the United States."[24] In avowedly Protestant imperial outposts such as Australia and New Zealand, where Catholics were tainted with charges of disloyalty following the Easter Rising, Irish nationalist aims were articulated in a more restrained fashion than in the United States. Emphasizing this diversity among diasporic Irish communities, Tim Meagher has cautioned against "essentializing a global Irishness, suggesting that the Irish in Australia, the United States or Britain, are merely versions of the Irish in Ireland."[25] Several contributors to this volume note the

importance of connections between diasporic outposts that often organized and acted independently of control from Dublin.

Nor should the "Irish world" be seen as exclusively nationalist.
Countervailing currents, including unionist, Orange, and imperialist
discourses and practices, must equally inform any understanding of Ireland's global revolution. Opposition to Irish self-determination across
Britain and the Anglosphere deserves greater attention in Irish-centered
and diasporic studies. Mirroring their republican rivals, Irish unionists toured the United States, celebrating Britain's historic links with
North America, while the Orange Order mobilized fraternal support
in dominions such as Canada and Australia.[26] After the revolution,
policemen, officials, and other loyal "refugees" departed Ireland for new
lives in Britain or its empire: their involvement in colonial policing and
administration, through "Irish" forces such as the British Palestine Gendarmerie, continued a long tradition of imperial service. While their
experiences were overlooked by post-independence narratives, recent
research on transnational imperial careers has brought into focus the
impact of Irish participation in the British imperial project.[27]

The British Empire also provided fertile ground for cultivating soli-
darities between anticolonial movements that, as several contributors
explore, looked to Irish republicanism as an exemplar of successful resistance. Radicals dedicated to causes such as socialism and suffrage forged
transnational connections across the British world. Sir Henry Wilson,
Chief of the Imperial General Staff, linked the domestic challenge from
Irish republicans with labor unrest in Britain, Bolshevism, and global
anticolonial agitation: Britain, he noted in his diary, "is fighting New
York & Cairo & Calcutta & Moscow who are only using Ireland as a
tool & lever against England, & nothing but determined shooting on
our part is any use."[28] Imagined or real, these connections shaped British decision making as to how the Irish war should be conducted and
concluded, with the implications for imperial rule in Egypt or India
frequently cited by figures such as Wilson: "If we lose Ireland we have
lost the Empire."[29] Britain's crisis of empire also limited the manpower,
resources, and political capital expended on Ireland.[30] Whether imperialist or anticolonial, these contemporary actors had a more integrated
worldview than their later historians.

The Irish diaspora was a vast and diverse entity. Between 1801 and 1921, some eight million people left Ireland, while their children and grandchildren often identified strongly with their ancestral homeland. For many, emigration was permanent, but the flow of people, money, and ideas was by no means one way.[31] A large proportion of Ireland's revolutionary leaders spent significant time outside of Ireland. Sojourns abroad, particularly in the United States, were frequent, and many people from ordinary backgrounds lived transnational lives. Although the Irish diaspora, particularly during the postwar era of unprecedented political mobilization, has been the subject of an extensive historiography (considered in the next section), the focus of this literature on the relationship between emigrant communities and their host societies has limited analysis of how diasporic nationalism, as an "imaginative" endeavor, contributed to a transatlantic dynamic of Irish nationalism.[32] Similarly, despite acknowledging the importance of the diaspora in shaping nationalism in Ireland, few studies of Irish nationalism assess how these influences and experiences shaped political thought and activism in Ireland.[33] Bridging the gap between the sophisticated historiographies of the Irish Revolution and diaspora, which developed largely in isolation to one another, global approaches enable us to explore how these important connections operated across the Irish world.

Ultimately, transnational approaches should achieve more than extending an Irish-centric focus from island to globe. Characterizing the "popular diasporic tendency to explore 'Irish people' scattered across the British world" as "a kind of ethnic trainspotting," Keith Jeffery urged greater attention to the role of "*Ireland* itself in that world." Just as Irish nationalist discourse drew on Boer nationalism or the Austro-Hungarian dual monarchy to articulate nationalist aspirations, a wide range of radicals and reactionaries engaged imaginatively with the Irish question for similar purposes. By making visible what Jeffery described as the "interconnectedness" of Irish experiences with those of other movements, and by highlighting how Irish nationalisms were shaped by contingency, reflecting the environments the Irish found themselves in, a wider canvas enables greater engagement with universal themes such as gender, class, and race. Making sense of revolutionary change in Ireland requires an understanding not only of the revolution in Ireland but of how the wider world was changing. In its precociousness, scale, and reach, Irish republicanism presents a compelling case study of the increasingly global character of twentieth-century nationalist movements.

Global approaches facilitate reassessment of temporal, as well as spatial, frameworks. In seeking to explain change, historians are wired to look back across time rather than out across space: our expertise lies more in the diachronic study of specific places than in analyzing moments of time over expansive spaces. The revolution in Ireland, for example, is more readily interpreted in terms of proximate cause—whether the Easter Rising, Ulster Crisis, and late nineteenth-century cultural revival, on the one hand, or the changes wrought by the Famine, including the emergence of Fenianism—than the sudden impact of the "Wilsonian moment" in 1919. Without dismissing the influence of these antecedents, an uncritical acceptance of nationalist chronologies accords too much weight to the legitimizing claims of revolutionaries keen to attribute their motivations to the influence of the "dead generations." For example, despite the tiny mobilization involved, hundreds of books have analyzed the Easter Rising, proclaimed by republicans and politicians as the point of origin of the revolution and southern state. In contrast, the two pivotal events of 1918, when the conscription crisis and general election marked the peak of popular nationalist mobilization, await a dedicated study.

If, however, unrest in Ireland was significantly bound up with international crises, the product less of local agency than "the inconstant fate of fluctuating empires,"[34] the impact of global forces must be evaluated. As Erez Manela observed in his study of anticolonialism in Asia and the Middle East, the practice of writing the history of a nationalist movement "as if it occurred solely within the boundaries of the emerging nation, or of the imperial enclosure from which it emerged" overlooks how wider international factors forged that history: "One of the central features of the Wilsonian moment was its simultaneity across the boundaries of nations, regions, and empires within which the histories of the anticolonial movements of the people are usually enclosed."[35] Without sufficient awareness of this contemporaneity, Manela argues, "the perceptions and actions of historical actors at the time, and much of what they saw and did at the time is rendered incomprehensible."[36]

Beyond Ireland, the "imperial turn" has resulted in a greater focus on the relationship between the First World War and revolutionary nationalism, increasingly analyzed within the temporal perspective of a "long decade" of war, revolution, and imperial decline—beginning with prewar upheavals in China, Mexico, and the Ottoman Empire, and concluding with the Treaty of Lausanne in July 1923.[37] The identical temporal framing of Ireland's Decade of Centenaries, although the invention of Irish policy makers keen to integrate foundational nationalist narratives within more pluralist contexts, illustrates how political instability in Ireland was profoundly shaped by broader international upheavals. Considerations of contemporaneity also have implications for understanding prewar nationalist developments. The striking parallels between the cultural and intellectual responses of nationalists in countries such as Ireland and India to imperial modernity at its early twentieth-century zenith indicate how this experience impacted the consciousness of nationalists in otherwise disparate societies.

### Toward a Transnational Historiography of the Irish Revolution

The Irish Revolution, then, was fundamentally a transnational event. Funds for the republican movement poured in via the expansive networks of diaspora nationalism; its leaders, in both their ideologies and their military tactics, were profoundly influenced by experiences abroad; and the violence that defined events in Ireland between 1916 and 1923 emerged against a backdrop of comparable revolutionary and anticolonial movements elsewhere in Europe and around the world. Despite emerging in such a fundamentally international context, much of the foundational historiography on the revolution engages only tangentially, or not at all, with its inherent transnationalism. As noted, the most prevalent methodology, best exemplified by the late David Fitzpatrick's study of the revolutionary decade in Clare, carried on by Peter Hart's work on the IRA in Cork and more recently by the Four Courts Press county-based series, "The Irish Revolution: 1912–1923," focuses on the complex and varied localism of conflict in Ireland during this period.[38]

If explicitly transnational methodologies remain underrepresented in the revolution's historiography, the ongoing Decade of Centenaries has produced an ever-increasing volume of work that places events in Ireland in a broader, global context. As Fitzpatrick cogently noted in his provocatively titled review article "We Are All Transnationalists Now," however, this trend in the historical literature is by no means a new phenomenon. Examining Ireland's past in a transnational perspective is "precisely what a great proportion of Irish historians have been doing over the past half century at least."[39] Undoubtedly, studies of diasporic Irish nationalism represent a distinct, long-standing subfield in their own right. Professional examinations of Irish America's role in the Irish Revolution emerged in the mid-twentieth century, led by Charles Callan Tansill's foundational study of the American Clan na Gael.[40] Building upon Thomas N. Brown's subsequent examination of nineteenth-century Irish American nationalism, many of the leading studies focus on the impact of the American setting as well as Irish immigrants' intergenerational search for respectability within American society.[41] More recent approaches have focused on the fascinating connections between Irish American nationalism and organized labor, socialism, women's suffrage, and other radical causes.[42]

How those of Irish birth and descent around the world engaged with Irish nationalism represents another significant branch of the diasporic literature. Irish nationalist associations thrived not only in Britain itself but also in the overseas dominions of Australia, New Zealand, Canada, Newfoundland, and South Africa—and, indeed, outside this "British world," in Argentina. Studies of the Irish republican movement in Britain are, unsurprisingly, the most adept at integrating diasporic nationalism with the struggle in Ireland. The IRA carried out extensive operations across the Irish Sea, in both raising funds and acquiring weaponry, while the Irish Self-Determination League of Great Britain rallied popular support for Irish independence from within the immigrant and ethnic community.[43] The foundational literature on Irish nationalism in Australia and New Zealand focuses on how Irish nationalism emerged as a key "domestic" question—an allegory for Irish Catholics' disillusionment with their position within Australasian society. More recent approaches have adopted a broader perspective, focusing on the connections between diasporic nationalism and other radical movements or causes. The South African literature, meanwhile, is far less developed than scholarship from the other former dominions, though initial studies of the small Irish republican movement there by Donal McCracken and more recent research by Ciaran Reilly represent important additions to the diasporic historiography.[44] Studies of Irish nationalism in Canada and Newfoundland survey the complex terrain of linguistic duality as well as the forceful and organized opposition to the republican movement led by groups such as the Orange Order, in addition to the intriguing relationship between Irish Canadian nationalist associations and the far larger movement in the United States.[45]

The historical literature on these diasporic communities is broad and varied, but a common theme is the tension between imperial identities and support for an increasingly radical and republican nationalist movement, particularly after 1916. Following Kevin Kenny's call for more explicitly comparative studies of the diasporic experience, works that compare expressions of diaspora nationalism in the American republic and British imperial settings emerged as an important feature of the literature. By examining how nationalist networks diffused across national boundaries and fostered an international exchange of ideas about Ireland and Irishness in overseas settings—essentially a diffusion of ethnicity from place to place—these studies are particularly valuable in establishing how the networks of diasporic Irish nationalism were truly global in scale.[46]

Research on engagement with nationalist movements by overseas Irish communities is particularly adept in illuminating and clarifying the complexity of the diaspora. At their greatest extent, between 1919 and 1921, the webs of Irish nationalism that spanned the globe bound disparate Irish communities in a common, cohesive movement. Through such communal engagement with the political destiny of the ancestral homeland, Irish identities rose, fell, and evolved.[47] The historiography on diaspora nationalism, as noted earlier, frequently falls short in assessing its overall impact on the fight for freedom in Ireland itself. There are exceptions, of course. Studies of nationalist fundraising endeavors, for example, examine the flow of money from the diaspora to Ireland, while works of historical biography on the revolution's key figures are frequently adept at highlighting the disparate, distant spaces in which their ideologies were shaped.[48] The most recent contributions to this literature move beyond the participation of Irish diasporic communities by applying more rigorously transnational and comparative methodologies to events in Ireland.[49] Beyond European contexts, there is likewise an expanding literature that examines connections between Ireland's Wilsonian moment and contemporary anticolonial struggles and radical movements in India, Africa, East Asia, and the Americas.[50]

Together with continuing local, regional, and national studies, transnational historiography is enhancing our understanding of the complex flow of money, information, and ideologies, through Ireland during the turbulent years that followed the Easter Rising. While this volume provides a sample of the breadth of emerging global scholarship on the Irish Revolution, some major themes, including loyalist mobilization, socialist engagements, and the role played by the Catholic Church, the most influential transnational organization to shape opinion on the Irish question, have not been addressed. Other themes, such as labor, deserve greater attention. Given the range of archives, languages, and historiographical expertise required to tackle topics such as the Catholic Church's global responses to the revolution, or comparative Irish engagement with anti-conscription, this book aims to spur further international scholarly collaborations.[51]

## A Global History of the Irish Revolution

Revolutionary Worlds, the opening section of this book, assesses Ireland's place in a newly reconfigured postwar world where empires appeared in irreversible decline. Comparing cases where connections between Ireland and other countries were explicitly acknowledged, as well as where they were more indirect or largely absent, this section explores issues of causality, context, and contemporaneity. Here, the extent to which different revolutionary movements drew on each other's rhetoric to legitimize their own struggles becomes apparent. Evaluating the accuracy of these parallels is less important than identifying the ideological and political work that shared narratives and common models of struggle performed. The adoption of similar strategies and techniques of struggle, reflecting in part contemporaneous international opportunities such as the Paris Peace Conference and the resulting American opposition to the League of Nations, is a striking feature of postwar nationalist movements.

The distinctive modes of anti-imperial ideology that emerged in Ireland, India, and Egypt and the manner in which they were shaped by the interplay of local and global forces are the concern of Martyn Frampton's essay. Affinities between these movements, he argues, extended beyond an awareness of a common enemy—empire—and a strategic response to the postwar crisis of empire. A rejection of anglicization and the efforts of more moderate nationalists to reach an accommodation with empire as well as an emphasis on the importance of culture and morality characterized militant nationalist discourses from the late nineteenth century in all three locales. An antimaterialistic "politics of authenticity," which emphasized how the pursuit of cultural independence through self-reliance formed a prerequisite for independent nationhood, informed the movements that gained the upper hand in each country in the postwar era. Too often, Frampton suggests, these movements have been understood through an exceptionalist lens that foregrounds a "national" or "religious" story; such perspectives fail to appreciate the extent to which these movements were the product of a distinct global conjuncture, constituting various aspects of a shared phenomenon. Consequently, the upheavals of 1919 should be understood not only as a response to the "Wilsonian moment." Sinn Féiners, Swadeshists, and Muslim Brothers, each in their own way, had long formed part of a global debate about empire, the role of the state, and how to build successful modern societies.

Comparing the efforts of Irish and Korean revolutionaries to win support abroad for the republics proclaimed in Dublin and Seoul in the spring of 1919, Fearghal McGarry assesses how transnational activism and global political developments shaped nationalism within both countries. Despite few connections between Ireland and Korea, and the differing outcomes of their struggles, comparison of both movements illustrates how, in the late 1910s and 1920s, nationalists embraced similar strategies, objectives, and discourses in response to the opportunities provided by the rise of Wilsonian self-determination. McGarry highlights the increasingly global character of postwar anti-imperial movements as the accelerating pace of the movement of people, ideas, and communications stoked nationalist expectations and weakened imperial resolve. He also considers the impact of "long-distance nationalism" on political developments at home. It was through their diasporic populations in the United States that Irish and Korean republicans most effectively wielded international influence, a development that shaped both countries' domestic politics in varying but significant ways.

In the wake of the 1916 Rising, Lenin was quick to rebuke Polish revolutionary Karl Radek for suggesting that events in Dublin amounted to no more than a bourgeois effort at a "putsch": only a pedant, Lenin argued, would vilify the Irish rebellion in these terms. Here, Anna Lively assesses Irish nationalist responses to the Russian Revolution, focusing in particular on the importance of imperialism and religion. Moving beyond the focus of existing Irish Soviet studies on socialist institutions and a narrow group of Irish radicals, she explores how many without strong socialist sympathies were interested in, and affected by, events in Russia, emphasizing in particular the idea of a shared anti-imperialism that influenced early Irish-Soviet relations. The emergence of a modern press accentuated the importance of the news from abroad, leading nationalists to draw more extensively on foreign events to fight domestic battles. Levels of Irish nationalist engagement with Russia varied widely over time and space, ranging from ideological commitments rooted in internationalism to more opportunistic expressions of rhetorical and strategic support. By 1921 there were signs of anticommunism developing in Ireland, particularly in response to news of religious persecution in Soviet Russia, with Bolshevism becoming a term of political abuse, used by the British government, unionists, and constitutional nationalists against Sinn Féin. Growing divisions among nationalists over Bolshevism by 1921 also reflected wider tensions over political strategy and questions of social change. Illustrating how the political translation of international news necessitates "imaginative work," this chapter identifies the need for a sophisticated contextualization of the reporting and consumption of foreign news.

The place of Ireland in the political imaginary of the Algerian nationalist movement demonstrates both the reach of the Irish Revolution and the Algerian embrace of the idea of global struggle. Exploring how Algerian nationalists were exposed to information about the Irish Revolution, Dónal Hassett analyzes how these narratives were interpreted and, most importantly, reconstructed to bolster visions of a future Algerian independence struggle. If, as Ernest Renan famously remarked, getting its history wrong is part of being a nation, reimagining other people's struggles is part of being a revolutionary. There are intriguing parallels with the use made in Ireland of the Russian Revolution explored by Lively, not least in how Algerians selectively crafted Irish precedents for their own purposes, and how these narratives changed over time. Neither cynical opportunists nor naïve imitators, Algerian nationalists saw the Irish struggle more as a source of inspiration than as a revolutionary template. By the 1970s, Irish republicans responded in kind, depicting Northern Ireland as the next Algeria.

How emigrant communities engaged with Irish nationalist movements is the concern of the collection's second section on Diaspora. Although the years between 1916 and 1922 witnessed a remarkable global mobilization that greatly strengthened Sinn Féin, the relationship between diasporic leaders and Irish-based nationalists was often acrimonious. In particular, sharply divergent attitudes on the League of Nations emerge as a significant fault line contributing to the rupture between Irish American and Irish leaders. Equally striking is the diversity of outlooks and identities across the diaspora, with tensions between progressive and conservative factions evident on issues such as race, class, and America's global role. The framing of discourses again emerges as an important theme: in order to gain traction among the diaspora or its host societies, the language of Irish self-determination was articulated in varying registers.

Analyzing the Irish Race Conventions that occurred across three continents between 1916 and 1921, Darragh Gannon assesses how Irish nationalists conceptualized, and institutionalized, the idea of a "global Ireland." Charting the development of the idea of an "Irish race," he assesses the ethnic assumptions underlying this term, and the reasons for its emergence as an organizing principle for nationalists around the Irish world. As with other contributors, Gannon emphasizes the importance of racial thinking and ethnic solidarity in framing ideas about the nation and national identity. Drawing on Akenson's idea of Irish nationalism as a global cultural system, he demonstrates how transnational Irish networks were as much the product of exchanges between diasporic networks and distinctive identities as of influences emanating directly from Ireland.

Exploring the activities of the Friends of Irish Freedom (FOIF), the United States' foremost Irish nationalist association, in the American-controlled Panama Canal Zone, Patrick Mannion provides a focused microstudy from the periphery of the Irish world. Formed by expatriate Irish American workers, the FOIF's Panamanian branches organized an extensive social program, placed nationalist propaganda in local newspapers, lobbied American and Panamanian politicians to recognize the Irish Republic, and raised funds by participating in the Dáil Éireann bond drive in early 1920. Robustly opposed by the British diplomatic mission in Panama, and closely observed by American military intelligence officers, their efforts represented a unique front in the fight for Irish self-determination.

Centered on the much-mythologized Charlie McGuinness, Breandán Mac Suibhne's essay analyzes divergent accounts of a bank raid in a small town in west Donegal. His essay demonstrates how carefully recently available archival material on the revolution, compiled decades after the events it describes, needs to be evaluated, not least given its impact on recent historiography. It also sheds light on the exodus of veterans from Ireland, particularly from among the ranks of the losing side, after the revolution, and their multitude of experiences around the world through the mid-twentieth century—themes that until recently were neglected by scholars.[52] Bridging the methodological chasm between "local" and "global," this intimate assessment of revolutionary lives illustrates the frequently transnational dimensions of the experiences of people from ordinary rural backgrounds. Of the four men who entered the bank, one became an adventurer and traveled around the world, one shot a police officer in Australia, one disappeared, it seems, in apartheid South Africa, and one became a respected pillar of the establishment, an Aer Corp commandant, after first becoming an executioner.

Links between imperialists have received less attention than those between anticolonialists. This reflects, in part, historiographical fashions, although the sources also present greater challenges. Archives and contemporary newspapers record the activities of revolutionaries in greater detail than the secretive or mundane work of spymasters and bureaucrats who rarely generate biographical sources. Imperialists, moreover, tend to be rivals while national revolutionaries are often not.

Nonetheless, as is explored in the third section of this book, Imperial Perspectives, similar themes can be identified. The impact on diasporic and domestic nationalist movements of the transnational circulation of imperial officials, methods, and ideas is evident. Just as Irish nationalists were emboldened by the Wilsonian moment, British concerns about nationalist revolt in Ireland reflected broader anxieties prompted by an international crisis of empire.

Michael Silvestri explores how Indian policemen and intelligence officials sought to apply experience gained in the campaign against revolutionaries in the Indian province of Bengal elsewhere in the empire, and beyond, during a formative period for British intelligence agencies. Officials such as the Indian Civil Service officer Robert Nathan and Charles Tegart, an Irish-born Indian police officer and expert on Indian "terrorism," sought not only to understand and neutralize Indian revolutionaries' global networks but to analyze and counter what they perceived as the connected activities of Irish republicans, communists, and Pan-Africanists during and after the war. Silvestri's analysis of these cross-colonial connections illustrates the sophistication of imperial networks during Ireland's revolutionary decade. The efforts of British security services to utilize intelligence and counterinsurgency experience gained in different global contexts illustrate that approaches to colonial governance within the British Empire did not simply emanate from the imperial center, nor were they confined within a single colony.

The First World War transformed imperial power relations and cultural beliefs, changing in the process the meaning of empire. Here, Heather Jones examines the impact of these changes on Irish republican and unionist agency and attitudes. The deployment of the British monarch in Ireland, north and south, highlights how the country formed part of a wider transnational postwar reconfiguration of the relationship between monarchy and empire reflecting the more assertive claims of dominions. Both the king's speech at the opening of the Northern Irish parliament and the debates around the oath of allegiance during the treaty negotiations demonstrate the shift in British imperial ideas that was occurring in—and also *through*—Ireland. As George V noted on the former occasion: "Everything which touches Ireland finds an echo in the remotest parts of the Empire."[53] It was not by chance that the term "British Commonwealth of Nations" first received legal recognition when it was substituted for "British Empire" in the Irish oath of allegiance. Transnational exchanges, such as those between South African prime minster Jan Smuts and King George V on the Irish question, played a key role in rethinking the empire. The concept of monarchy as the "arch" that might hold the empire together, and how this was understood, was at the core of the oath of allegiance's significance both in Ireland and in Britain, and helps to explain why efforts to settle the Irish question resulted in civil war. A picture emerges of a dialogue of the deaf that fatally eroded the potential for compromise: if Irish republicans were oblivious to the British notion that the role of the monarch might provide for shared allegiances and minority safeguards in a reconfigured empire, British politicians failed to appreciate the growing significance of anti-monarchist sentiment within nationalist politics after the Easter Rising. Only by recontextualizing these imperial meanings, and their transnational resonances, can the Irish Revolution be fully understood.

Not only did the Irish Revolution transcend Ireland, it impacted radical movements with little direct connection to the island. Demonstrating how the Irish question influenced the thinking and strategies of other movements, the concluding section, Radical Lives, Global Networks, illustrates how the transnational movement of people and ideas produced its own political dynamics. Focusing on activism in postwar America, the essays in this section employ predominantly biographical methodologies to explore the diverse ways in which Irish nationalism intersected with broader social movements on questions such as class, suffrage, and race. Contrasting with the conservative Irish American activists in Panama explored by Mannion, American radicals drew on Ireland to critique US practices of informal and economic imperialism in Latin America and Asia. A similarly complex picture emerges from the intersection of Irish nationalism with Black rights movements. Despite identifying Irishness with slavery, racism, and imperialism, the significance that several prominent Black rights activists came to attach to the republican struggle highlights the salience of progressive interpretations of the Irish question.

In her chapter on anti-imperialist women of the transatlantic Irish left, Elizabeth McKillen argues that the three activists she profiles were "organic intellectuals" whose ideas developed from their experiences.

Their activism, she argues, contributed to the anti-imperialist outlook of Irish American women's organizations, social reform movements, and trade unions in the heady period immediately before and after women's suffrage was enacted in the United States in 1920. Situating these activists as part of a distinctive movement of American reformers and left activists who politicized Irish Americans outside the conservative Catholic sphere of organizations such as the Ancient Order of Hibernians, McKillen assesses how the differing visions of self-determination articulated by Wilson and Lenin impacted their outlook. Her essay demonstrates how diasporic and radical networks served to cross-fertilize political ideas, discourses, and identities.

David Brundage charts the dramatic shift in W. E. B. Du Bois's views on Ireland between 1916 and 1920. Despite his admiration for Britain's role in the First World War, stemming from both the relatively liberal and democratic character of the United Kingdom and his consciousness of Irish American racism, Du Bois became an active supporter of Irish independence. In explaining this transition, Brundage emphasizes his interaction with Irish American republicans in New York's anticolonial networks and his experiences as an organizer of a Pan-African Congress in Paris where he made common cause with Irish revolutionaries. The role of "transnational connectors," such as Frank Walsh, in linking movements across borders and the importance of the shared methodologies of protest that emerged from these interactions are clear. The impact on Du Bois of the ideas and actions of Terence MacSwiney demonstrates how the Irish question stimulated global anticolonial activism and thought in an age of radical change.

Illustrating how Irish republicans proved a source of organizational inspiration as well as ideological influence for radical movements, Miriam Nyhan Grey's essay provides a compelling counterpoint to that of Brundage. Like Du Bois, Marcus Garvey graduated from support for the British Empire and its war effort to an enthusiastic endorsement of Irish self-determination. Probing issues of empire, race, and organizational culture, Grey identifies how the Irish struggle provided "a roadmap for Garveyism," illustrating how a powerful empire could be challenged from within. Garvey's writings and rhetoric make clear the influence of Irish initiatives such as global congresses, international fundraising campaigns, and the harnessing of diasporic support. Demonstrating how transnational solidarity could be cultivated, Irish nationalism offered a revolutionary model that Garvey drew on to link the causes of Caribbean self-government with Black American rights. The dual and interrelated reach of empire and diaspora, Grey concludes, galvanized Garvey's interest in the Irish question. Jamaica, Africa, and Ireland were connected both as components of the British Empire and as exponents of a diaspora nationalism espoused most visibly in New York City.

## Conclusion

How does a global history reshape the traditional narratives, interpretations, and chronologies of the Irish Revolution? First and foremost, it reveals how power was contested across a variety of spaces beyond the island. The postwar transition from a world dominated by empire to an international community of democratic nation-states was central to determining the outcome of the Irish struggle for independence. Tracking how this global shift played out across diverse sites where Irish revolutionaries and their opponents mobilized requires an international geography of the Irish Revolution. Although global history is criticized for its broad-brush approach, mapping how world historical forces interacted with national and local circumstances to effect political change requires close attention to how individuals, movements, and networks transmitted ideas about how the world should be governed, and the importance of local conditions and identities in determining how these ideas were received and adapted.

Involving people, Irish and non-Irish, across the world, the Irish Revolution constituted one of the great transnational moments in Irish history, encompassing a diverse range of actors, objects, places, and ideas. Irish revolutionaries influenced diverse social and political movements, just as those movements influenced them. Globalizing Ireland's revolution shifts our focus from the military to the political and cultural spheres, directing our attention to the role of ideology and political and literary discourse. It restores agency to the suffragists, labor activists, and other radicals often excluded from nation-centered histories despite their influential roles as transnational connectors. Any such analysis must acknowledge their complex motivations, ranging from progressive notions of solidarity to more opportunistic or chauvinistic factors, as well as the relative privileges bestowed on Irish nationalists through considerations of race and power. Thinking transnationally and comparatively can promote more inclusive and diverse histories of the revolution, illuminating how the transformation of Ireland formed part of a wider political and ideological moment in world history.

Highlighting the relevance of debates about universal ideas such as self-determination, race, and empire to the Irish Revolution has implications that extend beyond the historiographical. Shaped by the reconciliatory imperatives of the Good Friday Agreement, one of the most striking innovations of the Decade of Centenaries has been the Irish state's shift from articulating a narrow nationalist narrative of the struggle for independence to a more pluralist interpretation that places greater emphasis on the idea of the revolution as constituting a tragic period of "shared history," shaped by "multiple identities and traditions."[54] In this irenic framing, which requires more egalitarian forms of remembrance, the goal of transcending present-day animosities is accorded greater weight than frank interrogation of the ideological issues at stake in the conflict. It was surely this commemorative mode that explains the Irish state's biggest misstep during the Decade of Centenaries, the decision to formally commemorate the Royal Irish Constabulary's fatalities, including (possibly inadvertently) those Black and Tans who died while serving within that force. The ensuing public outcry prompted an unseemly reversal, recalling the government's earlier recalibration of its initially anodyne Easter Rising centenary program.[55] Rather than a dignified remembrance signaling post-nationalist Ireland's "maturity" about its history, the date of the planned ceremony saw the re-release of the Wolfe Tones' recording of "Come Out, Ye Black and Tans" top the UK charts.[56]

Some months later, the Irish president Michael D. Higgins offered a more insightful engagement with the divisive legacy of the revolution in a speech marking the centenary of the Sack of Balbriggan by the Black and Tans in September 1920. Outlining how collective punishment formed "a key aspect of empire rule and its imposition of colonial powers, laws, attributes and ideologies," which was implemented from India to Kenya, Higgins asserted that such methods were "rooted in ideological assumptions, of superiority and inferiority in terms of race, culture or capacity, in the notion of the collective as a disloyal, hopeless or threatening version of the 'Other.'"[57] Observing that "peoples and nations manage forgiveness easier than empires," burdened as they are by privilege, title, and "atrocities too great to recall," Higgins suggested that a form of ethical remembering leading to a "shared island at peace" requires recognition of Britain's imperialist role in Ireland. Given the decision of the British-government-appointed chair of the First World War centenary advisory board, against the advice of its historical advisors, not to extend the United Kingdom's commemorative program to encompass postwar violence in Ireland and India, this seems an unlikely prospect.[58] A willingness to reconsider exceptionalist narratives is noticeably less evident across the Irish Sea, where a mythologized "island story" remains substantially intact and attitudes to empire continue to be inflected by nostalgia, racism, and amnesia.[59] Although English forgetfulness of Ireland is hardly a new phenomenon, the reemergence of the Irish border as a destabilizing factor in British politics—along with the return of customs posts exactly one century after partition—demonstrates the continuing relevance of the revolution's legacy not just for the two Irish states, but for the third political entity that resulted from that conflict, the present-day United Kingdom.[60]

## NOTES

The editors would like to thank Enda Delaney and Breandán Mac Suibhne for their comments on earlier drafts of this article.

1  Cited in David Fitzpatrick, *Harry Boland's Irish Revolution* (Cork: Cork University Press, 2003), 179.

2  American Commission on Conditions in Ireland, "Evidence on Conditions in Ireland: Comprising the Complete Testimony, Affidavits and Exhibits Presented Before the American Commission on Conditions in Ireland" (Washington, DC, 1921).

3  Maurice Walsh, *Bitter Freedom: Ireland in a Revolutionary World, 1918–1923* (London: Faber & Faber, 2015), 11.

4  Both of these collections can be accessed at the (Irish) Military Archives website: www.militaryarchives.ie.

5  Recent works such as Senia Pašeta, *Irish Nationalist Women 1900–1918* (Cambridge: Cambridge University Press, 2013), and Linda Connolly, ed., *Women and the Irish Revolution: Feminism, Activism, Violence* (Dublin: Irish Academic Press, 2020), have focused greater attention on the role of women. On the overshadowing of political thought, see Richard Bourke, "Political and Religious Ideas during the Irish Revolution," *History of European Ideas* 46, no. 7 (2020): 997–1008.

6   Department of Culture, Heritage and the Gaeltacht, "Decade of Centenaries—Public Call for Submissions," Appendix A (2017).

7   Patrick Maume, "MacSwiney, Terence James," in *Dictionary of Irish Biography*, ed. James McGuire and James Quinn (Cambridge: Cambridge University Press, 2009).

8   For the international impact of MacSwiney's hunger strike, and the contrast between global and Irish remembrance, see Dave Hannigan, *Terence MacSwiney: The Hunger Strike That Rocked an Empire* (Dublin: O'Brien Press, 2010).

9   Maurice Walsh, *The News from Ireland: Foreign Correspondents and the Irish Revolution* (London: Bloomsbury, 2008), 104.

10  Edward Madigan, "'An Irish Louvain': Memories of 1914 and the Moral Climate in Britain during the Irish War of Independence," *Irish Historical Studies* 44, no. 165 (2020): 91–105.

11  Quoted in Seán Donnelly, "Ireland in the Imperial Imagination: British Nationalism and the Anglo-Irish Treaty," *Irish Studies Review* 27, no. 4 (2019): 496.

12  Arie M. Dubnov and Laura Robson, "Introduction," in *Partitions: A Transnational History of Twentieth-Century Territorial Separatism*, ed. Dubnov and Robson (Stanford, CA: Stanford University Press, 2019), 1–27.

13  Michael Collins to George Gavan Duffy, 18 June 1921, quoted in Peter Hart, *Mick: The Real Michael Collins* (London: Macmillan, 2005), 274.

14  On this, see the first volume of the Documents in Irish Foreign Policy (www.difp.ie).

15  Macready to General Sir Peter Strickland, 1 Jan. 1921, quoted in M. A. Doherty, "Kevin Barry and the Anglo-Irish Propaganda War," *Irish Historical Studies* 32, no. 126 (2000): 225.

16  Niall Whelehan, "Playing with Scales: Transnational History and Modern Ireland," in *Transnational Perspectives on Modern Irish History*, ed. Niall Whelehan (New York: Routledge, 2014), 7–29.

17  Robert Gerwarth and John Horne, eds., *War in Peace: Paramilitary Violence in Europe after the Great War* (Oxford: Oxford University Press, 2012); Robert Gerwarth, *The Vanquished: Why the First World War Failed to End, 1917–1923* (London: Allen Lane, 2016).

18  This is a key theme of Stephen Howe, *Ireland and Empire: Colonial Legacies in Irish History and Culture* (Oxford: Oxford University Press, 2000). Over the past two decades, a substantial historiography of Ireland and Empire has developed. A useful starting point is Keven Kenny, ed., *Ireland and the British Empire* (Oxford: Oxford University Press, 2004), which observed that "the great Irish national histories" have not taken Ireland's "wider imperial context to be an essential framework for interpreting the Irish past" (94).

19  Gemma Clark, "Violence Against Women in the Irish Civil War, 1922–3: Gender-Based Harm in Global Perspective," *Irish Historical Studies* 44, no. 165 (2020): 75–90; Anne Dolan, "Killing in 'The Good Old Irish Fashion'? Irish Revolutionary Violence in Context," *Irish Historical Studies* 44, no. 165 (2020): 11–24.

20  T. K. Wilson, *Frontiers of Violence: Conflict and Identity in Ulster and Upper Silesia, 1918–1922* (Oxford: Oxford University Press, 2010); Ian McBride, "The Peter Hart

Affair in Perspective: History, Ideology, and the Irish Revolution," *Historical Journal* 61, no. 1 (2018): 249–271.

21 C. A. Bayly et al., "AHR Conversation: On Transnational History," *American Historical Review* III, no. 5 (2006): 1444.

22 Enrico Dal Lago, Róisín Healy, and Gearóid Barry, eds., *1916 in Global Context: An Anti-Imperial Moment* (London: Routledge, 2018); Keith Jeffery, *1916: A Global History* (London: Bloomsbury, 1916), 8.

23 Michael Goebel, *Anti-Imperial Metropolis: Interwar Paris and the Seeds of Third World Nationalism* (Cambridge: Cambridge University Press, 2015).

24 D. H. Akenson, "Stepping Back and Looking Around," in *Irish Nationalism in Canada*, ed. David Wilson (Montreal: McGill-Queen's University Press, 2009), 186.

25 Cited in Whelehan, "Playing with Scales," 2.

26 Patrick Mannion, *A Land of Dreams: Ethnicity, Nationalism, and the Irish in Newfoundland, Nova Scotia, and Maine, 1880–1923* (Montreal: McGill-Queen's University Press, 2018), 208–212, 217–220.

27 See, for example, Seán William Gannon, *The Irish Imperial Service: Policing Palestine and Administering the Empire, 1922–1966* (London: Palgrave Macmillan, 2019).

28 Keith Jeffery, "The Road to Asia, and the Grafton Hotel, Dublin: Ireland in the 'British World,'" *Irish Historical Studies* 36, no. 142 (2008): 252.

29 Quoted in Kevin Kenny, "The Irish in the Empire," in Kenny, *Ireland and the British Empire*, 91.

30 Ibid.

31 David Fitzpatrick, *Irish Emigration, 1801–1921* (Dundalk: Economic and Social History of Ireland, 1984), 1; David Fitzpatrick, *The Americanisation of Ireland: Migration and Settlement, 1841–1925* (Cambridge: Cambridge University Press, 2020).

32 The transatlantic dynamic of Irish nationalism is a theme skillfully explored in David Brundage's *Irish Nationalists in America: The Politics of Exile, 1798–1998* (Oxford: Oxford University Press, 2016).

33 Tom Garvin, *Nationalist Revolutionaries in Ireland 1858–1928* (Dublin: Gill and Macmillan, 2005); Enda Delaney and Fearghal McGarry, "Introduction: A Global History of Irish Revolution," *Irish Historical Studies* 44, no. 165 (2020): 2–4.

34 Richard Bourke, "Introduction," in *The Princeton History of Modern Ireland*, ed. Richard Bourke and Ian McBride (Princeton: Princeton University Press, 2016), 15.

35 Erez Manela, *The Wilsonian Moment: Self-Determination and the International Origins of Anticolonial Nationalism* (Oxford: Oxford University Press, 2007), xi, 10.

36 Ibid., 222.

37 Robert Gerwarth and Erez Manela, eds., *Empires at War: 1911–1923* (Oxford: Oxford University Press, 2014).

38 David Fitzpatrick, *Politics and Irish Life, 1913–1921: Provincial Experiences of War and Revolution* (London: Gill and Macmillan, 1977); Peter Hart, *The IRA and Its Enemies: Violence and Community in Cork, 1916–1923* (Oxford: Oxford University Press, 1998). Okan Ozseker's *Forging the Broder: Donegal and Derry in Times of Revolution, 1911–1925* (Dublin: Irish Academic Press, 2019) adopts a more novel regional focus.

39  David Fitzpatrick, "We Are All Transnationalists Now," *Irish Historical Studies* 41, no. 159 (2017): 123. For other perspectives on the ongoing transnational turn in Irish historiography, see Enda Delaney, "Our Island Story? Towards a Transnational History of Late Modern Ireland," *Irish Historical Studies* 37, no. 148 (2011): 599–621; Delaney and McGarry, "Introduction," 1–10; and Whelehan, "Playing with Scales," 7–29.

40  Charles Callan Tansill, *America and the Fight for Irish Freedom, 1866–1922: An Old Story Based upon New Data* (New York: Devin-Adair, 1957).

41  Thomas N. Brown, *Irish-American Nationalism, 1870–1890* (New York: J.B. Lippincott, 1966). Important works that cover the Irish Revolution in the United States include Francis M. Carroll, *American Opinion and the Irish Question, 1920–1923* (New York: St. Martin's Press, 1978); Michael Doorley, *Irish American Diaspora Nationalism: The Friends of Irish Freedom, 1916–1935* (Dublin: Four Courts Press, 2005); Kevin Kenny, *The American Irish: A History* (London: Routledge, 2000); David Emmons, *The Butte Irish: Class and Ethnicity in an American Mining Town, 1875–1925* (Urbana: University of Illinois Press, 1989); Timothy J. Meagher, *Inventing Irish America: Generation, Class, and Ethnic Identity in a New England City, 1880–1928* (Notre Dame: Notre Dame University Press, 2001); Kerby Miller, *Emigrants and Exiles: Ireland and the Irish Exodus to North America* (Oxford: Oxford University Press, 1988).

42  Examples include Brundage, *Irish Nationalists in America*; Elizabeth McKillen, "Divided Loyalties: Irish American Women Labor Leaders and the Irish Revolution, 1916–23," *Eire-Ireland* 51 nos. 3–4 (2016): 165–187; Elizabeth McKillen, "The Irish Sinn Féin Movement and Radical Labor and Feminist Dissent in America, 1916–1921," *Labor: Studies in Working Class History* 16, no. 3 (2019): 11–37; Joanne Mooney Eichacker, *Irish Republican Women in America, 1916–1925* (Dublin: Irish Academic Press, 2003); Bruce Nelson, "Irish Americans, Irish Nationalism, and the 'Social' Question, 1916–1923," *boundary 2* 31, no. 1 (2004): 147–178; Bruce Nelson, *Irish Nationalists and the Making of the Irish Race* (Princeton: Princeton University Press, 2012); Miriam Nyhan Grey, ed., *Ireland's Allies: America and the 1916 Easter Rising* (Dublin: University College Dublin Press, 2016); Robert Schmuhl, *Ireland's Exiled Children: America and the Easter Rising* (Oxford: Oxford University Press, 2016).

43  Examples include Darragh Gannon, "Rise of the Rainbow Chasers: Advanced Irish Political Nationalism in Britain, 1916–1922," *Eire-Ireland* 69 (2014): 112–142; Peter Hart, "'Operations Abroad': The IRA in Britain, 1919–1923," *English Historical Review* 115, no. 460 (2000): 71–102; Keiko Inoue, "Dáil Propaganda and the Irish Self-Determination League of Great Britain during the Anglo-Irish War," *Irish Studies Review* 6, no. 1 (1998): 47–53; Donald MacRaild, *The Irish Diaspora in Britain, 1750–1939* (Basingstoke: Palgrave Macmillan, 2011); Gerard Noonan, *The IRA in Britain, 1919–1923, "In the Heart of Enemy Lines"* (Liverpool: Liverpool University Press, 2014); Iain D. Patterson, "The Activities of Physical Force Organizations in Scotland, 1919–1921," *Scottish Historical Review* 72, no. 193 (1993): 39–59; Thomas Tormey, "Scotland's Easter Rising Veterans and the Irish Revolution," *Studi Irlandesi: A Journal of Irish Studies* 9 (2019): 271–302.

44  Examples include Richard P. Davis, *Irish Issues in New Zealand Politics, 1868–1922* (Otago: University of Otago Press, 1974); Dianne Hall, "Irish Republican Women in Australia: Kathleen Barry and Linda Kearns's Tour in 1924–25," *Irish Historical Studies* 49, no. 163 (2019): 73–93; Stephanie James, "The Evolution of Adelaide's Irish National Association, 1918–1950: From Security Threat to Cultural Force?," *Journal of the Historical Society of South Australia* 45 (2017): 31–49; Elizabeth Malcolm and Dianne Hall, *A New History of the Irish in Australia* (Sydney: New South Publishing, 2018); Patrick O'Farrell, *The Irish in Australia: 1788 to the Present* (Sydney: University of New South Wales Press, 2000); Rory Sweetman, "Who Fears to Speak of Easter Week? Antipodean Irish Catholic Responses to the 1916 Rising," in *The Impact of the 1916 Rising among the Nations*, ed. Ruan O'Donnell (Dublin: Irish Academic Press, 2008), 71–90; Jimmy Yan, "The Irish Revolution, Early Australian Communists and Anglophone Radical Peripheries: Dublin, Glasgow, Sydney, 1920–1923," *Twentieth Century Communism* 18, no. 18 (2020): 93–125. On South Africa, see T. K. Daniel, "Erin's Green Veldt: The Irish Republican Association of South Africa, 1910–22," *Journal of the University of Durban-Westville* 3 (1986): 89–98; D. P. McCracken, "The Irish Republican Association of South Africa, 1920–22," *Southern African-Irish Studies* 3 (1996): 46–66; Ciaran Reilly, "'The Magna Hibernia': Irish Diplomatic Missions to South Africa, 1921," *South African Historical Journal* 67, no. 3 (2015): 255–270.

45  Examples include Simon Jolivet, *Le Vert et le Bleu: Identité Québécoise et Identité Irlandaise au Tournant du XXe Siècle* (Montreal: La Presse de L'Université de Montréal, 2011); Patrick Mannion, "Contested Nationalism: The 'Irish Question' in St. John's, Newfoundland, and Halifax, Nova Scotia, 1919–1923," *Acadiensis* 44, no. 2 (2015): 27–49; Robert McLaughlin, *Irish Canadian Conflict and the Struggle for Irish Independence, 1912–1925* (Toronto: University of Toronto Press, 2013); Peter Toner, "The Fanatic Heart of the North," in Wilson, *Irish Nationalism in Canada*, 34–51.

46  Kevin Kenny, "Diaspora and Comparison: The Global Irish as a Case Study," *Journal of American History* 90, no. 1 (2003): 134–162. Examples include Malcolm Campbell, *Ireland's New Worlds: Immigrants, Politics, and Society in the United States and Australia, 1815–1922* (Madison: University of Wisconsin Press, 2007); William Jenkins, *Between Raid and Rebellion: The Irish in Buffalo and Toronto, 1867–1916* (Montreal: McGill-Queen's University Press, 2013); Mannion, *Land of Dreams*.

47  Donald H. Akenson, *The Irish Diaspora: A Primer* (Toronto: P.D. Meany, 1993), 3. On the importance of nationalist networks serving as "nodes" that connected overseas diasporic populations, see Kevin Kenny, *Diaspora: A Very Short Introduction* (Oxford: Oxford University Press, 2013).

48  On fundraising, see Francis M. Carroll, *Money for Ireland: Finance, Diplomacy, Politics, and the First Dáil Éireann Loans, 1916–1936* (Westport, CT: Praeger, 2002) and Robin Adams, "Shadow of a Taxman: How, and by Whom, Was the Republican Government Financed in the Irish War of Independence (1919–1921)?" (DPhil thesis, University of Oxford, 2018). Examples of biography and biographical case studies include Catherine Burns, "Kathleen O'Brennan and American Identity in the Transatlantic Irish Republican Movement," in *The Irish in the Atlantic World*, ed. David

T. Gleeson (Columbia: University of South Carolina Press, 2012), 176–194; David Fitzpatrick, *Harry Boland's Irish Revolution, 1887–1922* (Cork: Cork University Press, 2004); Shane Lynn, "Osmond Esmonde's Dominion Odyssey: Irish Nationalism in the British Empire, 1920–21," *Australasian Journal of Irish Studies* 14 (2014): 69–90; Mary MacDiarmada, *Art O'Brien and Irish Nationalism in London, 1900–25* (Dublin: Four Courts Press, 2020); Mary McAuliffe, *Margaret Skinnider* (Dublin: UCD Press, 2020); Padraig Ó Siadhail, *Katherine Hughes: A Life and a Journey* (Newcastle, ON: Penumbra Press, 2014).

49 Studies that examine the Irish Revolution alongside comparable movements overseas are particularly elucidating in this regard. Resonant examples include comparisons with revolutionary activities in Finland, as first suggested by Joseph J. Lee in his landmark *Ireland, 1912–1985: Politics and Society* (Cambridge: Cambridge University Press, 1989), and more recently in a special issue of *Irish Historical Studies* ("Ireland and Finland, 1860–1930: Comparative and Transnational Histories") 41, no. 160 (2017). Examples of transnational, comparative approaches include Julia Eichenberg, "The Dark Side of Independence: Paramilitary Violence in Ireland and Poland after the First World War," *Contemporary European History* 19, no. 3 (2010): 231–248; Gerwarth and Horne, *War in Peace*; Brian Hanley, "'The Irish and the Jews have a Good Deal in Common': Irish Republicanism, Anti-Semitism and the Post-War World," *Irish Historical Studies* 44, no. 165 (2020): 57–74; Róisín Healy, "Early Risers and Late Sleepers: The Easter Rising and the Poznian Uprising of 1918/1919 Compared," in Dal Lago, Healy, and Barry, *1916 in Global Context*, 208–221; Róisín Healy, *Poland in the Irish Nationalist Imagination, 1772–1922: Anti-colonialism within Europe* (Basingstoke: Palgrave Macmillan, 2017); Walsh, *Bitter Freedom*; Wilson, *Frontiers of Violence*; Lili Zach, "'The First of the Small Nations': The Significance of Central European Small States in Irish Nationalist Political Rhetoric, 1918–22," *Irish Historical Studies* 44, no. 165 (2020): 25–40.

50 The idea of a broader, transnational Wilsonian moment is drawn from Manela, *Wilsonian Moment*. Examples of studies that place the Irish Revolution in a global context include David Brundage, "Lala Lajpat Rai, Indian Nationalism, and the Irish Revolution: The View from New York, 1914–1920," in Dal Lago, Healy, and Barry, *1916 in Global Context*, 62–75; Clark, "Violence Against Women in the Irish Civil War"; Jeffery, *1916*; Kate O'Malley, *Ireland, India and Empire: Indo-Irish Radical Connections, 1919–1964* (Manchester: Manchester University Press, 2008); Kate O'Malley, "Violent Resistance: The Irish Revolution and India," in *Ireland's Imperial Connections, 1775–1947*, ed. Daniel Sanjiv Roberts and Jonathan Jeffrey Wright (Basingstoke: Palgrave Macmillan, 2019), 213–221; Danielle Ross, "From Dublin to Turgai: Discourses on Small Nations and Violence in the Russian Muslim Press in 1916," in Dal Lago, Healy, and Barry, *1916 in Global Context*, 131–145; Michael Silvestri, *Ireland and India: Nationalism, Empire and Memory* (London: Palgrave Macmillan, 2009); Niall Whelehan, "Sacco and Vanzetti, Mary Donovan and Transatlantic Radicalism in the 1920s," *Irish Historical Studies* 44, no. 165 (2020): 131–146.

51 This volume results from a UK Arts and Humanities Research Council–funded research project, "A Global History of Irish Revolution, 1916–1923" (2017–2020), led by historians at Queen's University Belfast, the University of Edinburgh, and Boston College. Other project publications include Enda Delaney and Fearghal McGarry, eds., *The Irish Revolution 1919–21: A Global History* (Dublin: Wordwell, 2019) and a special issue of *Irish Historical Studies* 44, no. 165 (2020). The editors are grateful to Professor Rob Savage and the Irish Studies program at Boston College for supporting the conference (canceled due to COVID-19) initially scheduled to facilitate this publication.

52 Recent studies include Gavin Foster, *The Irish Civil War and Society: Politics, Class, and Conflict* (London: Palgrave Macmillan, 2015), 203–221; Síobhra Aiken, "'Sinn Féin Permits . . . in the Heels of Their Shoes': Cumann na mBan Emigrants and Transatlantic Revolutionary Exchange," *Irish Historical Studies* 44, no. 165 (2020): 106–130.

53 *Belfast Newsletter*, 23 June 1921, 9.

54 For an example of this rhetoric, see Department of Tourism, Culture, Arts, Gaeltacht, Sport and Media, "Decade of Centenaries Programme" (n.d.), www.decadeofcentenaries.com. For a critique of "shared history," see Fearghal McGarry, "The Limits of Pluralism: Historians, Commemoration, and Easter 2016," *Eire-Ireland* (forthcoming).

55 Fearghal McGarry, *The Rising. Ireland: Easter 1916* (Oxford: Oxford University Press, 2017), iv–xv.

56 "How Alan Partridge Helped Come Out Ye Black and Tans Top the Charts," *Guardian*, 14 Jan. 2020.

57 "Statement by President Michael D. Higgins on the Centenary Anniversary of the Sack of Balbriggan," 20 Sept. 1920, Media Library (www.president.ie).

58 "Row Over Bid to Extent Centenary Events to Cover Ireland and India," *Guardian*, 1 Apr. 2019.

59 On the misremembering of the British Empire, see Priya Satia, *Time's Monster: How History Makes History* (Cambridge, MA: Harvard University Press, 2020) and Priyamvada Gopal, *Insurgent Empire: Anticolonial Resistance and British Dissent* (London: Verso, 2019).

60 On English "forgetting" of Ireland, see Mo Moulton, *Ireland and the Irish in Interwar England* (Cambridge: Cambridge University Press, 2014), 1–4; on UK indifference to the centenary, see Fintan O'Toole, "Beyond Amnesia and Piety," in *Towards Commemoration: Ireland in War and Revolution 1912–1923*, ed. John Horne and Edward Madigan (Dublin: Royal Irish Academy, 2013), 160.

# PART ONE

# Revolutionary Worlds

# 1

# Beyond "Slavish" Imitation

## *The Politics of Cultural Authenticity and the Global Struggle Against Empire*

MARTYN FRAMPTON

The onset of the Irish Revolution after 1916, set amid the geopolitical upheavals of the First World War and its aftermath, has often been seen as a watershed: the first decisive blow to the edifice of British imperial power, heralding a long process of decolonization.[1] At the time, many were filled with a sense that a new world was being born out of the wreckage of the Great War.[2] Wherever one looked, it was possible to identify the collapse of centuries-old empires and the birth of nation-states. As historians have recognized, those charged with steering the British state through these choppy waters were acutely conscious that they faced a "crisis of empire" that took multiple different forms: revolt in the recently conquered territory of Iraq; the assertion of independence from the hitherto client state of Afghanistan; Mustafa Kemal's challenge to the postwar settlement in Turkey; the mobilization of Chinese nationalist energies through the May Fourth Movement; and of course the specter of sustained anti-imperialist insurgency in countries deemed vital to the health of the empire, notably Ireland, India, and Egypt.

British imperial administrators bemoaned the parallel activities of the "infernal trio" of Saʿd Zaghlul, Mohandas Gandhi, and Éamon de Valera; and responses in one territory were calibrated with a view to their likely impact on another.[3] Officials in India would later express their concern over the adoption by India's National Congress (INC) of "Sinn Féin methods."[4] Egypt, meanwhile, came to be seen as "another Ireland" because of its refusal to acquiesce to British control.[5] To some observers, this was a clear case of contagion—of the dissemination and uptake of dangerous ideas, which threatened imperial cohesion. The itinerant journalist Valentine Chirol thus spoke of the "slavish" imitation by Indian nationalists of radicals in "the West"—by which he meant particularly the Irish Fenians and Russian Anarchists.[6] On this reading, instability at the imperial center helped trigger unrest at the periphery.

And yet as scholars have noted in other contexts, ideas of imitation and contagion can take us only so far. In trying to explain why different countries, in radically dissimilar historical circumstances, nevertheless experienced analogous episodes of anti-imperial resistance, it is important not to lose sight of the local context—or rather to be clearer on the interplay between global and local forces. Moreover, just as the present volume is in keeping with the welcome historiographical shift toward placing events in Ireland within broader perspective, so too is it crucial to set the interlocking crises of the years 1919 to 1923, or indeed 1916 to 1923, within a wider temporal focus.

It is with this in mind that the current chapter extends its chronological horizons—focusing especially on the earlier moment of crisis of 1905–1906. The justification for so doing lies in the assertion that what occurred in Ireland during the revolutionary period marked the eruption of a mode of politics that had gathered strength around the globe over the preceding decades. Sinn Féin and the Irish Republican Army with which it became indelibly associated were embodiments of a distinct mode of anti-imperialist politics, grounded fundamentally in a project for cultural authenticity that emerged to challenge British imperial rule in diverse settings, and which remained potent thereafter.

To explore these issues further, the next section examines the contours of that mode of politics as it developed in Ireland under the banner of Sinn Féin. Thereafter, attention is drawn to the self-conscious internationalism of many Sinn Féiners and the extent to which they saw themselves as engaged in a shared struggle with movements elsewhere. This is followed by closer consideration of one such movement: that associated with the idea of Swadeshi in India. Finally, the chapter reflects on what all this can tell us about the emergence of the "politics of cultural authenticity," as a vehicle for anti-imperialist struggle, at the global level.[7]

## Sinn Féin: Ourselves Alone

As scholars like Roy Foster and Patrick Maume have underlined, the Irish Revolution was the work of a particular generation, which was forged through the "long gestation" of the late nineteenth and early twentieth centuries.[8] When Arthur Griffith founded his newspaper, *Sinn Féin*, in 1905, he imagined it as the mouthpiece for a number of associations and organizations, promising to provide a "summary and chronicle of the work done by the National Council, the Gaelic League, Cumann na nGaedheal, the Gaelic Athletic Association, the Industrial Development Association, and all other bodies, whatever the field of their labours, the object of which is the re-creation of an Irish Ireland."[9] Griffith hoped his journal would serve as the "inclusive compound" of a movement that was, as one writer observed, "comprehensive and many-sided, split up, so to speak, into sections which mutually react on one another."[10]

What united this sprawling social movement was the conviction that Ireland was possessed of a discrete cultural identity that was under existential threat. British control of Ireland was held to rest on much more than physical occupation. According to *Sinn Féin*, "British anglicisation schemes" had been designed to "convert Irish children into 'little Johnny Bulls.'"[11] Indeed, one enthusiast for the movement, Arthur Clery, described anglicization as "that most deadly of mental opiates," which was denuding the country of its national spirit.[12]

Against this backdrop, Sinn Féiners committed themselves to "rebuilding Irish nationhood" and forging a "new mind," which might resist "the spirit of Anglicisation."[13] A "nation in the true sense of the word," it was argued, must be "self-reliant and separate from other nations, not only in regard to its political institutions, but [also] in regard to its language and mental outlook and industries."[14]

Frequently, the alleged "materialism" of English culture was juxtaposed to the inherent "spirituality" of the Irish nation.[15] Clery thus saw "English culture" as "superficial," "shallow," and "sterile."[16] "Bourgeois England" was, he felt, dominated by purely material considerations. "The English mind," D. P. Moran likewise suggested, was "essentially one which justifies the means by the end. . . . It is narrow and bigoted by nature, and it is bloated by the fat traditions of success."[17] Its highest aim was said to be to "find new markets."[18] As Foster and Tom Garvin have pointed out in their respective works, a key impulse here was the readiness of Irish intellectuals to condemn "bourgeois" life as irredeemably materialistic and unspiritual. To this was added a certain ambivalence about "the city" in the abstract. Despite the fact that their movement was strongest in towns, Sinn Féiners tended to revere a rural cultural ethos and identity, while seeing the urban environment as alien and English.[19]

This antiurban and anticommercial ethos could be detected in the later writing of Aodh de Blácam, who described the great crowded industrial cities of Britain and America as "horrible perversions of the natural order." Capitalism in general, de Blácam wrote, was "unnatural, like the drink curse," and he yearned for a new "rural polity."[20]

Such arcadian visions were far from ubiquitous across the Irish Ireland movement—and indeed were explicitly repudiated by figures like Griffith and Moran. Even so, de Blácam's words were indicative of the strong moral dimension, which was frequently bound up with critiques of the British order in Ireland.[21] To many Sinn Féiners, what was required was a concerted effort to "strengthen the character of the Irish people"—and this was reflected in an emphasis on moral probity.[22] There was, for instance, a marked hostility toward gambling—described variously as the "betting nuisance" and the "betting evil." The prevalence of this pastime was said to reflect the "pernicious atmosphere" of the "Garrison" as opposed to that of the "Gael." Sinn Féin bewailed this "foreign importation" that was deemed no less damaging than "the degrading vice of intemperance." It was claimed that the ships that carried "British goods into Ireland" also brought "British vices," including that "damnable passion for gambling."[23]

"Foreign dances" were likewise judged by one Irish Ireland activist to be suspect, on account of their "insidiously debasing" and "denationalising influences." It was maintained that the "giddy whirl of the fantastic waltz, pandering as it does to the softer attributes of the sex," exercised "a most baneful influence over its devotees, warping their powers of concentration, weakening their faculties of imagination and fancy, deflecting the course of their higher thoughts and impulses, and leaving them in a condition of indefinable inanlioquence [*sic*]—call it idiotic amorousness, if you will."[24] It should be said that the editors of *Sinn Féin* did themselves disavow a belief in the "immorality of the waltz," but it seems clear that comments like those cited above were fairly typical within the movement—reflecting as they did particular ideas about morality, gender, and national identity.[25] And the newspaper did opine that social gatherings held by Irish Ireland organizations should properly confine themselves to "native dances," while all public or semipublic functions in Ireland should contain a majority of the same. Irish men and women who danced "foreign dances to the exclusion of native ones" were labeled "unpatriotic and culpable." Foreign dances were, in the words of another columnist, to be left "to the Seoinini [West Britons] and the Garrison."[26]

The latter reference was scarcely incidental. *Sinn Féin* averred that recruits into the British army were presented with an array of "opportunities and temptations for the gratifying" of a man's "worst and most degrading propensities." It was claimed that nearly a third of British soldiers were "the victims of their own vices" and that military bases were "plague spots" of venereal disease—a "foul ulcer" that was "spreading through the land."[27]

In keeping with this language, many drawn into the ambit of Irish Ireland activism evoked a sense of urgency—or what Garvin has called a fear of "cultural death."[28] Moran argued that the "very existence" of Ireland as a nation was under threat from the advance of the "Anglo-Saxon race, or, as it is now being called, the English-speaking race."[29] He expressed his dismay that the Irish took "all our ideas from England" and were "afraid to have any of our own."[30] Clery likewise worried that they were losing everything that made them "distinctively Irish" and were becoming "merely a discontented body of Britons."[31] And *Sinn Féin* lamented that "intellectual stagnation" had overtaken the "Irish race" when "it substituted the English language for the Irish as its vehicle of thought."[32]

It was to change this state of affairs that Douglas Hyde had established his Gaelic League in 1893, his goal being to reverse the "Englishing of Ireland."[33] Hyde called for an "Irish Revival"—a "general renaissance" that would see the awakening of "national consciousness."[34] In a similar vein, *Sinn Féin* urged its readers to foster a sense of "the larger nationality" through a cultural revival across "language, industries, music, art, habits and customs."[35] For writers like Clery, the value of the Irish language lay in the fact that it was "the one really distinctive thing we have."[36] As one *Sinn Féin* columnist put it, "A nation which possesses a national tongue, and gives it up, is itself voluntarily giving up its right to a free, unfettered national life. When, in addition, it adopts the language of its conqueror, it is locking the door of freedom on itself and handing over the key to its jailor."[37]

Moran, too, claimed that twenty minutes into his first Irish language class in 1896 he was struck by the realization: "Well hang them for Sassenachs, we have at least one thing they can't lay claim to, any way."[38] In his *The Philosophy of Irish Ireland*, he described a "distinct language" as "usually the most prominent mark of a nation," coupled with the existence of a broader set of "national traditions," customs, and culture.[39] He went on to assert that "Ireland will be nothing until she is a nation, and, as a nation is a civilization, she will never accomplish anything worthy of herself until she falls back upon her own language and traditions."[40] The "foundation of Ireland," according to Moran, was necessarily "the Gael"; this, he said famously, "must be the element that absorbs."[41]

In this way, the profound sense of civilizational crisis that animated adherents of Sinn Féin was matched only by their faith that all was not lost—indeed, that the moment of deliverance was at hand. A 1906 article in *Sinn Féin* stated that they faced a "critical moment in Ireland to-day." "We are awakening," the author observed, "from a long, long sleep. Many are still sleeping around us while others are rubbing their eyes dreamily and asking themselves where they are." In this context, the piece went on, those people who were "wide awake" bore a "great responsibility," for they had to "teach the sleepy folk where they are, and what they have to do, while those who are still asleep have to be aroused and taught their duty to their country."[42]

Prominent Sinn Féiners like Micheál Ó hAnnracháin urged individuals to "apply the principles" of the movement in their "everyday life." People were called to "think on national matters"; and Ó hAnnracháin criticized those who were "living-without-thinking." He demanded that his readers "Raise Sinn Féin . . . as our watch-cry . . . [m]orning, noon, and night" and be "Sinn Féiners in practice as well as preaching."[43] Another writer, meanwhile, argued that Sinn Féin's purpose was to engage in "practical rather than theoretical work." It was the "duty of each Sinn

Féiner," it was suggested, "to do the work that is to be done rather than say it should be done."[44] A later pamphlet on the *Ethics of Sinn Féin* appealed for everyone to "put into practice within himself or herself what might be called a Me Féin policy"—seeing themselves as "the Irish nation in miniature" and working to be "self-reliant and free."[45]

Sinn Féiners were convinced that the "revival" of an authentic and more virtuous Gaelic-Irish, cultural self—both on the part of the individual and across society as a whole—would foster a new sense of national self-worth and confidence. Griffith's introduction to *The Sinn Féin Policy* spoke explicitly about the recovery of "national dignity."[46] In calling his policy "Sinn Féin," he had deliberately invoked the Young Ireland movement of the 1840s and Thomas Davis' newspaper, *The Nation*. It was within that newspaper that the poet John O'Hagan articulated the English words that later came to be associated with the term "Sinn Féin," when he wrote, "Yet on 'ourselves' do we rely . . . 'Ourselves alone' our rallying cry!" This phrase, "ourselves alone," was rendered into Gaelic by *The Nation*'s editors as "Sinn Féin." Half a century later, when Griffith was looking to encapsulate his policy, it is claimed that Maire Butler suggested the name to him.[47] Davis, said Griffith, had sought to make Ireland a "self-governing nation" in the truest sense—rather than the shallow vision offered by parliamentarians.[48] And it was this ideal that he, Griffith, hoped to revive.

The essence of his Sinn Féin policy was to be the "nation's faith in itself." This was said to mark a departure from the ethos of the previous thirty years when Ireland had been "taught to regard herself as too weak to rise by her own efforts" and instead to "centre her hope and place her reliance in the generosity of her enemies."[49] As a poem in one early edition of the *Sinn Féin* newspaper declared—in an obvious echo of the early period:

> Not by slavish fellowship, not by hired prste [*sic*] . . .
> We will not be freedmen by a master's leave . . .
> Here we strive and, fighting, for the land we own,
> As we hope for freedom, trust Ourselves Alone.[50]

Elsewhere, Moran urged the recovery of "national pride," "self-respect," and "self-dependence," which had purportedly been lost by having been "brought up from our cradles in a half-hearted Anglo-Saxon civilization."[51] A 1907 pamphlet sought to mobilize the people around a doctrine of "national self-reliance."[52] And *Sinn Féin* saw itself as incubating the "spirit of revolt."[53]

In adopting this ethos of self-assertion, Sinn Féiners offered a strident critique of the hitherto dominant Irish nationalist elite, represented by the Irish Parliamentary Party (IPP). This was dismissed as possessing "little popular strength and no popular respect."[54] The voice of the IPP was labeled "the beggar's whine"—indicative of those statesmen who preferred to "apologise" for the existence of the Irish nation, rather than demand "full political emancipation."[55] Another *Sinn Féin* columnist wrote in vitriolic fashion of the "traitorous parliamentarian on the spouting platform, or the . . . spouting floor of a foreign legislature," who held up "to the gaze of her ravishers, the torn and naked body of his Motherland, and asks for pity, with the crying lip of a beggar and a slave, when he could, by a more direct attention to her wants, and under the influence of a salutary shame, staunch her wounds, steady the palpitating beat of her heart, and present her clothed and armed before the world."[56] Implicit in such words was the militancy that would later come to define the Sinn Féin movement during the years of the Irish Revolution. And it is clear—the impact of contingent events notwithstanding—that its later "radicalisation" was encouraged by a certain reverence for martial imagery and what Foster terms "hyper-masculinity," which were present from the outset.[57]

More immediately, the kind of language deployed in reference to the IPP made plain the inherently political nature of the Sinn Féin project. This was not merely something that came later as a consequence of external influences. Although a body like the Gaelic League *was* founded as an avowedly apolitical entity, the subsequently acknowledged truth was that its members could not ignore the "political aspects of the Irish Language movement."[58] Indeed, even in Hyde's formulation, the league stood above "all petty politics"—rather than politics per se.[59] As one writer for *Sinn Féin* put it, "Political unity and independence—Statehood—are the first and chief requisites of Nationality."[60] The newspaper and the National Council with which it was associated were committed to supporting the establishment of "a National Legislature endowed with the Moral Authority of the Irish Nation."[61] And to this end *Sinn Féin* insisted that it was right to resist the exercise of the British state's "usurped" authority in Ireland.[62]

Prior to the First World War, such talk remained largely speculative and at the margins of political debate. When tested at the polls, it proved unsuccessful. In 1907, C. J. Dolan, the IPP MP for North Leitrim, resigned his seat and joined the freshly inaugurated Sinn Féin party. At the ensuing by-election he was handsomely defeated by the IPP candidate. Nevertheless, Dolan did secure some 27 percent of the vote and the result was suggestive of a constituency for the Sinn Féin message.[63] Furthermore, in Sinn Féin's calls for a tax boycott and for a refusal to administer the machinery of state, it was possible to identify the seeds of the policies that would be brought to fruition in the revolutionary years.

From the beginning, then, the idea of Sinn Féin became associated with a readiness to challenge the entire edifice of British power in Ireland. This included a demand for the creation of new political institutions—but the vision for an alternative Ireland ran far wider than that. As Roy Foster has observed, the "revolutionary generation" sought to bring about a transformation of their collective "self" through the embrace of an authentic Irish identity, defined against the perceived materialism and immorality of British cultural colonialism.[64] And as the next section explores, many Sinn Féiners were conscious of the extent to which their project was of a piece with a broader, global moment.

### "We Are All in the Same Boat": An Ethos of Solidarity

As a recent biographer of Arthur Griffith has made clear, his politics were shaped by international events—not least by the Boer War of 1899–1902.[65] It was partly Griffith's sympathy for the Boer cause that impelled him to establish the *United Irishman*, the forerunner newspaper to *Sinn Féin* (though some have questioned the depth of his engagement with the substance of the conflict in southern Africa).[66] Certainly, to many Irish republicans, anti-imperialism abroad was a natural corollary of their opposition to British rule at home. This was reflected in the pages of *Sinn Féin* where the articulation of an internationalist perspective was also a means by which to assert precisely the kind of self-confident identity which was at the core of the movement's being.[67]

For this reason, the newspaper regularly ran an "Over the Frontier" feature, which carried news of purportedly like-minded struggles. Ireland was said to be "emerging from the insularity imposed on her for the last couple of hundred years." It was, *Sinn Féin* said, paying new attention to the "smaller Continental nations" whose "successful efforts on behalf of nationality and national characteristics [had] given her heart of hope in her own struggle." Special mention was made of "the brilliant examples set by Hungary and Belgium."[68] Elsewhere, readers were informed about the plight of the Basques—foreshadowing a sense of shared endeavor that would endure down to the twenty-first century—as well as the Poles, Bessarabians, and Bohemians.[69] In each instance, it seems clear that what drew the eye—and sympathy—of Sinn Féiners was the perception of shared nationalist struggle, in the face of established imperial power. Contemporary events in Europe were read through this lens.

More broadly, too, *Sinn Féin* closely followed the attempts made by other peoples to protect indigenous languages against "anglicising" processes of social change—particularly in terms of education. This included the Sinhalese in Ceylon and once more the Boers in South Africa—whose respective efforts to preserve their culture were seen as parallel to those of Irish Ireland.[70] In June 1906, for instance, a lengthy article described the "particularly interesting" situation in Ceylon, where the British faced Buddhist opposition to "anglicisation" and an effort to establish the "compulsory teaching of the national language in all the schools of the island"; the same movement was said to be intent on challenging "the thoughtless imitation of Western ways and habits."[71] With regard to South Africa, meanwhile, Sinn Féin welcomed the fact that a "a very fine anti-British-goods spirit" seemed to be "permeating the colony."[72]

Most significantly for present purposes, attention was also regularly drawn to events in India, with an emphasis on the iniquities of British rule and attempts there to repress the nationalist movement.[73] In 1906, *Sinn Féin* reprinted a lengthy editorial from the Calcutta-based newspaper *Amrita Bazar Patrika*, which asserted, "We are all in the same boat—the Indians, the Irish, and the masses in England. We all are ruled by the governing caste of England, not in our own interests but in that of theirs . . . the Irish and the Indians are very much in the same condition. So what is good for Ireland ought to be good for India in many respects." The same piece urged its readers toward action, rather than mere words, noting that "solid work and self-sacrifice" were essential for success. It further suggested that Griffith's notion of Sinn Féin was a "model" upon which the advocates of Swadeshi could usefully draw.[74]

In early 1907, *Sinn Féin* reported enthusiastically on a speech given by the Indian nationalist activist Bipin Chandra Pal, in which he had praised the Swadeshi movement for having encouraged his countrymen to look past English narratives about their own weakness and degeneracy. Swadeshists were said to be infused with an ethos of "benevolent indifference" akin to that of Sinn Féin, with their preference for Indian over English-made goods and their inculcation of national spirit.[75] Swadeshi, readers in Ireland were informed, was nothing less than the "India Sinn Féin movement."[76]

This ethos of international solidarity was also evident in relation to events in Egypt. In August 1906, *Sinn Féin* carried an account of the "cruel" and "barbarous" floggings and hangings that had been handed out by the British authorities to the villagers of Dinshaway—an episode that became a key driver of Egyptian nationalist mobilization.[77] In the aftermath, the newspaper quoted the nationalist leader Mustafa Kamil Pasha and his demands for Egyptian self-government.[78] And it also endorsed the Egyptian claim to Sudan, referring to the latter as territory that had been "torn" away by British policy, in what amounted to a calculated assault on "the soul of Egypt."[79]

A few months later, another article pointed to the "bloodstained regime" established by the British (and especially Lord Cromer) in Cairo, the instruments of which were "the lash and the gallows and the bribe." It was clear, said *Sinn Féin*, that "England will not yield until Egypt learns to rely upon herself—learns to think and act for herself, and then she will yield because she cannot do otherwise. How far Egyptian nationalism can translate itself into Sinn Féin remains to be seen. If its performance is as good as its promise, shown in the overthrow of Cromer, the Egyptian bondage will not last another decade."[80]

In Egypt, as much as in India, then, Sinn Féiners seemed convinced that they had found kindred spirits. How to explain such far-flung affinities? Statements of solidarity of the kind identified above can of course be dismissed as little more than cynical posturing—cost-free exercises that were framed solely by local exigencies. But the contention here would be, first, that they do reveal something important about the worldview of their protagonists; and second, perhaps more importantly, that the comparisons being drawn were not without merit. For in India, Egypt, and elsewhere, it was possible to identify the emergence of movements committed to the politics of authenticity.

### Swadeshi: "Ourselves Alone" in India

The Swadeshi movement that rose to prominence in India during the first decade of the twentieth century was, rather like its Sinn Féin counterpart, a rather diffuse phenomenon, one more or less united around a series of core precepts. "Swadeshi" became the watchword for a new generation of nationalists who demanded an end to India's presumed cultural erosion. As one of its leading lights, the aforementioned Bipin Chandra Pal argued, "Not only had our territories been conquered by the English, but by this English education even our mind, our mental ideas, our spiritual aspirations, all these had been got hold of by this foreign Government, this foreign culture, this foreign civilisation."[81] For Pal—in an obvious echo of Irish Sinn Féiners—India's problem was above all a "psychological" one. The British, he said, ruled India "not by force of arms," but through "hypnotism," or "maya." The goal of the new movement therefore was to "dispel the illusion, to kill and destroy this hypnotism"—to persuade the people that they were strong and capable of overcoming the British.[82] The battle for "swaraj," or self-rule, Pal declared, was being waged around the "citadel" that was the "the heart, [and] the mind of the people, of the masses."[83] Even more evocative were the words of another ardent Swadeshist, Sri Aurobindo Ghosh, who described British control of India as "no ordinary rough-riding despotism, but [rather] quiet, pervasive and subtle"; it had, he said, "fastened its grip on every detail of our national life and will not easily be persuaded to let go, even in the last degree, its octopus-like hold."[84]

According to men like Pal and Aurobindo, India's liberation would never come through the "imitation of European ideals and institutions." Such an approach, they believed, would only strengthen "the hold of the alien political authority established in the country."[85] In a striking turn of phrase, Pal declared that it was only "by our own exertions that we should improve our good. As one fruit cannot borrow the juice or taste of another fruit, so I began to think that our improvement depended upon ourselves alone."[86]

One aspect of this desire for self-sufficiency was the call for people to use vernacular languages and avoid the medium of English wherever possible.[87] Aurobindo decried the fact that there were people in Bengal who spoke "no other language than English." "This," he said, showed how "unnatural our way of life has become," and flowed from a situation of "foreign dependence." He urged Swadeshi activists to speak primarily in Bengali.[88] In similar fashion, the poet and novelist Rabindranath Tagore, an early (and later disillusioned) advocate of Swadeshi, worried about the impact of anglicization on India and hoped for an all-encompassing Indian cultural "renaissance."[89]

Even more than was the case in Ireland, meanwhile, the protagonists of Swadeshi emphasized that theirs was "essentially a spiritual movement." To see it as merely "economic or political," Pal averred, was "to misunderstand it altogether."[90] "India," said Aurobindo, needed to be "made conscious of her greatness by an overmastering sense of the greatness of her spirituality." This, Aurobindo believed, was "the main feeder of all patriotism."[91]

As was the case among Sinn Féiners, Swadeshists routinely identified the British with materialism, utilitarianism, individualism, "Manchester," and the industrial capitalist system.[92] Aurobindo referred to the "commercial vigour and expansive energy" of the "English mind," noting that it had "not any habit of entertaining clear and high ideals." Its horizons, he said, were "limited to the visible and material," and the English had "put their whole force into mechanical invention." The result, he acknowledged, had been "stupendous material Success," but at the cost of a great "defect of speculative imagination."[93] For Aurobindo, there was no doubting the "superiority of Eastern civilisation" with its "humanitarian and socialistic aspect," its "predominating feature of spirituality," and "the absence of a militant Materialism."[94]

It was a view to which Tagore and others, including Mohandas Gandhi, would subscribe, with India, and indeed Asia, imagined to possess a distinct, more spiritual form of civilization than the mechanized, soulless, and materialist "West."[95] "We, in the East," Tagore wrote, "believe in personality. In the West you have your admiration for power."[96] On another occasion, he cautioned against the "degradation which labourers face when they migrate to town to work in the factories set up by capitalists." Such factories were, Tagore argued, "like whirlpools," drawing "into their vortex the poor villagers" who were then confined to the "joyless and mechanical work of tending machines." It was to the "moribund" villages of India—the repository of the nation's spiritual heritage—that he looked for cultural renewal. Self-government could be achieved, Tagore averred, only by making people self-reliant and prosperous.[97] Even more strident were the views of Gandhi, who believed that the "tendency of Indian civilization" was "to elevate the moral being," while that of Western civilization was "to propagate immorality." The latter, he suggested, was "godless," whereas the former was "based on a belief in God."[98]

Furthermore, as in Ireland, there was an urgency to the Swadeshi cause. Aurobindo warned that India was facing "imminent national death." It had, he said, been brought to the "verge of exhaustion and decay" by "bureaucratic rule"—though he insisted that there was still hope for salvation if they acted now.[99] What this meant, according to Pal, was making Indians "conscious of their own power and strength."[100] He told one audience that he did not favor "*swaraj* [self-rule] obtained as a favour from Government"; rather, it "must be obtained by the strength of character and of purpose" of the people.[101] Pal urged his followers to set aside the "old faith of the people in the British Government as the saviour of their country," and instead to acquire a "new and intrepid faith in themselves."[102]

Others similarly claimed that Swadeshi meant learning "the value of standing on one's own legs" and developing "self-reliance, self-help and self-confidence."[103] The charismatic nationalist leader Bal Gangadhar Tilak often stressed the ideas of "self-help," "determination," and "sacrifice."[104] Elsewhere, Aurobindo called for "self-development by self help," as the only means by which Indians might free themselves from "the fatal dependence, passivity and helplessness" that flowed from a century of "all-pervasive British control."[105] The newspaper he helped found and edit, *Bande Mataram*, inveighed its readers, "We must help ourselves . . . we must depend on our own strength."[106]

As in Ireland, this posture offered a clear challenge to the established nationalist political elite that dominated the INC, and which had tended to press for only moderate concessions. Since the 1890s Aurobindo had been arguing that India would "not get from the British Parliament anything better than nominal redress, or at the most a petty and tinkering legislation." "If we are indeed to renovate our country," Aurobindo asserted, "we must no longer hold out supplicating hands to the English Parliament, like an infant crying to its nurse for a toy, but must recognise the hard truth that every nation must beat out its own path to salvation with pain and difficulty, and not rely on the tutelage of another."[107] He was unsparing in his critique of the INC, describing it as "a middle-class organ selfish and disingenuous in its public action and hollow in its professions of a large and disinterested patriotism."[108] Congress, said Aurobindo, had shown its commitment to a "purely mendicant policy," which revealed only its "own weakness."[109] Others echoed this criticism. Even Tagore noted, "We were, at one time, overwhelmed by the splendour of Europe and accepted its gifts without discrimination, like beggars. That was not the way to make any real gain. Whether it is knowledge or a political right, it must be earned; that is, it can be real for us only if we win it by struggle with obstructing forces."[110]

Against this backdrop, and as was the case with Sinn Féin, there was no denying the fundamentally political nature of Swadeshism. Indeed, Aurobindo dismissed the notion of "unpolitical Swadeshism" and attempts to "ignore the unignorable."[111] "Everything that concerns the welfare of the polis," said Aurobindo, "is political."[112] After 1905, the political character of Swadeshism was reinforced as key leaders preached "passive resistance" and noncooperation in response to the partition of Bengal and demanded immediate self-rule for India.[113] Aurobindo talked now of a "prolonged struggle" to challenge the authority of the "despotic foreign bureaucracy" in all spheres of life.[114]

"For a subject people," Aurobindo insisted, there was "no royal road to emancipation. They must wade to it through struggle, sacrifice, slaughter, if necessary. History suggests no short-cut."[115] He dismissed that "party of men" who still clung to the notion that they might "obtain Swaraj by asking for it." The reality, maintained Aurobindo, was that they had to "acquire it by their own efforts"; for just as "we cannot master the art of swimming unless we struggle in water," so they should "be prepared to undergo hardships in the struggle for Swaraj as there is no other alternative."[116] Similarly, another Swadeshist, Lala Lajpat Rai, stated plainly, "I believe in struggle—a righteous, stern, and unyielding struggle."[117] And one leading newspaper declared that what were required were "deeds and not words"—for words alone would "not save the dying nation."[118]

As in Ireland, when considering such rhetoric, the roots of the more militant posture that would evolve later were again only too evident. But what was perhaps most significant was the extent to which Swadeshism, as Manu Goswami has emphasized, marked not a retreat from the political but rather the embrace of a much broader conception of the political. It marked the rejection of a classically liberal idea of the relationship between the individual and society, or the individual and the state. Instead, it urged Indians to recover a more fulfilling mode of being, through the realization of their "true selves." Such authentic identities, it was imagined, would serve as the foundation for an alternative model of state and society.[119] And they would, it was hoped, bring about liberation in the fullest sense.

At this point it is worth pausing to emphasize that none of the foregoing should be taken to suggest that these movements were in any way derivative or imitative of one or another. Louise Williams has shown, by a close study of Tagore and W. B. Yeats, how very similar ideas could emerge in parallel between two men who—at least initially—were not in contact with one another.[120] The point might usefully be drawn in relation to the wider movements of Sinn Féin and Swadeshi; for, as Michael Silvestri has made clear, synergies between India and Ireland were not the product of direct relationships—or only rarely so.[121] It is true that individuals like Sri Aurobindo were conscious of events in Ireland. But the reality is that he had been articulating key ideas that would inform "Swadeshi" since the 1890s—long before Sinn Féin became an identifiable phenomenon. And as he did so he was influenced as much, if not more so, by Indian writers like Bankimchandra Chatterjee, who had advocated for a more authentic form of national identity, one rooted in both the Bengali language and Hinduism.

There was, then, no linear diffusion of ideas from Ireland to India. In each country, the politics of authenticity manifested in different ways, shaped by local circumstance—even as the resulting movements remained recognizable as part of a shared, global phenomenon.[122]

## The Global Revolt Against Empire

A number of scholars have noted the emergence of a culturalist discourse in the late nineteenth and early twentieth centuries. Andrew Sartori, for instance, has described this as a reaction to the structural logic of global capitalism as refracted through the lens of a *soi-disant* "liberal" imperialism.[123] Elsewhere, Goswami has observed that Swadeshi was the product of a specific conjuncture, which he framed as 1870–1914, and in which there flourished "widely shared particularistic and organic conceptions of nationhood."[124] Dominic Sachsenmaier has similarly referred to the "Age of Anxiety" in the decades leading up to and beyond the First World War, which saw the rise of "cultural alternatives" to Western-led modernity.[125]

The war itself of course exacerbated many of the sociopolitical trends already in evidence. It turbo-charged the growth of "the state"; it shattered the self-confidence of European empires; it encouraged and transformed anti-imperialist movements in a variety of ways; and it brought forth a new language for talking about "self-determination."[126] And yet for all that, the war was not the *fons et origo* of what eventuated in countries like Ireland. While the years after 1918 proved effervescent, it would be a mistake to overstate the impact of any "Wilsonian moment."[127] Instead, the politics of cultural authenticity were a response to empire—and especially British empire—as experienced over a much longer time span and at a more profound level.

For similar reasons, I would argue that it is useful to extend the chronological boundaries accorded to the conjuncture in question, tracing it all the way down to 1945. This again has the benefit of mitigating an over-focus on the First World War—or even, in the Irish context, the "long decade" of 1911–1923—while recognizing that this era, written broadly, was one of decisive change.[128] The years between 1870 and 1945 witnessed both the apex of Western imperial power but also an array of challenges to that power.

As Hedley Bull has noted, Western dominance of the international system perhaps peaked around 1900.[129] Even as it did so, numerous movements sought to contest imperial rule and imagined a different world order; they critiqued, too, the effect that modernity, as experienced through the Western lens, was having on their social, cultural, and economic landscapes.[130] This era had seen the first great wave of globalization, powered by the "second industrial revolution." The spread of steam, railways, and the telegraph in turn fueled the new imperialism and industrial-capitalist expansion. And this brought new forms of sociability and social relations into being; so too, new modes of power, order, and violence.[131] As societies across the planet were bound into the worldwide capitalist system, the period was experienced by many as one of intense, ongoing transformation and crisis.[132]

In 1907, the Swadeshi activist Sri Aurobindo alluded to this awareness of contemporary upheavals when he observed, "There are periods in the history of the world when the unseen Power that guides its destinies seems to be filled with a consuming passion for change and a strong impatience of the old." These were, he said, "periods of rapid destruction and energetic creation . . . the crash of great downfalls and the turmoil of swift and violent revolutions." In the process, the "world is thrown into the smelting pot and comes out in a new shape and with new features . . . in such a period we find ourselves at the dawn of this twentieth century."[133] On another occasion, Aurobindo wrote of the "Zeitgeist, the Time-Spirit," which was working "to bring about a mighty movement of which the world at the present juncture has need."[134] In India's confrontation with the British, he drew arresting parallels with events elsewhere:

In Egypt, in India, in Ireland the most Radical Government of modern times is bracing itself to a policy of repression. It thinks England has only to stamp her foot and all the trouble will be over. Yet only consider how many ideas are arising which find in British despotism their chief antagonist. The idea of a free and self-centred Ireland has been reborn and the souls of Fitzgerald and Emmett are reincarnating. The idea of a free Egypt and the Pan-Islamic idea have joined hands in the land of the Pharaohs. The idea of a free and united India has been born and arrived at full stature in the land of the Rishis, and the spiritual force of a great civilisation of which the world has need, is gathering at its back.[135]

Needless to say, such words would have been welcomed, and endorsed, by many in both Egypt and Ireland.

In this way, Aurobindo offered just one iteration of the widely held view that humanity was being enveloped by a "crisis," but one that raised the prospect that a new order might arise—one built on alternative foundations to those of Western-led imperialism. Amid the global circulation of ideas, groups and individuals reacted to these shared stimuli and embraced certain key concepts, while modifying them to suit local contexts.[136]

With this in mind, it is striking that for both Sinn Féin and the Swadeshi movement, the year 1905 proved decisive. What Harald Fischer-Tiné called the "annus mirabilis" of anti-imperial nationalism, was galvanized by the 1905–1906 war between Russia and Japan. This was a "global moment," which challenged the hitherto dominant, Eurocentric geopolitical and moral world order.[137] As Cemil Aydin has underlined, the war was experienced as an episode of "world-historical significance."[138]

For its part, *Sinn Féin* watched with interest the outcome of the 1905–1906 conflict and what this implied about the rise of anti-imperial nationalism. It welcomed the prospect of a newly assertive Japan, challenging the British and other entrenched imperial interests.[139] Perhaps more significantly, Japan's victory over Russia mobilized a swathe of nationalist activists across "the East"—who came increasingly to imagine themselves as "Eastern" and thereby distinct from "the West." Japan was heralded as the avatar of an alternative, non-Western form of modernity. It stirred hopes that Western power could be overcome, through an awakening of latent Eastern strength.[140]

One vernacular Indian newspaper in the Punjab thus observed that "no one ever thought of Japan winning the day, but all the same she administered the Muscovites a very severe beating."[141] Similarly, in a 1907 speech, Bipin Chandra Pal commented that their "drooping spirits" were raised by "contemplating the rise of Japan."[142] And Aurobindo wrote enthusiastically of the "swift, irresistible and impetuous bounding into life of Japan," stating that there was "no instance in history of a more marvelous and sudden up-surging of strength in a nation than modern Japan."[143] As the British later noted, "the Asiatic world" was "electrified and amazed by the victories of Japan over Russia."[144]

In Egypt, as mentioned above, there had already emerged a counterpart to Swadeshi and Sinn Féin, with the flowering of Mustafa Kamil's nationalist movement and party (Hizb al-Watan). Kamil talked in familiar terms about the need for self-strengthening and was especially impressed by the rise of Japanese power. He authored a book, *The Rising Sun*, which encouraged emulation of the Asian model. And Kamil hoped that Japan's defeat of Russia in the 1905–1906 war might prefigure a shift in the global balance of power against the West and, in particular, against the British, whom he saw as "enemy no. 1."[145]

Unfortunately, there is not the space here to explore the contours of Egypt's own experience with the politics of cultural authenticity—as a particular mode of anti-imperialist politics—other than to note that it is possible to identify an ethos and enduring set of impulses, akin to those that were operating in the cases of Swadeshi and Sinn Féin, but which came to take a very different format in subsequent years.

More generally, there were, throughout this period, numerous utopian movements that framed distinct anti-imperialist projects that drew together an eclectic mix of anticolonial, socialist, nationalist, and romantic ideas. Many of them were expressed through a discourse centered on ideas of "civilizational" and "cultural" authenticity, articulated in a local idiom.[146] Whether in Ireland, India, or Egypt—or indeed China, Korea, Iran, or elsewhere—"self-strengthening" movements sought to challenge European imperialist hegemony through an insistence on their own authentic character.[147]

They were all, in their own way, part of the global "revolt" against the West and what that West was perceived to represent, in terms of a worldwide capitalist, "liberal" order, structured *by* and *for* the imperialist powers. Dilip Menon is therefore right to refer to the "worldwide insurgency against empire" that drew in Swadeshists, Sinn Féiners, and others who were prepared to question European, and especially British, "hegemony."[148] Such insurgents imagined a culturally more authentic alternative that might provide the foundation for a new and better world.[149] And the launch of the Irish Revolution marked but one attempt to make those dreams a reality.

NOTES

1 For a good example of this kind of narrative, see Jan Morris, *Farewell the Trumpets: An Imperial Retreat* (London: Faber & Faber, 2012), 219: "It was in Ireland, even before the Great War ended, that the prototype of imperial revolution was launched—the precursor of all coups, rebellions and civil wars which were to harass the British Empire from now until the end."

2 For an evocative and wide-ranging account of this moment, see Adam Tooze, *The Deluge: The Great War and the Remaking of Global Order, 1916–1931* (London: Penguin, 2015).

3 John G. Darwin, "The Fear of Falling: British Politics and Imperial Decline since 1900," *Transactions of the Royal Historical Society* 36 (1986): 34. On the interweaving of crises, see also John Gallagher, "Nationalisms and the Crisis of Empire, 1919–1922," *Modern Asian Studies* 15, no. 3 (1981): 355–368; Keith Jeffery, "Sir Henry Wilson and the Defence of the British Empire, 1918–22," *Journal of Imperial and Commonwealth History* 5, no. 3 (1977): 270–293.

4 Cited in Gallagher, "Nationalisms and the Crisis of Empire," 367. See also Michael Silvestri, *Ireland and India: Nationalism, Empire and Memory* (Basingstoke: Palgrave Macmillan, 2009), esp. 46–75. On the Indian National Congress, see Peter Heehs, *India's Freedom Struggle, 1857–1947: A Short History* (New Delhi: Oxford University Press, 1988), 60–75.

5 High Commissioner Edmund Allenby in Sept. 1920, cited in Jeffery, "Sir Henry Wilson."

6 Chirol, cited in Silvestri, *Ireland and India*, 56.

7 In reflecting on the "politics of cultural authenticity," I am building in part on the work of the American philosopher Marshall Berman who defined this as an attempt to reconcile individuality with the "dream of an ideal community." For Berman this was a new phenomenon that emerged in the context of the fluid, mobile, capitalist societies that came into being from the late eighteenth century onward. See Marshall Berman, *The Politics of Authenticity: Radical Individualism and the Emergence of Modern Society* (London: George Allen & Unwin, 1970), vii–viii, xiv–xvi, 31–32, 75–88. On the subject of authenticity as shaping a particular mode of politics, see also Robert D. Lee, *Overcoming Tradition and Modernity: The Search for Islamic Authenticity* (Boulder, CO: Westview, 1997).

8 Patrick Maume, *The Long Gestation: Irish Nationalist Life, 1891–1918* (Dublin: Gill & Macmillan, 1999); R. F. Foster, *Vivid Faces: The Revolutionary Generation in Ireland, 1890–1923* (London: Allen Lane, 2014).

9 "Irish Ireland," *Sinn Féin* [hereafter *SF*], 5 May 1906.

10 "Ways and Means," *SF*, 7 July 1906. See also "Sinn Féin and Irish Trades Unionists," *SF*, 30 Mar. 1907; and Seán Ó Lúing, "Arthur Griffith and Sinn Féin," in Francis X. Martin, *Leaders and Men of the Easter Risings, Dublin 1916* (London: Methuen, 1967), 56–57.

11 "The Larger Nationality," *SF*, 1 Dec. 1906.

12  Arthur Clery, *The Idea of a Nation*, ed. Patrick Maume (Dublin: University College Dublin Press, 2002), 47.

13  "Irish Ireland," *SF*, 5 May 1906; "The External Relations of Gaelic Leaguers," *SF*, 29 Sept. 1906.

14  "The Economics of Nationalism," *SF* 38, no. 2 (19 Jan. 1907).

15  Arthur Griffith, *The Sinn Féin Policy: Fortieth Thousand* (Dublin: James Duffy, 1907), 7–8, 19. See also Tom Garvin, "Great Hatred, Little Room: Social Background and Political Sentiment among Revolutionary Activists in Ireland, 1890–1922," in *The Revolution in Ireland, 1879–1923*, ed. D. G. Boyce (Basingstoke: Macmillan, 1988), 91–114.

16  Clery, *Idea of a Nation*, 39.

17  D. P. Moran, *The Philosophy of Irish Ireland*, ed. Patrick Maume (Dublin: University College Dublin Press, 2006), 45. A journalist and founder of *The Leader* newspaper, Moran became, in the words of his biographer, perhaps the most "aggressive and articulate exponent of a Catholic Gaelic vision of Irish identity." Though a critic of Arthur Griffith and *Sinn Féin*, Moran nevertheless echoed many of their views and was part of the broader Irish Ireland movement. See Patrick Maume, *D. P. Moran* (Dundalk: Historical Association of Ireland / Dundalgan Press, 1995), 3.

18  Moran, *Philosophy of Irish Ireland*, 13. Griffith held to a similar view. See Paul Bew, *Ireland: The Politics of Enmity, 1789–2006* (Oxford: Oxford University Press, 2007), 363; Maume, *Long Gestation*, 49.

19  R. F. Foster, *Modern Ireland: 1600–1972* (London: Allen Lane, 1988), 455; Foster, *Vivid Faces*, 19; Tom Garvin, "The Anatomy of a Nationalist Revolution: Ireland, 1858–1928," *Comparative Studies in Society and History* 28, no. 3 (1986): 474; Tom Garvin, *Nationalist Revolutionaries in Ireland 1858–1922* (Dublin: Gill & Macmillan, 1987), 8–12, 103–107; Tom Garvin, "Priests and Patriots: Irish Separatism and Fear of the Modern, 1890–1914," *Irish Historical Studies* 25, no. 97 (1986): 68–72.

20  Aodh de Blácam, *What Sinn Féin Stands For* (London: Mellifont Press, n.d.), 151–156. On this strand of antimodernist Catholicism, see also Maume, *Long Gestation*, 166–167.

21  Maume, *Long Gestation*, 164–166, 208–214; Ben Novick, "Propaganda," in *The Irish Revolution, 1913–23*, ed. Joost Augusteijn (Basingstoke: Palgrave, 2002), 39–44; Foster, *Vivid Faces*, 48–58.

22  "Economics of Nationalism."

23  "The Gaelic Athletic Association: The Betting Nuisance," *SF*, 26 May 1906; "The Betting Evil," *SF*, 6 Apr. 1907.

24  "Irish Ireland: The Gaelic League: Foreign Dances," *SF*, 29 Sept. 1906.

25  Ibid.

26  "On the Dance," *SF*, 13 Oct. 1906.

27  "Anti-Enlistment," *SF*, 4 Aug. 1906; "Disease and the British Army in Ireland," *SF*, 23 Mar. 1907.

28  Garvin, *Nationalist Revolutionaries*, 59–82; Garvin, "Priests and Patriots."

29 Moran, *Philosophy of Irish Ireland*, 12. Moran, though a critic of Griffith and his newspaper, can fairly be said to have inhabited the same intellectual universe that animated the Sinn Féin movement.

30 Moran, *Philosophy of Irish Ireland*, 48. On this point, see also Donal McCartney, "Hyde, D. P. Moran and Irish Ireland," in Martin, *Leaders and Men*, 51–54.

31 Clery, *Idea of a Nation*, 5–6.

32 "Irish Ireland: The Gaelic League: New Gaelic Books," *SF*, 9 Feb. 1907. On a similar theme, see "The Gaelic League: The National Teachers," *SF*, 19 May 1906.

33 Douglas Hyde, "The Return of the Fenians," in *Ideals in Ireland*, ed. Lady Gregory (London: At the Unicorn, 1901), 65–73.

34 "Ways and Means."

35 "Larger Nationality."

36 Clery, *Idea of a Nation*, 13.

37 "Nationality," *SF*, 27 Apr. 1907.

38 D. P. Moran, "The Confessions of a Converted West Briton," *Leader*, 8 Sept. 1900, reprinted in Moran, *Philosophy of Irish Ireland*, 121–126. See also Maume, *Moran*, 8.

39 Moran, *Philosophy of Irish Ireland*, 1–2, 70.

40 Ibid., 112–113.

41 Ibid., 37.

42 "The Drama as a Nationalising Force," *SF*, 10 Nov. 1906. On a similar theme, see "The Song of the Celt," *SF*, 1 Sept. 1906; and "Irish Ireland: The Gaelic League: New Gaelic Books," *SF*, 9 Feb, 1907.

43 "Irish Ireland: The National Council," *SF*, 4 May 1907.

44 "Propaganda," *SF*, 30 Mar. 1907.

45 Riobard Ua Fhloinn, *The Ethics of Sinn Féin* (Limerick: An Comhiarle Naisiunta, n.d.), 4–5.

46 Griffith, *Sinn Féin Policy*, 2.

47 Ó Lúing, "Arthur Griffith," 58–59.

48 Griffith cited in "Irish Ireland: The National Council," *SF*, 23 Mar. 1907.

49 "The Sinn Féin Policy," *SF*, 5 May 1906.

50 "Sinn Féin Amhain," *SF*, 5 May 1906.

51 Moran, *Philosophy of Irish Ireland*, 21, 114.

52 Griffith, *Sinn Féin Policy*, 33–34.

53 "Editorial: The Situation," *SF*, 5 Jan. 1907.

54 "Editorial: The Galway Election," *SF*, 10 Nov. 1906.

55 "The Castle Catholic and Devolution," *SF*, 13 Oct. 1906.

56 "The Betting Evil," *SF*, 6 Apr. 1907.

57 Foster, *Vivid Faces*, 198.

58 "Ard-Chraobh," *SF*, 15 Dec. 1906.

59 "The Gaelic League: The Return of Dr. Hyde," *SF*, 30 June 1906.

60 "Nationality."

61 Griffith, *Sinn Féin Policy*, 33–34; "Editorial: To the Irish People," *SF*, 10 Nov. 1906.

62 "The Sinn Féin Policy in Practice," *SF*, 26 May 1906.

63 Ciarán Ó Duibhir, *Sinn Féin: The First Election 1908* (Dublin: Dumlin, 1993), 82. See also Bew, *Ireland*, 366.

64 Foster, *Vivid Faces*, 10; R. Foster, "The Irish Literary Revival," in *The Cambridge History of Ireland*, vol. 4: *1880 to the Present*, ed. Thomas Bartlett (Cambridge: Cambridge University Press, 2018), 175.

65 See Owen McGee, *Arthur Griffith* (Dublin: Irish Academic Press, 2015), 32–52.

66 Andries Wessels, "The Rhetoric of Conflict and Conflict by Rhetoric: Ireland and the Anglo-Boer War (1899–1902)," *Literator* 20, no. 3 (1999): 161–174.

67 Silvestri, *Ireland and India*, 49.

68 "Over the Frontier [hereafter OTF]: Ireland and the Continent," *SF*, 4 Aug. 1906.

69 "OTF," *SF*, 12 May 1906; "OTF," *SF*, 21 July 1906; "Irish Ireland: The Gaelic League," *SF*, 4 Aug. 1906. "OTF: The Basques," *SF*, 16 Feb. 1907.

70 "OTF," *SF*, 9 June 1906; "OTF: Ceylon," *SF*, 16 June 1906; "The Gaelic League: The Boers and Their Language," *SF*, 16 June 1906. See also in the latter "Repressive Methods in the Cape and in Ireland."

71 "OTF: Ceylon," *SF*, 23 June 1906. Again on the situation in Ceylon, see "OTF," *SF*, 25 Aug. 1906; "OTF," *SF*, 1 Sept. 1906.

72 "The Department and Protection," *SF*, 21 July 1906.

73 "OTF," *SF*, 19 May 1906; "OTF: India," *SF*, 29 Sept. 1906.

74 "OTF," *SF*, 4 Aug. 1906.

75 "OTF: India," *SF*, 2 Mar. 1907.

76 "OTF: India," *SF*, 30 Mar. 1907.

77 "OTF: Egypt," *SF*, 18 Aug. 1906.

78 "OTF: Egypt," *SF*, 11 Aug. 1906.

79 Ibid.

80 "OTF: Egypt," *SF*, 20 Apr. 1907.

81 Bipin Chandra Pal, *Swadeshi and Swaraj: The Rise of New Patriotism* (Calcutta: Yugayatri Prakashak, 1954), 191.

82 Ibid., 138–146.

83 Ibid., 188–189.

84 "The Doctrine of Passive Resistance," in *Political Writings and Speeches, 1890–1908—The Complete Works of Aurobindo*, vols. 6 and 7 (Pondicherry: Sri Aurobindo Ashram Trust, 2002), 263–303 (originally published serially in *Bande Mataram*, 11–23 Apr. 1907).

85 Bipin Chandra Pal, *Memories of My Life and Times*, vol. 1: *In the Days of My Youth (1857–1884)* (Calcutta: Bipin Chandra Pal Institute, 1973), 209–216.

86 "A Collection of Speeches Delivered by Babu B. C. Pal after His Return to Calcutta from the Madras Presidency," included with "Letter D.O. No. 43, H. H. Risley, Calcutta to A. Godley, London," 19 Dec. 1907 (speech given 3 Aug. 1907) (India Office Records and Private Papers, available at the British Library [hereafter IO], L/PJ/6/841, File 56).

87 Pal, *Memories I*, 209–216.

88  Sri Aurobindo, "Swadeshi and Boycott" (speech delivered in Dhulia on 26 Jan. 1908). Text noted down in shorthand and later typed by a police agent. This transcription was submitted as evidence in the Alipore Bomb Trial (1908–9), in *Political Writings and Speeches*, 837–844.

89  Louise B. Williams, "Overcoming the 'Contagion of Mimicry': The Cosmopolitan Nationalism and Modernist History of Rabindranath Tagore and W.B. Yeats," *American Historical Review* 112, no. 1 (2007): 69–100.

90  Bipin Chandra Pal, *Memories of My Life & Times*, vol. 2: *1886–1900* (Calcutta: Bipinchandra Pal Institute, 1973), 633–644.

91  "The Main Feeder of Patriotism," *Bande Mataram*, 19 June 1907, in *Political Writings and Speeches*, 511–513.

92  Andrew Sartori, *Bengal in Global Concept History: Culturalism in the Age of Capital* (London: University of Chicago Press, 2008), 140, 158.

93  Sri Aurobindo, "New Lamps for Old-V," *Indu Prakash*, 1893–94, in *Political Writings and Speeches*, 32–39.

94  "The Main Feeder of Patriotism," *Bande Mataram*, 19 June 1907, in *Political Writings and Speeches*, 511–513.

95  Carolien Stolte and Harald Fischer-Tiné, "Imagining Asia in India: Nationalism and Internationalism (ca. 1905–1940)," *Comparative Studies in Society and History* 54, no. 1 (2012): 65–92.

96  Uma Das Gupta, ed., *The Oxford India Tagore: Selected Writings on Education and Nationalism* (New Delhi: Oxford University Press, 2009), 168. See also Tagore's comments on the "mechanical" and materialistic character of the West in the same volume, 191–202.

97  Ibid., 134–135, 260–269.

98  Mohandas Gandhi, *Hind Swaraj, or Indian Home Rule* (Ahmedabad: Navajivan Karyalaya, 1938), 52–53, 98–101.

99  Sri Aurobindo, *The Doctrine of Passive Resistance* (Calcutta: Arya, 1948), 26–33.

100  "Annexure (xiv) to Enclosure No. 1: H. A. Stuart, Eastern Bengal and Assam: Abstract of Reports Regarding the Anti-partition Agitation during the First Half of March 1907," 15 Apr. 1907, included with "Copy of Letter from Government of India, to Secretary of State for India," 16 May 1907 (IO, L/PJ/6/836, File 4060).

101  "Annexure (xv) to Enclosure No. 1: Extracts from the Eastern Bengal and Assam Police Abstracts, Dacca," 9 Mar. 1907, included with "Copy of Letter from Government of India, to Secretary of State for India," 16 May 1907 (IO, L/PJ/6/836, File 4060). For another call for "self-help and self-reliance," see the *Amrita Bazar Patrika*, cited in "Means and Methods," in Jagadish Chandra Ghosh, ed., *A Book for the Swadeshi OR The National Problem and Its Solution* (Dacca: Self-published, 1906), 88–91.

102  Pal, *Swadeshi and Swaraj*, 55. On a similar theme, see also in the same volume, 124–138.

103  "The Hon. Rao Bahadur R. N. Mudholkar" [Presidential Address to the Third Central Provinces and Berar Provincial Conference], in *The Swadeshi Movement—A*

*Symposium: Views of Representative Indians and Anglo-Indians*, 2nd ed. (Madras: G. A. Natesan, 1919), 269–272. See also on these themes Sri Aurobindo, "Fragment of a Pamphlet," in *Political Writings and Speeches*, 67.

104 "Mr. Bal Gangadhar Tilak" (speech to the Calcutta Congress 1906, in support of the resolution on the Swadeshi movement), in *Swadeshi Movement*, 275–277.

105 Aurobindo, *Doctrine of Passive Resistance*, 8.

106 "Mr. A. Chaudhuri's Policy," *Bande Mataram*, 22 June 1907, in *Political Writings and Speeches*, 523–526.

107 "India and the British Parliament," *Indu Prakash*, 26 June 1893, in *Political Writings and Speeches*, 7–10.

108 Cited in Sartori, *Bengal*, 140.

109 Sri Aurobindo, "Is Mendicancy Successful?," *Bande Mataram*, 18 Sept. 1906, in *Political Writings and Speeches*, 173–175.

110 Gupta, *Oxford India Tagore*, 283.

111 "Mr. A. Chaudhuri's Policy," *Bande Mataram*, 22 June 1907, in *Political Writings and Speeches*, 523–526.

112 "Political or Non-political," *Bande Mataram*, 25 June 1907, in *Political Writings and Speeches*, 538–539.

113 R. C. Majumdar, "The Genesis of Extremism," in *Studies in the Bengal Renaissance: In Commemoration of the Birth Centenary of Bipinchandra Pal*, ed. Atulchandra Gupta (Jadavpur: National Council of Education, Bengal, 1958), 187–202.

114 Aurobindo, *Doctrine of Passive Resistance*, 5–7.

115 "The Leverage of Faith," *Bande Mataram*, 25 Apr. 1907, in *Political Writings and Speeches*, 346–348.

116 Sri Aurobindo, "The Meaning of Swaraj" (speech delivered in Nasik, 24 Jan. 1908). Text published in Marathi translation in the *Nasik Vritta* the next day. Retranslated into English and included in the Bombay Presidency Police Abstract of Intelligence, in *Political Writings and Speeches*, 833–836.

117 Lala Lajpat Rai, "Presidential Speech at the All-India Swadeshi Conference Held in December 1907 at Surat," in *Selected Documents of Lala Lajpat Rai*, vol. 1, ed. Ravindra Kumar (New Delhi: Anmol, 1992), 93–99.

118 *Amrita Bazar Patrika*, cited in "Means and Methods," in Ghosh, *Book for the Swadeshi*, 88–106.

119 Manu Goswami, *Producing India: From Colonial Economy to National Space* (Chicago: University of Chicago Press, 2004), 251–254.

120 Williams, "Overcoming the 'Contagion of Mimicry.'"

121 Silvestri, *Ireland and India*, 47. Kate O'Malley has shown that later, during the 1920s and 1930s, Indian and Irish nationalist activists *were* in contact with one another—to the consternation of the British. But the argument here would be that such connections were the product of certain shared perspectives, rather than their cause. See Kate O'Malley, "Ireland, India and Empire: Indo-Irish Separatist Political Links and Perceived Threats to the British Empire," in *Ireland and India: Colonies, Culture and*

*Empire*, ed. Tadhg Foley and Maureen O'Connor (Dublin: Irish Academic Press, 2006), 225–232.

122 Bernard Bate, "Swadeshi in the Time of Nations: Reflections on Sumit Sarkar's 'The Swadeshi Movement in Bengal, India and Elsewhere,'" *Economic and Political Weekly* 47, no. 42 (2012): 42–43.

123 Sartori, *Bengal*, 4–8, 51–52, 230–233.

124 Goswami, *Producing India*, 262.

125 Dominic Sachsenmaier, "Searching for Alternatives to Western Modernity—Cross-Cultural Approaches in the Aftermath of the Great War," *Journal of Modern European History* 4, no. 2 (2006): 241–260.

126 Philippa Levine, "Age of Imperial Crisis," in *The Ashgate Research Companion to Modern Imperial Histories*, ed. Philippa Levine and John Marriott (Farnham: Ashgate, 2002), 75–96.

127 Erez Manela, *The Wilsonian Moment: Self-Determination and the International Origins of Anticolonial Nationalism* (Oxford: Oxford University Press, 2007), 99–135.

128 John Horne, "James Connolly and the Great Divide: Ireland, Europe and the First World War," *Saothar* 31 (2006): 75–83.

129 Hedley Bull, "The Revolt against the West," in *The Expansion of International Society*, ed. Hedley Bull and Adam Watson (Oxford: Clarendon, 1984), 217–228.

130 Levine, "Age of Imperial Crisis," 80–81.

131 Tony Ballantyne and Antoinette Burton, "Empires and the Reach of the Global," in *A World Connecting 1870–1945*, ed. Emily Rosenberg (Cambridge, MA: Harvard University Press, 2012), 285–431, 348ff.

132 Giddens reminds us that this is perhaps the defining feature of modernity: ceaseless, rapid change. See Anthony Giddens, *Modernity and Self-Identity: Self and Society in the Late Modern Age* (Cambridge: Polity, 1991). See also Marshall Berman, *All That Is Solid Melts into Air: The Experience of Modernity* (London: Verso, 1983), 21.

133 Sri Aurobindo, "The Old Year," *Bande Mataram*, 16 Apr. 1907, in *Political Writings and Speeches*, 311–315.

134 Sri Aurobindo, "The Question of the Hour," *Bande Mataram*, 1 June 1907, in *Political Writings and Speeches*, 469–472.

135 Sri Aurobindo, "The Strength of the Idea," *Bande Mataram*, 8 June 1907, in *Political Writings and Speeches*, 493–496.

136 Manela, *Wilsonian Moment*, 16–52; C. A. Bayly, *Recovering Liberties: Indian Thought in the Age of Liberalism and Empire* (Cambridge: Cambridge University Press, 2012), 1–9, 346–347; Samuel Moyn and Andrew Sartori, "Approaches to Global Intellectual History," in *Global Intellectual History*, ed. Samuel Moyn and Andrew Sartori (New York: Columbia University Press, 2017), 3–30; David Armitage, "The Contagion of Sovereignty," *South African Historical Journal* 52, no. 1 (2005): 1–18.

137 Harald Fischer-Tiné, "Indian Nationalism and the 'World Forces': Transnational and Diasporic Dimensions of the Indian Freedom Movement on the Eve of the First World War," *Journal of Global History* 2, no. 3 (2007): 325–344. See also Cemil

Aydin, *The Politics of Anti-Westernism in Asia: Visions of World Order in Pan-Islamic and Pan-Asian Thought* (New York: Columbia University Press, 2007).

138 Cemil Aydin, "A Global Anti-Western Moment? The Russo-Japanese War, Decolonization, and Asian Modernity," in *Competing Visions of World Order: Global Moments and Movements, 1880s–1930s*, ed. Sebastian Conrad and Dominic Sachsenmaier (Basingstoke: Palgrave Macmillan, 2007), 213–236.

139 "OTF: Japan," *SF*, 18 Aug. 1906. See also "OTF," *Sinn Féin*, 2 June 1906.

140 Steven G. Marks, "'Bravo, Brave Tiger of the East!' The Russo-Japanese War and the Rise of Nationalism in British Egypt and India," in *The Russo-Japanese War in Global Perspective: World War Zero*, ed. John W. Steinberg et al. (Leiden: Brill, 2005), 609–627.

141 "Appendix I: Selections from Vernacular Papers Published in the Punjab," included with "Copy of Letter from Government of India, to Secretary of State for India," 16 May 1907 (IO, L/PJ/6/836, File 4060).

142 "Annexure (xiv) to Enclosure No. 1: H. A. Stuart, Eastern Bengal and Assam: Abstract of Reports Regarding the Anti-partition Agitation during the First Half of March 1907," 15 Apr. 1907, included with "Copy of Letter from Government of India, to Secretary of State for India," 16 May 1907 (IO, L/PJ/6/836, File 4060).

143 Sri Aurobindo, "Bhawani Mandir," in *Political Writings and Speeches*, 77–92. See also, in the same volume, "Eastern Renascence," *Bande Mataram*, 3 Sept. 1907, 670–671. On all this, see T. R. Sareen, "India and the Ear," in *The Impact of the Russo-Japanese War*, ed. Rotem Kowner (London: Routledge, 2007), 239–250.

144 *The Sedition Committee, 1918: Report* (Calcutta: Superintendent Government Printing, India, 1918), 17.

145 Marks, "'Bravo, Brave Tiger of the East!'."

146 Andrew Sartori, "The Resonance of 'Culture': Framing a Problem in Global Concept-History," *Comparative Studies in Society and History* 47, no. 4 (2005): 698. See also Sachsenmaier, "Searching for Alternatives," 254.

147 Manela, *Wilsonian Moment*, 99–135; Mehrzad Boroujerdi, "'The West' in the Eyes of the Iranian Intellectuals of the Interwar Years (1919–1939)," *Comparative Studies of South Asia, Africa and the Middle East* 26, no. 3 (2006): 391–401.

148 Dilip Menon, "The Many Spaces and Times of Swadeshi," *Economic and Political Weekly* 47, no. 2 (2012): 44–52, esp. 47, 50.

149 Seán Farrell Moran, "Patrick Pearse and the European Revolt Against Reason," *Journal of the History of Ideas* 50, no. 4 (1989): 625–643. For a similar point, see Goswami, *Producing India*, 270–271.

## 2

# "The Ireland of the Far East?"

*The Wilsonian Moment in Korea and Ireland*

FEARGHAL McGARRY

On 21 March 1919, exactly two months after the establishment of the revolutionary assembly, Dáil Éireann, at Dublin's Mansion House, the *Irish Independent* published a Chinese press agency report outlining the Japanese authorities' suppression of pro-independence protests in Seoul. A somewhat parochial headline pitched for its readers' attention: "SINN FEIN IN KOREA."[1] Although few Korean nationalists are likely to have considered their efforts in this light, at least one East Asian English-language newspaper, the Kobe-based *Japan Chronicle*, also noted similarities between the disturbances unfolding in both countries.[2] Focusing on how transnational activism and global political shifts shaped the development of nationalism in both countries, this chapter argues that the efforts of Irish and Korean nationalists to win international support do bear comparison. It explores how—in response to the rise of Wilsonian ideals and the expectation that a peace conference would institute a new world order based on the principle of self-determination—postwar revolutionaries embraced similar strategies, objectives, and rhetoric to advance their claims for independence on the international stage. It considers also why this "Wilsonian moment" resulted in very different outcomes for each movement.

## Easter 1916 and March First

How comparable were the Irish and Korean uprisings? On the eve of the First World War, the British government was finally poised to grant Ireland its own parliament. Under Home Rule, Ireland would remain part of the UK state and firmly within the folds of the British Empire, but the promise of a significant measure of self-government satisfied the aspirations of most Irish nationalists at that time. Two obstacles stood in the way. First, a militant campaign by (Protestant) unionists, who formed a majority in Ulster opposed to any diminution of the political union between Ireland and Great Britain, had prevented London from implementing Home Rule for the entire country. By the summer of 1914 it was widely, if bitterly, acknowledged by (Catholic) nationalist politicians that some form of partition would be necessary for southern Ireland to achieve its own parliament. The Ulster crisis saw the formation of unionist and nationalist paramilitary organizations, which heightened political tensions, undermined the moderate nationalist Irish Party, and energized a determined minority of separatists who believed that only violence could secure an independent republic.

The second obstacle came with the outbreak of the First World War, which saw Britain defer the implementation of Home Rule for the duration. Ireland, however, was transformed when fewer than two thousand poorly armed republicans occupied the center of Dublin in April 1916. Although vastly outnumbered, the rebels held out for six days. Their doomed insurrection—depicted as a romantic gesture of self-sacrifice led by high-minded intellectuals—won global attention. The British government's decision to execute its leaders ensured that they came to be seen as martyrs despite the initial unpopularity of the rebellion that devastated the center of the Irish capital. Against the backdrop of an unpopular war, which eroded support for the pro-enlistment Irish Parliamentary Party, and Britain's inept attempt to impose conscription on Ireland in 1918, the Easter Rising proved pivotal, generating mass support for separatism. As the war came to an end, Ireland stood on the verge of revolution.

In Korea the events that would become known as March First began as a popular protest against Japanese rule rather than a conspiratorial uprising. Korea had lost its independence in 1905, following Japan's defeat of Russia, when it became a protectorate. At the time many international observers, including the United States, which accepted Japan's claims in return for its acquiescence to American authority over the Philippines, regarded the occupation of Korea as an inevitable consequence of its prolonged decline. Despite its formal annexation in 1910, patriotic Korean societies and religious organizations (including Christians, Buddhists, and Cheondogyo) continued to resist Japanese rule.

The immediate catalyst for March First was the sudden death of the former emperor of Korea, Kojong, who was rumored to have been poisoned by Japanese officials. The presence of up to two hundred thousand mourners in Seoul provided the opportunity for a mass demonstration against Japanese rule. Thirty-three prominent civil and religious leaders gathered at Pagoda Park, where a Declaration of Independence was proclaimed to cheering crowds. A second, more militant, student-authored manifesto—blaming Japan for Kojong's death—circulated through Seoul. These events triggered a wave of demonstrations that saw up to two million Koreans participate in some two thousand protests across the peninsula over the next two months. Caught off guard, the Japanese authorities responded ruthlessly to these initially nonviolent protests, resulting in almost eight thousand deaths and fifty thousand arrests.[3] Despite its brutal suppression, March First saw nationalist sentiment, previously confined to an intellectual elite, gain popular support.

There were striking parallels between Easter 1916 and March First notwithstanding the greater scale of violence in Korea. Seen as marking "the birth of Korean nationhood," March First provided a foundational moment for the South Korean state that subsequently emerged, much as the Easter Rising did for the independent Irish state.[4] As both uprisings ended in failure, much of their importance lay in their propagandistic impact, which had been central to their organizers' calculations. Just as protesters in Seoul gathered in prominent locations to display revolutionary manifestos, the Easter rebels had proclaimed a republic outside Dublin's General Post Office and distributed their Proclamation across the city. Exploiting modern global communications, their propaganda was aimed at an international as much as a national audience. The impact of both events also stemmed from how they were remembered: the description of March First as a "watershed" whose "memory and influence has reverberated through the national psyche since and shaped the development of national identity and mythology" describes the impact in Ireland of the Rising.[5]

A final parallel concerns how historians now emphasize the importance of the contemporary international context of both events despite their organizers' efforts to frame their actions within longer national narratives.[6] In their Proclamation, the Easter rebels depicted themselves as embodying an insurrectionary tradition stretching back to the seventeenth century. Subsequent nationalist historiography in Ireland also downplayed the importance of its wartime context, interpreting the rebellion as the culmination of generations of struggle. Only in recent decades has the interconnected nature of Ireland's contemporaneous experiences of war and revolution been foregrounded: "As surely as Verdun or the Somme, Dublin in 1916 was a First World War battlefield."[7]

Korean historiography has witnessed a similar shift from exceptionalist interpretations. Noting how March First was commonly thought of "within the framework of Korean national history," an event "preceded by the earlier resistance to the Japanese occupation and annexation," historian Erez Manela observed how, viewed within a different context, it could be seen to form part of a wider wave of anticolonial resistance across Asia: if you "expand your frame of reference spatially rather than temporally, an extraordinary confluence of events comes into view." Might this expansive vista be usefully extended, ten thousand kilometers west of Korea, to a small island on the edge of Europe?

Any comparison of events in Ireland and Korea should acknowledge important differences between both countries, their histories, and geopolitical circumstances.[8] While Ireland had been subject to English influences for over seven hundred years, Japanese dominance over Korea—which, unlike Ireland, was surrounded by several powerful countries—was more recent. Korea had a longer and closer relationship with China than Japan; nor was there any Korean equivalent to Ireland's large pro-British Protestant minority. Koreans endured much greater repression than the Irish. Under General Terauchi Masatake, Korea's first governor-general, an aggressive policy of linguistic and cultural assimilation and radical reform was imposed in 1910.[9] British rule, in contrast, weighed more lightly on early twentieth-century Ireland. Whereas Koreans were largely excluded from political representation in Japan or Korea, Irish representatives sat in the British parliament at Westminster. Irish people enjoyed much the same civil rights, such as a free press, as other UK citizens, and shared in the opportunities of a prosperous British state in possession of a vast empire.

These differences reflected both the comparatively liberal nature of the British state and the differing constitutional relationships between both pairs of countries. Irish separatists nonetheless regarded themselves as enduring "the longest agony suffered by any people in history," a perception reinforced by a personal identification by many among the revolutionary generation with a traumatic national history.[10] Memories of seventeenth-century conquest and religious persecution informed Irish nationalists' understanding of their history, identity, and politics. And few Irish (or, for that matter, British) people perceived Ireland—governed by a colonial-style viceroy, British chief secretary, gendarmerie, and heavy military presence—as an integral part of the United Kingdom. The union with Britain had been imposed from London following the brutally suppressed 1798 uprising; Ireland had subsequently endured impoverishment and neglect (epitomized by the death of one million people and the emigration of another million during the catastrophic Great Famine of 1845–1851); and popular nationalist demands for self-government had been disregarded for decades.

Finally, nationalism was more deeply rooted in Ireland than in Korea. Republican insurrections had periodically occurred since 1798, while nonviolent nationalist mass movements dated back to the 1830s. In contrast, Korean nationalism remained confined to a small intellectual and professional elite by the late nineteenth century when the Independence Club was founded by activists such as the Christian civil servant Syngman Rhee. These Western-influenced advocates of nationalism and modernization were repressed by the socially conservative Korean court and, subsequently, the Japanese authorities. Nonetheless in Korea, as in many other East Asian nations, "influential groups of literate, socially mobile individuals, whose members were conversant in Western languages and ideas and had begun to develop and circulate notions of national identity articulated in modern idioms" by 1914.[11]

Despite these and other important differences, many contemporaries—including dissatisfied nationalists, vigilant imperialists, and academic observers—identified parallels between the vexed relationships of Ireland and Korea with their more powerful neighbors. "Frequently, in the rest of the world," Japanese scholar Yanaihara Tadao observed in 1936, "Korea is referred to as our Ireland."[12] Nor were those who acknowledged this similarity necessarily opposed to Japanese domination of Korea. In the age of empire it was widely accepted that powerful nations absorbed less successful peoples. Clarence Gilliland, a history professor at the University of Southern California, sympathized with an expanding Japan's need "to annex Korea in self-defense" to protect itself from rival powers: "Unprotected, she was a constant menace to Japan because of her close proximity. Her relation to Japan geographically is not unlike that of Ireland to England."[13] Nonetheless, most who drew such parallels agreed that nationalist grievances in both countries required some form of resolution: the *Japan Chronicle*, for example, warned that if Japan failed to emulate Britain's conciliatory approach to South Africa, "Korea would go the same way as Ireland and become an insoluble problem to Japan."[14] Significantly, it was only after international condemnation of Japanese repression of the March First protests that Korea first came to be described as "the Ireland of the Far East."[15] Censorship of press reports of Ireland's progress to independence and bans on the staging of patriotic Irish plays in Korea, which continued throughout the 1920s and 1930s, attest to official Japanese awareness of these troubling parallels.[16]

## A Wilsonian Moment?

Central to Erez Manela's groundbreaking study of the international origins of anticolonial nationalism is his thesis that global nationalist expectations were raised—and, with violent consequences, dashed—by President Wilson's advocacy of national self-determination.[17] Although Wilson never used this term in his seminal Fourteen Points speech, and gave little thought to its application beyond Europe, his advocacy of an international order of democratic states supplied a new language that came to underpin revolutionary challenges to the old order. The belief that their cause could be placed before the international community undermined the legitimacy of empires, encouraging nationalists to reject their offers of limited reform in favor of full independence. Imperial intransigence in the face of these demands fueled further resistance, broadening the social base of nationalist movements and reinforcing their commitment to goals that had been widely seen as unrealistic before the First World War. Manela's comparative analysis of nationalist movements in Egypt, India, China, and Korea highlighted the shared methodology of anticolonial activists who mobilized domestic mass movements and diasporic networks in support of self-determination.

An outpouring of pamphlets drew on Wilsonian language to articulate long-standing nationalist grievances, while the prospect of a seat at the Peace Conference incentivized popular mobilization. Much of this activism took the form of interactions across territorial boundaries, particularly within the "contact zones" of anti-imperial metropolises such as Paris, London, and New York.[18]

Although Manela's study has been criticized for underplaying the agency of anticolonial activists, and the significance of anti-capitalist critiques of Wilson's global liberalism,[19] the unrest that swept much of Asia in 1919 was clearly linked to expectations raised by the end of the war. The March First protests, for example, "began as an effort to draw the attention of Wilson and the peace conference to Korean claims for independence."[20] But how relevant is this model of non-Western anticolonial protest to a revolution that took place within the United Kingdom? Central to Manela's thesis is his claim that the "language of self-determination and the international forum afforded by the peace conference prompted nationalist leaders to rethink their strategies, redefine their goals, and galvanize larger domestic constituencies than ever before behind campaigns for self-determination."[21] Was this also the case in Ireland?

Irish separatist ambitions were initially stoked by the outbreak of the First World War rather than Wilson's ambitious postwar vision. The quixotic 1916 rebellion had partly been rationalized by the belief that the victorious Central Powers (described in the Proclamation as "our gallant allies in Europe") would look favorably on Ireland after the war. But the United States' entry into the war in April 1917 impacted the calculations of Irish nationalists who had previously dismissed Britain's claim to be fighting for "the freedom of small nations" as perfidious humbug. "From the time of the first declarations by Woodrow Wilson referring to the rights of small nations," one nationalist recalled, republicans "raised the question of the possibility of appealing to international opinion, and, especially, to support from the United States."[22] Wilson's Fourteen Points, another remembered, were "received delightedly by a keenly interested Ireland where it became a prime text, a veritable doctrine of faith for political speakers and writers of the advanced and progressive nationalist school."[23] After the war, popular enthusiasm for the "messiah of progress" swept Ireland, as elsewhere in Europe, with some forty town councils inviting the American president to visit Ireland.[24]

Given that Wilson had not listed Ireland among those countries deserving of independence, why did his vision prompt such enthusiasm? Both Irish republicans and British imperialists understood the radical implications of American commitment to a democratic world order. Such was the impact of Wilson's speech, Britain and France had felt it necessary to affirm (insincerely) that postwar governments in the former Ottoman territories should derive "their authority from the initiative and free choice of the indigenous population."[25] Even Irish unionist newspapers such as the *Irish Times* acknowledged that the legitimacy of states would increasingly come to rest on the consent of their inhabitants: "America not England will be the interpreter of the thoughts and visions of the world re-born."[26] This ideological shift had profound implications for Ireland.[27] Home Rule, to which the Irish Party remained committed, now appeared a relic of a fading imperial era, while the announcement of a postwar conference to redraw European boundaries according to the nationality principle made the separatist aims of republicans, previously derided as "rainbow-chasers," appear more realistic. So too did the rapidly transforming political landscape. Republics—rare in early twentieth-century Europe—became the postwar norm. In the weeks prior to the UK general election in December 1918 republics were proclaimed in Germany, Austria, Czechoslovakia, and Hungary. In demanding independence, Irish republicans knew history was on their side.[28]

The transformative 1918 general election demonstrated the impact of Wilsonian rhetoric in Ireland. Candidates for Sinn Féin (which had previously advocated an Austro-Hungarian model of dual monarchy prior to embracing republicanism after the Easter Rising) referred frequently to self-determination. Their election leaflets highlighted how their demands had been achieved by other oppressed peoples: "Poland Free! An Object Lesson For Ireland. Poland is Now Sinn Fein."[29] Indeed, republicans felt that Ireland, with its ancient culture and island boundaries, had a stronger case for nationhood than many postwar successor states: "The Czecho-Slovaks are demanding independence. Nobody is quite sure who the Czecho-Slovaks are but the whole world knows who the Irish are."[30]

Sinn Féin's manifesto identified four methods by which it would achieve a republic: abstention from Westminster, the use of "any and every means available" (implying the possibility of armed struggle), the establishment of an Irish parliament, and an appeal "to the Peace Conference for the establishment of Ireland as an Independent Nation."[31] As Manela concluded in relation to Asia, the rise of self-determination and the prospect of a peace conference prompted nationalist leaders to rethink their strategies, and galvanized popular support behind their more radical goals. Republicans could now appeal for a mandate at home to place their case before the world: "vote so that President Wilson may have overwhelming proof of Ireland's demand to be free."[32] Sinn Féin's election literature emphasized how this message resonated across the Atlantic: demanding Irish self-determination at a packed Friends of Irish Freedom rally at Madison Square Garden in December 1918, Cardinal O'Connell warned England that "the eyes of the world were upon her."[33] In short, the Peace Conference made Sinn Féin's radical strategies, such as abstention and the establishment of a revolutionary government, appear more credible, while undermining the reformism of their moderate nationalist rivals.[34] How, Sinn Féin asked, could the Irish Party demand a seat at Paris while confirming Ireland's status as "a province" by sitting at Westminster?

Wilson may have made anti-imperialism respectable, but the Peace Conference was never going to deliver Irish independence.[35] That the other Allies would side, against Britain, with a movement that had identified itself with Germany during the war was fanciful. Moreover, self-determination had always been intended only for the oppressed nationalities of the defeated Austro-Hungarian, Russian, and Ottoman empires rather than those of their victors. Sinn Féin's demand for representation at Paris may have been unrealistic, but by indicating a route to independence that bypassed the British parliament, it was tactically astute. Consequently, in Ireland, as in Korea, the Wilsonian moment proved significant, contributing to Sinn Féin's obliteration of the once-dominant Irish Party in the 1918 UK general election.

Having achieved this mandate, Sinn Féin proceeded to implement its republican manifesto. On 21 January 1919, five weeks before disturbances began in Seoul, its elected representatives gathered in Dublin, where they established a national parliament, formed a revolutionary government, and declared independence. Orchestrated before a gathering composed mainly of foreign journalists, this spectacle was intended for an international, as much as a domestic, audience. On the same day Dáil Éireann first assembled, Irish Volunteers killed two policemen in rural Ireland, ushering in two and a half years of guerrilla war that crucially sustained international interest in the Irish question.

In East Asia, the weeks after March First saw "a string of declarations of Korean independence," often generated by expatriates due to Japanese repression at home.[36] On 11 April 1919 the Provisional Government of the Republic of Korea (KPG) was proclaimed in Shanghai. Syngman Rhee—now exiled in the United States—was named president and Kim Kyusik—an American-educated Christian convert—was nominated foreign minister. With only seven hundred Koreans in Shanghai, the KPG's claim to represent a self-governing state was even more symbolic than that of the Dáil: "its members saw bringing the case of Korean independence before world opinion as their main task." They also sought to unify diasporic activism across China, Russia, Japan, and the United States.[37] Meanwhile, in Seoul, activists gathered secretly on 23 April to proclaim the Republic of Korea. They established (another) Korean government, also headed by Rhee, who was described as president of the Republic of Korea. Having proclaimed independence, Korean and Irish nationalists turned to winning recognition for it on the international stage.

### Proclaiming Independence

As striking as the parallels between the methods of nationalists in Seoul and Dublin were those between their arguments. The Korean and Irish Declarations of Independence (analyzed here alongside the accompanying Message to the Free Nations of the World) outlined the same rationale for independence.[38] Shared themes included a claim to nationhood rooted in a distinct ancient culture; repudiation of a foreign oppressor; divine sanction; the principles of democracy, justice, morality, law, and equality; and a Wilsonian-inspired vision of a stable international community of democratic nation-states. The documents' shared vocabulary of liberation included the following terms: ancient, blessing, destiny, force, foreign, freedom, inalienable right, independence, justice, nation, peace, rights, tyranny, and will of the people.

Both sets of documents articulated the assumption that civilized peoples, possessing the recognized cultural attributes of nationality, deserved statehood. Alluding to its "five-thousand-year history," the Korean declaration drew attention to Japanese efforts to dismiss its "great dynastic achievements in order to prop up its claim that our history began as a foreign colony with a primitive civilization." Despite "seven centuries of foreign oppression," the Message to the Free Nations noted, Ireland—"one of the most ancient nations in Europe"—had preserved its "national integrity." Whereas the Easter 1916 Proclamation had rooted Ireland's claim to independence in its insurrectionary tradition ("the dead generations from which she receives her old tradition of nationhood"), the 1919 Declaration upgraded Irish claims by citing the "overwhelming majority" secured for the republic. Although lacking a similar electoral mandate, the Korean declaration also rooted its claims in "the will of the Korean people."

Products of the second of four global waves of Declarations of Independence that had swept over more than one hundred nations since 1776, the inspiration of the American template was evident.[39] Like that document, they asserted before world opinion the right of states (based on natural and positive law) to secede from a repressive imperial state to membership of the international community of independent states. In contrast to the American original, but like most of its imitators, the declarations were outward- rather than inward-looking: that is, they were concerned more with the collective right of aspiring states to sovereignty than the human rights of their citizens. Their central message—aimed squarely at an international audience—was "the assertion of sovereignty as independence." Essential to this conception of independence, as David Armitage's seminal study has demonstrated, was not simply the severing of ties with empire but a public claim to an equal political and diplomatic place among the community of nations.[40]

American influence was further reflected by both movements' references to specific Wilsonian ideas such as the understanding (described by N. Gordon Levin as "liberal-capitalist internationalism") that a stable world order depended not merely on a community of democratic nation-states but on economic development and global interdependence.[41] Korean independence was accordingly presented as "an indispensable step towards the stability of East Asia" and "the attainment of world peace," while Irish independence was claimed to constitute "a condition precedent to international peace hereafter." Appeals were made not merely to Wilsonian idealism but to American self-interest. In a subsequent document, Korea's representative to the Paris Peace Conference, Kim Kyusik, warned that Japan sought to control Korea in order to turn the Pacific into a "Japanese lake."[42] Citing one of Wilson's Fourteen Points, "the Freedom of the Seas," the Message to the Free Nations claimed that English domination of Ireland, "the gateway of the Atlantic," was intended to ensure its control of the "great sea routes between East and West."

Both declarations emphasized the transformed postwar context. Juxtaposing Japan's "outdated notions of aggression" with Korea's desire "to take part in the global reform rooted in human conscience," the Korean declaration observed that a "new world is approaching before our very eyes. The age of might has receded, and the age of morality has arrived." Just as the Korean declaration welcomed the opening of "a new chapter in world history," the Irish declaration announced "the threshold of a new era in history," while the Message to the Free Nations declared "the dawn of the promised era of self-determination and liberty." The declarations were targeted not merely at a global audience but at the delegates gathering at Paris: from the outset, the attainment of independence was seen as synonymous with its international recognition. The Message to the Free Nations began by calling on "every free nation to support the Irish Republic by recognising Ireland's national status and her right to its vindication at the Peace Congress." Indeed, an awareness of the opportunities offered by a peace conference, even one that excluded Ireland, had preceded American involvement in the war. In 1916, Sinn Féin leader Arthur Griffith noted, "If we don't get in—which I suspect is possible—we shall stand on the stairs and harangue the world outside."[43] Writing from an English prison cell, following the first meeting of the Dáil, Griffith continued to prioritize international support: "Above all concentrate on the Peace Conference. . . . Mobilise the poets. Let them address Wilson, and let them remind him in their best verse that he has the opportunity and the duty of giving the world true peace and freedom."[44]

Irish and Korean efforts to secure representation at Paris were also characterized by their strongly transnational nature. The Korean representative to Paris, Kim Kyusik, was nominated by the Shanghai-based New Korea Youth Association.[45] Based in China, where he had fled from occupied Korea, his first challenge was to reach Paris. He eventually secured passage by traveling incognito among a sympathetic Chinese delegation. Neither of Korea's other US-based delegates, Syngman Rhee and Henry Chung, made it to France as they were denied passports on the advice of Secretary of State Robert Lansing.[46] Much of the Korean propaganda that circulated in Paris was also generated by expatriate organizations: for example, the Japanese-based Korean Youth Independence Association drafted Korean, Japanese, and English versions of another declaration of independence, which was sent to politicians, academics, and journalists in Seoul, Tokyo, and Paris.[47]

Irish efforts, enthusiastically mapped out by Griffith in a detailed memorandum, were similarly global in scale. If Irish representatives could not get to Paris, Irish American senators, congressmen, and cardinals should be sent in their stead. An international network of consuls, working with the Irish diaspora, would mobilize international opinion. Sympathetic states, particularly those with Irish associations, would be lobbied. South Americans should be told of Ireland's support for Bolivar: "Remind Liberia and Haiti that Ireland is the only European country that never engaged in the Negro slave trade. Remind Bohemia, Poland, Roumania and Bulgaria of the similarity of our struggles."[48] Remarkably, much of this ambitious agenda would come to pass with a "foreign ministry" emerging as one of the few successfully functioning arms of a largely symbolic Dáil government.[49]

The Dáil government's representatives faced similar challenges to those of the KPG. Its original nominees—Dáil president Éamon de Valera, Griffith, and Foreign Affairs minister Count Plunkett—were denied visas. However, Seán T. O'Kelly did make it to Paris, exploiting his status as a city councilor bearing (on the suggestion of republican leader Michael Collins) an invitation to Wilson to receive the freedom of Dublin. Like the Koreans, the Irish also relied on diasporic connections to bypass imperial obstacles. An American Commission on Irish Independence, consisting of four Irish Americans with influence in the Democratic Party and labor circles, lobbied (unsuccessfully) for the Irish delegates' safe passage, and it was this commission (rather than O'Kelly) that secured meetings with the otherwise elusive Wilson in New York and Paris.

The Irish and Korean representatives in Paris adopted much the same methods. The Irish mission, although modest in comparison to those of established states, had far more staff and resources at its disposal than other revolutionary missions. Instructed to demand his country's inclusion in the conference, and to "create worldwide opinion regarding the necessity of Korea's liberation," Kim sought interviews with conference delegates, journalists, and other influencers.[50] Liaising with his revolutionary government in Dublin, O'Kelly embarked on a sophisticated effort to mobilize global opinion, win diplomatic support, and cultivate the international press. He sent elaborate parchment copies of the Declaration of Independence, Message to the Free Nations, and case for Ireland's independence to the Peace Conference's 71 delegates and to 140 journalists and newspapers.[51] Both envoys circulated petitions, appeals, and letters that—much to the irritation of Wilson—quoted his own speeches.[52] A Korean Information Bureau was established to compile and disseminate press summaries publicizing Korea's plight, while from Dublin an *Irish Bulletin* was distributed to nine hundred newspapers and opinion formers.

Despite his impressive title, "the accredited envoy of the Provisional Government of the Irish Republic" was—like Kim—snubbed by Wilson (and every other delegate) who refused to acknowledge his correspondence. O'Kelly quickly surmised that the prospects of securing a formal hearing at Paris were "very slight." Nor was this due solely to British objections: even before the conference, Robert Lansing, the US secretary of state, had grasped the incendiary implications of Wilson's rhetoric: "The more I think about the President's embrace of the principle of self-determination, the more convinced I am of the danger of putting such ideas into the minds of certain races. . . . What effect will it have on the Irish, the Indians, the Egyptians. . . . The phrase is simply loaded with dynamite. It will raise hopes which can never be realised. It will, I fear, cost thousands of lives."[53] Wilson, whose own commitment to self-determination had waned, also foresaw "a tragedy of disappointment" at Paris.[54] The US delegation regarded appeals by countries such as Ireland and Korea as fundamentally misunderstanding the purpose of the conference, which was intended not to establish "a new world order" but merely to settle "questions arising out of the war." Moreover, it had been agreed that no delegations could be accepted without the unanimous consent of the Big Four allies. The undoubted wrongs of countries like Ireland, Wilson's advisors insisted, must await adjudication by the League of Nations that the president was fighting to establish.[55] A more cynical interpretation of the postwar settlement agreed at Paris would see it as marking the beginning of an alliance "in which London would accommodate American power and Washington would defer to the interests of the British Empire."[56] Although Wilson reportedly conceded that Ireland's case was "the great metaphysical tragedy of today," he undertook to do no more than apply informal pressure on London to seek a political settlement in Ireland.[57] Privately, his attitudes to the Irish, who he believed were fortunate to live in a democracy, were unsympathetic: he told one advisor he felt like "telling them to go to hell."[58]

But much was achieved at Paris. O'Kelly reported that Ireland's appeal "created quite a big sensation in official and journalistic circles."[59] His efforts to secure "the ear of the press," despite relying heavily on biased British news agencies, gained traction even if the wheels had to be greased by "money and plenty of it."[60] He forged useful working relationships with South African and Egyptian representatives including Sa'd Zaghlul. Reporting to Dublin in June, as his unsuccessful mission wound down, O'Kelly claimed he was not downhearted: "On the contrary, I feel quite hopeful. I am satisfied that we are not going to secure recognition for the Republic before the Conference now sitting comes to an end, but I am equally satisfied that we have advanced considerably along the road towards that goal."[61]

Had the Irish and Koreans really believed the route to the promised land of self-determination lay through Paris? Or was their presence there merely intended to internationalize their struggles? Propaganda lay at the heart of both strategies, rendering Paris principally a site of political theater.[62] Portraits of O'Kelly and Kim, dressed identically in formal diplomatic attire, illustrate the performative dimension of their roles on this international stage. On arrival in Paris, O'Kelly placed a note in the press announcing his presence as Ireland's official representative. Installing himself in "one of the most important hotels," he held press conferences, handed out business cards, and extended hospitality to "great men."[63] This was a new form of revolutionary politics reflecting hopes that, at the world's first modern peace conference, staged in front of the global media, public opinion rather than realpolitik and secret deals might count for something. Intended to project the illusion of statehood, the mimicking of diplomatic conventions by revolutionary governments strengthened their claims to legitimacy: "At a time when states were being made and unmade, this was important."[64]

Nonetheless, the failure to achieve recognition, and the double standards on display in Paris, proved frustrating: "All these delegations great and slight are solely interested in grabbing all they can of the spoils for themselves," O'Kelly complained: "They have no time to listen to anyone like myself who wants justice and right to prevail."[65] Korea's interests, Kim complained, had been sacrificed to those of Japan: "How can anyone in his senses imagine that these swashbucklers will help to make the world safe for democracy?" Syngman Rhee, familiar with Wilson from his Princeton days, was dismayed to realize that "the architect of peace based upon justice, was planning to sacrifice Korean independence for the sake of power politics."[66] Sinn Féin's newspaper described the Peace Conference as working hard "to make the world safe for hypocrisy," while Irish and international journalists noted parallels between the treatment of Ireland and other stateless nationalities.[67] For example, Article 10 of the League of Nations—which guaranteed the territorial integrity of existing states—was criticized as binding its members "to respect and preserve both the newly acquired freedom of the Poles and Bohemians and the newly affirmed subjection of the Irish and the Coreans."[68]

What were the consequences of failure at Paris? In Korea, the March First protests had been quashed by the time the Treaty of Versailles was signed on 28 June 1919, but embarrassment arising from international press coverage of Japanese atrocities saw the introduction of a more conciliatory "cultural policy" in Korea that summer.[69] In Ireland, the failure at Paris may have contributed, along with the more significant suppression of the Dáil and Sinn Féin by the British authorities, to the shift from politics to violence taking place: in a controversial press interview de Valera warned that "violence will be the only alternative remaining to Irish patriots if the Peace Conferences at Paris fail to take steps to extend self-determination to Ireland."[70] Despite the setback, international propaganda continued to remain central to both movements' strategies, with the United States now superseding Paris as the key site of global struggle. Acknowledging that "we have little or nothing to hope from Wilson's efforts on our behalf," O'Kelly advised that the time was now right for de Valera to cross the Atlantic: "Our American friends are satisfied the fight must be transferred to the United States, and they are prepared to do their share in making the issue a burning one."[71]

## Diasporic Nationalism

Due to Japanese repression on the peninsula, the Korean diaspora had come to exert an important cultural and political influence by the early twentieth century. Nationalists in Korea increasingly looked to their overseas compatriots as "the foundation of our future independence." More widely read in Korea than America, US-based newspapers such as *SinHan minbo* (*New Korea Daily*) were described as "organs of our Korean independence."[72] With an impure peninsula "unable to function as a true homeland," some intellectuals concluded that the diaspora was best placed to act as the nation's custodians: "paradoxically, the nation could exist only outside the nation."[73]

Although numbering fewer than six thousand, Korean Americans had been galvanized by March First. Drawn from a Western-educated elite, leaders such as Syngman Rhee and Henry Chung argued the case for self-determination, presenting Korea's struggle as analogous with earlier American revolutionary efforts. Their appeals drew on the strong Protestant missionary links between both countries. "The Korean situation is without parallel in modern history," claimed one Methodist organization: "Unlike Ireland, Korea is dominated by a nation that is Anti-Christian in sentiment and addicted to the most brutal practices that characterised our late world war."[74]

The highpoint of this campaign was the First Korean Congress in April 1919. Attended by nearly two hundred delegates (including reportedly from Ireland and England) representing twenty-seven expatriate organizations, its name and location evoked the revolutionary-era Continental Congress. Gathered in Philadelphia, the "cradle of liberty," they ostentatiously committed themselves to American ideals.[75] Parading with American and Korean flags to Independence Hall, where the American Declaration of Independence had been signed, delegates observed as Rhee proclaimed the Korean Declaration of Independence and establishment of the Provisional Government of Korea. "An Appeal to America" was drafted, while speakers emphasized democratic and Christian values: "Our cause is a just one before the laws of God and man. Our aim is freedom from militaristic autocracy; our object is democracy for Asia; our hope is universal Christianity."[76] Korean independence, it was made clear, would advance "U.S. ideological, economic and political interests in East Asia."[77] Following the congress, the League of the Friends of Korea was formed to publicize conditions in Korea, and a Korean Commission was established in Washington, D.C., as the diplomatic arm of the KPG. A *Korean Review* was launched to present the "true facts" of Korea's case and to influence American press coverage.[78] The KPG president, Rhee, toured the United States in autumn 1919, while activists like Chung churned out articles and pamphlets. By June 1920 the league had established eighteen branches with ten thousand members in cities such as Boston and San Francisco.

Just as Korean nationalists celebrated their compatriots for creating "a new Korea in North America," a British home secretary had complained in the late nineteenth century of "an Irish nation in the United States . . . absolutely beyond our reach."[79] The emigration of almost four million Irish people to the United States between 1851 and 1921 allowed Irish republicans to harness one of the world's most formidable diasporas. Throughout many northern cities Irish Americans exerted an enviable grip over municipal politics and employment, the Democratic Party, the labor movement, and the Catholic Church. They also exercised influence through militant revolutionary organizations such as Clan na Gael and fraternal societies like the Ancient Order of Hibernians. At its peak, the Friends of Irish Freedom (FOIF) and its larger rival, the American Association for the Recognition of the Irish Republic, claimed almost one million members. Whether through money, propaganda, or other forms of support, Irish America's impact on political nationalism in Ireland was profound.[80]

Two months before the Korean Congress, an Irish Race Convention had also gathered at Philadelphia. Organized by the FOIF, the public face of Clan na Gael, it was chaired by Daniel Cohalan, a New York State Supreme Court justice with close links to Congress via Tammany Hall, New York's notorious Democratic Party machine. Attended by five thousand delegates from a broad range of Irish American organizations, the convention voiced its support for Irish efforts in Paris and passed a Declaration of Principles and Policies emphasizing the American loyalties of the Irish race from "the revolution to the present day."[81] Religion also played a significant role at the Irish convention, which was attended by over thirty bishops including the influential cardinal James Gibbons of Baltimore. This clerical involvement had a moderating influence, ensuring that the convention's key resolution, proposed by Gibbons, called for self-determination rather than recognition of the Irish Republic.

The centerpiece of the Irish campaign was an eighteen-month mission to the United States by Éamon de Valera. Although he was an innately dignified figure, the artifice underlying his statesmanlike demeanor in America was exemplified by his transformation following a horrendous journey where, smuggled in the hold of a passenger ship, he had endured seasickness and the ignominy of rats gnawing on his clothes. On arrival, de Valera took a suite at the Waldorf Astoria, where, fitted out by tailors, he was unveiled to the international press. A slick whistle-stop tour saw crowds of up to fifty thousand attend rallies in "Irish" cities such as Boston and Chicago.

Against the background of a broader wave of postwar radicalism, the mobilization of diasporic support generated links between anti-imperialist nationalists and supporters of causes such as labor, suffrage, and socialism. The championing of Irish independence by advocates ranging from Black rights activists like Marcus Garvey to prominent Zionists demonstrated how extensively the Irish question was debated in radical circles at that time. The death in London of hunger striker Terence MacSwiney, for example, prompted a protest against British shipping by Irish, Italian, and African American longshoremen that shut down New York's waterfront. A rally in New York to honor Mac-

Swiney, presided over by a Jewish judge, was attended by one hundred thousand supporters including German Americans, Japanese, and East Indians.[82] Speaking at such occasions, de Valera sought to extend support beyond the diaspora, calling on Americans—"a spiritual people with interests second to none in humanity's future"—to provide global moral leadership.[83]

Although Irish nationalists in America identified most strongly with other movements struggling for freedom from British rule, sympathy for Korea was voiced at some meetings. In San Francisco, for example, de Valera told his American audience, "In your fight for liberty everywhere we felt that you entered our cause—were fighting for our cause as well as your own. But the people of India, Egypt, Korea, and Ireland are in the same thraldom as in the past." Henry Chung shared a platform with Irish speakers at a public meeting in the same city organized by the Women's Irish Education League.[84] In late 1919 New York–based radicals formed a League of Oppressed Peoples to link Ireland's cause with those of India, Egypt, Persia, Korea, Russia, and China. At its meetings Irish activists like Harry Boland spoke alongside Korean supporters such as the socialist Presbyterian minister Norman Thomas.[85]

Whereas nationalists were heartened by such displays of international solidarity, imperialists detected a global conspiracy: "Britain was fighting New York and Cairo and Calcutta and Moscow who are only using Ireland as a tool and lever against England," claimed the Irish-born Chief of the Imperial General Staff, Sir Henry Wilson.[86] Such projections of the Irish conflict onto the international stage demonstrate how revolutionaries and imperialists were more attuned than later historians to the significance of contemporary transnational connections. This wider context presented difficulties as well as opportunities for revolutionary nationalists. Wilson's exaggerated claim paralleled popular anxieties manifested, in the United States, by a backlash against communists, hyphenated Americans, and other "un-American" subversives triggered by anarchist bombings in 1919 that had led to the arrest of one thousand suspects in America's First Red Scare orchestrated by J. Edgar Hoover's "Radical Division."[87]

In part arising from this fraught context, there were limits to Irish solidarity with radical causes. Race, for example, remained an important facet of the reactionary discourse of nationhood in this era. Although willing to proclaim his support for Asian anti-imperialists, de Valera could also ask American audiences why "Ireland is now the last white nation that is deprived of its liberty."[88] Despite receiving public support for their cause from prominent African American intellectuals,[89] Irish nationalists in America were silent on Irish American complicity in the murderous 1919 Chicago race riots. On the international stage, Dáil diplomats also took care to ensure that what they saw as Ireland's superior claims to nationhood were not conflated with those of colonized and "colored" peoples.

While support from any quarter was welcome, Irish—and Korean—efforts focused on mainstream American politics. If de Valera's mission was an attempt to appeal, over Wilson's head, to the American public, there were some grounds for optimism given Irish America's political clout. In March 1919 the House of Representatives had resolved (by 246 to 45 votes) that the Peace Conference should favorably consider Ireland's claim to self-determination, while the Republican-controlled Senate called on the conference to admit the Irish delegates. Debates on the Irish were bound up with other nationalities including the Koreans. Although some politicians hostile to Wilson's foreign policy made much of the denial of self-determination to Ireland and Korea, the president's supporters highlighted the double standards arising from their greater commitment to Ireland's cause. Opposing a resolution sympathizing with Irish independence in June 1919, one senator noted, "There are stories in the newspapers about Korea having national aspirations, but you have not yet introduced any resolution against Japan, providing for the independence of Korea, lately conquered and very much oppressed. Why? Because you know Great Britain will be good-humored with you and Japan will not be, and, while there are a lot of Irish-American votes, there are no Korean votes in America."[90] Noting the Senate's failure to support Korea, another senator observed that there were no "hyphenated Americans from Korea, with votes to re-elect Senators and representatives."[91] Such barbs also reflected Democrat resentment of Irish American senators from their own party who had joined the Republican majority in opposing Wilson's peace settlement.

With elections imminent and a growing isolationist mood, Irish republicans hoped that Irish American pressure might yet shift the ailing president's position on Ireland, notwithstanding continuing charges of double standards. In March 1920 a Senate proposal by Charles Thomas, a Republican from Colorado, that "Great Britain, and Japan, respectively, will forthwith recognize the existence and political independence of the republic of Ireland and the ancient kingdom of Korea" was unsuccessful.[92] In contrast, a resolution supporting Irish independence passed by thirty-eight to thirty-three votes. After an amendment to record the Senate's sympathy for Korean independence was rejected, the outspoken Republican isolationist William Borah cynically described the result as "a proposition of the U.S. Senate with nearly 20,000,000 people in the United States of Irish blood, just at the beginning of a political campaign, applying the great principle of self-government to no-one except those who can vote."[93]

Although Korean activists attracted public attention in America, thereby "increasing the momentum of international interest in the March First Movement," without an ethnic vote to mobilize they were unable to exert effective political pressure.[94] De Valera's American tour generated extensive press coverage, financial support, and—through the Irish American vote—political pressure but proved ultimately no more successful in achieving formal recognition. The Irish campaign in America did, however, result in significant domestic and international consequences. George Creel, Wilson's troubleshooter in Europe, was appalled by the delegations "of Irish, Italians, Egyptians, Hindus, and other races . . . brought to Washington and given elaborate hearings under the false assumption that the Senate had power to redress their grievances." Their efforts, he claimed bitterly, destroyed Wilson's settlement but did little to secure their freedom: "Blind with prejudice and passion, and urged on at every step by the hypocritical applause of the Republican group," they opposed "the League in which lay their one hope."[95] Shortly before the broken president departed the White House, Wilson confided to his biographer that he held "the foolish Irish" in America responsible for the rejection of the Versailles Treaty and the League of Nations.[96]

The campaign in America also had implications for Irish nationalist politics. The failure of Irish efforts to win the support of the Republican and Democratic presidential candidates to succeed Wilson later that year resulted not, as in Korea's case, from American indifference but rather from deep divisions between Irish and Irish American political leaders, demonstrating how transnational activism and the globalized political discourse of the Wilsonian era created tensions as well as opportunities. If nationalist movements increasingly operated across borders, where did authority within them reside? If claims for sovereignty could be more successfully articulated beyond the nation, where would political power rest?

In Korea, the effectiveness of Japanese repression sharpened such questions: "If the peninsula was not the best location for preserving the nation, who then would lead the struggle for independence?"[97] The question was discussed at the Korean Congress. Observing that Syngman Rhee, the KPG president, was in Philadelphia rather than Shanghai (where his nominal government was located), the congress president Philip Jaisohn—an American-trained doctor who became Korea's first naturalized US citizen—reassured the delegates:

> It does not make any difference whether the President of the Provisional Government is in prison or whether he is in France; he may be in America. . . . It does not make the government non-existent, because it is not generally known where it is located. It is the will of the people that makes the government. . . . When the Revolutionary War broke out, you will recall that the Government was not established in any one place, they were forced to move around. When the British chased them from one place, they moved their capital to another. They had a capital in Yorktown, and then they came to Philadelphia. . . . It does not make any difference whether the Government is located in Manchuria, Philadelphia or Paris.[98]

Although the congress sought to present the KPG as the sovereign government of Korean people wherever it resided, and from whatever background its activists came, Richard S. Kim has argued that it did ultimately matter where political authority resided: "Diasporas, like globalization . . . transcend the boundaries of the nation-state and often challenge territorialized notions of identity and political participation. Paradoxically, though highlighting the deterritorialized dimensions of migrant experiences, diasporas also are founded upon nation-based discourses that enshrined the principle of the exclusive territoriality of the sovereign state. Diaspora and globalization thus are not antithetical tendencies to the nation-state but rather inextricably embedded within the nation-state system."[99] American influence on Korean nationalists, Kim argues, amounted to something more substantial than an awareness of the benefits of framing their aims within a Wilsonian discourse: "With the 'globalizing of America' following World War One, the adoption and promotion of American democratic values displayed during the Korean Congress became central rhetorical and political strategies for the Korean independence movement as whole."[100] Consequently, US-based expatriates "came to hold disproportionate political influence and power," with Western-educated figures—such as Rhee and Jaisohn—defining "the ideological contents and political agenda of a burgeoning Korean nationalism within the context of American global power."[101] Although none of these figures played a significant role in Korea itself, their reputation there "as international leaders of the national resistance endowed them with supreme legitimacy."[102] Backed by the United States, Rhee would become the founding father of the Republic of Korea after the Second World War.

There are some parallels here with Ireland, not least the appeal of a republican form of government to leading Irish revolutionaries: five of the seven signatories who proclaimed the republic in 1916, for example, had spent time in the United States. Similarly, de Valera's profile and status were enhanced by his presence and prestige in the United States. On arrival in New York, for example, the office he held was transformed from that of president of the Dáil Éireann ministry to the more impressive—if invented—role of president of the Irish Republic. But if the Korean Congress was successful in establishing Korean Americans "as an integral part of a diasporic political movement inextricably linked to their compatriots in and out of their homeland,"[103] relations between Irish and Irish Americans were characterized by sharper divisions. Money represented one source and symptom of conflict. While Irish American leaders sought to use most FOIF funds to pursue their political objectives within the United States, de Valera advocated an External Loan (or "bond drive") under Dáil authority to fund the struggle at home. Raising over five million dollars from 276,000 American subscribers (dwarfing the FOIF's one million dollars), this successful initiative—also adopted by the Korean Provisional Government—reinforced Irish pretensions to statehood.[104] Further conflict arose from de Valera's suggestion that an Irish government might agree with

Britain on an analogous arrangement to the Platt amendment whereby Cuba prevented its territory from being used by powers hostile to the United States. American dominance of Cuba enabled de Valera's Irish American rivals to disingenuously present this pragmatic accommodation of British security requirements as a betrayal of the aspiration to full independence.[105]

More rows ensued over rival tactics at the Republican and Democratic conventions in 1920. After de Valera's attempt (opposed by his Irish American rival Cohalan) to win Republican Party recognition of the Irish Republic failed, de Valera scuppered Cohalan's more viable effort to win support for Irish self-determination. Centering on whether Irish or Irish American politicians should direct the US campaign, these conflicts reflected not only factional rivalries but ideological differences arising from the divergent outlooks and objectives of the Irish in Ireland and America. For example, the League of Nations, which republicans in Ireland aspired to join, was seen by many Irish Americans as a threat to US sovereignty.

Compared to their Korean counterparts, Irish-based politicians were more successful in preserving their authority: de Valera, for example, established a new Irish-controlled movement that won over most Irish American support. However, de Valera's American mission did contribute to tensions at home, most notably the Cuban controversy that prefigured divisions over the Anglo-Irish Treaty.[106] His biographers have also attributed his remoteness from his colleagues at home and his increasingly authoritarian leadership style, which contributed to the treaty split and Civil War, in part to his American sojourn.[107] Although the importance of American diasporic influence in Irish politics would endure, the powerful alliance forged by the transatlantic campaign in support of the Irish Republic was not sustained: never again would a passionate commitment to the cause of Irish freedom occupy the same salience as a marker of Irish American identity or result in the "frenzied outpouring of devotion for the homeland" that characterized the postwar years.[108]

## Conclusion

Across the postwar world, the varying outcomes of the Wilsonian moment were shaped by multiple factors: geopolitics, realpolitik, the ability of nationalist movements to generate support, and the ability and willingness of imperial powers to resist international pressure and suppress internal dissent. Ireland and Korea, in contrast to the new republics of central and eastern Europe, sought independence from empires that had won the war, although Britain, beset by a global crisis of empire, had emerged from it weakened.

In contrast to Korea, Ireland was not subjected to colonial levels of violence. The liberal character of the British state and civic society—rarely extended to nonwhite parts of the empire—constrained repression in Ireland, which was widely condemned by sections of the British press, political class, and church leaders. Racial considerations curbed British violence and strengthened Ireland's claims to independence. Although the killing of fourteen people at Croke Park in 1920 was described as Ireland's Amritsar, there was some distance between that slaughter and the killing of more than four hundred Indians in Jallianwala Bagh in 1919—a massacre in which Irish colonial officials and military officers were implicated.

Despite the expectations raised by Wilson, neither Korea nor Ireland escaped the gravitational pull of empire. Acknowledging de Valera's success in America, Michael Collins had astutely warned, "Our hope is here and must be here. The job will be to prevent eyes turning to Paris or New York as a substitute for London."[109] British power blunted Ireland's revolution, frustrating republican aspirations for full independence. Having signaled its willingness to grant Home Rule in 1914, Britain conceded dominion status to southern Ireland in 1922. But as in colonial territories such as Egypt, and—more blatantly—in the new Middle Eastern mandates, this outcome was less a case of empire giving way to nationalism as the working out of new forms of political authority that masked how the rhetoric of self-determination had been subordinated to imperial exigencies.[110] But for many among the diaspora, and for other oppressed peoples, the Irish settlement appeared generous, and the implications of the Irish state's evolution to full independence over the next three decades were not lost on nationalist leaders in Asia and Africa.[111]

Ruthlessly suppressed at home, and mobilizing only limited support abroad, the March First movement was crushed by a more implacable empire. The paths of Korea and Ireland did not again converge until after the Second World War, when the further ebbing of empire saw the two republics declared in 1919 finally gain recognition on the world stage. That both countries were, by then, partitioned testified to the continuing limitations on sovereignty for small states with big neighbors.

What was most noteworthy about Irish and Korean revolutionary nationalism in 1919? Its global character is striking. The accelerating pace of the transnational movement of "people, modern communications, and the exchange of ideas, information" and money raised nationalist aspirations and undermined imperial resolve.[112] Republican efforts at home were strengthened by support from the "Irish world," with events in one sphere, such as the death of MacSwiney, resonating powerfully through the other. The impact of "long-distance nationalism" on domestic developments was evident.[113] It was primarily through its diaspora in America, Britain, and across the empire that Irish republicans wielded most influence on Britain's Irish policy. In his influential Caird Hall speech advocating a peace settlement in Ireland that extended his government "to the utmost limit possible," Churchill argued that it would "not only be a blessing in itself estimable, but with it would be removed the greatest obstacle which has ever existed to Anglo-American unity, and that far across the Atlantic Ocean we should reap a harvest sown in the Emerald Isle."[114]

Equally striking is the extent to which the postwar rhetoric of self-determination buttressed Irish and Korean challenges to empire. Noting the limited impact of the First World War on Korea, Erez Manela observed that "it was not merely the impact of the war but the emerging discourse of the peace—especially the rapid spread of the principle of self-determination as the bedrock of international legitimacy—that is crucial for understanding the events of 1919 in the colonial world." Ireland's revolution, like March First, formed part of the postwar high tide of national self-determination that saw the world's borders redrawn. The parallels between Irish and Korean efforts indicate the need to integrate transnational and global factors into national narratives: "One of the central features of the Wilsonian moment was its simultaneity across the boundaries of nations, regions, and empires within which the histories of the anticolonial movements of the people are usually enclosed."[115] Ultimately, these global perspectives will help us to appreciate how nationalist revolutionaries experienced the same ideological moment in world history.

NOTES

1 *Irish Independent* [hereafter *Independent*], 21 Mar. 1919.

2 Cited in Susan C. Townsend, "Yanaihara Tadao and the Irish Question: A Comparative Analysis of the Irish and Korean Questions, 1919–36," *Irish Historical Studies* 30, no. 118 (1996): 197.

3 Tae-eok Kwon, "Imperial Japan's 'Civilization' Rule in the 1910s and Korean Sentiments: The Causes of the National-Scale Dissemination of the March First Movement," *Journal of Northeast Asian History* 15, no. 1 (2018): 116.

4 Kyung Moon Hwang, "The Birth of Korean Nationhood," *New York Times*, 1 Mar. 2019. Cultivated by the South Korean state, this legitimizing narrative—tracing national sovereignty from the state's foundation in 1948, through the expatriate Korean Provisional Government, to a point of origin rooted in March First—has been revised in recent decades with greater emphasis placed on other forms of resistance such as that of the Tonghak peasants. In contrast, North Korea's genealogy centers on mythologized accounts of the role played by Kim Il-Sung in the guerrilla struggle in 1930s Manchuria (Andre Schmid, *Korea between Empires, 1895–1919* [New York: Columbia University Press, 2002], 253–257).

5 Erez Manela, "The Wilsonian Moment in East Asia: The March First Movement in Global Perspective," *Sungkyun Journal of East Asian Studies* 9, no. 1 (2009): 12.

6 Enrico Del Lago, Róisín Healy, and Gearóid Barry, eds., *1916 in Global Context: An Anti-Imperial Moment* (London: Routledge, 2018).

7 Keith Jeffery, *1916: A Global History* (London: Bloomsbury, 2015), 104.

8 Townsend, "Tadao," 195.

9 Jimin Kim, "Representing the Invisible: The American Perceptions of Colonial Korea (1910–1945)" (PhD diss., Columbia University, 2011), 89.

10 See "Ireland's Case for Independence," submitted by Seán T. O'Kelly to the Peace Conference in June 1919, in Ronan Fanning, Michael Kennedy, Dermot Keogh, and Eunan O'Halpin, eds., *Documents in Irish Foreign Policy*, vol. 1 [hereafter *DIFP*] (Dublin: Royal Irish Academy, 1998), 25.

11 Erez Manela, *The Wilsonian Moment: Self-Determination and the International Origins of Anticolonial Nationalism* (Oxford: Oxford University Press, 2007), 8.

12 Townsend, "Tadao," 202.

13 Clarence Vosburgh Gilliland, "Japan and Korea since 1910," *Annual Publication of the Historical Society of Southern California* 11, no. 3 (1920): 52.

14 Quoted in Townsend, "Tadao," 197.

15 "A Japanese Proposal for Free Korea," *Literary Digest* 63 (25 Oct. 1919): 23, cited in Kim, "Representing the Invisible," 88–89. See also Maurice Walsh, *Bitter Freedom: Ireland in a Revolutionary World, 1918–1923* (London: Faber & Faber, 2015), 38.

16 Chong Chin-sok, "Democratic Thought of the March 1st Independence Movement Inherited by the Press," in *The March 1st Independence Movement and the Korean Provisional Government, Revisited: Republicanism in the Global Context and the Develop-*

*ment of East Asian Independence Movements*, ed. H. C. Kim (Seoul: North East Asian History Foundation, 2020).

17 Manela, *Wilsonian Moment*.

18 Michael Goebel, *Anti-Imperial Metropolis: Interwar Paris and the Seeds of Third World Nationalism* (Cambridge: Cambridge University Press, 2015).

19 See, for example, Rebecca Karl in *American Historical Review* 113, no. 5 (2008): 1474–1476.

20 Manela, *Wilsonian Moment*, 9.

21 Ibid., 8–9.

22 Patrick J. Little witness statement, (Irish) Military Archives [MA], Bureau of Military History [BMH], witness statement [WS] 1769).

23 Kevin O'Shiel witness statement (MA, BMH, WS 1770).

24 Walsh, *Bitter Freedom*, 35–38.

25 Kristian Coates Ulrichsen, "The British Occupation of Mesopotamia, 1914–1922," *Journal of Strategic Studies* 30, no. 2 (2007): 366.

26 *Irish Times*, 28 Dec. 1918, cited in Walsh, *Bitter Freedom*, 35.

27 Charles Townshend, *The Republic: The Fight for Irish Independence* (London: Penguin, 2013), 3.

28 Walsh, *Bitter Freedom*, 37.

29 Sinn Féin election leaflet, 1918 (National Library of Ireland [NLI], ILB 300 p 1, Item 33).

30 Ibid., Item 75.

31 Sinn Féin election manifesto, 1918 (NLI, EPH F223). The manifesto's final slogan declared, "President Wilson is Coming to Europe!"

32 Ibid.

33 Sinn Féin election leaflet, 1918 (NLI, ILB 300 p 4, Item 12).

34 Michael Laffan, *The Resurrection of Ireland: The Sinn Féin Party 1916–1923* (Cambridge: Cambridge University Press, 1999), 250.

35 Walsh, *Bitter Freedom*, 38.

36 Manela, *Wilsonian Moment*, 199.

37 Richard S. Kim, "Inaugurating the American Century: The 1919 Philadelphia Korean Congress, Korean Diasporic Nationalism, and American Protestant Missionaries," *Journal of American Ethnic History* 26, no. 1 (Fall 2006): 51.

38 For the "Irish Declaration of Independence" and "Message to the Free Nations of the World," both 21 Jan. 1919, see Documents on Irish Foreign Policy (www.difp.ie). For the Declaration of Korean Independence, 1919, see Proclamation of Korean Independence (en.wikisource.org).

39 David Armitage, *The Declaration of Independence: A Global History* (Cambridge, MA: Harvard University Press, 2007).

40 Ibid., 22.

41 Quoted in Kim, "Inaugurating the American Century," 56.

42 Manela, "March First," 22.

43 Laffan, *Resurrection of Ireland*, 251.

44 Arthur Griffith letter, 23 Jan. 1919, *DIFP*, 3.

45 Manela, *Wilsonian Moment*, 129.

46 Ibid., 201.

47 Ibid., 129.

48 Arthur Griffith letter, 23 Jan. 1919, *DIFP*, 3–4.

49 Gerard Keown, *First of the Small Nations: The Beginnings of Irish Foreign Policy in the Interwar Years 1919–1932* (Oxford: Oxford University Press, 2016).

50 Manela, *Wilsonian Moment*, 206.

51 O'Kelly to Cathal Brugha, 7 Mar. 1919, *DIFP*, 7–8.

52 In the Irish appeal sent to Georges Clemenceau, the Peace Conference chair, six paragraphs cited Wilsonian rhetoric. Meeting Wilson in June, a member of the American Commission on Irish Independence repeatedly angered the president by quoting extracts from his speeches drawn from this document (*DIFP*, 23–24, 29).

53 Robert Lansing, *The Peace Negotiations: A Personal Narrative* (New York: Houghton Mifflin, 1921), 97.

54 George Creel, *The War, the World, and Wilson* (New York: Houghton Mifflin, 1920), 161–162.

55 Ibid., 190.

56 Walsh, *Bitter Freedom*, 219.

57 O'Kelly to Dublin, 15 June 1919, *DIFP*, 29.

58 Margaret Macmillan, *Paris 1919: Six Months That Changed the World* (New York: Random House, 2002), 11; Robert Schmuhl, *Ireland's Exiled Children: America and the Easter Rising* (Oxford: Oxford University Press, 2016), 75–118.

59 O'Kelly to Brugha, 7 Mar. 1919, *DIFP*, 8.

60 O'Kelly to Brugha, 7 Mar. 1919, *DIFP*, 10.

61 O'Kelly to Dublin, 15 June 1919, *DIFP*, 29.

62 Gerard Keown, "Global Horizons? The Irish Quest for International Recognition," in *The Irish Revolution 1919–21: A Global History*, ed. Enda Delaney and Fearghal McGarry (Dublin: Wordwell, 2019), 35.

63 O'Kelly to Cathal Brugha, 7 Mar. 1919, *DIFP*, 6; John Gibney, "Dressed to Impress: The Material Culture of the Dáil Éireann Foreign Service," in Delaney and McGarry, *Irish Revolution*, 41–42.

64 Gerard Keown, "'The Most Clamorous of All the National Groups': Ireland and the Paris Peace Conference" (Ireland, the Revolution and the First World War conference, Irish Cultural Centre, Paris, 27 June 1919).

65 *DIFP*, 8–9.

66 Quoted in Manela, *Wilsonian Moment*, 201.

67 *Nationality*, 19 Apr. 1919.

68 J. C. Walsh, "Ireland at the Peace Conference," *Studies: An Irish Quarterly Review* 8, no. 30 (1919): 178.

69 Manela, *Wilsonian Moment*, 211.

70 *Irish Press* (Philadelphia), 15 Mar. 1919.

71 O'Kelly to Dublin, 15 June, 24 May 1919, *DIFP*, 29, 17.

72 Schmid, *Korea between Empires*, 247–248.

73 Ibid., 252, 225.

74 Resolution passed at Methodist preachers' meeting, Chicago, 19 May 1919, Korean American Digital Archive, USC Digital Library (http://digitallibrary.usc.edu).

75 Kim, "Inaugurating the American Century," 53–54.

76 Manela, *Wilsonian Moment*, 202; Kim, "Inaugurating the American Century," 51; Korean Congress, *First Korean Congress* (Philadelphia, 1919), 29–30, cited in Kim, "Inaugurating the American Century," 57.

77 Kim, "Inaugurating the American Century," 54.

78 Ibid., 63–67.

79 Schmid, *Korea between Empires*, 46; Schmuhl, *Ireland's Exiled Children*, 17.

80 David Brundage, *Irish Nationalists in America: The Politics of Exile, 1798–1998* (Oxford: Oxford University Press, 2016); Fearghal McGarry, "'A Land Beyond the Wave': Transnational Perspectives on Easter 1916," in *Transnational Perspectives on Modern Irish History*, ed. Niall Whelehan (London: Routledge, 2015), 165–188.

81 Michael Doorley, *Irish American Diaspora Nationalism: The Friends of Irish Freedom, 1916–1935* (Dublin: Four Courts Press, 2005).

82 Brian Hanley, "Why Irish Revolutionaries Had to Go Global" (Century Ireland), www.rte.ie/centuryireland.

83 Walsh, *Bitter Freedom*, 210.

84 Press cutting (*San Francisco Chronicle*, 4 Sept. 1919), articles about Henry Chung, 1919, Korean American Digital Archive, USC Digital Library (http://digitallibrary. usc.edu). The league was founded by Kathleen O'Brennan, whose activism is analyzed in Elizabeth McKillen's essay in this volume.

85 *Irish People*, 8. Nov. 1919. I am grateful to Brian Hanley for this reference. On the league, see David Brundage, "Lala Lajpat Rai, Indian Nationalism and the Irish Revolution," in Dal Lago, Healy, and Barry, *1916 in Global Context*, 62–75.

86 Quoted in Keith Jeffery, *Field Marshal Sir Henry Wilson: A Political Soldier* (Oxford: Oxford University Press, 2006), 263.

87 Walsh, *Bitter Freedom*, 212–216.

88 Ibid., 49. See also Bruce Nelson, *Irish Nationalists and the Making of the Irish Race* (Princeton: Princeton University Press, 2012).

89 See the essays by Nyhan Grey and Brundage in this collection.

90 *New York Times*, 10 June 1919, quoted in Kim, "Representing the Invisible," 218.

91 Ibid., 218.

92 Kim, "Representing the Invisible," 216.

93 Ibid., 217.

94 Ibid., 218–219.

95 Creel, *The War*, 331.

96 Schmuhl, *Ireland's Exiled Children*, 115–116.

97 Schmid, *Korea between Empires*, 246.

98 Kim, "Inaugurating the American Century," 53.

99 Ibid., 52.

100 Ibid., 56.

101 Ibid., 52.

102 Hwang, "Birth of Korean Nationhood."

103 Kim, "Inaugurating the American Century," 53.

104 Robin Adams, "'Something Typically Irish as Well as Essentially Modern': The Irish Bond Drive in the United States," in Delaney and McGarry, *Irish Revolution*, 37–41.

105 Walsh, *Bitter Freedom*, 217–220.

106 Darragh Gannon, "Addressing the Irish World: Éamon de Valera's 'Cuban Policy' as a Global Case Study," *Irish Historical Studies* 44, no. 165 (May 2020): 41–56.

107 Ronan Fanning, *Éamon de Valera: A Will to Power* (London: Faber & Faber, 2015); David McCullough, *De Valera*, vol. 1: *Rise 1882–1932* (Dublin: Gill, 2017).

108 Timothy J. Meagher, "Irish America without Ireland: Irish-American Relations with Ireland in the Twentieth Century," in Whelehan, *Transnational Perspectives*, 189.

109 Laffan, *Resurrection of Ireland*, 251.

110 Arie Dubnov and Laura Robson, eds., *Partitions: A Transnational History of Twentieth-Century Territorial Separatism* (Stanford, CA: Stanford University Press, 2019).

111 Kenneth Shonk, "'The Shadow Metropole': Global Anti-colonialism and the Legacy of Ireland's Revolution," in Delaney and McGarry, *Irish Revolution*, 84–87.

112 Brundage, *Irish Nationalists in America*, 6.

113 Ibid.

114 David Stafford, *Oblivion or Glory: 1921 and the Making of Winston Churchill* (New Haven, CT: Yale University Press, 2019), 216–217.

115 Manela, *Wilsonian Moment*, 10.

# 3

# "Playing at International Politics?"

## *Irish Nationalist Responses to the Russian Revolution, 1917–1921*

ANNA LIVELY

The First World War hastened the collapse of the Russian, Ottoman, Habsburg, and Austro-Hungarian empires and fueled nationalist and anticolonial movements across the globe, in places as different as Egypt, India, China, Korea, and east-central Europe. As John Darwin argues, the "massive aftershocks of the First World War had a collective significance" and led to international discussions about self-determination, a term used by both V. I. Lenin and President Woodrow Wilson.[1] In Ireland, the 1916 Easter Rising and the British response, combined with the context of the war, helped drive a shift away from constitutional nationalism and the formerly dominant Irish Parliamentary Party and facilitated the growth of Sinn Féin.[2]

Against the background of this national and global reconfiguration, news reached Ireland of the abdication of Tsar Nicholas II and the creation of the Provisional Government in Russia in March 1917. Irish nationalists greeted enthusiastically what became known as the February Revolution in public meetings, newspaper articles, political commentaries, and private correspondence, praising the advent of a "New Russia."[3] In an unusual 1919 political manifesto, journalist and politician Aodh de Blácam even suggested that Bolshevism had its roots in Ireland. De Blácam, who was brought up as an evangelical Protestant but converted to Catholicism in 1913, argued that Bolshevism aligned with Catholic teaching. He emphasized the debt that Russian revolutionaries like Lenin owed to Ireland, particularly to the Irish socialist republican James Connolly, who was executed following the Rising. For de Blácam, "Ireland cried to Russia, and Russia to Germany, and Liberty, wakened in Ireland, has begun once again to walk the earth."[4]

This chapter considers the diverse strands of Irish nationalist re-sponses to Russia between the abdication of the tsar in March 1917 and the closing stages of the "Russian" civil wars in 1921 (a conflict extend-ing beyond Russia's borders). Priyamvada Gopal describes, aptly, how transnational and anticolonial solidarity involves "imaginative work" and the "interpretation, comprehension and reconstitution" of news from abroad.[5] This process is contested, with questions over whose voices should be privileged, what information should be believed, and how to deal with seemingly irreconcilable differences. Changes in com-munication technology, including submarine cables and later wireless telegraphy, allowed for faster dissemination of information across the globe by the late nineteenth and early twentieth centuries, forming part of strategies of imperial control.[6] Lines of communication between Russia and Ireland were mostly indirect, with Irish newspapers often obtaining news from Russia through international news agencies like Reuters and the London press. Irish commentators reinterpreted news from Russia to suit Irish domestic conditions and to make political points, such as about the war, British hypocrisy, or social change. News-papers engaged in "scissor-and-paste" journalism, whereby previously published material was reprinted, often with different headings and political insinuations.[7]

Through texts, speeches, and debate, the Russian Revolution gained political significance within Ireland, demonstrating the complex pro-cess of political translation across borders. Interest in the Russian Revo-lution was not the preserve of any single Irish political group, as it related to broader issues like empire, women's rights, nationhood, and religion. Existing Irish Soviet studies, such as by Emmet O'Connor, Maurice Casey, and Michael Quinn, show the importance of the net-works and connections established between Irish republicans, socialists, and Soviet organizations like the Communist International (Comin-tern) from 1919.[8] Beyond personal travel and institutional engagement, the transnational circulation of texts and news reports facilitated more fluid discussions among Irish nationalists about what the Russian Revo-lution meant for Ireland. Of course, Irish nationalists had a broad range of social and political views and were involved, sometimes simultane-ously, in constitutional, cultural, republican, suffragist, pacifist, and militant organizations on the island of Ireland and in the Irish diaspora.

This chapter draws on Irish nationalists' correspondence, diaries, and memoirs, Bureau of Military History (BMH) witness statements by revolutionary veterans, and newspapers from different branches of Irish nationalism. It also notes some comparisons between Irish commentary on Russia and Russian-language texts on Ireland.

Press coverage was influential in framing attitudes to Russia. The *Freeman's Journal* was established in 1763 and later became known as a "semi-official organ" of the Irish Party. After 1905 it struggled to compete with rival nationalist paper the *Irish Independent,* founded by businessman William Martin Murphy, a notorious opponent of trade unionism.[9] Published between 1918 and 1933, *An t-Óglách* was framed as "The Official Organ of the Irish Volunteer" and featured militant nationalist articles on warfare and national and international events.[10] Socially radical, feminist, and pacifist, the *Irish Citizen* was founded in 1912 by writer and activist Francis Sheehy Skeffington and poet and playwright James Cousins.[11] While politically varied, these texts tended to privilege elite voices, whereas the BMH witness statements, collected by the Irish state between 1947 and 1957, included some "rank and file separatists."[12]

The year 1917 did not mark the start of Russo-Irish relations, and there were preexisting cultural, economic, and political links between Russia, Ireland, and the Irish diaspora.[13] In the late 1870s the North American Irish republican organization Clan na Gael hoped to profit from Anglo-Russian tensions and sought Russian support for a possible military campaign. While these plans were not realized, Clan na Gael correspondence suggests the importance of the maxim of "England's difficulty as Ireland's opportunity" in shaping Irish nationalist responses to Russia.[14] As Carla King demonstrates, this maxim also influenced Irish nationalist responses to the 1905 Russian Revolution. Michael Davitt, the founder of the Irish Land League, traveled to Russia in a journalistic capacity in 1903, 1904, and 1905, initially to investigate the Kishinev pogrom in the Bessarabia region of the Russian Empire. Davitt's view of the 1905 Revolution was shaped by anti-British feeling and a desire to challenge what he saw as the "campaign of falsehood against Russia" in sections of the British press.[15] His reports downplayed Russian protests and strikes, although he was more sympathetic to Polish and Finnish revolutionary movements.[16] There was strong precedent for Irish nationalist engagement with Russian politics, but it was contingent on the national and international context, particularly Anglo-Russian and Anglo-Irish relations.

## Responses to the February Revolution

News of the February Revolution prompted significant excitement in Ireland. In early 1917, information from Russia came "sparingly," including "gloomy" reports from the Petrograd correspondent of the *Sunday Times*, the odd article from a "Stockholm newspaper," and "meagre reports" from meetings of the Duma.[17] The day after Nicholas II's abdication, this "reign of silence" was broken: a telegram from the British ambassador in Petrograd about the abdication reached the House of Commons and the Irish press.[18] The abdication followed strikes, including among female textile workers in Petrograd, and International Women's Day protests on 8 March 1917.[19] Yet, for many Irish contemporaries, the immediate significance of events in Russia was in relation to the First World War. More than a hundred Irish servicemen, mostly from the north of Ireland, served in an armored car division that supported the Russian Army on the Eastern Front between 1915 and 1918. Some of these servicemen witnessed the Russian Revolution firsthand alongside a handful of other Irish eyewitnesses, including Irish nurses and governesses in the region.[20] More widely, Russia's relationship with the Allies mattered to Ireland in terms of the outcome of the war and future peace negotiations. The Irish Volunteers split at the outbreak of the war in 1914, with a minority rejecting Irish Party leader John Redmond's support for the war effort. Responses to the February Revolution reflected these divisions, as supporters of Irish participation in the war hoped that the revolution would galvanize the Allied war effort. For John Dillon, Redmond's successor as Irish Party leader from March 1918, the February Revolution served as a "splendid justification to those of us who saw in this war a great fight for freedom and human right."[21]

In contrast, some opponents of Irish participation in the First World War hoped that the Russian Revolution would see Russia pull out of the conflict, thereby hastening the defeat of the Allies and the granting of Irish independence. The republican, journalist, writer, and diplomat

Robert Brennan recalled hearing news about Russia in 1917 while in Lewes prison in East Sussex, where he was imprisoned for his participation in the Rising in County Wexford, alongside (fellow rebel) Harry Boland. According to Brennan, Boland sneaked a copy of the daily papers from the priest's office in the prison and, after reading about the Russian situation, shouted that "Russia is out of the war, boys. That's one leg off o' the pot." In response, "the place rang with cheers and cries of 'up the Rebels!'"[22] The timing is confused here as Russia was not officially "out of the war" during Brennan's time in Lewes prison in 1917, although he would have welcomed Russian military failures on the southern section of the Eastern Front in June.[23] His statement suggests how memories of excitement about events abroad lasted, if not precise details or chronologies. Similar reports were interpreted in dramatically different ways depending on how and where the news was received. In a politically radicalized prison setting, these Irish nationalists anticipated events in Russia causing revolutionary ripples across Europe.

In 1917, the collapsing Russian Empire was in a state of flux, with a myriad of nationalist, socialist, and other political movements all jostling for position. The relationship between the Provisional Government and these movements was volatile. For example, by May 1917 the Provisional Government was under pressure from Finnish socialists and social democrats to offer greater independence to Finland, with debates intensifying over self-determination versus self-rule.[24] Irish nationalist commentaries often simplified the situation and remained optimistic about the Provisional Government's nationality policies. A reader of the *Irish Independent* called for a Finnish-style policy in Ireland, arguing this would deepen Irish loyalty to the Allied cause.[25] Similarly, the Irish historian and nationalist Alice Stopford Green celebrated "the triumph of liberty" in Poland, despite the fractured military and political situation in the region, which escalated into the Polish-Soviet War of 1919 to 1920. A Home Rule supporter from the 1890s, Green condemned British imperialism in her history books and as an activist during the Second Boer War of 1899 to 1902, when she visited prison camps in Saint Helena. This anti-imperialism shaped her view of Russia: in 1917, Green described "New Russia" as being on the side of progress, identifying Germany and Britain with backward, imperialist aggression.[26] Irish commentaries were selective, focusing on the elements of the Russian situation that seemed most relevant to Ireland and often distinguishing between Irish and English responses to Russia. As one *Freeman* editorial put it, "Irishmen" understood the February Revolution more deeply than "the average English man," as "they know, as only a nation in the shadow of the prison-house can know, the thrill with which a people sees the dawn of liberty flushing the sky."[27]

Prominent Irish nationalist politicians like Redmond and Dillon made public proclamations on the February Revolution, which they disseminated through the press to convey an impression of international prestige and political autonomy. This was as much about political optics as genuine interest in Russia. In a message to the Duma on behalf of the Irish Party on 22 March, Redmond celebrated the end of Tsarist autocracy and declared the support of the "Irish Nation" for the "Russian nation," emphatically placing both nations on an equal footing.[28] Replying to Redmond by telegram, Mikhail Rodzianko (the chairman of the Duma Committee) indicated Russia's support for "national emancipation" internally and in "its war ends," although he did not go into detail about Ireland.[29] Dillon also sent a message to the Petrograd paper the *Bourse Gazette* suggesting the similarities between Russia and Ireland, both "suffering under a bureaucracy and police rule."[30] In speeches and written interventions, supporters of Sinn Féin and the Irish Party sought to use international connections against each other, arguing that their party was best placed to represent Ireland on the international stage.[31] International engagement was a valuable political tool for conveying authority and legitimacy, but it was a competitive field, with rival groups hoping to capitalize on connections to Russia.

Russo-Irish relations were not one-way, and Irish newspapers reported on high levels of Russian interest in Ireland. Following the February Revolution, the British trade unionist and Labour MP Will Thorne was part of a British delegation to Russia, aimed at encouraging Russia to stay in the war. In May 1917, Thorne described how Russians in Petrograd, in Moscow, and on his way to the front asked him "why we called ourselves a democratic country, professing to be fighting for democratic ideals and human liberty when we did not give Home Rule to Ireland."[32] While Thorne probably exaggerated the extent of Russian interest, Ireland featured fairly regularly in early twentieth-century

Russian newspapers, and there was a tradition of Russian liberal and socialist interest in Anglo-Irish politics and Irish land reforms.[33] In Ireland, minor or vague expressions of international support could be depicted as highly significant. The constitutional nationalist bishop of Ross, Denis Kelly, referred to Thorne's comments in a sermon in Skibbereen and emphasized how Ireland had become a "test question" in Russia. For Ross, Russian interest in Ireland illustrated the significance of Irish Home Rule for the "white races" of the world and for the future of "civilisation."[34] Locating Ireland in a global context helped to convey Irish identity and agency. *An t-Óglách* praised the Volunteers as the "teacher of the nations," whose "deeds" were "spoken of in distant lands."[35] International self-positioning could be politically empowering as well as performative, encouraging optimism about Ireland's future.

The landmark granting of suffrage to women over twenty in Russia, which followed a mass suffrage demonstration in Petrograd in March 1917, was received enthusiastically by some Irish nationalists. The political activist and feminist Hanna Sheehy Skeffington compared events in Russia to the Easter Rising, citing the Proclamation of the Irish Republic, which promised a government "elected by the suffrages of all her men and women."[36] In a speech during a 1917 lecture tour in the United States, Sheehy Skeffington celebrated how the "proclamation gave equal citizenship to women, beating all records, except that of Russian Revolutionists, and their Revolution came later," thereby suggesting Ireland's international status and modernity.[37] The *Irish Citizen* also welcomed the granting of "universal suffrage" in Russia, although it questioned whether the "increasing emancipation of women" justified the costs of the war.[38]

In contrast, the mainstream Irish press paid little attention to the enfranchisement of Russian women, generally prioritizing high-political and military-focused British reports on Russia such as the Press Association's War Specials.[39] As 1917 wore on, the Irish constitutional nationalist press became more critical of the direction of the Russian Revolution and the growth of "anarchy," although there continued to be surges of optimism, such as after the Socialist Revolutionary (SR) Alexander Kerenksy became head of the Provisional Government in July.[40] During the turbulence of 1917, there was no single Irish expert in Russian affairs; eyewitness accounts were sporadic because of wartime disruptions, and news reports from Russia, while relatively frequent, were often contra-dictory. This allowed for multiple competing narratives on the Russian Revolution, ranging from those favoring constitutional moderation to support for female emancipation. News from Russia was co-opted for different political agendas as the Russian Revolution became a means of addressing broader political and social questions in Ireland.

## Responses to the October Revolution

On 7 and 8 November 1917, Bolsheviks famously seized post and tele-graph offices, railway stations, government buildings, and the Winter Palace in Petrograd. Lenin signed decrees on peace and land, the former promising a "just, democratic peace" without annexations or indem-nities and the latter calling for the seizure of land estates, either by peasants directly or through the state.[41] Suspicious of socialism and nonconstitutional methods, the *Freeman* and *Independent* depicted the Bolshevik takeover as an illegitimate "coup," rather than a revolution comparable to the French Revolution.[42] Their translation of the Bol-sheviks as "Maximalists" was misleading as, in a Russian context, the Maximalists were a far-left group within the SR party, which broke away to form the Union of SR-Maximalists in 1906.[43] The nuances of Russian revolutionary politics were lost in translation.

Nevertheless, optimism about the Russian Revolution continued on the left and among militant nationalists in Ireland, who were keen to define their international position against socially conservative sec-tions of the British and Irish press. In 1905, Irish nationalist attitudes to Russian revolutionaries were complicated by anti-Russian sentiment in Britain, which made Davitt and others more sympathetic to the Rus-sian state.[44] By late 1917, the war had created a very different context for Russo-Irish relations, in which support for Bolshevism played into anti-British and antiwar discourse in Ireland. *An t-Óglách* and the *Irish Citizen* generally trusted Bolshevik-controlled sources and British pro-labor publications like the *Daily Herald*, although the *Citizen* suggested the problems of seeing Soviet Russia as either "heaven" or "hell."[45] *An t-Óglách* emphasized how Ireland could contribute to a wider "revolu-tionary movement," which was "sweeping through Europe" and leaving imperialism "cracking and crumbling away."[46]

Similarly, Russian revolutionary commentaries on Ireland speculated about Ireland's potential to strike at the heart of the British Empire. Lenin and Trotsky commented on the short-term failings of the 1916 Easter Rising but implied that future unrest in Ireland could spread across the British Isles and the British Empire, drawing on Karl Marx's framing of Ireland as a possible revolutionary "lever."[47] The Bolshevik newspapers *Pravda* and *Izvestiia* placed Ireland within a colonial context, drawing comparisons between revolutionary movements in Ireland, India, Egypt, and South Africa. *Pravda* argued that the Irish struggle showed the "deep cracks" appearing in the "colonial system," using very similar language to *An t-Óglách*.[48] As Michael Silvestri emphasizes, there was a shared anti-imperial tone to Soviet commentaries on Ireland and some Irish nationalist writings on Russia in this period, both conveying international unrest as a moment of global opportunity.[49]

Irish nationalists and socialists showed support for the Russian Revolution (both February and October) in performative and symbolic ways, including through songs, flags, and the color red. In her diary, Anglo-Irish activist and writer Charlotte Despard (sister of John French, Lord Lieutenant of Ireland) described a British labor conference at which a "Russian told us the story of the Bolsheviks," prompting "much enthusiasm" and waving of the "Red Flag."[50] In Dublin, a "Russian Republic Reception: Mass Meeting" was held at Mansion House on 4 February 1918, featuring speakers like Constance Markievicz, the first woman elected as an MP to the British Parliament, and Maud Gonne, the actress and suffragette. The reception declared how Russian revolutionaries and the Irish people shared common principles of "democracy," "universal peace," and "liberty."[51] Dillon condemned this meeting in his first speech as leader of the Irish Party at Enniskillen in March 1918. He asked Éamon de Valera and other Sinn Féin politicians to clarify their position: did they believe "the liberty given to Russia by Lenin and Trotsky was the liberty that Ireland needs"? For Dillon, the "tyranny" in Russia served as a "lesson for the Irish people" to maintain their "common sense" and support the Irish Party.[52] His speech reflected how, by 1918, constitutional nationalists were using references to Bolshevism to criticize Sinn Féin. Publications like the *Freeman* deployed visual symbols to stir up fears of revolutionary disorder, accusing attendees of the Mansion House meeting of trying to replace the green flag with the red.[53]

Attendees at the Mansion House meeting also raised the thorny question of the relationship between Bolshevism and Christianity. In February 1918 the Irish press learned via Reuters about the Soviet decree on the separation of church from state, which included the civil registration of births and marriages. Somewhat paradoxically, the Irish constitutional nationalist press used this decree to suggest the impossibility of the Bolsheviks holding on to power (because of the religiosity of the Russian people) and to reiterate the severity of the Bolshevik threat.[54] Similar warnings about Russian "infidelity" and atheistic campaigns began to appear in sermons and articles by Irish clergymen.[55] Unsurprisingly, Irish sympathizers with Bolshevism disagreed with these interpretations. At the Mansion House meeting the medical practitioner and activist Kathleen Lynn warned that "some people were shy of acclaiming Russia, fearing that the cry of anti-clericalism might be levelled against them—a cry that had been raised against men and movements which the British Government had reason to fear." She suggested, fairly, that anxieties over the Russian Revolution were being manipulated for conservative political ends.[56] Also in February 1918, Gonne wrote a public letter critiquing the *Freeman*'s reports on "Bolshevik attacks on religion," arguing, with some justification at this stage, that Catholics in Russia had more rights after the revolution than under the tsar.[57] Defenders of the Bolsheviks emphasized prerevolutionary religious persecution in Russia, including violence against Jews and Armenians, while opponents lamented the impact of Bolshevism on religious life.[58] Even in early 1918, Bolshevik attitudes to religion were a point of a political vulnerability for Irish sympathizers with the Russian Revolution.

For critics of Bolshevism, "radical" Bolshevik women, most notably the revolutionary and People's Commissar for Social Welfare Alexandra Kollontai, exemplified the threat posed by socialism to the social order. The *Freeman* juxtaposed Kollontai's radicalism with an image of female piety; it described how devout Russian women protested against Kollontai's attempt to confiscate the Alexander Nevsky monastery in Petrograd by carrying icons through the streets.[59] Rev. P. J. Coleman, a Catholic curate from Croom, County Limerick, denounced Kollontai's measures as a "positive, direct and unbridled attack on religion."[60] Rumors circulated about Bolshevik degradation of women and plans for the "nationalisation of women," a claim that had strong sensationalist appeal.[61]

On the surface, the October Revolution was a turning point in terms of Irish nationalist perceptions of Russia. The broad nationalist consensus over the February Revolution broke down as debates raged over Bolshevik policies, particularly on gender and religion. However, many of these divisions had been evident in contrasting Irish nationalist interpretations of the February Revolution, which indicated very different understandings of "revolution" and "liberty." Irish nationalists used international references to articulate their positions on domestic political debates. The geographical and political distance from Russia allowed for considerable hyperbole and exaggerated positions. With news communication and details from Russia often unclear, rumors could turn into facts and isolated instances into general rules.

## The "Russian" Civil Wars

The "Russian" civil wars formed a "continuum of crises, wars, revolutions and civil wars that ebbed and flowed across the collapsing Russian Empire," involving a geographically and politically diverse range of participants, reaching far beyond Russia itself.[62] Between 1918 and 1921, self-determination and empire remained prominent themes in Irish-Soviet relations. Most directly, Irish republicans like Patrick McCartan explored the possibility of a treaty of mutual recognition with Soviet Russia, partly via contacts in the United States. This formed part of a major search for global allies among Irish republicans during this period, including in Egypt, India, and Argentina.[63] McCartan's memos and correspondence reveal careful consideration of the proposed Irish-Soviet treaty in Irish American circles and in Dublin, with close attention paid to its economic, political, diplomatic, and religious dimensions, including proposals for an "accredited representative of the Republic of Ireland" to represent Catholic interests in Russia.[64] While changing relations between the British and Soviet governments undermined the likelihood of a formal Irish-Soviet treaty by 1921, this does not negate the significance of Irish-Soviet relations at the time.

The Irish republican activist Kathleen O'Donovan (née Boland) attributed the Irish Republican loan to Soviet Russia in 1920, famously given in exchange for part of the Russian crown jewels, to a "sort of fellow feeling with poor downtrodden Russians who, like [our people] were struggling to throw off the yoke of slavery."[65] Ireland and Soviet Russia could be depicted as underdogs and pioneers on the international stage, both trying to preserve their fledgling republics against imperialism.

The "Russian" civil wars interested Irish nationalists partly because of the Allied intervention in Russia. Following the March 1918 Treaty of Brest-Litovsk between the Bolshevik government and Germany, British marines arrived in Murmansk, an accessible port a hundred fifty miles north of the Arctic Circle, which the British government hoped to protect from hostile forces. At various points between 1918 and 1920 there was also an Allied presence in Arkhangelsk, Vladivostok, south Russia, the Baltic, and elsewhere.[66] Some Irish-born participants were involved in this military intervention, such as Colonel Philip Woods from Belfast, a former Ulster Volunteer Force member who served in 1918 and 1919 in Karelia (an area between the White Sea and the Gulf of Finland). Woods led a Karelian regiment, raised from Karelians seeking Allied support against Bolsheviks, Germans, and White Finns in the region. This regiment was nicknamed the "Royal Irish Karelians" because of their shamrock regimental badges, designed by Woods from the cloth of an old billiard table, illustrating the unpredictability of transnational exchanges in this period.[67] The overlap between the First World War, the Russian Revolution, and "Russian" civil wars meant there were multiple, ongoing lines of connection between Russia and Ireland through the Allies and through Britain.

While Woods's experience was atypical, the British intervention in Russia had a wider political significance. As the Anglo-Irish War intensified in 1919 and 1920, there was considerable scope for comparisons between events in Russia and Ireland, including among the Irish diaspora. An Irish republican mass meeting in Philadelphia passed a resolution "requesting the withdrawal of occupation from Russia and Ireland," to be sent to "President Wilson, Premier Lloyd George, Premier Clemenceau, Premier Orlando and the King of the Belgians."[68] Lantern slides declared how "Ireland and Russia are the acid tests of our democracy," calling on the United States to oppose intervention in Russia and to recognize the Irish Republic.[69] North American liberal journalist and writer Lincoln Colcord, who spoke at the Philadelphia meeting, subsequently highlighted its success to the Finnish-born revolutionary Santeri Nuorteva, who was connected to Irish-Soviet treaty negotiations in 1920. Nuorteva served as a Social Democrat in the Finnish parliament before emigrating to North America in 1912. In 1919 he became secretary of the Russian Soviet Government Bureau, a body involved in propaganda efforts and fostering international commercial relations. Using the Philadelphia meeting as evidence, Colcord impressed on Nuorteva the political influence of Irish Americans and how, by recognizing the Irish Republic, Soviet Russia could combat the "present anti-Bolshevik madness" in the United States.[70]

The Philadelphia meeting and Colcord's response reflect the entangled, global nature of Irish nationalist responses to the "Russian" civil wars, in this case involving Finnish, Russian, North American, and Irish actors and interests. The high levels of press coverage of Russia and Ireland at this time, including in the United States and Britain, meant that Russo-Irish comparisons were likely to attract public interest and provoke a reaction. Contemporary commentators rarely viewed the Allied intervention in Russia in isolation; instead it became a reference point in wider campaigning and political rhetoric on self-determination and foreign policy.

The global context also influenced Irish methods of resistance against the British state. The Irish munitions strike from May to December 1920, when Irish dockers and railwaymen refused to transport munitions or armed military personnel, followed a British dockers' strike. In May 1920 British dockers refused to place munitions bound for Poland on the SS *Jolly George* due to fears that they would be used against the Bolsheviks. Although Allied troops were nominally withdrawing from north Russia, War Office telegrams published in the *Daily Herald* suggested the possibility of a campaign with White leader Admiral Kolchak. This revelation escalated the broader Hands Off Russia campaign within the British left.[71] The BMH witness statements of Christopher Moran, Volunteer and participant in the Rising, and Thomas Johnson, labor politician and trade unionist, indicate the influence of Hands Off Russia actions in Ireland. Following his imprisonment after the Rising, Moran—who worked on the railways—refused to transport munitions from a British gunboat at Dún Laoghaire, telling the traffic manager that "when Englishmen were refusing to handle munitions to kill Russians, I would not handle munitions to kill Irishmen."[72] Both he and Johnson implied that there was greater justification behind Irish actions than those on the *Jolly George* given the potential impact of the weapons on their own communities.[73]

National identities remained powerful in transnational interactions, with Irish nationalists sometimes creating hierarchies of need and deserving. A 1918 Sinn Féin handbill compared "Irishmen" to "the Ukraine," "the Poles," "the Esthonians," and "the Finns," arguing that these nationalities had gained their freedom even though they were "younger," with a less "glorious history" and less "awful" experiences of "oppression" than Ireland.[74] In this case, the rhetoric of transnational solidarity sat alongside assertions of national exceptionalism. This complex relationship between nationalism and internationalism was evident in Irish nationalist engagement with Ukrainian politics. Between 1918 and 1920, Ukrainian nationalists, White forces, Bolsheviks, Poles, Ukrainian communists, and others struggled for control over the region in a conflict that killed over a million people.[75] Despite this, de Blácam indicated that the Ukrainian question had been solved in 1919. His political manifesto *Towards the Republic* (1919) opened with the quotation "In the dear lost Ukrainia / Which is not ours, though our land," which he attributed to "Shevchenko, national poet of Ukrainia (now a free Republic)."[76] Taras Shevchenko was a celebrated Ukrainian poet of the nineteenth century, sometimes compared to Irish poet Thomas Moore.[77] For de Blácam, Shevchenko's poetry signified a deep-rooted cultural and territorial nationalism, with clear parallels to Irish nationalism. De Blácam's reference to Ukrainian nationalism was symbolic but fleeting, serving as a stepping-stone to his discussion of Ireland rather than a subject of analysis in its own right.

In comparison, republican, suffragist, and writer Rosamond Jacob developed a more nuanced understanding of Ukrainian politics through her activism with the Women's International League for Peace, an organization formed after the International Congress of Women in the Hague in 1915. In July 1921 Jacob wrote to Sheehy Skeffington from a league congress in Vienna, noting how "the Ukrainian delegates want us to write something for their papers about passive resistance in Ireland. They are very keen on passive resistance, they say they are using it against Russian aggression in Ukraine."[78] While Jacob continued to sympathize with Soviet Russia (traveling there in 1931 as a delegate of the Friends of the Soviet Union), she became aware of more contentious aspects of Soviet nationality policy during the civil wars. Irish responses to Russia mirrored domestic political concerns, which encouraged a focus on religion, the national question, and the future of the former Russian Empire. However, there were attempts to think and campaign on a much more international scale during this period, including through travel and engagement in international networks.[79]

Yet Jacob and others faced growing resistance in these efforts by 1920, as accusations of "Irish Bolshevism" and warnings of the dangers of communism gained momentum in the United States, Britain, and Ireland. Richard Dawson, the secretary of the London branch of the Irish Unionist Alliance, argued that there could be no doubt that Irish Republicans had an "understanding" with "Bolshevik revolutionists."[80] In his commercially successful *Red Terror and Green* (1920), he suggested that Sinn Féin and the labor movement had become indistinguishable.[81] In the north of Ireland, unionists framed Bolshevism in relation to partition and the perceived threat posed by Irish republicanism to the British Empire and the United Kingdom. In 1921, the moderate unionist *Belfast Newsletter* published details of a British government white paper on "Intercourse between Bolshevism and Sinn Fein," which included the draft Irish-Soviet treaty "captured" in a raid in Dublin.[82]

The effect of this anti–Sinn Féin propaganda should not be overstated as it largely reinforced existing opposition to Sinn Féin. Nevertheless, these political attacks provoked some concern among Irish republicans. As early as March 1918, de Valera warned that "capital was being made against us about [the] Russian Revolution" and the party should therefore focus on the "political machine."[83] During 1917 the Russian Revolution was not synonymous with socialism in the Irish press and public awareness of Bolshevism was limited (at least until the very end of the year). Initially, Irish nationalists could be fairly creative in their interpretations of the Russian Revolution, but by 1921 there was a clearer association in political discourse and the press between Russia, Bolshevism, and radicalism.

Concerns also emerged over political leadership, strategy, and the pace of revolutionary change in Russia. Even the generally pro-Soviet *Irish Citizen* indicated that Ireland might not want "a new order as sudden and as revolutionary as that of New Russia." Instead, Ireland should try to achieve a "gradual and bloodless revolution from within" and preserve elements of the "capitalist system" in the short term.[84] In his BMH witness statement, Brennan recalled the skepticism of journalist, politician, and Sinn Féin founder Arthur Griffith about Soviet politics: "[Griffith] said to me of the Russian Soviet system, then in process of formation, 'A dictatorship is bad enough but a proletarian dictatorship is infinitely worse. If there is to be dictatorship let it be one of the cultured classes.' 'The propertied classes?' I said. 'No' he replied, 'not the propertied classes—the cultured classes.'"[85] These comments are plausible in the context of Griffith's wider views, a mix of nationalism and meritocracy with (according to some) racist and anti-Semitic undertones.[86] However, the language of "proletarian dictatorship" rarely featured in Irish commentaries on Russia before 1921 and is more likely to be a reference to the Soviet Union rather than to the revolutionary period. In hindsight, Brennan, paraphrasing Griffith, put class struggle to the fore in his framing of the Russian Revolution. Yet for many Irish nationalists at the time, nationalism, empire, and self-determination were at least as important as class in their interpretations of events in Russia.[87] Later Irish accounts, whether in memoirs or BMH witness statements, often blurred together the February and October revolutions, the "Russian" civil wars, and the creation of the Soviet Union.[88] Irish responses to the Russian Revolution in "real-time" were more diverse and changeable, reflecting the differences between the messy realities of the time and memories of transnational connections.

## Conclusion

In July 1917 the *Irish Independent* declared that "there is an Irish problem in Russia, and that there are three Irelands concerned," going on to discuss the situation in Finland, the "Ukrainian question," and Russia itself.[89] This characterization of Russia, Finland, and Ukraine as "three Irelands" shows the use of the familiar to make sense of the unfamiliar and the distortion of Russian events to fit an Irish lens. This engagement often involved two strands. On the one hand, there were attempts to find parallels, promote solidarity, or articulate shared goals across borders. Yet there was also a tendency to play up differences for political reasons or to help articulate national identities. Russia had long served as an "Other" in British and Irish political debates, as seen in the nineteenth century and in responses to the 1904–1905 Russo-Japanese War and 1905 Russian Revolution.[90] Long-standing tropes regarding Russian backwardness, her "simple-minded" people, and her "lawlessness" fed into developing antisocialism and anti-Bolshevism within Irish political debate.[91] Emmet O'Connor's argument that it was only at the end of the 1920s that "people started to frown on association with Russia" ignores the deeper, historic roots of anti-Russian stereotyping.[92] Recorded in the 1940s and 1950s, the witness statements given by Irish revolutionaries to the Bureau of Military History often merged prerevolutionary, revolutionary, and Cold War stereotypes of Russia, including comments on the harshness of Russian punishments and the oppressive influence of the "Russian bear."[93] Anti-Semitism also featured in some Irish responses to Russia between 1917 and 1921 and remained a feature of Irish anticommunism.[94] Equally, Russian commentaries on Ireland often played on stereotypes of Irishness and the "tragedy" of Irish history, including themes like social conservatism, drunkenness, and the "simple" mentality of the Irish peasant. Like Irish tropes on Russian difference, many of these characterizations of Ireland persisted in the Soviet Union during the Cold War.[95] These two strands of engaging and "othering" coexisted in Irish debate during the revolutionary period, sometimes in an uncomfortable and jarring way, and influenced Irish nationalist perceptions of the wider world.

Events in Russia, as elsewhere, lent themselves to imaginings of global change and anti-imperialism. *An t-Óglách* depicted the collapse of the Russian Empire as indicative of a shift in the balance of power in Europe that would help secure an Irish Republic. In the process of constructing global narratives and positing comparisons, Irish commentators often omitted significant aspects of the Russian Revolution and the "Russian" civil wars such as the formation of Soviet political structures or economic questions. While this was partly because of limited information, selective interpretations served political purposes, particularly in terms of facilitating criticism of the British government or rival parties. This does not mean that Irish engagement with the Russian Revolution was "merely playing at international politics."[96] Rather, it reveals the dual process whereby Irish nationalists drew on news of foreign political movements, but also projected their own political assumptions and interests on external events. Transnational engagement and expressions of solidarity in texts and speeches were neither a sign of utopian, internationalist cooperation nor meaningless rhetoric. They were products of a contested and multifaceted process, involving fruitful debate as well as stereotyping and simplification. During this turbulent period, there was a strong sense of opportunity and uncertainty; the map of the world could be redrawn, and new societies could be born. Divisions over the Russian Revolution reflected competing visions for Ireland's future and place in the world.

## NOTES

1 John Darwin, *After Tamerlane: The Rise and Fall of Global Empires, 1400–2000* (London: Penguin, 2008), 369.

2 David Fitzpatrick, *The Two Irelands: 1912–1939* (Oxford: Oxford University Press, 1998), 63–75.

3 *Irish Citizen*, Nov. 1917, 387.

4 Aodh de Blácam, *Towards the Republic: A Study of New Ireland's Social and Political Aims* (Dublin: Thomas Kiersey, 1919), 31, 59, 73. I am grateful to Dr. Brian Hanley for bringing this source to my attention. Patrick Maume, "De Blacam, Aodh," in *Dictionary of Irish Biography [DIB]*, ed. James McGuire and James Quinn (Cambridge: Cambridge University Press, 2009), http://dib.cambridge.org.

5 Priyamvada Gopal, *Insurgent Empire: Anticolonial Resistance and British Dissent* (London: Verso, 2020), 19–22, 63–64, 79.

6 Daniel Headrick, *The Tentacles of Progress: Technology Transfer in the Age of Imperialism, 1850–1940* (New York: Oxford University Press, 1988), 97–109, 126–127.

7 Stephan Pigeon, "Arthur Griffith and His Censors: Evading Censorship with Scissors-and-Paste Journalism in the Irish Newspaper Press, 1914–5," *Publishing History* 80 (2019): 35–66.

8 Stephen White, "Ireland, Russia, Communism, Post-Communism," *Irish Studies in International Affairs* 8 (1997): 155–161; Emmet O'Connor, *Reds and the Green: Ireland, Russia and the Communist Internationals, 1919–43* (Dublin: University College Dublin Press, 2004); Michael Quinn, *Irish-Soviet Diplomatic and Friendship Relations, 1917–91* (Dublin: Umiskin Press, 2016); Maurice Casey, "Red Easter," *History Ireland* 24 (2016): 40–42; Jérôme aan de Wiel, "Ireland and the Bolshevik Revolution," *History Ireland* 25 (2017): 38–42; Michael Silvestri, "'Those Dead Heroes Did Not Regret the Sacrifices They Made': Responses to the Russian Revolution in Revolutionary Ireland," in *The Global Impacts of Russia's Great War and Revolution,*

*Book 2: The Wider Arc of Revolution*, ed. Choi Chatterjee et al. (Bloomington, IN: Slavica, 2019), 253–276.

9   Felix M. Larkin, "The Dog in the Night-Time: The *Freeman's Journal*, the Irish Parliamentary Party, and the Empire, 1875–1919," in *Newspapers and Empire in Ireland and Britain: Reporting the British Empire, c.1857–1921*, ed. Simon J. Potter (Dublin: Four Courts Press, 2004), 113; Patrick Maume, "The *Irish Independent* and Empire, 1891–1919," in Potter, *Newspapers and Empire*, 124–142.

10  "An tÓglach Magazine," *Óglaigh na hÉireann: Defence Forces Ireland: Military Archives* (2017), www.militaryarchives.ie.

11  Margaret Ward, *Fearless Woman: Hanna Sheehy Skeffington, Feminism and the Irish Revolution* (Dublin: University College Dublin Press, 2019), 113–114.

12  Fearghal McGarry, "'Too Many Histories?' The Bureau of Military History and Easter 1916," *History Ireland* 19 (2011): 26–29.

13  Eoin MacWhite, "Ireland in Russian Eyes under the Tsar," *ANV Historical Review* 1 (1965): 1–8; A. V. Prokhorenko, ed., *Sankt-Peterburg—Irlandiia: Liudi i sobytiia* (Sankt Peterburg: Evropeiskii Dom, 2011).

14  For example, see General F. F. Millen to the Supreme Council of the Irish Republican Brotherhood, 23 Dec. 1877 (National Library of Ireland [NLI], Dublin, John Devoy Papers, MS 18,008/8/4).

15  Michael Davitt notebook, Jan.–Feb. 1905 (Trinity College Dublin Archives [TCD], Michael Davitt Papers, MS 9582/51).

16  Ibid. Carla King, "'. . . In a Humble way, a Supporter of Russia': Michael Davitt in Russia. 1903, 1904 and 1905," in *Life on the Fringe? Ireland and Europe, 1800–1922*, ed. Brian Heffernan (Dublin: Irish Academic Press, 2012), 135–156.

17  *Freeman's Journal* [hereafter *Freeman*], 28 Feb. 1917, 6, 13 Mar. 1917, 4; *Independent*, 8 Mar. 1917, 2.

18  *Freeman*, 16 Mar. 1917, 4.

19  Jane McDermid and Anna Hilyar, *Midwives of the Revolution: Female Bolsheviks and Women Workers in 1917* (London: UCL Press, 1999), 147–151. Dates according to the Gregorian calendar (Russia followed the Julian calendar until 1918).

20  Royal Navy Armoured Car Division Papers, 1914–2000 (Public Record Office of Northern Ireland [PRONI], Belfast, D4467); Charlotte Alston, "Encounters on the Eastern Front: The Royal Naval Armoured Car Division in Russia 1915–20," *War in History* 25 (2017): 485–510; Peter Stevenson, ". . . From Bangor to Baku: Ulster Soldiers Fighting for the Royal Navy," *BBC*, 16 Oct. 2014, http://bbc.co.uk. On Irish female eyewitnesses, see, e.g., *Belfast Newsletter*, 10 Apr. 1917, 5; *Independent*, 12 July 1918, 2; *Freeman*, 13 July 1918, 3; *Skibbereen Eagle*, 10 Jan. 1920, 3.

21  *Independent*, 24 Mar. 1917, 3; Fitzpatrick, *Two Irelands*, 57.

22  Robert Brennan (Bureau of Military History [BMH], WS 779), 201, www.militaryarchives.ie; Michael Kennedy, "Brennan, Robert," in *DIB* (2009).

23  Robert Service, *A History of Twentieth-Century Russia* (London: Penguin, 1998), 49.

24  David Kirby, *A Concise History of Finland* (Cambridge: Cambridge University Press, 2006), 158–159.

25  *Independent*, 21 Apr. 1917, 3.

26  *Independent*, 24 Apr. 1917, 3; R. B. McDowell, *Alice Stopford Green: A Passionate Historian* (Dublin: Allen Figgis, 1967), 62–105; Alice Stopford Green, *History of the Irish State to 1014* (London: Macmillan, 1925), 420–421.

27  *Freeman*, 3 Apr. 1917, 5.

28  *Freeman*, 23 Mar. 1917, 5.

29  *Freeman*, 3 Apr. 1917, 5.

30  *Freeman*, 1 May 1917, 5.

31  For example, see *An t-Óglách*, 14 Oct. 1918, 4.

32  *Independent*, 26 May 1917, 2; G. D. H. Cole and Marc Brodie, "Thorne, William James," in *Oxford Dictionary of National Biography* (2004), www.oxforddnb.com.

33  For example, see G. E. Afanas'ev, *Istoriia Irlandii* (Sankt Peterburg: Brokgauz-Efron, 1907) and the front-page article on "Ulster" in the Russian Constitutional Democratic Party (Kadets) newspaper *Rech*, 10 (23) Aug. 1912, 1.

34  *Freeman*, 28 May 1917, 5; Patrick Maume, "Kelly, Denis," in *DIB* (2009).

35  *An t-Óglách*, 17 July 1921, 3.

36  "Proclamation of the Irish Republic," 24 Apr. 1916 (Conflict Archive on the Internet database, www.cain.ulster.ac.uk).

37  Hanna Sheehy Skeffington, *British Militarism as I Have Known It* (Tralee: Kerryman, 1946), 14; Rochelle Goldberg Ruthchild, *Equality and Revolution: Women's Rights in the Russian Empire, 1905–17* (Pittsburgh: University of Pittsburgh Press, 2010), 226–230.

38  *Citizen*, Apr. 1917, 253, Aug. 1917, 373.

39  For example, see *Newsletter*, 18 May 1917, 5; *Freeman*, 21 May 1917, 5.

40  For example, see *Freeman*, 17 May 1917, 4; 3 July 1917, 5.

41  Service, *History of Twentieth-Century Russia*, 62–68.

42  *Freeman*, 8 Nov. 1917, 3; 9 Nov. 1917, 4–5; *Independent*, 8 Nov. 1917, 3; 9 Nov. 1917, 2–4.

43  Anna Geifman, *Thou Shalt Kill: Revolutionary Terrorism in Russia, 1894–1917* (Princeton: Princeton University Press, 1993), 73.

44  Copies of Davitt's letters from Saint Petersburg, Jan.–Feb. 1905 (TCD, Michael Davitt Papers, 9524/6026).

45  *An t-Óglách*, 30 Sept. 1918, 4; *Irish Citizen*, Oct. 1917, 382–383, Apr.–May 1920, 87.

46  *An t-Óglách*, 15 Nov. 1918, 3, 30 Nov. 1918, 1.

47  Trotsky, "Lessons of the Events in Dublin," *Nashe Slovo*, 4 July 1916, in *The Communists and the Irish Revolution. Part 1: The Russian Revolutionaries on the Irish National Question, 1899–1924*, ed. D. R. O'Connor Lysaght (Dublin: Literéire, 1993), 58–60; Lenin, "The Irish Rebellion of 1916" (July 1916), in O'Connor Lysaght, *The Communists*, 61–65; John Rodden, "'The Lever Must Be Applied in Ireland': Marx, Engels and the Irish Question," *Review of Politics* 70 (2008): 609–640.

48  *Izvestiia*, 18 Sept. 1919, 3. Also see, for example, *Pravda*, 25 Jan. 1919, 1, 7 Feb. 1919, 1; *Izvestiia*, 20 Nov. 1920, 1.

49  Silvestri, "Those Dead Heroes," 254.

50  Charlotte Despard diary, 22 Jan. 1918 (PRONI, Charlotte Despard Papers, D2479/1/4).

51  William O'Brien diary, 4 Feb. 1918 (NLI, William O'Brien Papers, MS 15,705/11). "Circular Letter Regarding Meeting Held in Mansion House," 1918 (NLI, Thomas Johnson Papers, MS 17,120/1); "Russian Republic Reception," [1918] (NLI, LO P 114).

52  *Eagle*, 23 Mar. 1918, 1.

53  *Freeman*, 22 Mar. 1918, 2.

54  Service, *History of Twentieth-Century Russia*, 62; *Freeman*, 6 Feb. 1918, 2, 22 Mar. 1918, 2.

55  For example, see *Church of Ireland Gazette*, 18 Jan. 1918, 46, 1 Feb. 1918, 72; *Eagle*, 16 Feb. 1918, 3.

56  *Independent*, 4 Feb. 1918, 3.

57  *Independent*, 7 Feb. 1918, 3; James Zatko, "The Roman Catholic Church and Its Legal Position under the Provisional Government in Russia in 1917," *Slavonic and East European Review* 38 (1960), 476–492.

58  For example, see *Citizen*, Nov. 1917, 387.

59  *Freeman*, 6 Feb. 1918, 3.

60  *Freeman*, 16 Feb. 1918, 6.

61  *Independent*, 21 Mar. 1919, 4, *Freeman*, 7 Mar. 1919, 3, *Eagle*, 27 Dec. 1919, 2.

62  Jonathan Smele, *The "Russian" Civil Wars, 1916–26: Ten Years That Shook the World* (Oxford: Oxford University Press, 2016), 1.

63  Bruce Nelson, *Irish Nationalists and the Making of the Irish Race* (Princeton: Princeton University Press, 2012), 179–241; Alice Ginnell (BMH, WS 982).

64  "Ireland: Sinn Fein: Relations with Soviet Government," 1920–1921 (The National Archives, United Kingdom, HO 144/22379).

65  Kathleen O'Donovan (BMH, WS 586), 33; Quinn, *Irish-Soviet Diplomatic and Friendship Relations*, 9–10; "Memo by McCartan re Russian Treaty and Mission to Russia" (NLI, Count Plunkett Papers, MS 11,404/31); Patrick McCartan to L. A. Martens, 8 May 1919 (NLI, Patrick McCartan Papers [PMP], MS 17,682/5).

66  Evan Mawdsley, *The Russian Civil War* (Edinburgh: Birlinn, 2005), 49–52.

67  Nick Baron, *The King of Karelia: Col P. J. Woods and the British Intervention in North Russia, 1918–1919: A History and Memoir* (London: Francis Boutle, 2007), 6, 63–64. Also see Francis McCullagh, *A Prisoner of the Reds: The Story of a British Officer Captured Siberia* (London: J. Murray, 1921).

68  "Resolution by the Citizens of Philadelphia," 1919 (NLI, Joseph McGarrity Papers [JMP], MS 17,651/6/11).

69  "List of Suggested Lantern Slides," 1919 (NLI, JMP, MS 17,651/6/12).

70  Lincoln Colcord to Santeri Nuorteva, 1920 (NLI, PMP, MS 17,682/7); McCartan to Éamon de Valera, 20 July 1920 (JMP, MS 17,439/12); Auvo Kostiainen, "'A Wonderful Man' or 'A Dangerous Bolshevik' Santeri Nuorteva in the United States, 1912–1920," *American Communist History* 6 (2007): 197–207; Parker Bishop Albee et

al., "Portrait of a Friendship: Selected Correspondence of Samuel Eliot Morison and Lincoln Colcord, 1921–47," *New England Quarterly* 56 (1983): 166–199.

71  L. J. Macfarlane, "Hands Off Russia: British Labour and the Russo-Polish War, 1920," *Past & Present* 38 (1967): 126–152; Helene O'Keeffe, "The 1920 Munitions Strike: 'An Unusual Kind of Strike,'" *RTÉ History*, 21 May 2020, www.rte.ie.

72  Christopher Moran (BMH, WS 1438), 11–13.

73  Thomas Johnson (BMH, WS 1755), 12–13.

74  "Irishmen Look Around You!," 1918 (NLI, ILB 300 1).

75  Timothy Snyder, *The Reconstruction of Nations: Poland, Ukraine, Lithuania, Belarus, 1569–1999* (London: Yale University Press, 2003), 137–141.

76  De Blácam, *Towards the Republic*, 1.

77  Jurij Bojko and Victor Swoboda, "Taras Shevchenko and West European Literature," *Slavonic and East European Review* 34 (1955): 90.

78  Jacob to Sheehy Skeffington, July 1921 (NLI, Sheehy Skeffington Papers, MS 41, 177/27); Ward, *Fearless Woman*, xxi, xxxiii, xxxvii, xxx.

79  *Citizen*, Dec. 1919, 52. Maurice Casey, "'The Future of Feminism': The Irish Women's Franchise League and the World Revolution, 1917–20," in *The Irish Revolution 1919–21: A Global History*, ed. Enda Delaney and Fearghal McGarry (Dublin: Wordwell, 2019), 27–30.

80  Richard Dawson, *Red Terror and Green* (1920; London: New English Library, 1972), 124; Mo Moulton, *Ireland and the Irish in Interwar England* (Cambridge: Cambridge University Press, 2014), 266.

81  Dawson, *Red Terror and Green*, 142–145.

82  *Newsletter*, 10 May 1921, 4.

83  Michael Laffan, *The Resurrection of Ireland: The Sinn Féin Party, 1916–23* (Cambridge: Cambridge University Press, 1999), 258.

84  *Citizen*, June–July 1920, 103.

85  Brennan (BMH, WS 779), 512–3.

86  Michael Laffan, "Griffith, Arthur Joseph," in *DIB* (2009). Brian Maye challenges Griffith's "Frankenstein image" in *Arthur Griffith* (Dublin: Griffith College Publications, 1997), 356–372.

87  Also see O'Connor, *Reds*, 2.

88  For example, see Sean O'Casey, *Autobiography Book 4: Inishfallen, Fare Thee Well* (1949; London: Pan Books, 1972), 15–16.

89  *Independent*, 20 July 1917, 2.

90  For example, see *Eagle*, 29 Oct. 1904, 4, 14 Jan. 1905, 4. Martin Malia, *Russia under Western Eyes: From the Bronze Horseman to the Lenin Mausoleum* (London: Belknap, 1999), 3–6, 172, 184.

91  For example, see *Independent*, 27 Aug. 1917, 2, 15 Nov. 1917, 2.

92  O'Connor, *Reds and the Green*, 138–9.

93  For example, see Patrick Mullooly (BMH, WS 1087), 5, 14; James A. H. Irwin (BMH, WS 394), 9.

94   For example, see de Blácam, *Towards the Republic*, 63; *Newsletter*, 23 Dec. 1918, 2; *Church of Ireland Gazette*, 13 Feb. 1920, 102. Also see R. M. Douglas, "'Not So Different After All': Irish and Continental European Antisemitism in Comparative Perspective," in *Irish Questions and Jewish Questions: Crossovers in Culture*, ed. Aidan Beatty and Dan O'Brien (New York: Syracuse University Press, 2018), 31–46; and Brian Hanley, "'The Irish and the Jews Have a Good Deal in Common': Irish Republicanism, Anti-Semitism and the Post-war World," *Irish Historical Studies* 44, no. 165 (2020): 57–74.

95   For example, see E. Astori, *Angliia, Uel's' i Irlandiia* (Moskva: I. N. Kushnerev, 1912), 68–81; P. M. Kerzhentsev, *Revoliutsionnaia Irlandiia* (Moskva: Vserossiiskii tsentral'nyi ispolnitel'nyi komitet sovetov, 1918), 3; "Comments in Russia on Irish affairs" (1949) (National Archives of Ireland, Dublin, DFA/6/414/24/35).

96   McCartan to de Valera, 20 July 1920.

# 4

# "The Example of Valiant Little Ireland"

## The Irish Revolution in Algerian Nationalist Thought

DÓNAL HASSETT

In 1961, the seventh year of the long and bloody Algerian War of Independence, a Swiss publishing firm released a collection of texts by prominent Algerian nationalist Laroussi Khelifa. This *Manual for the Algerian Activist* was based on the material used by Khelifa and other intellectual cadres of the Front de Libération Nationale (FLN) in the movement's training schools in Morocco. In the section dedicated to "revolutionary doctrine," pride of place was given not to Marx nor to Fanon but rather to "the particularly significant example of valiant little Ireland." Khelifa presented the Algerian struggle as part of a broader international anticolonial movement that had first swept South America, then Asia, and finally Africa. In this historic process, Ireland stood out for its "unremitting struggle for over a century . . . to win its independence from the English colossus."[1] The integration of (a version of) Irish history into the FLN's revolutionary curriculum is indicative of both the international reach of the Irish Revolution and the Algerian nationalists' embrace of a global conception of their struggle.

Throughout the twentieth century, a variety of Algerian activists would evoke the Irish Revolution. Figures as diverse as Ahmad Tawfiq Al-Madani, a young nationalist intellectual living in exile in the Tunis of the 1920s, Hocine Aït Ahmed, a key political strategist for the nationalist movement in the post–Second World War era, Larbi Ben M'hidi, the most iconic martyr of the revolution, and Redha Malek, a key negotiator in the peace talks that secured Algeria's independence, all evoked Ireland in their writings. For them and many of their comrades, Irish history served, above all, as a means of negotiating and reinventing their own relationships—strategic, political, and emotional—with anticolonial struggle. As this chapter shows, while the Irish Revolution was a source of inspiration for Algerian nationalists, its primary role was not as a playbook that could be directly replicated in the very different coercive and racially discriminatory context of colonial Algeria. Algerians may have occasionally sought to reproduce the tactics deployed by Irish nationalists, but this was never the principal space occupied by Ireland in their revolutionary imaginary. Instead, Ireland stood out as a beacon of hope, *the* example of a settler colony that had defeated a mighty empire and secured a form, however limited, of freedom. In its story, or at least in the versions of its story that reached North Africa, Algerian nationalists saw the prospect that their sacrifices, both personal and collective, might one day be rewarded, that their country might one day be freed. Moreover, the complex blend of political and military strategies that underpinned Irish nationalism in the nineteenth and twentieth centuries allowed Algerian activists to evoke the elements of the Irish story that most closely aligned with the evolving political logics of anticolonial action in their country. In doing so they refracted and reimagined Ireland's history through the prism of Algeria's struggle for liberation.

### Ireland and Algeria: A Fair Comparison?

Before we delve into the multiple ways in which Algerian nationalists interpreted and mobilized the Irish Revolution in their own anticolonial politics, it is worth exploring the historical parallels that underlay their comparisons and the divergences that undermined them. Historians and political theorists have long highlighted the similarities in the legal status of Algeria and Ireland within the political structures of their respective empires. Over the course of the nineteenth century both colonies had been legally integrated into the metropolitan polity, with the Acts of Union of 1800 subsuming Ireland into the United Kingdom and the 1848 departmentalization of Algeria incorporating the colony into the French metropole. Both were marked by the presence of a minority settler community of a different ethnicity and religion whose arrival had been spurred by the expropriation of the lands of the indigenous population and who enjoyed or had enjoyed political, economic, and cultural hegemony. The nominal assimilation of Algeria and Ireland into their respective imperial metropoles was called into question in both territories by the existence of exceptional colonial institutions and repressive laws and practices not in place in the metropole. The economic effects of colonial rule were important drivers for mass emigration from both countries, while the cultural impact of colonialism meant that many of the prominent leaders of resistance in Algeria and Ireland received their education and articulated their opposition to colonialism in the language of the colonizer. These points of comparison have been explored in the work of Ian Lustick and led prominent historians of Algeria Hélène Blais, Claire Fredj, and Sylvie Thénault to conclude in a recent article that "Ireland is perhaps the closest case to that of Algeria."[2] The Algeria-Ireland comparison has been particularly embraced by literary scholars in the postcolonial tradition, including such important figures as Edward Said and Declan Kiberd.[3] They have drawn on the parallels between the Francophone literature of Algeria and the Anglophone literary production of Irish writers to make broader points about the long-term cultural, social, and political impact of settler colonialism. The weight of the evidence and the scholarship that has developed around it makes a convincing case for the comparison of these two colonial contexts.

However, a close examination of the concrete realities of colonial rule in Ireland and Algeria shows how the types of colonialism practiced in both contexts varied in scale, form, and temporalities. These variations shaped the lived experiences of the revolutionary generations in Ireland and in Algeria. Most importantly, the advent of Catholic Emancipation in Ireland removed the formal legal inequalities grounded in ethnoreligious discrimination, while the extension of the franchise during the revolutionary period empowered Irish men and women (over the age of thirty) to express their desire for change at the ballot box. Algerians, in contrast, were relegated to the status of colonial subjects, denied French citizenship until 1946. Even then, Algerians' political rights remained limited. The franchise was denied to Algerian women until 1958 and the use of separate electoral colleges was designed to ensure that a settler's vote was worth eight times that of an Algerian. In any case, the French authorities had no qualms about banning political parties, stuffing ballot boxes, and rigging elections in the colony.[4] While both the coercive power of the British administration in Ireland and the range of military, paramilitary, and armed policing forces available to impose it were unparalleled elsewhere in the United Kingdom, they remained, at least in theory, under the jurisdiction of the courts and/or subject to specific laws of exception. In Algeria, the vast majority of the subject population was governed by a harsh and arbitrary legal code known as the Indigénat that allowed local administrators to impose corporal punishment, collective fines, and internment, largely without judicial oversight.[5] The power of the code diminished over time and it was eventually abolished in 1946, but the colonial state in Algeria continued to deploy extensive coercive measures against the population, and the outbreak of the War of Independence saw the generalization of practices of torture, the use of napalm, the forced displacement of a significant proportion of the population, and frequent summary executions. The willingness of the French to deploy violent tactics with much greater frequency and intensity in Algeria than the British authorities had done in revolutionary Ireland was, in part, a reflection of the different processes of racialization and Othering that underpinned colonial rule in both territories. By the twentieth century, the Irish stood near the top of the hierarchy of colonized peoples in a British Empire increasingly defined by the concept of the color line. They held significant sway in the Parliament in Westminster, and some were active participants in the imperial project overseas. The Algerians, in contrast, continued to be regarded as racially different and culturally backward in the supposedly "colourblind" French imperial polity. Finally, the issue of land ownership, central to any settler colonial context, was, by the beginning of the twentieth century, radically different in Ireland and Algeria. Decades of political agitation and the increasing electoral power of the Irish population within the British polity had led to significant land reforms and the erosion of the power of the old landowner class. In Algeria, where both the colonial conquest and the subsequent expropriation of land were much more recent phenomena, there was no prospect of an equitable redistribution of land within the racialized settler colonial state. Acknowledging these fundamental differences is crucial to understanding the limits of the Algeria-Ireland comparison.

The visions of the Irish Revolution developed and promoted by various Algerian nationalists preceded much of the scholarship on which I have relied for my comparative analyses. They also relied on limited sources of information often drawn from openly political narratives that were far more concerned with denouncing British rule and celebrating Irish heroism than establishing an accurate account of the relationship between Ireland and the British colonial metropole. In any case, Algerian nationalists were not looking to be inducted into the historiographical debates of Irish history. What they sought, above all else, was a precedent that could legitimize and inform their own struggle. Thus, what matters most for our purposes is not how sustainable broad comparisons between Algeria and Ireland were from a historical perspective but rather the reasons why and the contexts in which Algerian nationalists chose to evoke the Irish Revolution.

### Ireland as a Warning for the Colonial Authorities

The radical social, economic, and political changes brought about by the Great War and that were so central to driving radicalization and revolutionary politics in Ireland did not leave Algeria untouched. Like Ireland, the war saw the mobilization of thousands of men from different ethnoreligious backgrounds to serve on the battlefields of continental Europe.[6] However, while recruitment in nationalist and unionist communities in Ireland took place on a voluntary basis, conscription was applied to Europeans and Algerians in France's North African departments. Both the European settlers and the unionist community in Ireland would stress their defense of their respective empires to advocate for the maintenance of the status quo in their territories, arguing that through their sacrifices, they had sealed their union with the metropole in blood.[7]

The responses in the Irish nationalist and Algerian communities were more complex. The leaders of mainstream constitutional nationalism in Ireland supported the war effort, arguing that it would reinforce Ireland's right to Home Rule once victory was achieved. More radical nationalists in the republican and socialist traditions opposed the war, eventually organizing an armed insurrection at Easter 1916. Although the Easter Rising ended in a dramatic military defeat, it would transform Irish politics as one of the key motors for the radicalization of Irish nationalism. Algerians' limited political rights meant that mass politics was nowhere near as developed in that territory as it was in

Ireland. The members of the educated elite, who were described as the "Young Algerians" in a homage to the "Young Turks" and the various liberal movements of mid-nineteenth-century Europe (including the Young Irelanders), largely supported the application of conscription to Algerians.[8] They hoped that Algerian service in the war would result in the extension of further political and civil rights.[9] Outside the severely restricted sphere of high politics, some Algerians met the increased encroachment of the wartime colonial state with open resistance. Efforts to enforce the draft resulted in a string of minor revolts and acts of civil disobedience.[10] In November 1916, only months after the failed Easter Rising in Dublin, locals in the Aurès mountains of southeastern Algeria staged an insurrection against the French colonial authorities, demanding an independent republic. The rebellion was brutally crushed and, unlike the Easter Rising, had limited immediate impact on politics in the colony, although it did live on in the folk memory of a region that would become the cradle of revolutionary activity during the Algerian War of Independence.[11]

In the aftermath of the Great War, as Ireland's revolution entered its most radical phase, a new political movement was emerging in Algeria around a charismatic member of the precolonial nobility, the Emir Khaled. Khaled, an officer of the French Army who was decorated for his service in the war, was the grandson of the Emir 'Abd al-Qādir, the iconic resistance leader who had led opposition to the French conquest of Algeria. He was able to take advantage of reforms in 1919 that saw the limited expansion of suffrage for local elections to members of the Algerian elite and some Algerian war veterans. Khaled's slate of candidates secured important victories in the Algiers region on a platform calling for enhanced political rights and a form of special citizenship for Algerians within the French Empire.[12] His attitude toward French rule was somewhat ambiguous, often blending nationalistic language with declarations of loyalty and appeals for the full integration of Algerians into the French polity.[13] He was willing to pursue some tactics that were similar to those adopted by Sinn Féin, including a failed effort to win support for the Algerian cause from President Wilson at the Paris Peace Conference, but did not embrace the kind of radical and often violent political program that underpinned the Irish Revolution.[14]

Khaled and his movement drew inspiration primarily from examples in the Muslim and Arab worlds, particularly celebrating the successes of Mustafa Kemal's Young Turks and Saʻd Zaghlul's Wafd Party in Egypt.[15] Where Egypt and Turkey were examples of Islamic countries embracing modernity and self-determination that Algerians should seek to emulate, Ireland served as a kind of cautionary tale of the consequences of ignoring the demands of colonial subjects. By critiquing the failures of a rival imperial power, Khaled and his followers could couch their attacks on colonial oppression in a language of imperial loyalty. As the movement grew increasingly frustrated, its newspaper, *L'Ikdam*, began to evoke the specter of Ireland's violent break with empire. Writing in November 1921, a French contributor to the newspaper warned of the dangers of repeating the mistakes of "Anglo-Saxon colonialism" by "persisting with oppression" and "making life impossible for the natives." A refusal to implement significant reforms would end "in a very violent explosion" of popular anger; the colonial authorities need only "look at what has happened in Ireland" to confirm this.[16] This message was echoed in even stronger terms the following year by columnist Ahmed Balloul, who urged the French to learn from the mistakes of their British rivals, arguing that "repression in Ireland did not succeed in snuffing out the revolt and proud England had to settle with the Irish" and pointing to its repercussions in Egypt, in India, and across the empire.[17] For Khaled and his followers, Ireland was not an example that they should follow but rather a precedent that their French rulers should avoid.

The effort to cast the campaign for change that he led as a means of preserving not ending empire would not spare Khaled from the repression of the colonial state. He was driven into exile by the French authorities and, despite efforts to stage a comeback in the late 1920s in an alliance with the anticolonial French Communist Party, never again exercised significant influence in Algeria. The fact that Khaled's efforts to avoid falling foul of the authorities by framing his calls for change as a means of preserving colonial rule failed is indicative of just how limited the scope for political activism was in the coercive settler colonial state of French Algeria. There was no room in postwar Algeria for a political activism that openly embraced the separatism, civil disobedience, and armed insurrection supported by Sinn Féin in Ireland. This did not mean, however, that Algerian activists could not draw inspiration from the successes of the Irish Revolution.

## Ireland as a Source of Romantic Inspiration

While the Emir Khaled and his supporters in colonial Algiers were trying to leverage the example of Ireland to secure immediate concessions from the French authorities, a young Algerian intellectual in neighboring Tunisia was arguing that France's North African subjects should draw on the example of Ireland to forge their own form of nationalism. Ahmad Tawfiq Al-Madani was born in 1899 into an Algerian family of the precolonial elite that had fled to Tunis following the defeat of the 1871 Mokrani Revolt against French rule in Algeria.[18] The establishment of the French protectorate over Tunisia in 1881 meant that the young Ahmad would grow up both in exile and under a repressive colonial system. He became involved in politics at a young age, publishing his first articles in a nationalist newspaper at fifteen. He soon came to the attention of the wartime authorities in Tunisia, serving a first prison sentence in the French colonial penitentiary system from 1915 to 1918. Upon his release, he quickly returned to political activism, playing a role in the foundation of the first Tunisian nationalist party, the Destour. Political activists in North Africa organized across national boundaries in this period, often calling for the unity of the three colonies of the French Maghreb. As a Tunisian of Algerian origin, Al-Madani played a role in coordinating and organizing opposition to French rule in both territories, though he is best remembered for his role in Algerian nationalism. Al-Madani's career as a publisher and activist was as long as it was fascinating, but he is most renowned as a crucial figure in the development of a form of Algerian cultural nationalism that in many ways mirrored the national revival that had paved the way for revolutionary politics in Ireland.[19]

In 1923, just as the Irish Free State was emerging from a bloody and bitter civil war, Al-Madani published a celebration of Ireland's fight for freedom in the pages of the Tunisian Arabophone paper *Al-Fajr*. His article, "Niḍāl Irlandā" (Ireland's Struggle), ran to a total of twenty-four pages and included a detailed description of the island's geography, climate, economy, and history.[20] The only source specifically referenced in the essay is the reporting of French journalist Ludovic Nadeau, who served as the Irish correspondent for *Le Temps* in Dublin in 1921.[21] Events in Ireland were covered extensively in the French press, which was widely available in Tunis. Furthermore, newspapers in Arabic from Egypt, where events in Ireland were followed with great interest, were available in Tunis and circulated in Al-Madani's familial milieu.[22] The existence of a somewhat laxer censorship regime regarding the Arabophone press in Tunisia than in Algeria made it possible for him to publish his essay on Ireland for an Arabic-speaking readership not just in Tunis but also in his ancestral homeland, where Tunisian newspapers were often consumed by intellectual elites.[23]

From the outset, Al-Madani made clear that "Niḍāl Irlandā" was far more than a historical account of Irish nationalism. The text opens with a bold and broad statement: "Freedom is the fruit of jihad."[24] This meant not that his study of Irish history had led Al-Madani to embrace violent struggle per se but rather that it reinforced his belief that freedom could be secured only through hard-fought spiritual, cultural, and political struggle. A keen student of history, Al-Madani cited the cases of the French, the Americans, and the Turks as examples that show that "freedom is not given to nations, nations take their freedom." By this logic, Egypt and India, both "stained with blood," would, he argued, surely "win freedom and blissful independence" in the future. But it was Ireland, a small nation that had "taken control of its own future,"[25] that Al-Madani saw as "a wonderful example from which" North Africans should "draw much wisdom."[26] The history of its recent struggle in a context of settler colonialism showed Algerians that "no obstacle can stand in the way" of the organized resistance of "a people determined to realise its will."[27]

Al-Madani offered his readers a narrative of Irish history that implicitly ran parallel to that of colonialism in North Africa. The "imposition" of a foreign culture, language, and religion was presented as having "sparked revolution" in the "souls" of the Irish, starting Ireland out on the path of true struggle for independence.[28] His assertion that the "English made a lot of efforts to leave the country in a state of poverty so that they could enslave it" must have resonated with readers in Tunisia and Algeria, where the expropriation of land and wealth by the colonial authorities was a recent, and in some cases ongoing, process.[29] His denunciation of the famines caused by colonialism in Ireland came at a time when Algeria itself was recovering from a disastrous famine due to the mismanagement of food supplies by the colonial authorities.[30] Al-Madani's North African audience would surely read between the lines, seeing in his blistering critique of British colonialism in Ireland an attack on French rule in their own region.

Al-Madani's analysis was not restricted to critiquing British rule in Ireland; he also offered a detailed account of Irish contestation of it. He recognized both the possibilities and the limits of the Irish using their position within the British polity to advocate for immediate reform. He acknowledged the improvements brought about by Gladstone, focusing in particular on the separation of church and state and freedom of religion, a cause dear to the heart of Islamic cultural revivalists in North Africa, but he argued that they were not sufficient for an Irish population "that did not want an alternative to independence."[31] Al-Madani denounced the "beautiful promises" made by the English to the Irish and by "others to others," an oblique reference to French wartime commitments to reform in North Africa, in the "hour of need" during the Great War.[32] The Irish, he argued, were never taken in by such promises, seizing on the "opportunity that arose from the context of the war" to stage a "revolution" in the capital. This may have failed, but it paved the way for a final acceptance that the "Irish could not rely on hope of help from the British" and would have to forge their own destiny under the leadership of Sinn Féin.[33] Nor could the Irish or other colonial peoples count on a just postwar order grounded in the "Fourteen Principles of the wise Wilson." They would have to "rely on themselves." For the Irish, this meant waging a "final war against England" to secure freedom.[34] What exactly it meant for the Algerians was less clear.

Al-Madani's account of the war celebrated the heroism of the Irish republicans and denounced British oppression without overly dwelling on the reality of combining political action with armed struggle. Unsurprisingly for someone who had recently spent a significant spell in the colonial penitentiary system, his focus was on the unifying effect the policy of repression had on its victims and on the broader Irish public. "Imprisonment, torture and executions were but a motivation for the Irish," he argued, adding that the coercive power of the British state served only to "spark a fire of patriotism . . . that is impossible to quell." Al-Madani paid special attention to the emblematic figure of Terrence MacSwiney, the lord mayor of Cork whose lengthy hunger strike ending in death made of him an international martyr for the Irish cause. He lauded MacSwiney's sacrifice, describing him as a *mujāhid*, a term that might be best translated as "spiritual warrior" and that would subsequently be used to describe the fighters of the FLN during the Algerian War.[35] However, the role of MacSwiney, de Valera, and Collins, figures he singled out for special attention as "Ireland's Most Famous Men," in organizing politically and militarily against British rule received little attention.[36] Al-Madani offered no real analysis of the tactics pursued by the IRA, an entity that, like Dáil Éireann, is not specifically discussed in the text. The mobilization of organized labor and of women behind the national cause, so central to the success of the Irish movement, went unmentioned. Al-Madani evoked Ireland not as a playbook that the Algerians might seek to reproduce but rather as an inspirational tale of heroism, bravery, and national revival that should ignite patriotism in the souls of his compatriots.

The lack of operational and organizational detail in "Ireland's Struggle" is indicative not just of a lack of historical accuracy but also of a broader political ambiguity at the heart of the text. Al-Madani tied together the different strands of Irish nationalism, presenting the advocates of Home Rule led by the "great nationalist Parnell," the rebels of 1916, and the heroes of the War of Independence as one, united historical movement. The question of the legitimacy and efficacy of the armed struggle, which would become central to debates within the Algerian national movement in the post–Second World War era, was simply elided in the text. Instead, Al-Madani recast the War of Independence as an abstract form of resistance to colonial oppression that was the direct result of the obstinance of the British government.[37] This suggests an intermediate position between the portrayal of revolutionary violence among Emir Khaled's supporters as a negative result of colonial intransigence and its enthusiastic celebration by a later generation of revolutionaries in the FLN. Al-Madani was neither endorsing nor denouncing violence; he was open to any path that might bring freedom to North Africa.

Al-Madani's pragmatic approach to anticolonial activism was evident in his narrative of the Civil War, portrayed as a political (not military) dispute between two camps led by great heroes, Collins and de Valera. While he acknowledged the integrity of the positions held by both men on the Anglo-Irish Treaty, the clauses of which are reproduced in full in the essay, he ultimately endorsed the agreement, claiming that the Free State "gives full life to the nation," allowing for the development of the "national spirit" so a republic can eventually be secured.[38] His embrace of the famous "stepping-stone" principle is hardly surprising. Throughout the interwar period, Al-Madani continued to favor a negotiated transition out of empire in which the reins of power were passed from French colonial officials to the existing Algerian elites.[39] His vision of an Arabo-Islamic Algeria ruled by these elites was not too distant from the Catholic and Gaelic Ireland that the first Free State government was trying to craft in 1923.

By the time Al-Madani published his memoirs in 1977 after a lengthy career as a writer and a politician, Algeria had secured its independence through a violent anticolonial insurrection that had become central to the identity of the postcolonial state. The text sought to reinvent its author as a lifelong revolutionary whose commitment to the use of any means necessary to overthrow colonialism was beyond question.[40] Describing himself as a "born rebel,"[41] Al-Madani specifically cited his publication on Ireland as evidence of his long-standing interest in revolutionary insurrection. His autobiography recast the Irish War of Independence as a popular struggle in which "the people crushed their internal and external enemies," denouncing those who opposed Sinn Féin in the name of "moderation" and reserving all his praise for "the hero Eamon de Valera."[42] Gone was the endorsement of the "stepping-stone" theory and the ambiguity around the armed struggle. In his old age, Al-Madani had, it seemed, embraced radical Irish republicanism. The roots of this Damascene conversion lay not in a more profound engagement with the historiography of the Irish Revolution but rather in the changing interpretation of the Irish precedent among Algerian nationalists. Al-Madani, who was the originator of the comparison with Ireland, now reimagined his past understanding of Ireland's struggle so it was more in line with the narrative dominant among Algeria's revolutionary generation. The path of Algerian history had transformed his vision of Irish history.

### Ireland as a Means of Legitimizing Political Strategy

While Al-Madani was laying the intellectual foundations for nationalism in North Africa, Algerian migrants in France were constructing a political movement to call for national liberation. Eager to build a base among the swelling ranks of Algerian migrant workers in the metropole, the French Communist Party give its financial and political support to a new nationalist movement called the Étoile Nord-Africaine (ENA; North Africa Star). The ENA advocated for the independence of Algeria, Morocco, and Tunisia, combining Leninist anti-imperialism with a celebration of Arabic and Islamic culture. Under the leadership of the charismatic Messali Hadj, the ENA broke with the Communist Party and built a mass nationalist movement first in France and subsequently in Algeria itself. Although the organization was closely linked to the nascent networks of international anti-imperialism throughout the interwar period, Ireland rarely featured in its rhetoric.[43] Messali and his followers focused primarily on anticolonial action elsewhere in the Arab and Islamic worlds, in Africa and in the colonies of the French Empire. The Irish Revolution barely featured, even as a fleeting reference, for the ENA.[44] It was only in the wake of the bloody repression that accompanied the end of the Second World War in Algeria that Ireland would come to occupy an important place in the movement's revolutionary imaginary.

While the end of the Second World War was supposed to usher in a new era of peace and prosperity in the French Empire, the events of May 1945 exposed the extent to which violence underpinned the colonial project in Algeria. On 8 May 1945, as crowds gathered in the city of Sétif in northeastern Algeria to celebrate the final defeat of Nazism in Europe, scuffles broke out between nationalists and the colonial police. The clashes rapidly escalated, with groups of Algerians violently attacking European civilians across the region, leaving one hundred two people dead.[45] The response of the colonial state was as brutal as it was disproportionate. Mass arrests were accompanied by summary executions and the bombardment of villages from the air and the sea, with an estimated death toll between fifteen and twenty thousand.[46] Although the scale of the repression was far more severe in Algeria than had been in the case in Ireland after Easter 1916, a similar dynamic of radicalization took hold in Algerian politics. Demands for a radical break with France grew and nationalists embraced strategies of civil disobedience and, in some cases, armed struggle. This coincided with limited but important reforms within the French Empire. As part of a broader effort to recast the empire as an egalitarian developmentalist project, the French colonial state granted a restricted form of citizenship to Algerians and expanded their representation in local political bodies. Universal suffrage was not extended to Algerian women and a racially discriminatory electoral college system grossly undervalued the votes of Algerian men, but for the first time an electoral strategy seemed possible for Algerian nationalists.[47] For a movement increasingly interested in the potential of combining radical civil resistance, possibly with a dose of armed struggle, with electoral activism, Ireland became a natural point of reference.

On 15 February 1947, Algerian nationalists gathered for a clandestine congress in a warehouse in central Algiers. Now operating under the name Movement for the Triumph of Democratic Liberties (MTLD), Messali's party had taken five of the seats reserved for Algerians in the French Assembly in the previous years' legislative elections. The party was now faced with the challenge of combining its parliamentary opposition to colonialism with a sustained campaign against French rule in the repressive context of the coercive colonial state. Ireland would be central to their discussion. Hocine Aït Ahmed, then a rising star in the movement and a subsequent founder of the FLN, summed up the mood of the meeting by declaring, "We may as well have been in a bar in Dublin, such was the spirit of patriotic conspiracy."[48] For Aït Ahmed and his comrades, Ireland's fight for freedom was not simply another tale of heroic resistance to colonialism. It was a precedent whose successes Algerians could emulate and whose failures they could avoid. After all, Ireland shared a common experience with Algeria as both "a settler colony and a colony of exploitation."[49] Evoking a version of the Irish national struggle, one that did not strictly align with the realities of Irish history, allowed the nationalists to justify pursuing a strategy combining electoral politics and revolutionary anticolonialism. In the narrative of Irish nationalism put forward at the congress, it was Sinn Féin's participation in their electoral process, and not their subsequent abstentionism, that was most important. Indeed, there was a blurring, whether deliberate or not, between the histories of the Home Rule and the republican movements to create a narrative that better fit with the situation of the Algerian nationalists. Sinn Féin's electoralism was evoked by Aït Ahmed to assert, paradoxically, that the five MTLD deputies could fulfil their "revolutionary roles" in Parliament by "filibustering, propagandising, and agitating . . . as the Irish deputies had done."[50] For Aït Ahmed and the MTLD, their celebration of Sinn Féin and de Valera did not prevent them from drawing on the strategies of the Irish Parliamentary Party.

The perceived military tactics of Irish nationalists held a lot less attraction for the strategists of the Algerian movement. Charged by the congress with setting up a clandestine paramilitary group, known as the Special Organisation (OS), Aït Ahmed was involved in the preparation of a secret report on the armed struggle in 1948. In preparation, the authors read a range of texts, including von Clausewitz's *On War*, extracts from Marx and Engels, reports on guerrilla warfare in America and Indochina, and an unidentified "old history book on the Easter Rising."[51] The resulting report argued that the Algerians should look to their own history of violent resistance, instead of modeling their armed struggle on foreign examples, including "the debacle of Easter 1916 and the terrorism that followed it."[52] The report acknowledged that the "Irish experience of patriotic combat offered rich lessons," but the insight in this case was about what strategy should be avoided.[53] The "revolutionary warfare" grounded in "guerrilla tactics" and rallied behind a political mass movement advocated in the report was, in fact, much closer to the reality of the Irish republican campaign during the War of Independence than was suggested.[54] It seems likely that the prominence of the Easter Rising in the limited sources available to the report's authors, coupled with their nationalist commitment to elevating Algerian historical experiences over that of other colonial peoples, led them to disregard the Irish insurrectionary experience. It was the political action, not the armed struggle, of Irish republicans that Algerian activists sought to emulate.

However, Algerian nationalists soon came to realize that the political tactics pursued by their Irish equivalents could not easily or effectively be reproduced. The political space available for them to operate in was far more limited than had been the case for generations of Irish nationalists. Where the Irish Parliamentary Party had wielded significant influence in Westminster due to its size and its occasional role as king-maker, the five nationalist deputies elected from the limited electoral college were marginal to the life of the French National Assembly and lacked both the power and the institutional knowledge to be anything more than a nuisance.[55] When, in 1948, the French moved to introduce a local assembly in the colony, with sixty delegates each for the European and Algerian electoral colleges, they forestalled the chance of a nationalist victory by engaging in a massive electoral fraud. In the end, the MTLD secured only nine of sixty seats, compared to the fifty-seven the authorities speculated they would have gained in free and fair elections.[56] The British may have banned Sinn Féin and related movements, rejected the mandate of their MPs, defunded republican local authorities, and imprisoned political activists en masse, but they did not stuff ballot boxes, effectively disenfranchising nationalist supporters. The electoral strategy pursued by Irish republicans was simply not possible in the intensely coercive and racist colonial context of Algeria.

Once Algerian nationalists learned this lesson, they abandoned electoral politics and returned to clandestine action, including the beginnings of the armed struggle. Ireland was relegated to its previous status as both a symbol of romantic inspiration and a cautionary tale. The party's internal bulletin celebrated Ireland's cultural and religious struggle, its "creation of a written national language: Gaelic," and its defense of Catholicism against "Anglican Great Britain."[57] It also pointed to the efforts of the British colonizer to promote moderates and divide the Irish national movement as a warning against similar moves by authorities in Algeria.[58] Ireland, however, was no longer seen as a precedent that should inform the political strategies of the nationalist movement. For members of the party's vanguard OS organization, charged with leading the armed struggle, Ireland remained a part of the "mosaic of references" that defined its revolutionary imaginary. Its centrality to the "applied science of revolution" may have faded, but it was still a key element of the international "revolutionary romanticism" in which members of the OS were immersed in their formative years.[59] When many of them would break with the party and its leader, Messali Hadj, to found their own revolutionary organization, the FLN, they would carry this knowledge and affinity for Ireland with them.

### Ireland's Contribution to Revolutionary Identity and Ideology

The founders of the FLN who launched the Algerian Revolution in November 1954 were keenly aware of the importance of situating their action historically and within the geopolitical context of the Cold War. The vanguard of armed and political resistance to French colonial rule in the 1950s and 1960s drew on a wide range of contemporary and historical references, combining evocations of Algeria's own history of resistance to foreign invasion with proclamations of solidarity with recent and ongoing struggles against colonialism throughout the so-called Third World. Undoubtedly, the military and political exploits of the Emir 'Abd al-Qādir, the Mokrani Revolt, the Viet Minh, and Nasser's Egypt had more immediate relevance in revolutionary Algeria than in Ireland. And yet the case of Ireland did contribute to the revolutionary identity and ideology of at least some of the leaders of the FLN during the War of Independence.

The group of men who initiated the violent insurrection against French rule in Algeria in November 1954 had come of age as activists in the late 1940s, the highpoint for engagement with Irish history in the Algerian nationalist movement. The long stints in prison that were the price of political resistance under the coercive colonial regime offered some the opportunity to deepen their knowledge of and identification with Ireland's struggle. We have already seen how Hocine Aït Ahmed, a founding member of the FLN, was a committed student of Irish history and how Ireland featured in the curriculum of the movement's training school for its cadres. Abane Ramdane, a key figure in shaping the movement's political strategy in its early years, was an ardent admirer of de Valera and reportedly spoke often of the Irish example.[60] While imprisoned by the French he undertook a lengthy hunger strike for recognition as a political prisoner and dedicated himself to the study of Irish history.[61] However, it is the case of Larbi Ben M'hidi, another founding father of the FLN and the iconic martyr of the revolution, that is the most striking.

Larbi Ben M'hidi was born in 1923 in Eastern Algeria and became involved in nationalist activities from a young age. Arrested during the 1945 repression, he subsequently became a member of the vanguard OS group, where he was exposed to the histories of a wide range of revolutionary movements across the colonial world.[62] Of all the documents that informed his vision of anticolonial revolution in this period, the only one that seems to have survived for posteriority is his copy of the 1935 book *Où va l'Irlande?* (Where to for Ireland?), by French journalist Étiennette Bueque.[63] The text, a staunchly pro–Fianna Fáil account of Irish history focused mainly on the post-independence period,[64] remained in the possession of Ben M'hidi's comrade in arms and biographer El Hachemi Trodi. The annotations on the text, briefly detailed in El Hachemi Trodi's book, offer fascinating insights into Ben M'hidi's vision of Ireland's struggle and its relevance to the Algerian Revolution. When de Valera's rejection of the assimilation of the Irish on the basis of their "distinct nationality" is cited, Ben M'hidi marks the text with the initials "F-M" for French Muslim, the legal term used to describe Algerians at the time. Likewise, when the author refers to the arbitrary nature of colonial rule that allegedly leaves the Irish subject to the whims of Englishmen, he draws the comparison with what he describes as the "colons/f," the French settlers.[65] Ben M'hidi does not hesitate to call out the blindness of the French reporter to the reality of the subjects of France's own empire, writing the word "false" beside her claim that the "French are long used to respecting an order established popular will." For this key figure of the Algerian Revolution, there was no denying the parallels between the struggles of Ireland and Algeria.

The sharp radicalization of Algerian nationalism in its revolutionary phase is clearly reflected in Ben M'hidi's unabashed critique of the Free State government. He denounces the Treatyites as "traitors" for compromising on Irish sovereignty and suggests a parallel between Cumann na nGaedheal's claim to be protecting Ireland from anarchy with the position of the moderate Algerian political leader Ferhat Abbas, who had not yet rallied to the FLN at this point.[66] Ben M'hidi's views are indicative of how his wing of the nationalist movement differed from the cultural nationalism promoted by a figure like Ahmad Tawfiq Al-

Madani. Although Al-Madani would subsequently rally to the FLN and reimagine his interpretation of Irish history, the impulse of a radical like Ben M'Hidi—toward the more absolutist revolutionary approach of a de Valera, at least as he appeared in the pages of *Où va l'Irlande?*—showed a shift in priorities for the revolutionaries of the FLN who were not prepared to settle for any form of truncated independence.

## Ireland and Algeria's Diplomatic Revolution

The Algerian Revolution would have a major impact not just on Algeria's future but on the global political order. Algeria's independence struggle was *the* global revolution of the post–Second World War era. As the work of both Matthew Connelly and Jeffrey Byrne has shown, the Algerian Revolution was fundamentally shaped by and shaped, in turn, the Cold War, the emergent institutions of international governance, and various Third Worldist conceptions of anti-imperial solidarity.[67] Ireland played its own small but not insignificant role in the internationalization of the Algerian struggle.

Ireland's diplomatic interventions in the Algerian Revolution would show both the possibilities and the limits for the conversion of imagined bonds of anti-imperial solidarity into concrete assistance. Unlike other European nations, Ireland did not feature in the FLN's extensive fundraising and arms-smuggling networks during the war.[68] The Irish government did not provide arms or financial support to the Algerians, nor did it officially recognize the Provisional Government of the Republic of Algeria, as other postcolonial states did. Nevertheless, the Irish were seen as distinct from other western European countries by the FLN, even categorized in one report as part of the "Afro-Asiatic" bloc,[69] a label the Irish themselves were keen to reject.[70] As Christophe Gillissen's research has shown, the Irish delegation at the UN sought to balance its ideological and historical commitment to anticolonialism and its desire to uphold a long-standing and important alliance with France. It was riven with tensions, with a young Conor Cruise O'Brien strongly advocating support for Algeria in the face of some of the older, more Francophile members of the Irish diplomatic corps.[71] Indeed, the Irish delegation at the UN tried to fight back attempts by pro-French elements to water down their support for the Algerians by evoking "similarity between Algeria's fight for independence and Ireland's own battle."[72] The Algerian diplomats consulted frequently with their Irish counterparts, discussing strategies to secure broad support for motions but also pushing back against efforts to temper their radicalism.[73] The enthusiasm of the Irish government for the Algerian cause may have ebbed and flowed throughout the course of the conflict, but the Irish state never rowed back on its commitment to the principle of self-determination for Algerians and its rejection of any form of partition in Algeria, two principles grounded in its own experience of the independence struggle.[74]

In the dying days of the Algerian War, Ireland appeared once more as a cautionary tale for Algerian nationalists. Redha Malek, one of the negotiators of the Evian Accords that brought the conflict to an end, recalls in his biography how the FLN delegation were eager to avoid the type of outcome that in their view defined the Anglo-Irish Treaty. They wanted an Algeria totally liberated from French rule, not some form of federation that would see their "sovereignty mortgaged by too close an allegiance to" the former colonial power, as they believed had happened to the Free State.[75] Ireland served above all as a warning of the perils of partition. Throughout the late colonial period, the French authorities raised the prospect of some form of partition to preserve French control of the Sahara and/or to create European enclaves on the coast. In an effort to legitimize their proposals, they cited various instances of partition in other empires, suggesting that the British could hardly condemn the division of Algeria when their own country included a statelet, Northern Ireland, that had been carved out of a former colony.[76] The FLN negotiators were also eager to draw this parallel. They asserted that the Irish example showed that partition would increase the likelihood of a post-independence civil war and would mean that the national question would continue to "fuel the frustration of a whole people" even after the conflict formally ended.[77] Ultimately, the FLN argument won out and plans to partition Algeria were abandoned. The decision of the French to abandon efforts to carve out a piece of Algeria for themselves had far more to do with realpolitik than any evocation of the Irish precedent, but its presence in the debate shows, once more, how Ireland was important to the politics of colonial comparison, mobilized by both the colonizer and the colonized in Algeria.

Epilogue: The Algerian Revolution in Irish Politics

Of course, Algerians were not the only self-styled revolutionaries who looked overseas for inspiration in the second half of the twentieth century. In 1973, the Irish radical Michael Farrell published a pamphlet called *The Battle for Algeria*.[78] In it, he analyzed the situation in Northern Ireland, where the Troubles had entered their bloodiest phase, through the lens of the Algerian Revolution. Farrell's narrative of the Algerian Revolution, while detailed, was reductive in places, blending the heady rhetoric of revolution with occasional uses of Orientalist language one would more readily associate with the French authorities than with the FLN. The conclusions he drew are not ones most historians of Algeria would share. Nor are the predictions of an anti-imperialist victory and unity behind the vanguard party of People's Democracy likely to be credible to historians of Northern Ireland. Farrell was reimagining the history of Algeria's struggle to legitimize his own vision of political and military struggle in Northern Ireland. He was simply doing with Algerian history what generations of Algerian nationalists had done with Irish history.

Conclusion

The story of Ireland's role in shaping Algerian nationalism is testament to the global nature of revolutionary anticolonialism and nationalism in the twentieth century. The fact that Algerians were able to lay their hands on so much information about the conflict in Ireland underlines the extent to which the Irish Revolution was an international media event whose reach extended far beyond the territorial spaces of the Irish diaspora and the bounds of the British Empire. A young journalist in post–First World War Tunis could read detailed accounts of life in Dublin during the War of Independence, while a nationalist prisoner in a jail in southeastern France in the 1950s could immerse himself in tales of Irish heroism. Certain events and figures appear to have had more prominence in the press that reached Algeria than others. The heroic failure of Easter 1916 seems to have stood out as the primary military action of the Irish Revolution. This led Algerian revolutionaries to avoid detailed discussion of—or to even write off—Irish military tactics in a way that undersold the success of the IRA. Press narratives of a people united in struggle behind the great men of the nationalist movement erased the important contribution of women and of labor to the revolution in Ireland and led to the enthusiastic celebration of de Valera by political activists whose socialist leanings would have seen them ostracized in the Ireland he governed. The narrative of the Irish struggle that was presented in the publications to which Algerians had access rarely accounted for the complex realities of colonialism and revolution on the island of Ireland. This would have implications for the way Algerians understood, represented, and mobilized Irish history. It would not, however, diminish their interest in Ireland's struggle.

The great attraction of Ireland for the Algerian nationalists was its unique position, at least in their understanding, as a settler colony that had achieved some form of freedom, however truncated, from imperial rule. They were far more attuned to the commonalities between the Irish and Algerian cases than the many differences that distinguished them. The central role that Protestants descendant from settler stock had played in the formation of Irish nationalism, and the place of the Protestant minority in the imagined community of the Irish nation, was ignored in favor of a clear binary between "settler" and "native" that was more reflective of the situation in Algeria than in Ireland. The fact that the Irish enjoyed far more freedoms, at least in the late nineteenth and early twentieth centuries, than was the case for Algerians was never expressly acknowledged. This would have implications for the limited and ultimately failed attempt to transpose some Irish political practices of resistance to a colonial context where the categories of "settler" and "native" had much more contemporary relevance and the coercive power of the state was far more overbearing.

For Algerian nationalists, the Irish Revolution was, thus, never primarily conceived of as a revolutionary playbook that could be directly applied to their country's struggle for freedom. Instead, different actors and movements chose to evoke it (or not) in line with their own readings of Irish history and their own understanding of its relevance to their personal and collective political projects. The diversity of tactics, policies, and personal experiences that defined Irish nationalism meant that it could be cited to legitimize any number of political, strategic, and ideological positions within the Algerian movement. The Algerian nationalist's narrative of Irish history was never simply a product of the limited information available to them. Instead, it showed how Algerians' understanding and mobilization of Irish history responded to the contingencies and the changing logics of political action in their own country. For the Emir Khaled and his supporters, Ireland could best serve their cause as a cautionary tale, a means of critiquing imperial intransigence without openly inviting the repression of the coercive colonial state. For a young Ahmad Tawfiq Al-Madani, the heroic tale of Ireland's struggle served to rally North Africans behind a nebulous form of nationalism, which was ambiguous about both violence and what independence really meant. In his old age, evoking Ireland would allow Al-Madani to reinvent himself as a lifelong radical revolutionary. His case illustrates how the visions of Ireland's history changed as the personal and political imperatives of activists in Algeria evolved over time. The attempt of post–Second World War nationalists to combine electoral and clandestine activities was the closest Algerians came to directly replicating Irish practices in their own struggle, but even then the case of Ireland was used to legitimize and inform a political strategy that was the expression of the internal logics of their nationalist movement. For leading FLN figures during the revolutionary period, the example of Ireland was evoked less as an instructional manual to inform their activism and more as a means of validating and legitimizing their personal and collective suffering and their radical nationalist vision of Algeria's future. The Algerian diplomats who sought Irish support at the UN or used the Irish example to push back against partition saw the mobilization of Irish history as a means of securing and protecting their own national independence. Algerians were neither cynical opportunists whose evocation of Irish history was purely functional nor naïve imitators of Ireland's historical struggles. They saw in Ireland's story a precedent that could inform, legitimize, and advance their own campaigns for freedom.

In the end, the Algerian nationalist movement succeeded in securing what the men and women of the Irish Revolution never could: a united and fully independent republic. Algerian activists were never simply the apprentices of other revolutionary movements, whether these were in France, Russia, Egypt, Vietnam, Ireland, or elsewhere. They forged their own path to freedom using their own limited resources, developing their own political and military strategies and drawing on both the historical experiences and the concrete assistance of other countries as they saw fit. In doing so, they were not mimicking the Irish. And yet their very insistence on standing alone, breaking with the dominant parties in France and rejecting the control of external powers, echoed the strategies deployed by Irish revolutionaries. Their successes would mean that some in the next generation of self-styled Irish revolutionaries would idealize them in much the same way as they had once glorified the famous protagonists of Ireland's War of Independence. By the 1970s, certain activists in bars in Belfast were dreaming of the atmosphere of patriotic conspiracy in revolutionary Algiers. They too would find that it was easier to draw inspiration from the anticolonial revolution of others than it was to emulate their successes.

## NOTES

All translations from French are mine. Translations from Arabic are mine also but have been verified and corrected by Dr. Abdelhamid Abbas, to whom I owe a debt of gratitude.

1 Laroussi Khelifa, *Manuel du militant algérien* (Lausanne: La Cité, 1961), 124.

2 Ian S. Lustick, *Unsettled States, Disputed Lands: Britain and Ireland, France and Algeria, Israel and West Bank-Gaza* (London: Cornell University Press, 1993); Hélène Blais, Claire Fredj, and Sylvie Thénault, "Désenclaver l'histoire de l'Algérie à la période coloniale," *Reveue d'histoire modern & contemporaine* 63, no. 2 (2016): 8.

3 Declan Kiberd, *Inventing Ireland: The Literature of the Modern Nation* (Cambridge, MA: Harvard University Press, 1995), 163; and Edward Said, *Culture and Imperialism* (London: Vintage, 1993), 273.

4 James MacDougall, *A History of Algeria* (Cambridge: Cambridge University Press, 2017), 84, 88.

5 Isabelle Merle, "Retour sur le régime de l'indigénat: Genèse et contradictions des principes répressifs dans l'empire français," *French Politics, Culture & Society* 20, no. 2 (2002): 77–97.

6 Historian Jacques Frémeaux estimates that 73,000 Europeans from Algeria and 173,000 Algerians served in French forces during the First World War. Frémeaux, *Les Colonies dans la Grande Guerre: Combats et Epreuves des Peuples d'Outre-Mer* (Paris: SOTECA, 2006), 55, 63.

7 For Algeria, see Dónal Hassett, *Mobilizing Memory: The Great War and the Language of Politics in Colonial Algeria, 1918–1939* (Oxford: Oxford University Press, 2019), 56–57; for Irish Unionism. see Jonathan Evershed, *Ghosts of the Somme: Commemoration and Culture War in Northern Ireland* (London: University of Notre Dame Press, 2018), 9–10.

8 Charles-Robert Ageron, *Genèse de l'Algérie algérienne* (Algiers: EDIF, 2000), 107.

9 Michelle Mann, "The Young Algerians and the Question of the Muslim Draft, 1900–1914," in *Algeria Revisited: History, Culture and Identity*, ed. Rabah Aissaoui and Claire Eldridge (London: Bloomsbury, 2017), 39–55, 41.

10 Gilbert Meynier, *L'Algérie Révélée: La guerre de 1914–1918 et le premier quart du XX siècle* (1981; Algiers: Editions El Maarifa, 2010), 568–591.

11 Ouanassa Siari Tengour, "La révolte de 1916 dans l'Aurès," in *Histoire de l'Algérie à la période coloniale, 1830–1962*, ed. Abderrahmane Bouchène, Jean-Pierre Peyroulou, Ouanassa Siari Tengour, and Sylvie Thénault (Paris: La Découverte, 2014), 255–260.

12 Mahfoud Kaddache, *Histoire du nationalisme algérien, Tome I, 1919–1939* (Algiers: EDIF, 2003), 89–95.

13 Charles-Robert Ageron, "Enquête sur les origines du nationalisme algérien. L'émir Khaled, petit-fils d'Abd El-Kader, fut-il le premier nationaliste algérien?," *Revue des mondes musulmans et de la Méditerranée* 2 (1966): 9–49, 46–49.

14 For the text of Khaled's letter to Wilson, see Mahfoud Kaddache, *L'Emir Khaled: Documents et Témoignages pour servir à l'étude du Nationalisme Algérien* (Algiers: Office des Publications Univesitaires, 1987), 121–125.

15 Gilbert Meynier and Jacques Thobie, *L'histoire de la France coloniale, Vol II: L'apogée, 1871–1931* (Paris: Armand Collin, 1991), 440.

16 A. D. de Beaumont, "Gare la casse!," *L'Ikdam*, 4 Nov. 1921.

17 Ahmed Balloul, "La faillite d'une politique," *L'Ikdam*, 31 Mar. 1922.

18 Ahmad Tawfiq Al-Madani, *Mémoires de Combat*, trans. Malika Merabet (Algiers: Office des Publications Universitaires, 1989), 19.

19 James MacDougall, *History and the Culture of Nationalism in Algeria* (Cambridge: Cambridge University Press, 2006), 24–25.

20 Ahmad Tawfiq Al-Madani, "Niḍāl Irlandā," *Al-Fajr* 2, nos. 4–5 (1923): 193–210. Available online thanks to the dedicated work of Al-Madani's grandson, Amine Sharif Zahar, at http://elmadani.org.

21 Rémy Serpolay, "Regards sur les relations franco-irlandaises: études des représentations de l'Irlande à travers un quotidien français: Le Temps (1912–1942)," in *Irlande Vision(s)/Révision(s)*, ed. Madelaine Pelletier (Tours: Presses Universtaires François Rabelais, 2017), 143n9.

22 MacDougall, *History and the Culture of Nationalism*, 37.

23 Arthur Asseraf, *Electric News in Colonial Algeria* (Oxford: Oxford University Press, 2019), 58–60.

24 Al-Madani, "Niḍāl Irlandā," 193.

25 Ibid., 194.

26 Ibid., 193.

27 Ibid., 194.

28 Ibid., 198.

29 Ibid., 195.

30 Ibid., 194. For details on the postwar famine in Algeria, see Kaddache, *Histoire du nationalisme algérien*, 23–25.

31 Al-Madani, "Niḍāl Irlandā," 200.

32  Ibid., 200.

33  Ibid., 200–201.

34  Ibid., 200–201.

35  Ibid., 200.

36  Ibid., 209.

37  Ibid., 202.

38  Ibid., 210.

39  James McDougall, "« Soi-même » comme un « autre ». Les histoires colonials d'Ahmad Tawfiq al-Madanî (1899–1983)," *Revue des mondes musulmans et de la Mediterranée* 95–98 (2002): 95–110.

40  MacDougall, *History and the Culture of Nationalism*, 230.

41  Al-Madani, *Mémoires de Combat*, 9.

42  Ibid., 259.

43  See Dónal Hassett, "An Independent Path: Algerian Nationalist and the League Against Imperialism," in *The League Against Imperialism: Lives and Afterlives*, ed. Michele Louro, Carolien Stolte, Heather Streets-Salter, and Sana Tannoury-Karam (Leiden: Leiden University Press, 2021).

44  Messali did draw a comparison between Ireland and Algeria as countries where colonization had taken place "under the pretext of civilising a people that were already civilised." Benjamin Stora, *Messali Hadj, 1898–1974* (Paris: Hachette Littératures, 2004), 99.

45  MacDougall, *History of Algeria*, 180.

46  Sylvie Thénault, *Histoire de la guerre d'indépendance algérienne* (Paris: Flammarion, 2012), 46.

47  MacDougall, *History of Algeria*, 183–184.

48  Hocine Aït Ahmed, *Mémoires d'un combattant: l'esprit d'indépendance (1942–1952)* (Paris: Sylvie Messinger, 1983), 93.

49  Ibid., 93.

50  Ibid., 93.

51  Ibid., 133.

52  Hocine Aït Ahmed, "Rapport d'Aït Ahmed, décembre 1948," in *Les Archives de la révolution algérienne*, ed. Mohammed Harbi (Paris: Éditions Jeune Afrique, 1981), 15–49, 18.

53  Ibid., 18.

54  Ibid., 22–24.

55  Malika Rahal, "Les représentants colonisés au Parlement français: le cas de l'Algérie (1945–1962)" (MA diss., Université Bordeaux-Montaigne, 1996), 52.

56  Mahfoud Kaddache, *Histoire du nationalisme algérien, Tome II, 1939–1951* (Algiers: EDIF, 2003), 743–746.

57  "Doctrine: La Révolution Nationale Moderne," *La voix algérienne*, July 1948.

58  "Bulletin Intérieur du MTLD," *La voix algérienne*, 20 June 1948.

59  Omar Carlier, *Entre nation et jihad: Histoire sociale des radicalismes algériens* (Paris: Presses de Sciences Po, 1995), 293–294.

60   See Belaïd Abane, *L'Algérie en guerre: Abane Ramdane et les fusils de la rébellion* (Paris: L'Harmattan, 2008), 216; and Clément Henri Moore, *Combat et solidarités estudiantins: L'UGEMA (1955–1962)* (Algiers: Casbah Editions, 2010), 294.

61   Abane, *L'Algérie en guerre*, 216.

62   El Hachemi Trodi, *Larbi Ben M'Hidi: L'homme des grands rendez-vous* (Algiers: ENAG, 1991), 167.

63   Ibid.

64   Étiennette Bueque, *Où va l'Irlande?* (Paris: Editions Sociales Internationales, 1935).

65   Trodi, *Larbi Ben M'Hidi*, 168.

66   Ibid.

67   Matthew Connelly, *A Diplomatic Revolution: Algeria's Fight for Independence and the Origins of the Post–Cold War Era* (London: Oxford University Press, 2003); Jeffrey James Byrne, *Mecca of Revolution: Algeria, Decolonization, and the Third World Order* (London: Oxford University Press, 2016).

68   See Gilbert Meynier's account of support networks in *Histoire intérieure du FLN (1954–1962)* (Paris: Fayard, 2002).

69   Mohammed Harbi, "Synthèse des rapports des sections 1 sur la politique extérieure du GPRA, 1960," in *Les Archives de la Révolution Algérienne*, ed. Mohammed Harbi (Paris: Jeune Afrique, 1981), 389–391.

70   Con Cremin, Note 1 on Algeria, 12 Dec. 1959 (National Archives of Ireland [NAI], DFA/10/2/346).

71   Christophe Gillissen, "Ireland, France and the Question of Algeria at the United Nations, 1955–62," *Irish Studies in International Affairs* 19 (2008): 151–155, 151–167.

72   "Ireland Abstains from Voting," *Irish Times*, 8 Dec. 1959.

73   "Ireland Abstains from Vote," *Irish Independent*, 8 Dec. 1959.

74   Con Cremin, Note on discussion with M. Blanchard, 24 Sept. 1959 (NAI).

75   Redha Malek, *L'Algérie à Evian* (Paris: Seuil, 1995), 211.

76   Arthur Asseraf, "A New Israel: Colonial Comparisons and the Algerian Partition That Never Happened," *French Historical Studies* 41, no. 1 (2018): 105–108.

77   Malek, *L'Algérie à Evian*, 211.

78   Michael Farrell, *The Battle for Algeria* (Belfast: People's Democracy, 1973).

PART TWO

Diaspora

# 5

# Inventing Global Ireland

## The Idea, and Influence, of the Irish Race Convention

DARRAGH GANNON

Working from his New York office on 2 May 1919, Daniel Cohalan, the president of the Friends of Irish Freedom, wrote a letter to Archbishop Daniel Mannix in Melbourne:

> Recent events have resulted in making very clear to the world that the racial solidarity of those of Irish blood throughout the world, and to strengthen that solidarity in the interest of liberty, is one of the aims and hopes of the men and women of Irish blood here in America. . . . I bring these matters at this time to your attention, feeling that through you the liberty-loving people of Australia will be informed fairly of the conditions here in America and will do all that lies in their power to strengthen the hands of those who are in Paris in the effort to bring to Ireland the liberty to which so many people throughout the world feel that she is entitled.[1]

Among the recent events to which Cohalan referred was the Irish Race Convention held in Philadelphia in February 1919, which five thousand Irish American delegates attended. The Friends of Irish Freedom would declare it the "epoch making" event of Irish nationalism.[2] However, it was Cohalan's injunction to "racial solidarity" in Melbourne, ten thousand miles away, which is of greater interest to this study, for it suggests a global Irish nationalism developed as much through diasporic networks, and identities, as through Irish-island influences.

Writing Ireland globally has been a both nationalist and historiographical project. Over the course of the Irish Revolution, Irish nationalists around the world conceptualized, and institutionalized, the idea of a "global Ireland." Between 1916 and 1921, Irish Race Conventions were convened successively in New York (1916), Philadelphia (1919), Melbourne (1919), and Buenos Aires (1921). The Irish Race Congress held in Paris in January 1922, most impressively, was coordinated by Irish nationalist conference organizers in Pretoria, London, Dublin, and Toronto. "I have had the world conference of the race idea in mind for a long time," Éamon de Valera wrote in 1921.[3] What exactly was the "idea" of the Irish Race Convention? This chapter charts the development of the Irish Race Convention as political concept. Where was the Irish Race Convention politically conceived? How did nationalists around the Irish world negotiate the ethnic tensions underlying this term? What transnational influences did the Irish Race Convention exert during the Irish Revolution?

To address these questions, in turn, is to reflect upon a broader range of conceptual and thematic approaches to the study of modern Ireland, advanced by scholars around the world. Charting future directions in the study of the global Irish, American-based historian Kevin Kenny concluded that "wherever the Irish settled, nationalism became a means of expressing not only an ethnic but also an international or diasporic sense of Irishness that transcended any simple desire for acceptance in the host land. The development of diasporic sensibilities within nationally specific ethnic identities is an ideal subject for comparative inquiry."[4] The argument for decentering Irish historiography has been further developed by Canadian-based scholar Donald Akenson: "Our collective mission should be to chart Irish nationalism as a small, but not insignificant, *global* cultural and social system."[5] Elsewhere, British-based scholar Enda Delaney has identified the theme of power as central to the negotiation of any "greater Ireland" history: "Reconstructing the dynamics of power in late modern Ireland in all its multifaceted complexity will require a transnational approach, not least to investigate if they operated in different ways in different environments."[6] Surveying the field from New Zealand, finally, Angela McCarthy has underlined the analytical value of networks by which to situate histories of Ireland in the world: "Communication exchanges, flows of information . . . and the role of social networks are all fundamental."[7] The salience of diasporic approaches and transnational themes in the scholarship of internationally based Irish historians is suggestive of alternative perspectives on Ireland fostered by scholarly distance from the island. Irish nationalists in centers around the world, similarly, conceived their identity a century ago in terms of both global and national politics. The idea, and influence, of the Irish Race Convention connected the "global" and the "local."

## The Idea of the Irish Race Convention

If the influence of the Irish Race Convention was global, its ideological base was American. The Irish American relationship with race has been the subject of extensive historiographical debate over the past thirty years. Scholars such as David Roediger and Noel Ignatiev have explicated the nineteenth-century Irish experience of migration to the United States as one of alienation. To overcome the barriers to assimilation, these scholars have argued, the Irish situated themselves within preexisting racial hierarchies in the United States, "becoming white."[8] Recent scholarship, foregrounding Irish nationalism in America, has presented race as a more capacious category of analysis. In his study of mid-nineteenth-century Irish nationalism in the United States, Cian McMahon has argued that the idea of the "Irish race" "was for the most part a language of Celts and Saxons rather than blacks and whites, because from the perspective of Irish migrants, the differences between the white races were just as important as those separating whites from people of color."[9] Bruce Nelson's study Irish Nationalists and *the Making of the Irish Race* presented race as a reflexive identity among Irish American nationalists: "This discourse of race as national (and sometimes multinational) character coexisted with the more familiar discourse of race as colour."[10] David Brundage, meanwhile, has discerned a "significant change in the racial thinking" of Irish nationalists in America from the late nineteenth century toward accommodation with African American activists.[11] The idea of the Irish Race Convention coexisted alongside many of these ideological strands of Irish nationalism in the United States. More significantly, however, the Irish Race Convention would come to define the influential identification of Irish American nationalists with Ireland, America, and the global Irish diaspora. As Kevin Kenny concluded, "Race is a powerful way of interpreting the world and explaining how it works."[12]

On 4 March 1916, twenty-three hundred Irish American delegates assembled in the Hotel Astor, New York, for two days of discussion under the banner of the Irish Race Convention. The gathering had been orchestrated by Clan na Gael, John Devoy reminding its members, "It is hardly necessary to point out to you that such a Conference, if successful, will afford a rallying point for the union of the entire Irish race at home and abroad and that on the result of its action will probably depend the whole future of the Irish cause."[13] The issue of unity was a key motivating factor in the call for an Irish Race Convention. The First World War had divided the Irish nationalist movement in the United States. As the "leader of the Irish Race," John Redmond nominally retained the support of the Irish in America. Despite growing disillusionment with Redmond's endorsement of the British war effort, the United Irish League of America (UILA) remained the predominant public manifestation of Irish nationalism, counting on two hundred branches across the country.[14] The New York–based Clan na Gael, bitterly opposed to Redmond's "recruitment" of nationalist Ireland for the British war effort, were determined to unite Irish Americans in support of an Irish Republic during the war.

The holding of an Irish Race Convention would afforce the legitimacy of that political position. "I am strongly opposed to admitting any but those whose sentiments are in accord with ours," one supporter wrote to John Devoy, "The Convention will neither be the time nor the place to argue who is right, or who is wrong. We're right, and let the other fellows keep away."[15] Absent the UILA, the delegates at the convention denounced the Home Rule movement, unifying instead around a new republican-inspired organization, the Friends of Irish Freedom (FOIF): "They have inseparably allied those dearest interests with the base interests of England . . . for an empty formula labelled Home Rule Ireland has abandoned her historic attitude and kissed the rod that has scourged her."[16] Within six months, the FOIF had attracted almost three thousand members.[17] "On the strength of the mandate given by the convention," F. M. Carroll observed, "constitutionalism was publicly rejected and a new basis was laid for revolutionary agitation."[18] The Irish Race Convention thereafter would become the recognized political forum by which to unite Irish nationalist forces in the United States. In the wake of the later Irish American split between Devoy and de Valera, Irish political leaders in the United States would propose the holding of an Irish Race Convention to effect nationalist unity.[19]

The staging of the Irish Race Convention in March 1916, moreover, was of strategic temporal importance. Devoy, who had been covertly meeting with German officials in New York, had financed Roger Casement's expedition to Berlin with a view to securing German military aid for an Irish rebellion during the war. The significance of Devoy's interventions has been summarized authoritatively by Joe Lee: "no America, no New York, no Easter Rising."[20] The organization of the Irish Race Convention marked a further intervention in preparations for the Rising. Assurances from Joseph Plunkett in September 1915 that a rebellion would soon take place prompted Devoy to issue a national call for the Irish Race Convention three months later; Clan na Gael colleagues, unaware of the impending Rising in Dublin, had been urging Devoy to call an Irish Race Convention since the beginning of the year.[21] Further details of the Rising arrived by Irish Republican Brotherhood (IRB) courier in February 1916: "A short time before the Convention I had received from the Supreme Council of the IRB the announcement that they had decided to strike on Easter Sunday, 23 April but only four men in America knew that fact. They were all present at the Convention, but, of course, no hint of it could be given to anyone else. The only indirect allusion I made to the subject was in a short speech delivered just before the Convention adjourned."[22] In his remarks, Devoy proclaimed, "I not alone hope that Germany may decisively defeat England on both land and sea, but I hope that Ireland will contribute a reasonable share in bringing about that result."[23] The staging of the Irish Race Convention, and the establishment of the Friends of Irish Freedom, six weeks before the Rising, ensured that the movement in Ireland would not be without support in the event of the rebellion being defeated. The FOIF indeed would stage important public events at Madison Square Garden, in solidarity with the interned 1916 rebels, while Ireland remained under martial law in the months that followed the Rising.[24]

Timing would remain a critical consideration in the staging of future Irish Race Conventions in the United States and elsewhere. A further Irish Race Convention was organized in New York in May 1918 in sync with nationalist opposition to conscription in Ireland. "The menace of conscription has had its good effects," FOIF secretary Diarmuid Lynch declared, "it showed the world in an illuminating flash what self-determination and small nations mean as applied to Ireland today and furnishes a concrete proposition for submission to the American people." A petition for Ireland's right to self-determination was issued on behalf of the "Irish Race" to Woodrow Wilson.[25] The formula of the Irish Race Convention had been established. If Irish American identity was publicly constructed in specific temporal contexts, as Timothy Meagher has written of the Irish in Worcester,[26] the idea of the Irish Race Convention in the United States was defined by public demonstrations of ethnic unity and nationalist solidarity. In the aftermath of the First World War, the idea, and influence, of the Irish Race Convention would extend beyond the boundaries of Irish America, throughout the "Irish world."

## The Influence of the Irish Race Convention: Philadelphia, Melbourne, Buenos Aires

The inaugural meeting of Dáil Éireann on 21 January 1919, and the establishment of the Department of Foreign Affairs in April, provided an Irish focus to the idea of global Ireland. The issue of a "Message to the Free Nations of the World" and a "Declaration of Independence" couched in the Wilsonian rhetoric of "self-determination" offered initial promise to the aspiration of international recognition of the Irish Republic. Dáil Éireann TDs (Teachtaí Dála—elected representatives to the Dáil) Seán T. O'Kelly and George Gavan Duffy were dispatched to Versailles accordingly.[27] Elsewhere, an Irish Self-Determination League was set up in Great Britain under the leadership of the Dáil Éireann envoy to London Art O'Brien: "The purpose of the League is to keep a running fire of publicity on the question of self-determination throughout Great Britain in order to strengthen the hands of our representatives in Paris."[28] Éamon de Valera would issue a public call to this effect: "League yourselves together so that, flung world-wide though we are, we may all act together in co-operative unison. . . . Irishmen and Irishwomen are doing their duty nobly though they suffer. Children of the Irish race in England, unite and assist them!"[29] However, it would be a further year before the Self-Determination for Ireland League of Canada and Newfoundland was established in Montreal and two years before the Self-Determination for Ireland League of Australia was formed in Sydney. The legitimation of Ireland's case before the Paris Peace Conference required immediate global influence and a recognizable political imprint. It would be the Irish Race Convention, rather than the Irish Self-Determination League, that would become the defining global brand of Irish nationalism in 1919.

On 22 February 1919, the FOIF convened the third Irish Race Convention in the United States in four years. Taking place in Philadelphia ("the Cradle of American liberty"), the event was organized to coincide with Woodrow Wilson's convening of the Paris Peace Conference. In this political context, Irish nationalists in the United States were best placed to lobby Wilson to facilitate the entry of Dáil Éireann's representatives to Versailles. "To give that lead the necessary political direction and force," Dáil envoy to the United States Patrick McCartan noted, "[Joseph] McGarrity urged that a race convention should be summoned at once."[30] The Philadelphia-based Clan na Gael leader was determined that the Race Convention would be as representative as possible of the Irish American community: "We should go carefully over the list of delegates so as to pick out men from various States and sections not now represented even one name left out may do great harm."[31]

Attended by over five thousand delegates from across the United States, the convention was intended not only to demonstrate the breadth of Irish American support for the Irish Republic but to reinforce the ethnic standing and racial respectability of Irish Americans. Issuing resolutions in favor of self-determination for Ireland, delegates invoked their American citizenship before their Irish nationality. "It is absolutely essential that Self-Determination be given to Ireland at this time," Daniel Cohalan declared, "in doing that we are acting as Americans first. In saying that, the twenty odd million of Irish men and women who are American citizens [should] be put upon the plane of all the other great races." Delegates used the platform of the Irish Race Convention, further, to chronicle the racial discrimination which the Irish had historically experienced in American society: "Because of the incessant Irish propaganda for the last fifty or sixty years they came to America handicapped as no other race comes to America, and that therefore an Irishman must have twice or three times the brains of his fellow-citizens in order to get along and overcome that handicap." The 1919 Convention, however, was represented as the apotheosis of the Irish race in America. While nineteenth-century migrants were characterized as "the great animals for the American labor market . . . the best blood of our people thrown on the slave market of America," attention was now called to the "high place which the Irish race has won throughout the country." Reading the résumés of the speakers—Cardinal Gibbons, Justice Gadigan, Congressman Gallacher—the conference chairman described the delegates as among "the most distinguished citizens of the West."[32] A delegation of those "distinguished citizens," among them former mayor of Chicago Edward F. Dunne and former chairman of the National War Labor Board Frank P. Walsh, were deputed to present the resolutions of the Irish Race Convention before Woodrow Wilson.

The magnitude of the Irish Race Convention caught the attention of the American public. The events in Philadelphia were widely reported in the American press: "Self-Determination Demand of Convention of Irish Race"; "Irish Race Convention Inspires Eloquence"; "Speakers Plea for Freedom of the Irish Race."[33] Resolutions from ordinary Americans in support of the convention's aims, further, were sent to US congressmen.[34] The strength of public reaction to the Irish Race Convention was noted in the White House. Writing on 1 March, Wilson's private secretary, Joseph Tumulty, advised the president, "During the past few days men of all races have come to me, urging me to request you to see this committee."[35] Wilson, en route to New York during a break in the Peace Conference, had already discerned the impact of the Irish Race Convention. "Every day we receive resolutions of this kind," he confided to Tumulty, "regardless of what we may think of Cohalan and his crowd, there is a deep desire on the part of the American people to see the Irish question settled."[36] The ethnic unity and racial respectability invoked by the Irish Race Convention conferred upon it a political legitimacy in American terms; its timing leveraged contemporary political events. Wilson, consequently, would agree to meet the Irish Race Convention delegates in Paris, acknowledging the significance of their representations of Irish self-determination: "You have touched upon the great metaphysical tragedy of today."[37]

Not only did the Irish Race Convention communicate the influence of the Irish in America, but its title proffered a diasporic identity that transcended Irish American politics. The Irish Race Convention in Philadelphia was projected as an exemplar to be followed by Irish nationalist communities around the world. At the conclusion of its proceedings a cablegram was sent to Thomas Ryan, the premier of Queensland: "This Convention is a call of the blood. It reaches out to every land and it shows to the world today the united race demand absolute independence for Ireland . . . that the Irish race of the world over is a power that must be reckoned with." A further resolution was issued to Archbishop Mannix in Victoria: "This cablegram is more than a message from you to a distinguished prelate at the other side of this globe. It is a clarion call to Irishmen all the world over."[38] Public communication with Irish nationalists in Australia invoked both the diasporic identity of the Irish Race Convention and its global influence as a transnational network of Irish nationalist organization. The realization of these ideas depended on the response of Irish nationalists around the world. "There has been for some time a widespread feeling that we should hold an Australasian Irish Race Convention on the lines of the Great Convention held some months ago at Philadelphia," Mannix wrote to Bishop Michael Kelly in Sydney in September 1919, "the time has come for Australia and New Zealand to take their stand by the side of America."[39]

The Irish Race Convention in Melbourne was organized for 3 November 1919, with the stated purpose of "pressing to a conclusion the matter of self-determination for Ireland."[40] The nationalist position of the Irish in Australia and New Zealand remained unclear in late 1919. The idea of Home Rule self-government, which had generated political movements in Australia since the 1880s, remained the stated objective of nationalists in the Antipodes.[41] It was notable, indeed, that the Sinn Féin–inspired Irish National Association failed to become a mass public organization in Australia in the aftermath of the 1918 general election.[42] The "Sinn Fein rebellion," and the controversial battles over conscription between Archbishop Mannix and Australian Prime Minister Billy Hughes, conflated "self-determination" with the disloyalty of the Irish Republic in the minds of the Australian public in particular. The Irish Race Convention was organized in part to legitimate the demand for Irish self-determination.

The convention, which was attended by over one thousand delegates from Australia and New Zealand, was opened by Archbishop Mannix, who declared, "This is no time for halting words or balanced phrases. We are with the Irish people or we are against them. We help them openly or we leave them to their fate. . . . Self-determination, which is really Sinn Feinism—is on everybody's lips." The necessity to clarify the position of the Irish in Australia was reinforced by T. J. Ryan, who chaired the proceedings: "This is a time when we should speak in language which not only can be understood, but which cannot be misunderstood." Patrick Farrell has described "Sinn Fein" as "one of the languages of controversy" in Australia during the First Word War.[43] Delegates at the convention framed their support for Irish self-determination in terms of loyalty to the Commonwealth accordingly. "I am not here as representing any political party," Ryan added, "but as a citizen, and as an Australian of Irish descent." The Australian and New Zealand Army Corps (ANZAC) experience, specifically, was deployed to emphasize the loyalty of the Irish in Australia. J. T. Murphy, the New South Wales representative, averred that "we Australians of Irish birth, will stand loyal to the sacrifices of our fellows and see, if it is in our power to do it, that Ireland is granted the same privilege for which Australians fought and died." Representations of ethnic sacrifice and imperial loyalty served as a prelude to the issue of resolutions asserting Ireland's right to self-determination. "We here enjoying the full fruits of self-government and living 716,000 miles away from Ireland get the true perspective of Ireland's self-determination," Tasmanian representative Charles O'Connor concluded: "We can render a service to the Empire by using our weight and influence in endeavouring to heal the running sore that exists in the centre of the Empire."[44] The convention was an exercise in Australian political citizenship. A rally of 150,000 Melburnians in Fitzroy Gardens later that evening illustrated the point emphatically.

The specter of a mass "Sinn Fein" rally, and the idea of an Irish Race Convention, in the capital of Victoria, nonetheless, prompted critical press headlines across the Antipodes: "Irish Convention. Republic for Ireland. Self-Determination Urged"; "Irish Voices Too Far Off to Be Heard"; "A Question of Loyalty."[45] The Race Convention, however, was not intended only for Australian public consumption. Archbishop Mannix had coordinated the event with the view to signaling the support of the Irish in the Antipodes to policy makers in the imperial metropole: "Their voice would reach not merely Collins Street; it would reach London. It would be a message which they had long been expecting to receive in England."[46] The London dailies covered the Irish Race Convention as an event of imperial significance. "Reports have been telegraphed from Melbourne of an event with an important bearing on Empire politics," *The Times* reported, noting "the gathering from all parts of the continent of 2,000 delegates to an 'Irish Race Convention.'"[47] The resonance of the event in Melbourne, moreover, prompted the governor general of Australia to wire the secretary of state for the colonies in London: "I have the honour to bring to your Lordship's notice . . . what is described as the 'Australasian Irish Race Convention' . . . the Convention was attended by the whole of the Roman Catholic Archbishops and Bishops in Australia and New Zealand."[48] The Australian Commonwealth Government, Basil Thomson reported to the British Cabinet, were considering taking legal action against the organizers of the Race Convention for the circulation of "disloyal Irish propaganda within the Commonwealth."[49] The assembly of Irish nationalists in Australia and New Zealand, under the banner of the Irish Race Convention, was intended to arrest the attention of policy makers across the "British world."

The holding of an Irish Race Convention, furthermore, was intended to communicate the strength, and connectivity, of the global Irish diaspora. The final resolution agreed upon by the convention in Melbourne was a message to Éamon de Valera, then in the United States: "We in Australia . . . send our message across the leagues of ocean to tell De Valera and the people who support him that we stand behind them in that great cause of freedom that we are fighting today."[50] This resolution reciprocated the messages received from the Irish Race Convention in Philadelphia, signifying the communication of distant diaspora communities. The Irish American press highlighted this transnational connection. "Great Irish Race Convention in Australia Modelled on Historic Gathering in Philadelphia," John Devoy's *Gaelic American* commented.[51] Daniel Cohalan's Washington-based *News Letter* would observe of the events in Melbourne, "This final phase of Ireland's struggle for freedom is being fought out on many fronts—wherever descendants of the exiled Irish race gather."[52] The Irish American press would urge the Irish in Canada to follow in the footsteps of the United States and Australia by staging an Irish Race Convention.[53] An Irish Race Convention planned by the Self-Determination for Ireland League of

Canada was to take place in Montreal in November 1921, attended by Irish nationalists from Great Britain, Australia, and South Africa in order "to focus public attention on the solidarity of the Irish race and its determination to sustain Ireland in the fight."[54] However, it would be in South America, not North America, where the idea of the Irish Race Convention was next presented.

Irish migration to South America had been recurrent throughout the nineteenth century. Between forty and fifty thousand Irish people migrated to Argentina and Uruguay over this period alone. A significant number of those who settled in Argentina were middle-class farmers (*estancieros*) who purchased large ranches cheaply on the fertile land along the River Plate. Migrants from the midlands were particularly noticeable among the Irish in Argentina, the consequence of decades of chain migration.[55] The most prominent of these, the Offaly-born William Bulfin, published his experiences in *Tales of the Pampas*.[56] His Buenos Aires–born son Eamon would later be appointed as Dáil Éireann envoy to Argentina in 1920.[57] Éamon de Valera himself took considerable interest in leveraging the Irish community in Argentina, and the governments of the Latin republics, on behalf of the Irish Republic while in America, going so far as to countenance a South American tour.[58] The significance to which de Valera attached this South American project was evidenced by his appointment of the Westmeath-born Laurence Ginnell and Patrick Little as Dáil envoys to Argentina in the summer of 1921.

The principal mission with which Ginnell and Little were tasked was the raising of the Dáil loan in South America. The Irish communities in Latin America, it was hoped in Dublin, would raise half a million pounds for Dáil Éireann. Based in Buenos Aires, Little was less sanguine: "I had one day in Rio de Janeiro. But it was enough as there is only a handful of Irish there. . . . Paraguay is very poor and in an unstable condition as they had a revolution not so long ago. . . . Peru—there is one doubtful Irishman actually discovered. . . . Uruguay—which although so near the Argentine and so rich, yet no Irish from there make any attempt to approach or get in touch with the diplomatic mission at B[uenos] A[ires]."[59] The strongest connections were developed with Irish nationalists in Chile and Bolivia. Frank Egan, who had been appointed as Dáil envoy to Chile in August 1920, wrote encouragingly to

Laurence Ginnell on the potential for the Dáil loan in South America: "Everything points to success, if Argentine comes forward all will follow."[60] Further support came from Jasper ("Gaspar") Nicolls, an Irishman operating from Oruro, Bolivia: "By acting in concert rather than as isolated groups the Irish of the various Republics could do much more effective work in many ways e.g. in assisting the Irish Republic in enforcing its decree against emigration from Ireland."[61]

The principal challenge facing the success of the Dáil loan in Argentina, however, was not geography but social class. "The idea which works much against an Irish mission," Patrick Little submitted in his report to Dublin, "is that we only come here for money and we don't care a jot what happens the Irish."[62] This was the predominant outlook of the Irish rancher class: "The work in the Argentine was much more difficult, because we were dealing with the very rich Irish there, who were owners of large estates and land, and raised cattle and sheep. It required diplomacy to prevent them from getting offended by statements of a very democratic nature. . . . They were extremely conservative and with pro-British tendencies, for serious economic reasons."[63] The floating of the Dáil loan, Little concluded, could succeed in Argentina only through "the idea of Race pride—love of traditions and Irish dead, etc and Irish culture and future of Irish Race."[64]

The Irish Race Convention was held in Buenos Aires on 29 November 1921. Attended by ninety delegates, the event was chaired by Laurence Ginnell, who addressed the lack of organization in the Irish-Argentine community and the best means of levying the support of the Argentine population for the Irish cause. He criticized those present for their "almost complete lack of knowledge about Irish life. Your deficient organisation would not help to support the human ideal of freedom, and would not maintain your distinct and valued identity."[65] The Irish loan, however, was successfully issued at the meeting and five delegates were appointed to represent Argentina at the Irish Race Congress in Paris in January 1922. The Irish Race Convention in Buenos Aires was to serve as a rallying cry for the organization of the Irish in South America more broadly. Building on the success of the convention, a bespoke issue of the *Irish Bulletin* was published in Buenos Aires for circulation throughout Latin America. "Allow me to congratulate you and co-workers on the grand success of the Irish-Argentine Convention, the organising work for future operations, and the successful sending of delegates to the All-World Conference of the Irish Race," Frank Egan wrote from Santiago on receipt of *El Boletín Irlandés*.[66] Delegates from Argentina, Brazil, Chile, and Mexico would depart South America, in turn, to attend the Irish Race Congress in Paris.

## Global Ireland: Paris, 1922

The Irish Race Congress held in Paris between 21 and 28 January 1922 demonstrated both the global scope and national differences inherent in the concept of the Irish Race Convention. The Race Congress was originally proposed by the Irish Republican Association of South Africa (IRASA), which had been established in Pretoria in 1920.[67] From the viewpoint of Irish nationalists on the Cape, Ireland appeared on the horizon a worldwide Irish community: "It is not the Ireland of four millions that we are thinking of now . . . we are thinking also of the greater Ireland, the Magna Hibernia across the seas, the millions of Irish people throughout the world. Though these Irish are now citizens of their adopted lands, they must not be, and they are not, wholly lost to Ireland. They are also to share in the great destiny of their mother-land."[68] The discourse of Irish nationalists in South Africa soon shifted from ideas of global Ireland to its potential strategic influence. Writing to Art O'Brien in London in March 1921, the IRASA's honorary secretary Eugene Scallan proposed that "in spite of the rapidity of events in Ireland we feel that there is a danger of a deadlock . . . the summoning of a World Conference of the Irish Race at this juncture to support the just claim of Ireland would be a dramatic stroke which could not fail to influence political opinion everywhere in favour of Ireland."[69] O'Brien was in complete agreement, writing to de Valera of this diasporic initiative: "Apart altogether from our desire to render direct service to Ireland it would be of immense advantage to the Irish people in every land to be in touch with one another and to enter into communion and rivalry in presentation and fosterage of their common inheritance of history and ideals."[70] The Irish Self-Determination League of Great Britain (ISDL) and IRASA would collaborate over the next six months with a view to cohosting the Irish Race Congress in Paris, Madrid, or the Hague. The most effective political strategy underpinning the Irish

Race Congress, its South African organizers emphasized, lay in its presentation as an initiative of the global Irish diaspora:

> The great point my Association would like to make is that we who attend this Conference have not rallied at the call of the motherland nor are we convinced at the request either expressed or implied of An Dail but as citizens of dozens of different countries throughout the world, and being in addition of the Irish Race, united by ties of sentiment to Ireland and recognising that a deadlock was in danger of developing, have spontaneously agreed to meet in some neutral place to devise some means of assisting the people of Ireland to attain the realisation of their hopes. . . . It will be obvious that the moral force behind this appeal will be immeasurably greater if the convocation were the result of a spontaneous effort, than if it could be regarded as merely the meeting of Irish exiles convened by one of the belligerents to its aid in the difficult situation that has arisen. The first essential for success, namely spontaneity and detachment from Irish control would be absent.[71]

The Dáil Department of Foreign Affairs, however, soon took charge over the convening of the Irish Race Congress, marginalizing its original organizers. "With regard to the question of control," Assistant Under-Secretary for Foreign Affairs Robert Brennan wrote to Art O'Brien, "it is thought best that the guidance should be in the hands of the people at home here who are best acquainted with the situation and know best what is required."[72] In reality, Éamon de Valera had selected the Canadian-born Irish nationalist Katherine Hughes to coordinate the Irish Race Congress to be held in Paris in January 1922.[73] Hughes had previously established the Self-Determination for Ireland League of Canada and Newfoundland and accompanied de Valera on his southern tour of the United States, before being redeployed by de Valera to the Antipodes, wherein she established Irish Self-Determination Leagues: "She gives a glowing account of the young League in these countries and reports the establishment of 400 branches in Australia and 100 in New Zealand."[74] Arriving in Paris in September 1921, Hughes would establish the Central Secretariat of the Irish Race Congress in the Grand Hotel, liaising directly with de Valera and the Department of Foreign Affairs in Dublin.

The potential for the Irish Race Congress to contribute to the resolution of the ongoing British-Irish conflict was heightened in the summer of 1921 with the declaration of a military truce. It was in the sphere of international diplomacy that the diaspora card could be best deployed to Irish nationalist advantage. The global significance of Ireland's diaspora had been acknowledged in the initial proposals prepared by the British cabinet in July 1921: "There is no part of the world where Irishmen have made their home but suffers from our ancient feuds: no part of it but looks to this meeting between the British government and the Irish leaders to resolve these feuds in a new understanding honourable and satisfactory to all."[75] Basil Thomson, meanwhile, reported to the British Cabinet on the influence of Irish American nationalists over de Valera's positioning on negotiations.[76] The British negotiating team evidently expected the influence of the global Irish diaspora to be raised by the Irish plenipotentiaries, in view of the impending Irish Race Congress. However, in the official accounts of the negotiations only Michael Collins is on record as having addressed the issue, in a memorandum on a new League of Nations titled "International Aspects of the Anglo-Irish Settlement": "Ireland is herself a mother country with worldwide influence . . . the Irish in Ireland would be joined by the Irish in America, and they would share in a common internationality with the people of America, England and the other free nations of the League."[77] While it is often asked why de Valera did not "go to London," perhaps the greatest missed opportunity of the Anglo-Irish Treaty negotiations was de Valera's failure to include a representative of Ireland's diaspora community among the plenipotentiaries. The signing of the Anglo-Irish Treaty on 6 December 1921, before the Irish Race Congress had taken place, sidelined the potential influence of "global Ireland." Divisions in Ireland over the signing of the Anglo-Irish Treaty, and its subsequent ratification by Dáil Éireann on 7 January 1922, moreover, threatened to undermine the holding of the Irish Race Congress.

Between 21 and 28 January 1922, one hundred Irish nationalist delegates descended on Paris from Australia, New Zealand, Newfoundland, Great Britain, Argentina, Brazil, Chile, Mexico, Belgium, France, Spain, Italy, Java, and Ireland. The representatives of the Self-Determination for Ireland League of Canada and the American Association for the Recognition of the Irish Republic ultimately refused to travel to Paris "in the belief that the division of opinion in Ireland would nullify the Congress and its effectiveness."[78] For those who did attend, the failure to refer to the Irish Race Congress before signing the Anglo-Irish Treaty was the first item on the agenda. Opening his remarks, Rev. Dr. O'Reilly commented of the Australian delegation: "We have come from the ends of the Earth and it has taken a long time to do it. When we left Australia it was taken for granted that the main purpose to be served by this Congress was that this meeting of the Irish assembled from all the seas of the world would be the most powerful lever for the effecting of that surrender of Dublin Castle."[79] Benjamin Farrington, who followed, outlined the disillusionment of the South African delegates: "The idea of calling the Conference came to us in South Africa because we felt that in the struggle Ireland was maintaining against England she could only succeed through something that amounted to a revolution in the political constitution of the world."[80] Art O'Brien captured the disillusionment of many in attendance from around the world: "It is unfortunate that by an accident we were not called upon to do something which we should have been called upon to do at the time."[81]

Deprived of their original political objective, delegates turned their attentions to coordinating the global development of Irish culture and heritage. The compiling of an Irish dictionary of biography, the return of Irish manuscripts from imperial institutions, and the establishment of university chairs in Irish history around the world were discussed by delegates, who eventually agreed to set up a new global organization to pursue these matters: Fine Ghaedheal. The committee of the worldwide organization, ultimately, would include one representative from Ireland, three representatives from Great Britain, and one representative from the United States.

The clearest divisions arose, however, not over the Anglo-Irish Treaty but from the different national allegiances and ethnic identities invoked in the name of the "Irish race." Returning to the podium, Fr. O'Reilly adverted to the national loyalties of the Irish in Australia: "We must frankly and unequivocally accept the nationality of the country we are living in . . . it would be a vain thing for me to ask any young Australian to be an Irishman first and an Australian after."[82] The representative from the Cape framed activism on behalf of the Irish race in terms of citizenship: "We took our stand as South African citizens . . . we who come from abroad come here owing an undivided political allegiance to the country of our permanent residence."[83] Other representatives rejected identifications with the Irish race in terms of a transnational citizenship. Patrick Little commented of the Irish experience in South America: "You have them far away, this Irish community fighting continually against absorption into a very attractive civilisation, namely the Spanish civilisation of South America."[84]

The delegations from Great Britain, however, were vociferous in their opposition to a correlation between residency and citizenship. "We Irish in Scotland do not accept the nationality of the country in which we reside," the Glasgow-based Sean O'Sheehan insisted, "they continue to be nationals of Ireland, temporarily resident in a foreign country."[85] In bringing together delegates from across the "Irish world," the Irish Race Congress served to highlight the innate differences in national outlook between its diaspora communities. Removed from these tensions, delegates from Ireland were rendered silent observers to this diaspora-led discourse. "You must be patient with us who have come from distant places," an American delegate advised the onlooking Countess Markievicz, "but we have to tell you of certain things that we have to encounter and that we are encountering all the time."[86]

Tensions between nationalists from Ireland and its diaspora, however, would emerge over the course of the weeklong Irish Race Congress. Membership of the new Fine Ghaedheal executive caused dissension among non-Anglophone delegates, the Brazilian representative proposing that Sinn Féin TD Michael Hayes resign from the committee, to which the latter tersely replied, "I will not be interrupted by a Brazilian from Ireland."[87] Others were dissatisfied that the election proceedings presided over by Éamon de Valera had not allowed for sufficient representation from Irish diaspora communities in Europe and South America: "there are about six hundred in France"; "there is an organisation complete in Chili"; "I want Brazil to be in."[88] The predominance of Irish-island voices and issues was reinforced on the last day of the proceedings, wherein pro- and anti-Treaty delegates exchanged barbed comments over the signing of the Anglo-Irish Treaty. "The only thing we have to do is to agree to disagree," de Valera remarked to Eoin Mac-Neill.[89] Several items on the agenda, including the location of the next Race Congress, consequently, went unresolved. For diaspora-based delegates who had traveled weeks, and thousands of miles, to be in Paris, the internecine disputes over the minutiae of the Anglo-Irish Treaty were deeply underwhelming. A representative from Brazil would intervene in the rerun of the Treaty debates, commenting, "We are treated here at this Conference as if we were little children."[90]

The signing of the Anglo-Irish Treaty before the Irish Race Congress had convened in Paris ultimately undermined the political influence of "global Ireland" over the Irish question. The removal of the global Irish diaspora from the negotiating table was noted by British policy makers. "The recent party split is likely to have a dampening effect on the Congress," Basil Thomson reassuringly briefed the British Cabinet.[91] The architects of previous Irish Race Conventions, further, were frustrated by the erosion of political influence in Paris. Writing in the *Gaelic American*, John Devoy characterized the congress as "De Valera's new scheme to keep himself afloat. An 'Irish World League' to boom his fake Irish Republic . . . the plan fails."[92] Archbishop Mannix, whose niece served as a secretary to the congress, briefed the Australian delegates before their departure for Paris: "The opinion he had at present would scarcely entitle him to set his name to the bottom of the treaty . . . he had his own opinion and because it was his own he kept it to himself."[93] The waning political influence of the Irish Race Convention idea was captured sharply in the *New York Times*:

> The Irish Race Congress at Paris was called long before the settlement with Great Britain. Its intention was undoubtedly to stir up international feeling in favour of Ireland and to set flowing new streams of anti-English propaganda. . . . Whether in Paris or Dublin or New York, sensible Irishmen must be aware that the final test of their capacity to govern themselves is now upon them. . . . It is of no use to make eloquent speeches about Ireland's historic wrongs or to dilate with emotion upon the great things which the Irish race would do if only freed from British fetters. . . . The only Irish Race Congress which the world will note, or long remember, is not the one in Paris but the one in Dublin.[94]

The Anglo-Irish Treaty reduced the Irish Race Congress to a cultural exhibition of "global Ireland." However, as Gerard Keown has noted, "it is surely too simplistic to represent the Irish Race Conference as an altruistic if naïve South African scheme wrecked by Republican saboteurs."[95] The divisions that defined the Irish Race Congress were not between pro- and anti-Treaty positions but the differences of perspective on the idea of the "Irish race" on the part of nationalists around the "Irish world." The idea of a cohesive diasporic nationalism, which brought delegates together under the banner of the Irish Race Congress, was underwritten by distinct nation-centered views on citizenship, ethnicity, and nationality. The differences in discourse between delegates from Ireland and those among its diaspora, further, underlined a significant ideological cleavage in the Irish nationalist experience. The congress in Paris marked a break in the idea, and influence, of the Irish Race Convention.

## Conclusion

The Irish Race Convention, politically conceived in the United States, would become the totemic representation of Irish nationalist influence around the world between 1919 and 1922. Although seeking to construct and mobilize a global diasporic Irish identity, the Irish Race Convention struggled to subsume ethnic discourses specific to each host nation within this vision: America (race), Australia (empire), Argentina (class). "What was often distinctive about Irish nationalism," Fearghal McGarry has observed, "was not its rhetoric or values but how, and to what end, this discourse was deployed."[96] Irish nationalists invoked the political idiom of the Irish Race Convention at strategic moments, with the view to influencing national and international policy makers. The organization of the Irish Race Congress in Paris by Irish nationalists in South Africa and Great Britain, parallel to the Anglo-Irish Treaty negotiations, constituted the most significant attempt to leverage the influence of global Ireland on behalf of the Irish Republic. The political oversight of Dublin, and the signing of the Anglo-Irish Treaty in London, effectively undermined the potential political impact of the Irish Race Congress in Paris. The idea of the Irish Race Convention, nonetheless, exerted significant transnational influence. The organization of Irish Race Conventions in Philadelphia, Melbourne, and Buenos Aires attested to the development of a global network of Irish nationalists, mobilized as much by diasporic connections, and identities, as by

Irish-island influences. The Irish Race Congress signified the apogee of this global Irish movement. The gathering of representatives from twenty-two countries ultimately reinforced the global scope, and great divergences on issues of citizenship, ethnicity, and nationality, that defined Irish nationalism around the world. A century on, the ideas, and influences, of "global Ireland" remain open to historical enquiry and contestation.

NOTES

I would like to thank the editors, Patrick Mannion and Fearghal McGarry, for the invitation to contribute to this volume. I would like to further thank Mark McGowan and Cian McMahon for giving so generously of their time and thought in their reading of my essay.

1 Daniel Cohalan to Archbishop Mannix, 2 May 1919 (Melbourne Diocesan Historical Commission Archives, Archbishop Mannix Papers, Box 2).

2 Friends of Irish Freedom report, 27 Dec. 1919 (American Irish Historical Society Archives, Friends of Irish Freedom Papers, Box 1, Folder 2).

3 Éamon de Valera to Art O'Brien, 30 May 1921 (National Library of Ireland [NLI], Art Ó Briain Papers, MS 8429/1).

4 Kevin Kenny, "Diaspora and Comparison: The Global Irish as a Case Study," *Journal of American History* 90, no. 1 (2003): 159–160.

5 Donald Akenson, "Stepping Back and Looking Around," in *Irish Nationalism in Canada*, ed. David Wilson (Montreal: McGill-Queen's University Press, 2009), 180.

6 Enda Delaney, "Directions in Historiography: Our Island Story? Towards a Transnational History of Late Modern Ireland," *Irish Historical Studies* 37, no. 148 (2011): 617.

7 Angela McCarthy, "Introduction," in *Ireland in the World: Comparative, Transnational, and Personal Perspectives*, ed. McCarthy (New York: Routledge, 2015), 4.

8 David Roediger, *The Wages of Whiteness: Race and the Making of the American Working Class* (New York: Verso, 1991); Noel Ignatiev, *How the Irish Became White* (New York: Routledge, 1996).

9 Cian McMahon, *The Global Dimensions of Irish Identity: Race, Nation and the Popular Press, 1840–1880* (Chapel Hill: University of North Carolina Press, 2015), 3.

10 Bruce Nelson, *Irish Nationalists and the Making of the Irish Race* (Princeton: Princeton University Press, 2012), 7.

11 David Brundage, *Irish Nationalists in America: The Politics of Exile, 1798–1998* (Oxford: Oxford University Press, 2016), 119–121.

12 Kevin Kenny, "Race, Violence and Anti-Irish Sentiment in the Nineteenth Century," in *Making the Irish American: History and Heritage of the Irish in the United States*, ed. J. J. Lee and Marion Casey (New York: New York University Press, 2006), 365.

13 Clan na Gael circular, 29 Dec. 1915 (New York Public Library Archives and Manuscripts [NYPLA], William Maloney Papers, Box 7).

14 Brundage, *Irish Nationalists in America*, 143–144.

15  Joseph McLaughlin to John Devoy, 21 Feb. 1916 (NLI, John Devoy Papers, MS 18,007/33/3).

16  *Gaelic American*, 11 Mar. 1916.

17  Michael Doorley, *Irish-American Diaspora Nationalism: The Friends of Irish Freedom, 1916–1935* (Dublin: Four Courts Press, 2004), 50.

18  Francis M. Carroll, *American Opinion and the Irish Question, 1910–23: A Study in Opinion and Policy* (Dublin: Gill and Macmillan, 1978), 53.

19  Patrick McCartan to Joseph McGarrity, 22 June 1920 (NLI, Joseph McGarrity Papers, MS 17,617/1/27); Éamon de Valera to Bishop Michael J. Gallagher, 6 Aug. 1920 (University College Dublin Archives [UCDA], Éamon de Valera Papers, P150/987).

20  J. J. Lee, "Foreword," in *Ireland's Allies: America and the 1916 Easter Rising*, ed. Miriam Nyhan Grey (Dublin: University College Dublin Press, 2016).

21  John Devoy to Joseph McGarrity, 1 Dec. 1915 (NLI, Joseph McGarrity Papers, MS 17,609/3/10).

22  John Devoy, *Recollections of an Irish Rebel* (New York: Chas P. Young, 1929), 449.

23  *Gaelic American*, 11 Mar. 1916.

24  Friends of Irish Freedom, "Madison Square Garden Irish Relief Fund Bazar" program, 14 Oct. 1916 (National Museum of Ireland, Easter Week Collection, HE:EW.473).

25  *Gaelic American*, 25 May 1918.

26  Timothy J. Meagher, *Inventing Irish America: Generation, Class, and Ethnic Identity in a New England City, 1880–1928* (Notre Dame: Notre Dame University Press, 2001).

27  Gerard Keown, *First of the Small Nations: The Beginnings of Irish Foreign Policy in the Interwar Years* (Oxford: Oxford University Press, 2016), 37–40.

28  Art O'Brien to Rev. P. Campbell, 29 Apr. 1919 (NLI, Art Ó Briain Papers, MS 8436/16).

29  Éamon de Valera, "To the Irish Race in England," Mar. 1919 (UCDA, Éamon de Valera Papers, P150/630).

30  Patrick McCartan, *With de Valera in America* (New York: Brentano, 1932), 79.

31  Joseph McGarrity to Diarmuid Lynch, 6 Mar. 1919 (American Irish Historical Society Archives, Friends of Irish Freedom Papers, Box 27, Folder 3).

32  *Irish Press*, 1 Mar. 1919.

33  *San Francisco Chronicle*, 23 Feb. 1919; *Kentucky Courier*, 23 Feb. 1919; *Buffalo Times*, 23 Feb. 1919.

34  Resolutions to the Committee on Foreign Relations, 1919 (National Archives of the United States, US Senate Records, SEN 65A-J17).

35  Joseph P. Tumulty to Woodrow Wilson, 1 Mar. 1919 (Library of Congress [LOC], Joseph P. Tumulty Papers, Box 3).

36  Woodrow Wilson to Joseph P. Tumulty, 28 Feb. 1919 (LOC, Joseph P. Tumulty Papers, Box 49).

37  Diary of the American Commission of Irish Independence, 11 June 1919 (NYPLA, Frank P. Walsh Papers, Box 124).

38  *Irish Press*, 1 Mar. 1919.

39  Archbishop Mannix to Bishop Kelly, 22 Sept. 1919 (Sydney Diocesan Archives, Bishop Kelly Papers, A0 548).

40  *Melbourne Age*, 16 Sept. 1919.

41  Malcolm Campbell, *Ireland's New Worlds: Immigrants, Politics and Society in the United States and Australia, 1815–1922* (Madison: University of Wisconsin Press, 2008), 180.

42  Dianne Hall and Elizabeth Malcolm, *A New History of the Irish in Australia* (Sydney: NewSouth, 2018), 323–324.

43  Patrick O'Farrell, *The Irish in Australia* (Kensington: New South Wales University Press, 1987), 270.

44  *Sydney Catholic Press*, 6 Nov. 1919.

45  *Melbourne Argus*, 4 Nov. 1919; *Sydney Sun*, 4 Nov. 1919; *Auckland Star*, 5 Nov. 1919.

46  *Sydney Catholic Press*, 6 Nov. 1919.

47  *The Times*, 17 Nov. 1919.

48  Governor-General of Australia to the Secretary of State for the Colonies, 7 Nov. 1919 (National Archives of Australia, Governor-General's Office Records, A11804).

49  Home Office Director of Intelligence, "A Monthly Review of Revolutionary Movements in Foreign Countries," Dec. 1919 (National Archives, United Kingdom [NAUK], Cabinet Records, CAB 24/95/8).

50  *Sydney Catholic Press*, 6 Nov. 1919.

51  *Gaelic American*, 22 Nov. 1919.

52  *News Letter*, 2 Jan. 1920.

53  *News Letter*, 9 Jan. 1920, 22 May 1920.

54  Lindsay Crawford to Art O'Brien, 27 July 1921 (NLI, Art Ó Briain Papers, MS 8460/46). For more on the Self-Determination for Ireland League of Canada and Newfoundland, see Patrick Mannion, *A Land of Dreams: Ethnicity, Nationalism, and the Irish in Newfoundland, Nova Scotia, and Maine, 1880–1923* (Montreal: McGill-Queen's University Press, 2018).

55  Edmundo Murray, *Becoming Irlandés: Private Narratives of the Irish Emigration to Argentina (1844–1912)* (Buenos Aires: Literature of Latin America, 2005), 7–20.

56  William Bulfin, *Tales of the Pampas* (London: Fisher and Unwin, 1900).

57  Eamon Bulfin to Éamon de Valera, 20 Apr. 1920 (UCDA, Éamon de Valera Papers, P150/735).

58  See Darragh Gannon, "Addressing the Irish World: Éamon de Valera's 'Cuban policy' as a Global Case Study," *Irish Historical Studies* 44, no. 165 (2020): 41–56.

59  Patrick Little to Robert Brennan, 4 Dec. 1921 (National Archives of Ireland [NAI], Department of Foreign Affairs Papers, DFA ES Box 32, File 216(4)).

60  Frank Egan to Laurence Ginnell, 23 Dec. 1921 (NLI, Laurence Ginnell Papers, MS 49,810/7).

61  Gaspar Nicolls to Laurence Ginnell, 23 Sept. 1921 (NLI, Laurence Ginnell Papers, MS 49,810/7).

62  Patrick Little to Robert Brennan, 4 Dec. 1921 (NAI, Department of Foreign Affairs Papers, DFA ES Box 32 File 216(4)).

63  Patrick Little statement (Military Archives of Ireland, Bureau of Military History, WS 1769).

64  Patrick Little to Robert Brennan, 4 Dec. 1921 (NAI, Department of Foreign Affairs Papers, DFA ES, Box 32, File 216(4)).

65  *El Boletín Irlandés*, 10 Dec. 1921.

66  Frank Egan to Laurence Ginnell, 23 Dec. 1921 (NLI, Laurence Ginnell Papers, MS 49,810/7).

67  See Ciaran Reilly, "'The Magna Hibernia': Irish Diplomatic Missions to South Africa, 1921," *South African Historical Journal* 67, no. 3 (2015): 255–270.

68  *The Republic*, 12 Mar. 1921.

69  Eugene K. P. Scallan to Art O'Brien, 11 Mar. 1921 (NLI, Art Ó Briain Papers, MS 8460/44).

70  Art O'Brien to Éamon de Valera, 25 May 1921 (NLI, Art Ó Briain Papers, MS 8429/1).

71  Eugene K. P. Scallan to Robert Brennan, 6 Oct. 1921 (NLI, Art Ó Briain Papers, MS 8460/44).

72  Robert Brennan to Art O'Brien, 19 Aug. 1921 (NLI, Art Ó Briain Papers, MS 8429/1).

73  Pádraig Ó Siadhail, *Katherine Hughes: A Life and a Journey* (Newcastle, ON: Penumbra Press, 2014).

74  Robert Brennan to Department of Publicity, 9 Aug. 1921 (NAI, Department of Foreign Affairs Papers, DFA ES 2/201/41).

75  British Cabinet, "Proposals of the British Government for an Irish Settlement," 20 July 1921 (NAUK, Cabinet Records, CAB 24/126/50).

76  Director of Intelligence, Reports on Revolutionary Organizations in the United Kingdom (DIRROUK), no. 123, 15 Sep. 1921 (NAUK, Cabinet Records, CAB 24/128/9).

77  Michael Collins, "The International Aspects of the Anglo-Irish Settlement," 23 Nov. 1921 (NAI, Dáil Éireann Secretariat Records, DE 2/304/1/62).

78  Fine Ghaedheal, *Proceedings of the Irish Race Congress in Paris, 1922* (London: Fine Ghaedheal, 1922), 28.

79  Ibid., 37.

80  Ibid., 39.

81  Ibid., 44.

82  Ibid., 36.

83  Ibid., 41.

84  Ibid., 43.

85  Ibid., 50.

86  Ibid., 56.

87  Ibid., 204.

88  Ibid., 176.

89  Ibid., 224.

90  Ibid., 192.

91  DIRROUK, no. 139, 19 Jan. 1922 (NAUK, Cabinet Records, CAB 24/132).

92  *Gaelic American*, 5 Feb. 1922.

93  *Brisbane Telegraph*, 20 Jan. 1922.

94  *New York Times*, 23 Jan. 1922.

95  Gerard Keown, "The Irish Race Conference, 1922, Reconsidered," *Irish Historical Studies* 32, no. 127 (2001): 375.

96  Fearghal McGarry, "'A Land Beyond the Wave': Transnational Perspectives on Easter 1916," in *Transnational Perspectives in Modern Irish History: Beyond the Island*, ed. Niall Whelehan (London: Routledge, 2015), 177.

# 6

# "A Most Obnoxious Campaign Against Everything British"

## The Curious Case of the Friends of Irish Freedom in the Panama Canal Zone, 1918–1921

PATRICK MANNION

As we mark the centenary of Ireland's War of Independence, the critical role played by the overseas diaspora is attracting increased attention from historians. Both foundational and emerging scholarship has tended to focus on areas where Irish emigrants settled in large numbers and where well-supported Irish nationalist associations were established and thrived: Great Britain, Australia, New Zealand, Canada, and, especially, the United States.[1] Investigations of popular engagement with Irish nationalism from other colonized portions of the British Empire, such as India, have further enhanced our understanding of the remarkably diverse and variable transnational movement for Ireland's freedom.[2] This article is concerned with how the networks of global Irish nationalism extended to the diaspora's spatial and demographic periphery. It examines the activities of three branches of the Friends of Irish Freedom (FOIF), as well as their successor organization, the American Association for the Recognition of the Irish Republic (AARIR) in the American-controlled Panama Canal Zone from 1918 to 1921.

Although they attracted, at most, between two and three hundred formal members, their unique situation within an American enclave in Latin America provides a fascinating opportunity for a microstudy of diasporic nationalism. How did a movement that directly opposed British imperialism operate inside of what was essentially an American colonial outpost, ridden with class and racial tensions in the early twentieth century? Did Irish nationalists in the Zone extend their lobbying, fundraising, and propaganda efforts beyond American territory? How were their efforts opposed, from both within and beyond the Canal Zone?

Driven by a small number of deeply committed individuals, the Zonian FOIF achieved remarkable success given the relatively small Irish population there. In order to gain support from beyond the Irish American community, the group's public rhetoric was steeped in the language of American patriotism, and only rarely did it carry out any activity outside of the Zone. Despite its remote setting, this was an inherently American engagement with Irish nationalism. Nevertheless, supported by the Foreign Office in London as well as by key figures within the Canal Zone government, British diplomats in the Republic of Panama waged a sustained, though ultimately unsuccessful, campaign to derail the FOIF's local efforts. A study of the Panama Canal Zone FOIF, then, reveals not only the remarkable spatial spread and adaptability of Irish American nationalism but also the complex set of local, national, and transnational factors that influenced support for and opposition to the republican movement during the Irish Revolution.

### Ethnicity, Race, and the Panama Canal Zone

The American presence on the Isthmus of Panama began in the mid-nineteenth century, with the construction of the American-owned Panama Railroad from 1848 to 1855, designed to move passengers and cargo between the Atlantic and Pacific Oceans. Even with the railroad in place, there remained a long-standing interest in building a canal that would allow vessels to pass through the Isthmus, thereby eliminating the need for the lengthy circumnavigation of Cape Horn. Late nineteenth-century French efforts to construct such a canal had failed, and with renewed interest in a maritime link following the acquisition of the Philippines in 1898, the United States stepped in to complete it.[3] The Isthmus was then part of Colombia, but in November 1903, as a proposed treaty that would grant the United States rights to build the canal stalled in the Colombian senate, a small group of Panamanian nationalists declared the country's independence. Perceiving an opportunity to gain more favorable terms than the Colombians were willing to offer, the United States immediately recognized the Panamanian Republic and American naval vessels blocked Colombian efforts to retake the territory. On 18 November 1903, the hastily arranged Hay-Bunau-Varilla Treaty was signed, granting the United States rights to build the canal and, critically, exclusive rights to administer a zone extending five miles from each side of the canal.[4]

The Zone was thus established as an unincorporated territory of the United States. Its administration was based in the town of Balboa, on the Pacific terminus of the canal and adjacent to the capital of the republic, Panama City. There were several towns through the interior of the Isthmus, including Pedro Miguel, Gamboa, and Gatun; while Cristóbal, next to the Panamanian city of Colón, was on the canal's Atlantic terminus, known locally as the "Atlantic side." Following the canal's completion in 1914, the Zone was placed under the authority of an appointed governor, usually an officer from the Army Corps of Engineers. Reporting to the secretary for war, the governor was responsible for maintenance and the smooth operation of the canal as well as the civilian governance of the American enclave. Although this system of governance was briefly interrupted by US involvement in the First World War, it was maintained into the 1920s.[5]

Following the establishment of the Canal Zone, both skilled and unskilled workers flocked to the Isthmus. Most skilled workers and canal administrators were white Americans, the vast majority of whom lived within the American-controlled Canal Zone. Most manual laborers were transplanted West Indians, almost 150,000 of whom arrived during the construction phase of the canal between 1904 and 1914. Many returned home following its completion, but tens of thousands remained, either working on the canal or as laborers in the Panamanian Republic.[6] Their living and working conditions "ranged from difficult to appalling." The Isthmian Canal Commission (ICC)—the administrative body tasked with building the canal—also recruited laborers from southern Europe, Greeks, Italians, and especially Spaniards, but most had either returned to Europe or settled elsewhere in Latin America by the beginning of the 1920s.[7] Although there were some exceptions, Panamanians themselves were generally excluded from canal work.[8]

In 1920, the US census recorded 22,858 inhabitants of the Canal Zone. The population had been in freefall since the completion of the canal, down from 31,048 in 1916 and 62,810 in 1910. Of the 12,370 persons recorded as "white," 10,763 (87 percent) were American-born. The foreign-born white population was diverse. Those of British birth predominated (212 persons), followed by individuals from the Scandinavian countries (139 persons) and 103 white Panamanians. There were just 87 Irish-born people in the Canal Zone in 1920—56 men and 31 women. While it is difficult to gauge the population of Americans of Irish descent, the Zone's demographics suggest that republican activism there was primarily the product of an intergenerational engagement with Irish nationalism.[9]

From the beginning, labor on the canal was strictly divided by race—in many ways a reproduction of the early twentieth-century Jim Crow American South.[10] Racial segregation in the Zone was epitomized by the "gold" and "silver" employment rolls. As construction began in 1904, the ICC realized that they would have to offer generous salaries and benefits to American skilled workers in order to persuade them to relocate to the Isthmus. Americans who moved to the Canal Zone were placed on the "gold" roll, where they earned between 25 and 50 percent more than equivalent positions back home. Moreover, they enjoyed free accommodations, utilities, health care, and access to education.[11] Silver employees, predominantly West Indians, earned approximately half of the wages of an equivalent worker on the American mainland.[12]

Social life in the Zone was similarly segregated by race. Gold employees lived in comfortable housing inside the enclave, while those on the silver roll were more likely to live in rudimentary accommodation within Panama. Institutions such as hospitals, schools, and post offices were segregated by roll, which essentially meant by race.[13] White Americans, both men and women, joined a wide array of social clubs, mostly transplanted from the United States, such as the Elks, the Loyal Order of Moose, and, for Catholic men, the Knights of Columbus. Well-provisioned YMCA clubs in each Canal Zone town provided additional amusements and entertainments.[14] There was even access to American goods through a commissary system that provided the comforts and luxuries of home, from basic foodstuffs and clothing to cigars and ice cream.[15] White employees of the Panama Canal, including those of Irish descent, lived comfortable, "almost cloistered lives under American aegis."[16]

The postwar era, when the networks of Irish nationalism extended into the Canal Zone, was a period of particularly acute class and racial tension on the Isthmus. Unsurprisingly, the completion of the canal in 1914 prompted a considerable reduction in both gold and silver employment rolls. The silver roll was reduced from approximately 38,000 workers in 1913 to just 8,000 by 1921, and those who kept their jobs had to endure a reduction to their already dismal wages.[17] Gold employees maintained their salaries and generous benefits, but their numbers were likewise reduced from 5,300 in 1911 to 3,300 by 1918.[18] White labor unions in the Zone redoubled their efforts to ensure that both West Indian and Panamanian workers would be fully excluded from the gold rolls. Meanwhile, many West Indian silver roll employees joined the American Federation of Labor (AFL)–affiliated United Brotherhood of Maintenance of Way Employees and Railway Shop Workers. On 24 February 1920, about eleven thousand silver roll employees went on strike, demanding a seven-cent hourly wage, an eight-hour workday, and equal pay for women.[19] Mississippi-born governor Chester Harding steadfastly refused the workers' demands and, as the strike went on, began evicting West Indian employees and their families from homes within the Zone.[20] The strike was ultimately defeated thanks largely to the gold roll employees' efforts to keep the canal operational.

In the Panama Canal Zone, then, there was little chance of cross-racial social or labor solidarity. Most white gold roll employees were comfortable and did not wish to risk any threat to the status quo.[21] It was in this American enclave, a "close-knit, defensive . . . white supremist society," that the FOIF was established in 1919, gaining considerable support from the Zone's small cadre of Irish Americans.[22]

## The Establishment of the Friends of Irish Freedom in the Panama Canal Zone

Although an organized, public campaign in support of Irish independence did not develop in the Canal Zone until 1919, initial connections to republican nationalism were already in evidence by mid-1918. Within the historiography of global Irish nationalism, the role of particularly dedicated individuals operating at a local level in driving broader, popular engagement with Irish affairs is often overlooked. A single, passionate person could often be the difference between a nationalist association taking hold and thriving, versus latent concern with Ireland's political destiny gradually petering out. In the Canal Zone, initial communication between American-based Irish nationalists and those on the Isthmus was almost exclusively through Rhode Island–born Michael Hamill—a mechanic working on the dry docks at Cristóbal. Toward the end of the war, Hamill's letters about Ireland drew the attention of the Zone's postal censors, and several were passed on to American military intelligence officers. According to one report, he had been "very active in the Sinn Fein movement" during the well-publicized trial of Roger Casement following the Easter Rising of 1916.[23] In a virulently Anglophobic June 1918 letter to a Dr. Ailene Hughes of Holyoke, Massachusetts, Hamill claimed that he was "the first one to join the Sinn Fein movement, and [am] empowered by the New York board to represent them on the Isthmus of Panama—they will all know Mike Hamill, 'R.I. Red' and the work I did on getting over six hundred signers to the petition for President Wilson for the freedom of Ireland."[24]

Later in 1918, Hamill engaged in a more formal communication with US-based Irish nationalists. The postal censor intercepted a 20 August letter from Diarmuid Lynch, national secretary of the FOIF. Lynch enclosed copies of the constitution and bylaws of the FOIF as well as membership cards and an addressed envelope.[25] By the end of 1918, the FOIF had emerged as the United States' foremost Irish nationalist organization. It was originally established in March 1916 in New York by members of the radical Clan na Gael—intended as a more public, open republican organization than the secretive clan.[26] Initial growth of the FOIF was relatively slow, but it began to expand rapidly following the end of the First World War in November 1918, as large numbers of Irish Americans became engaged with the question of Ireland's self-determination. Swelled further by the popularity of Éamon de Valera's tour of the United States, the FOIF had grown into a formidable organization by late 1919, surpassing 225,000 members spread across an astonishing 753 branches in virtually every American state—a formidable lobbying and propaganda network.[27]

It is likely that the communication between Lynch and Hamill was a key step in the formal establishment of a branch of the FOIF in the Panama Canal Zone. Although Hamill was almost certainly the foremost figure involved in establishing a local branch, he faded from the organization—or at least from its public activities—rather quickly.

This may have been owing to his personality. One intelligence report described him as "fairly well educated," but also "reclusive." From an American perspective, at least, Hamill was not deemed disloyal. The Canal Zone's Department of Intelligence recorded that he viewed Sinn Féin's revolutionary tactics as "comparable to the methods and models of the American Revolution. . . . He has an air of sincerity about him which appears to be genuine as far as his Americanism is concerned. He is out and out for Ireland against England in the matter of her rule of Ireland. However, he makes no radical statements or threats."[28] A close association of American and Irish revolutionary nationalisms would quickly emerge as a primary rhetorical feature of the Canal Zone FOIF branches.

While Hamill received the material necessary to start a branch in November 1918, FOIF organizational activity did not begin until the early months of 1919. A public meeting, "calling every friend of liberty for Ireland on the Isthmus of Panama," was set to take place at the Balboa Lyceum on 9 February 1919, organized by John P. Corrigan, J. P. Donovan, and T. J. Owens—all of whom would remain leading figures within the Canal Zone FOIF. Corrigan, who would later serve as the first president of Balboa's FOIF branch, was born in England of Irish parents and was listed in the 1920 census as an "inspector."[29] Donovan, a foreman, was likewise English-born with Irish parents, while Owens, who would serve as the local FOIF's secretary, was a clerk with the United Fruit Company, born in Ireland and immigrated to the United States as a child.[30] The meeting never took place. Upon hearing about the plans to establish a branch, General Richard M. Blatchford, acting governor of the Canal Zone, informed Corrigan that "as the United States and England are Allies and friends, he could not sanction a meeting as proposed to take place as the Canal Zone is a federal territory and not an independent state of the American union." Corrigan agreed to cancel the meeting, but Blatchford nevertheless dispatched soldiers to the Lyceum on the evening of 9 February to break up any assembly that may have taken place.[31]

The committee of Corrigan, Donovan, and Owens had drafted a series of resolutions that they intended to pass at the meeting. The language of American patriotism was prominent. The resolutions read in part that it was "against this unjust form of Government Americans rebelled, Washington took his glorious stand, Lincoln fought, and President Wilson has aroused the noble determination of the free; Be it therefore resolved that we, the Friends of Irish Freedom living under a flag that has always represented liberty, do hereby give our sincere and hearty support to our brothers in every land enlisted in the noble cause of Irish independence, that they can count on our support no matter what the danger or cost."[32] With the meeting's cancellation, however, it does not appear as though this resolution was ever publicly disseminated.

Despite this early setback, Irish nationalist speeches were delivered at that year's Saint Patrick's Day celebration at the Balboa Lyceum. The event included addresses by a leading Panamanian attorney, Oscar Terón, who discussed Irish revolutionaries who fought with Simon Bolivar, before concluding with a strong endorsement of Irish independence. The Roman Catholic priest serving St. Mary's parish, New York–born Father T. J. McDonald—another devout Irish republican who would remain involved with the FOIF throughout this period—vociferously attacked the League of Nations, a common concern amongst Irish American nationalists in early 1919. The most interesting speech, however, was by visiting New York congressman Anthony J. Griffin, who bemoaned the fact that "Canal military authorities stopped an Irish meeting by force of arms," and assured the audience that Congress would endorse Irish self-determination.[33] This piqued the interest of the British diplomatic delegation in Panama City. Perhaps fearing a turn in public opinion over perceived British interference in American affairs, an exchange between Britain's long-serving minister to Panama, Sir Claude Mallet, and the Foreign Office encouraged Mallet to distance himself from Blatchford's decision to cancel the meeting. Blatchford, it seems, was concerned about possible backlash and sent his aide-de-camp to enlist British support should "he be called to account."[34] Although Blatchford's tenure in the Canal Zone would end the following month, his successor, Chester Harding, was similarly willing to cooperate with the British to suppress engagement with Irish nationalism.

After this fractured beginning, the FOIF in the Canal Zone made little headway until the final months of 1919. A successful meeting finally took place in Balboa on 16 November, which resulted in the establish-

ment of an official branch. Reflecting its distinctly American orientation, the branch was named in honor of Commodore John Barry—an
Irish Catholic from Wexford and hero of the American Revolution,
remembered as the first commander of the American Navy. J. P. Donovan, another prominent FOIF member, stated at the meeting that
"[Barry's] name ought to be brought before the public so that everyone would be made aware that the founder of the American Navy was
an Irishman." At the following monthly meeting, a second branch in
Cristóbal, on the Atlantic side, was set up and named for George Washington.[35] Several months later, in May 1920, a third FOIF branch was
established in the interior town of Pedro Miguel and named for Francis
Scott Key, author of "The Star-Spangled Banner."[36]

December 1919 saw the organization's first attempts at political lobbying and also a rare effort on the part of the Canal Zone FOIF to
extend their local activity beyond the American enclave. A deputation
from the group met with the Panamanian National Assembly's committee charged with debating the Treaty of Versailles and the League
of Nations. The FOIF submitted a memorandum, dated 10 December
1919 and signed by Fr. McDonald, Corrigan, James M. Courtney, and
Owens, representing both branches of the organization and on behalf
of "the American citizens of Irish blood on the Isthmus of Panama." It
presented a strong argument against the Panamanian Republic joining
the League of Nations. The FOIF in the United States, and Irish Americans more broadly, were vehemently opposed to the league, particularly
Article 10 of its covenant, which guaranteed the territorial integrity and
political independence of all member nations, and, as such, could be
interpreted as guaranteeing Ireland's position within the United Kingdom.[37] In order to dissuade Panamanian politicians, the memorandum
stated:

> . . . that Panama should undertake to guarantee with its blood and treasure
> the perpetuation of monarchies and empires should be unthinkable to every
> sound Panamanian mind. . . . We point out that if France desired to help
> Ireland as she did in the seventeenth and eighteenth centuries, or if Spain,
> the land from which your fathers sprung, wished to extend aid to Ireland
> as she did in the sixteenth century, they would be unable to do so. . . . And
> it is necessary for us to remind you that if the League of Nations was in

existence when your own dear country was fighting for her independence it
would have been impossible for the United States of America to have helped
her. . . . We confidently hope and pray that your National Assembly will not
allow that light of hope to be extinguished.

According to the new British minister in Panama, Andrew Percy
Bennett, the FOIF deputies received a rather cold reception, and were
"promptly informed" that the committee would not consider the
memorandum as it was "inimical to a country which the Republic of
Panama had the honour of calling an Ally."[38] The Panamanian foreign
minister, meanwhile, passed the full text of the memorandum on to
Percy Bennett.

It was, perhaps, naïve of the intensely American Canal Zone FOIF
to approach the Panamanian government in this way. Beyond the obvious reality that such a small deputation from a relatively minor society
was unlikely to hold much sway, relations between the republic and
American Canal Zone were particularly sour in the immediate postwar
period. Many of the Panamanians who worked along the canal had lost
their jobs following its completion, and by 1919 they were frozen out of
the more lucrative gold employment roll entirely. The American system
of commissary, moreover, badly hurt Panamanian merchants and businesses and was a long-standing point of contention on the Isthmus.[39]
Despite the FOIF's best efforts to appeal to the Panamanians' own revolutionary legacy, there was no real chance of persuading them to abandon the League of Nations. Panama ratified the Treaty of Versailles in
January and joined the league as a founding member.

## FOIF Activity and the British Response

The opening six months of 1920 saw the most concerted activity on
the part of the Canal Zone FOIF, and also the most determined efforts
by both British and American statesmen to disrupt it. A meeting in
Cristóbal on 11 January, which was attended by US military intelligence
officers, formalized plans to raise funds for Dáil Éireann by selling
bonds of the Irish Republic.[40] Launched in New York on 17 January
1920, the bond certificate drive was intended to capitalize on the substantial upswelling of support for the nationalist cause in the midst of

de Valera's American tour. Although away from the public eye there were considerable disagreements between de Valera, his entourage, and the Irish American leaders of the FOIF, the local administration of the campaign was, in many cases, left to individual FOIF branches. The national drive was a tremendous success, raising approximately $5.1 million from across the United States.[41]

As plans for the bond drive developed, the FOIF's local activities became increasingly public and visible. A letter in the *Star and Herald* on 14 February outlined the cause as one that should appeal to all Americans, not just to those of Irish Catholic birth or descent. The Irish question, it said, "was not a religious one," and the organization "admits to its membership persons of all religious beliefs." The report also highlighted the number of women who attended the meeting and announced a fundraising ball to be held at Balboa's Tivoli Hotel on 21 February—the eve of Washington's birthday.[42] A directive from Washington instructed the Canal Zone's Intelligence Department to keep the group under surveillance and, if possible, to place an agent within its ranks to investigate any potential connection to communist radicals.[43]

The FOIF ball was intended as the primary, public fundraising event in the bond certificate drive. Over one thousand tickets to the event were sold, but again, owing to interference from Percy Bennett and the British diplomatic mission in Panama, it did not take place as scheduled. Upon hearing about the proposed event, Percy Bennett "called upon Colonel Chester Harding, the Governor of the Canal Zone, and represented to him the impropriety of the Tivoli Hotel—which is the property of and run by the United States government—hiring out its ballroom for the purpose of swelling the funds of a society whose openly declared policy was the dismemberment of the United Kingdom." Harding agreed with the British minister's assessment and informed the association that the ball could not take place at the venue. The FOIF were understandably outraged and cabled Harding's immediate superior, Secretary of War Newton D. Baker, to protest this decision. According to Percy Bennett, the FOIF were so confident of Baker overturning Harding's decision that they neglected to inform their thousand ticket holders of the potential problem with the venue. Baker did not reply, and "hundreds turned up at the Tivoli on the evening of the 21st instant only to find the doors shut against them." Although Percy Bennett's involvement "was naturally treated as an official secret," the Canal Zone FOIF wasted little time in apportioning blame.[44] In a statement published on the front page of the *Star and Herald*—coincidentally on the same day that the canal's silver roll employees went on strike—the executive claimed that Percy Bennett was directly responsible for Harding's decision. The matter, they said, "has been referred to our national headquarters with the view of ascertaining whether American citizens on the Panama Canal are to be stifled in their efforts to offset the propaganda of the government of Great Britain against the efforts of Ireland to have a government based upon the will of her citizens."[45] The national FOIF board were keen to exploit an obvious case of British interference in their affairs. Details of the Tivoli Hotel incident were published in leading Irish American newspapers, while the national executive discussed it at their meeting in New York on 23 July, with the decision that they, too, would register a formal complaint with Secretary Baker.[46]

Despite another rather significant setback, the Canal Zone FOIF branches carried on with the business of raising the Dáil loan and distributing Irish republican propaganda. Advertisements for the bond drive appeared in the *Star and Herald* from mid-February, generally adopting a language of American patriotism. An example from 29 February included excerpts from Benjamin Franklin's 1788 address "to the good people of Ireland" and concluded with an appeal: "Americans can personally help redeem this pledge by subscribing to the Irish Liberty Loan."[47] Similar calls appeared in the paper throughout March.[48]

American military officers, meanwhile, continued to monitor the FOIF, sending examples of the association's propaganda back to Washington. These included a pamphlet titled "What Is Sinn Fein" and another that juxtaposed the Continental Congress's 28 July 1775 appeal "to the people of Ireland," which called for Irish sympathy with the grievances of the American colonies, with de Valera's message "to the liberty-loving people of America," in another direct attempt to link republican Irish nationalism with the objectives and rationale of the American Revolution.[49] This tactic is not surprising. Given the relatively small number of Irish Americans in the Zone, extra efforts were required to draw support from the broader Anglo-American community. According to Philadelphia's nationalist newspaper, the *Irish Press*, republican leaflets had been circulated "to every resident of the Canal Zone."[50] As material was distributed from the central FOIF organization to the branches in the Canal Zone, the networks of global diaspora nationalism were in full effect.

As the bond drive gained momentum, the activities of the FOIF yet again drew the ire of British diplomats in Panama. On this occasion, Percy Bennett approached the Panamanian minister of foreign affairs regarding the advertisements that were regularly appearing in the *Star and Herald*. Although the paper was published within the Canal Zone, it and its Spanish-language copublication, *La Estrella*, circulated widely in the republic as well. Percy Bennett "pointed out that the publication of such notices in Panama's principal newspaper might give rise to impressions in the public mind of which the Panamanian Government, as an ally of Great Britain, would by no means approve." The minister agreed to pass Percy Bennett's concerns on to the Panamanian president, Belisario Porras, who was a close "personal friend" of the paper's owner. In his triumphant report to the Foreign Office, Percy Bennett passed on assurances that no further Irish republican propaganda would be printed in the *Star and Herald*. This would not be the case, however, as advertisements for the bond drive continued throughout the remainder of March.[51]

The 1920 celebration of Saint Patrick's Day, in the midst of the bond certificate drive, was similarly contentious. Father McDonald's address to the Knights of Columbus was virulently anti-British, the priest referring to the Union Jack as "a flag of murder" that ought to be torn down "wherever you see it flying." Englishmen, he said, "are pirates, robbers, and murderers." Percy Bennett's report—understandably apoplectic—noted that the text of this speech had been passed on to Governor Harding. In a response to Percy Bennett, perhaps aware of the negative press that had followed the canceled ball in February, Foreign Office assistant secretary Roland Sperling advised the minister to ignore any similar utterances by "Sinn Fein agitators." He also noted that the address had been forwarded to the British envoy in Rome, John Francis Charles de Salis. He, in turn, passed it on to Monsignor Boneventura Ceretti, papal undersecretary of state, who "expressed fear as to the mischief which might result from raving of this sort."[52] The transnational networks of Irish diaspora nationalism were formidable, but so too were those employed by the British state to counter the republican movement.

The bond drive was relatively successful in the Canal Zone. It was extended by six weeks in order to allow for additional canvassing, and on 19 May secretary T. J. Owens wrote to Éamon de Valera announcing that $3,515, subscribed by over two hundred Zonian residents, had been remitted to national bond drive manager Frank P. Walsh. Although this was a small sum in absolute terms, Owens wanted de Valera to be personally aware of the Canal Zone's "great work for the cause," as it demonstrated the global reach of republican nationalism: "Men and women of the Irish race, wherever they live, in the prairies of Canada or the jungles of the tropics, are determined to see you win."[53] Owing to the great distances involved, however, the actual bond certificates did not reach Canal Zone subscribers until mid-September.[54]

With the bond drive winding down, the next objective for the Canal Zone branches of the FOIF was to stage the ball that had been scuppered by Percy Bennett and Chester Harding in February. A new date of 7 August was set. To avoid accusations of political fundraising, which had derailed the previous effort, attendance was by invitation rather than by selling tickets. According to the *Star and Herald*, over a thousand guests were expected and special late-night trains were arranged to give supporters in Cristóbal and Colón a chance to participate.[55] The press reports suggested a successful event: "Words of praise were on lips everywhere."[56] A later statement published by the FOIF executive described the ball as "more than a success," and suggested a significant increase in membership in its aftermath.[57] British diplomats had again attempted to intervene. Consul Constantine Graham, at that time standing in for Percy Bennett, met with Harding in another attempt to get the event canceled. He was informed that this was impossible, as no tickets had been sold. Harding did assure Graham that "proper measures would be taken to avoid any anti-British demonstrations." Graham's description of the ball itself contrasted with the enthusiastic reporting of the *Star and Herald*, stating simply "it was attended by nobody of importance and passed off quietly."[58]

## The End of the FOIF, the AARIR, and the Decline of Irish
## Nationalist Networks in the Panama Canal Zone

The FOIF maintained its activity and momentum throughout the latter months of 1920. Monthly meetings continued and were regularly reported in the press. In a similar vein to some branches on the US mainland, a special committee was established to investigate the way Irish history was being taught at Canal Zone schools. This culminated with a report in November calling for an "Americanization drive" to reduce what the FOIF perceived as British propaganda within the curricula.[59] Meanwhile, the organization carried out a membership drive throughout September—placing advertisements in the *Star and Herald* calling on "all freedom-loving Americans" to join.[60] Another formidable event took place that autumn—a memorial service for Terence MacSwiney, the nationalist lord mayor of Cork who died on a hunger strike at London's Brixton Prison on 25 October. MacSwiney's death was a global event, as individuals of Irish descent across the diaspora came together for Masses, vigils, and public memorials. The Canal Zone memorial event took place on 7 November at the baseball stadium in Balboa. Given the tremendous publicity that surrounded MacSwiney's hunger strike, it is unsurprising that the event attracted, according to the *Star and Herald* at least, "the most representative crowd of Americans that had ever come together for such a purpose in the Canal Zone." Father McDonald presided, and his strongly nationalist speech asserted that Americans in the Zone "would not stand for imperialism."[61]

Despite the best efforts of the Canal Zone FOIF branches to frame Irish nationalism in American language in order to attract support from beyond the Irish American community, there is evidence to suggest that the organization was rather aggressively opposed from within the enclave. Following the memorial event for MacSwiney, a series of letters appeared in the *Star and Herald* arguing against Irish self-determination and defending the position of unionists in Ulster.[62] These were carefully countered by members of the FOIF, including Courtney and Henry McKeown, who, though not on the executive, was an active member of the organization and was singled out for particular praise in T. J. Owens's letter to de Valera regarding the bond certificate drive.

Reflecting the insular nature of the white, American Canal Zone, the exchanges eventually devolved into petty, even personal squabbles. In one anonymous letter, McKeown was referred to as "the most irascible person to be met."[63] Amid arguments over the position of Ulster in an Irish republic and the civilizing influence of the British government in Ireland, the American orientation of the Zonian FOIF was maintained, as the most intense aspect of these debates was about the role of Irish Catholics in the American Revolution.[64]

In 1921, long-standing disagreements between de Valera and the American FOIF leaders such as John Devoy and Judge Daniel Cohalan resulted in a split in the organization. De Valera maintained that the FOIF's key objectives ought to be fundraising and lobbying for a fully independent Ireland. The American leadership, though, was increasingly using the organization's networks both to promote a more domestically oriented political agenda and to improve social and economic conditions for Irish Americans. At the end of 1920, de Valera established the rival AARIR as an exclusively Ireland-focused organization. Across the United States, the vast majority of FOIF branches were converted into AARIR ones in the early months of 1921.[65] Despite their distinctly American orientation, the Canal Zone branches did likewise—formalizing their affiliation with the association by mid-February—an example of grassroots support for Irish rather than Irish American leadership.[66]

Regular meetings continued across the Zone and, for a time, took place alongside another Irish-oriented group, the Canal Zone branch of the Committee for Relief in Ireland. This group was expressly humanitarian—focusing on the financial relief of families affected by the violence of the Irish Revolution, rather than on Ireland's political independence. There was considerable overlap between the executives of both organizations, and former FOIF president J. P. Corrigan served as chairman.[67] The presence of several Panamanians and active fundraising within the republic suggest a broader appeal, and this was reflected in the final tally, which saw $4,225 raised in the Zone—a substantially higher sum than the bond certificate drive.[68]

For the new AARIR, by far the most significant activity that spring was an Irish nationalist speech by visiting congressman William E. Mason. Mason is best known for preparing a bill, generally known as

the Mason Bill, that would have provided funds for an American diplomatic delegation to the Republic of Ireland—essentially a recognition of Irish independence. He was part of a congressional delegation
that toured the Canal Zone in March 1921 and gave an impromptu,
strongly nationalist speech to the members of the AARIR on 22 March.
Given the unique setting of the Canal Zone, the British diplomats were
angered yet again. Constantine Graham complained that the AARIR,
"sheltering under the privilege afforded to its members as employees of
the Canal Zone, has carried out a most obnoxious campaign against
everything British." As it was "made by a member of old standing such
as Senator Mason, within a mile of a foreign country," the incident
"acquires special significance and goes beyond the region of home political controversy."[69] Graham wrote a strongly worded complaint to
the Canal Zone's new governor, Jay Morrow, as well as to the American
envoy to the Republic of Panama, William Jennings Price. Clearly furious, Graham was in fact chided by his superiors at the Foreign Office
for sending these protests without consulting them.[70] They saw potential, no doubt, for further Irish republican propaganda should the
example of a British diplomat protesting the speech of an elected American official, delivered in American territory, become publicly known.

Mason's speech, however, was the final major public action by Irish
nationalists in the Panama Canal Zone. Following the truce of July 1921
and the subsequent Anglo-Irish Treaty signed in December, organized
republican activity in the Canal Zone gradually slowed. Meetings continued until at least early September, when a republican resolution was
printed in the *Star and Herald*. In the aftermath of the Treaty's signing,
however, the AARIR in the Panama Canal Zone was silent, perhaps
reflecting a growing disillusionment with the cause that had spread
throughout many diasporic nationalist groups by the beginning of 1922.

## Conclusion

An examination of the Friends of Irish Freedom in the Panama Canal
Zone reveals how engagement with the Irish Revolution on the diasporic periphery could be both inherently local, even insular, and at
the same time expressly transnational. The mode of Irish nationalism
displayed by the Canal Zone branches was strongly influenced by its

setting within an American colonial enclave. With FOIF composed almost entirely of Americans of Irish descent, a distinctly American conception of Irish republicanism, with a strong parallel between colonial America's and Ireland's independence as a foremost rhetorical point, was their most distinctive feature. As local agents in a global fight for Irish freedom, the Zonian FOIF was also the primary point of contact between local activists and the international networks of Irish nationalism. Propaganda pieces, produced either in New York or in Dublin, were widely distributed within the Zone, while the local branches also raised funds for the broader movement via the bond certificate drive of spring 1920.

Within the Isthmus of Panama, the activities of Irish nationalists rarely extended beyond the American-controlled Zone—the sole exception being the almost preposterous attempts by the local branches to lobby the Panamanian government to reject the League of Nations. This insularity is ultimately unsurprising, given the tense racial divisions in early twentieth-century Panama. White Americans, whether Irish or not, were deeply invested in maintaining their privileged status, so cross-community or cross-border support for an old-world political question was never likely to materialize, and, similarly, the Zonian FOIF did not apply their anti-imperialist rhetoric to domestic issues. While in many respects "radical," expressions of republican Irish nationalism existed comfortably within a context of class and racial privilege. Equally intriguing in this case are the robust efforts on the part of Andrew Percy Bennett and his fellow British diplomats to disrupt this relatively minor Irish nationalist group—an example of the equally transnational operation on the part of the British state to oppose Irish independence.

The Irish Revolution was a global event. As in communities across the diaspora, a wide variety of local personalities and events had a substantial influence on day-to-day engagement with the "Irish question" in the Canal Zone, but the brief existence of the local FOIF branches also demonstrates the transnational networks of the diaspora at their fullest extent. Although the FOIF was by no means a major force in the movement for an independent Irish Republic, their passionate and resilient activities provide another example of the vast spatial extent of Irish nationalist networks in the early twentieth century.

NOTES

1   Some examples of key work on Irish American nationalism include David Brundage, *Irish Nationalists in America: The Politics of Exile, 1798–1998* (Oxford: Oxford University Press, 2016); Francis M. Carroll, *American Opinion and the Irish Question: A Study in Opinion and Policy* (New York: St. Martin's, 1978); Michael Doorley, *Irish-American Diaspora Nationalism: The Friends of Irish Freedom, 1916–1935* (Dublin: Four Courts Press, 2005); Elizabeth McKillen, "The Irish Sinn Fein Movement and Radical Labor and Feminist Dissent in America, 1916–1921," *Labor: Studies in Working Class History* 16, no. 3 (2019): 11–37; Kerby Miller, *Emigrants and Exiles: Ireland and the Irish Exodus to North America* (New York: Oxford University Press, 1985); Joanne Eichacker Mooney, *Irish Republican Women in America, 1916–1925* (Dublin: Irish Academic Press, 2003); Miriam Nyhan Grey, ed., *Ireland's Allies: America and the 1916 Easter Rising* (Dublin: University College Dublin Press, 2016); Robert Schmuhl, *Ireland's Exiled Children: America and the Easter Rising* (Oxford: Oxford University Press, 2016). In Canada, Australia, and, to a lesser extent, Great Britain, much of the historical literature on republican Irish nationalism in the early twentieth century focuses on conflicting loyalties to Ireland and empire. Key works include Simon Jolivet, *Le Vert et le Bleu: Identité Québécoise et Identité Irlandaise au Tournant du XXe Siècle* (Montreal: Les Presses de L'Université de Montréal, 2011); Patrick Mannion, *A Land of Dreams: Ethnicity, Nationalism, and the Irish in Newfoundland, Nova Scotia, and Maine, 1880–1923* (Montreal: McGill-Queen's University Press, 2018); Pádraig Ó Siadhail, *Katherine Hughes: A Life and a Journey* (Newcastle, ON: Penumbra Press, 2014); Mark McGowan, *The Imperial Irish: Canada's Irish Catholics Fight the Great War* (Montreal: McGill-Queen's University Press, 2017); Robert McLaughlin, *Irish Canadian Conflict and the Struggle for Irish Independence, 1912–1925* (Toronto: University of Toronto Press, 2013); David A. Wilson, ed., *Irish Nationalism in Canada* (Montreal: McGill-Queen's University Press, 2009); Malcolm Campbell, *Ireland's New Worlds: Immigrants, Politics, and Society in the United States and Australia, 1815–1922* (Madison: University of Wisconsin Press, 2007); M. Stephanie James, "'Deep Green Loathing?' Shifting Irish-Australian Loyalties in the Victorian and South Australian Irish Catholic Press, 1868–1923" (PhD diss., Flinders University, 2014); Elizabeth Malcolm and Dianne Hall, *A New History of the Irish in Australia* (Cork: Cork University Press. 2019); Patrick O'Farrell, *The Irish in Australia, 1788 to Present* (Sydney: University of New South Wales Press, 2000); Jimmy Yan, "Revolutionary Ireland and Transnational Labour Solidarity on the Victorian Railways: The Case of Alex Morrison and Tom Wilson, 1921–22," *Labour History: A Journal of Labour and Social History* 114 (May 2018): 17–39; Peter Hart, "'Operations Abroad': The IRA in Britain, 1919–1923," *English Historical Review* 115, no. 460 (2000): 71–102; Keiko Inoue, "Dáil Propaganda and the Irish Self-Determination League of Great Britain during the Anglo-Irish War," *Irish Studies Review* 6, no. 1 (1998): 47–53; Donald MacRaild, *The Irish Diaspora in Britain, 1750–1939* (Basing-

stoke: Palgrave Macmillan, 2011); Gerard Noonan, *The IRA in Britain, 1919–1923, "In the Heart of Enemy Lines"* (Liverpool: Liverpool University Press, 2014).

2 See, for example, David Brundage, "Lala Lajpat Rai, Indian Nationalism, and the Irish Revolution: The View from New York, 1914–1920," in *1916 in Global Context: An Anti-Imperial Moment*, ed. Enrico Dal Lago, Roisin Healy, and Gearoid Barry (Oxford: Routledge, 2018), 62–75; Kate O'Malley, *Ireland, India and Empire: Indo-Irish Radical Connections, 1919–1964* (Manchester: Manchester University Press, 2008); Kate O'Malley, "Violent Resistance: The Irish Revolution and India," in *Ireland's Imperial Connections, 1775–1947*, ed. Daniel Sanjiv Roberts and Jonathan Jeffrey Wright (Basingstoke: Palgrave Macmillan, 2019), 213–221; M. C. Rast, "'Ireland's Sister Nations': Internationalism and Sectarianism in the Irish Struggle for Independence, 1916–1922," *Journal of Global History* 10, no. 3 (2005): 479–501; Michael Silvestri, *Ireland and India: Nationalism, Empire and Memory* (Basingstoke: Palgrave Macmillan, 2009).

3 Michael E. Donoghue, *Borderland on the Isthmus: Race, Culture, and the Struggle for the Canal Zone* (Durham, NC: Duke University Press, 2014), 12; John Major, *Prize Possession: The United States and the Panama Canal, 1903–1979* (Cambridge: Cambridge University Press, 1993), 4. See also David McCullough, *Path between the Seas: The Creation of the Panama Canal 1870 to 1914* (New York: Simon & Schuster, 1977).

4 Major, *Prize Possession*, 49–51.

5 Ibid., 35–36.

6 Michael L. Conniff, *Black Labor on a White Canal: Panama, 1904–1981* (Pittsburgh: University of Pittsburgh Press, 1985), 4.

7 Julie Green, "Spaniards on the Silver Roll: Labor Troubles and Liminality in the Panama Canal Zone, 1904–1914," *International Labor and Working-Class History* 66 (Fall 2004): 82, 94.

8 Major, *Prize Possession*, 5.

9 *Fourteenth Census of the United States, 1920*, vol. 1, "Total Population, 1920," 691, and vol. 3, table 6, "Foreign-Born Civilian Population, by Color, Sex, and Country of Birth," 1244–1245 (US Census Bureau, 1920).

10 Conniff, *Black Labor on a White Canal*, 7.

11 Carla Burnett, "'Unity Is Strength': Labor, Race, Garveyism, and the 1920 Panama Canal Strike," *Global South* 6, no. 2 (Fall 2013): 42–43; Major, *Prize Possession*, 78–79; Conniff, *Black Labor on a White Canal*, 32.

12 Major, *Prize Possession*, 81.

13 Burnett, "Unity Is Strength," 43; Stephen Wolff Frenkel, "Cultural Imperialism and the Development of the Panama Canal Zone, 1912–1960" (PhD diss., Syracuse University, 1992), 153.

14 Katherine A. Zien, *Sovereign Acts: Performing Race, Space and Belonging in Panama and the Canal Zone* (New Brunswick, NJ: Rutgers University Press, 2017), 54–55; Green, "Spaniards on the Silver Roll," 80.

15 Major, *Prize Possession*, 103.

16 Frenkel, "Cultural Imperialism and the Development of the Panama Canal Zone," 111.

17 Conniff, *Black Labor on a White Canal*, 49.

18 Ibid., 51.

19 Burnett, "Unity Is Strength," 40.

20 Ibid., 59; Conniff, *Black Labor on a White Canal*, 59.

21 Major, *Prize Possession*, 92.

22 Conniff, *Black Labor on a White Canal*, 51.

23 Guy Johannes [Chief, Police and Fire Division, Panama Canal Zone], "Confidential Memorandum No. 534: Michael Hamill," 20 Aug. 1918 (National Archives and Records Management, College Park, MD [NARA], Record Group [RG] 165, Records of the War Department, Military Intelligence Division Correspondence, 1917–1941, File 9771-A-8, Box 2193).

24 Michael Hamill to Ailene Hughes, 16 June 1918, US Postal Censorship Report, #64965 (NARA, RG 165, Records of the War Department, Military Intelligence Division Correspondence, 1917–1941, File 9771-A-8, Box 2193).

25 Diarmuid Lynch to Hamill, US Postal Censorship Report # 89496 (NARA, RG 165, Records of the War Department, Military Intelligence Division Correspondence, 1917–1941, File 9771-A-8, Box 2193).

26 Doorley, *Irish-American Diaspora Nationalism*, 37.

27 Ibid., 87–88, 188–190. The figure of 225,728 members in September 1919 includes "associate members" drawn from other Irish ethnic associations such as the Ancient Order of Hibernians.

28 Hiram B. Crosby [Canal Zone Department of Intelligence] to Acting Director of Military Intelligence, 29 Jan. 1919 (NARA, RG 165, Records of the War Department, Military Intelligence Division Correspondence, 1917–1941, File 9771-A-8, Box 2193).

29 Corrigan was listed as president of the Commodore Barry branch in the FOIF's list of branch contact details. At some point during 1920, he was replaced as president by Massachusetts-born James M. Courtney. See "Friends of Irish Freedom Branch List," n.d. (American Irish Historical Society [AIHS], Friends of Irish Freedom Papers, Box 23, Folder 8).

30 Biographical details were compiled using the ancestry.com genealogical database. Original data are from the *Fourteenth Census of the United States, 1920*. Owens's place of birth, Drogheda, was recorded in "Passenger and Crew Lists of Vessels Arriving at New York, New York, 1897–1957" (National Archives at Washington, DC [database online], Records of the Immigration and Naturalization Service), http://ancestry.com.

31 Sir Claude Mallet to Foreign Office (FO), 19 Feb. 1919 (National Archives of the United Kingdom [NAUK], No. 45688, FO 371/4248).

32 Mallet to FO, 19 Feb. 1919 (NAUK, No. 45688, FO 371/4248).

33 *Star and Herald*, 17 Mar. 1919.

34 Mallet to FO, 22 Mar. 1919; FO to Mallet, 5 May 1919 (NAUK, No. 61897, FO 371/4248).

35 *Irish Press*, 13 Dec. 1919.

36 *Star and Herald*, 8 May 1920.

37 Doorley, *Irish-American Diaspora Nationalism*, 96–97.

38 Andrew Percy Bennett to FO, 24 Feb. 1920 (NAUK, A1746/1746/32, FO 371/5663).

39 Major, *Prize Possession*, 103, 107, 137.

40 Norman Randolph to Director of Military Intelligence, 13 Jan. 1920 (NARA, RG 165, Records of the War Department, Military Intelligence Division Correspondence, 1917–1941, File 9771–56, Box 2184).

41 Doorley, *Irish-American Diaspora Nationalism*, 108–112. See also Francis M. Carroll, *Money for Ireland: Finance, Diplomacy, Politics, and the First Dáil Éireann Loans, 1919–1936* (Westport, CT: Praeger, 2002), 15–30; Robin J. C. Adams, "Shadow of a Taxman: How, and by Whom, Was the Republican Government Financed in the Irish War of Independence (1919–21)?" (PhD diss., University of Oxford, 2018).

42 *Star and Herald*, 14 Feb. 1919.

43 Director of Military Intelligence to Intelligence Officer, Panama Canal Department, 24 Jan. 1920 (NARA, RG 165, Records of the War Department, Military Intelligence Division Correspondence, 1917–1941, File 9771–56, Box 2184). A fear of communism pervaded American military intelligence reports in the postwar period—a product of America's First Red Scare.

44 Percy Bennett to FO, 24 Feb. 1920 (NAUK, A1746/1746/32, FO 371/5663); *Star and Herald*, 22 Feb. 1920.

45 *Star and Herald*, 24 Feb. 1920.

46 See "Minutes of National Executive Meeting," 23 July 1920 (AIHS, Friends of Irish Freedom Papers, Box 23, Folder 9); *Irish World*, 17 Apr. 1920.

47 *Star and Herald*, 29 Feb. 1920.

48 See, for example, *Star and Herald*, 1, 8 Mar. 1920.

49 Randolph to Director of Military Intelligence, 5 Mar. 1920 (NARA, RG 165, Records of the War Department, Military Intelligence Division Correspondence, 1917–1941, File 9771–56, Box 2184).

50 *Irish Press*, 17 Apr. 1920. See also *Irish World*, 10 Apr. 1920.

51 Percy Bennett to FO, 5 Mar. 1920 (NAUK, A1889/1746/32, FO 371/5663).

52 Percy Bennett to FO, 24 Apr. 1920; Roland Sperling to Percy Bennett, 31 May 1920 (NAUK, A3375/3375/32, FO 371/4540); John Francis Charles de Salis to FO, 6 July 1920 (NAUK, A4781/3375/32, FO 371/4540).

53 Owens to de Valera, 19 May 1920 (University College Dublin Archives, Éamon de Valera Papers, P150/982).

54 *Star and Herald*, 16 Sept. 1920.

55 *Star and Herald*, 5 Aug. 1920.

56 *Star and Herald*, 9 Aug. 1920.

57 *Star and Herald*, 8 Sept. 1920. A laudatory report was also included in the *Irish Press*, 28 Aug. 1920.

58 Constantine Graham to FO, 11 Aug. 1920 (NAUK, A6298/1746/32, FO 371/5663).

59 *Star and Herald*, 29 Nov. 1920.

60  See, for example, *Star and Herald*, 14 Sept. 1920.

61  *Star and Herald*, 9, 10 Nov. 1920.

62  See, for example, *Star and Herald*, 11, 14 Nov. 1920.

63  *Star and Herald*, 9 Dec. 1920.

64  See, for example, *Star and Herald*, 11, 13, 22, 24 Nov., 3, 7 Dec. 1920; 14, 19 Jan. 1921.

65  Doorley, *Irish-American Diaspora Nationalism*, 134–135.

66  *Star and Herald*, 18 Feb. 1921. Months earlier, in July 1920, the Barry branch had passed a strongly worded resolution expressing their confidence in de Valera. See *Irish Press*, 31 July 1920.

67  See *Star and Herald*, 28, 29, 31 Jan., 10 Feb. 1921. On the Committee for Relief in Ireland, see Carroll, *Money for Ireland*, 24; Francis M. Carroll, "The American Committee for Relief in Ireland, 1920–22," *Irish Historical Studies* 23, no. 89 (May 1982): 30–49.

68  Carroll, "American Committee for Relief in Ireland," 35.

69  Graham to FO, 25 Mar. 1921 (NAUK, A2757/2146/32, FO 371/5601).

70  Graham to Jay Morrow, 24 Mar. 1921 (NAUK, A2757/2146/32, FO 371/5601); FO to Graham, 31 Mar. 1921 (NAUK, A2146/2146/32, FO 371/5601).

# The Generation that Lost

*The Ulster Bank, Ardara, County Donegal, 16 June 1921, and
Long After, and Far Away*

BREANDÁN MAC SUIBHNE

Naked, Charlie McGuinness was spectacular. Bob Briscoe, lord mayor of Dublin in the late 1950s and early 1960s, said as much. The two had met in Hamburg in October 1921. It was the time of the Truce, and the IRA was trying to run guns from Germany during what some reckoned might prove only a "lull." Michael Collins had sent out Briscoe, the son of a Dublin shopkeeper, to handle the business end of things, and then McGuinness, a seaman from Derry, to look after shipping.

On arrival, McGuinness had presented Briscoe with sealed orders from Liam Mellows, who would soon split with Collins over the Treaty. The orders, Briscoe later remembered, were most peculiar. First, they explained that the bearer had an anchor tattooed on the back of his left hand and a ring on the fourth finger. Those tattoos were known to the British, and Briscoe was to get them removed. Second, the orders further informed him that though McGuinness was a Catholic, "he had not been to confession for fourteen years, during which time he had committed just about every sin in the calendar." Now that McGuinness was to command a desperate undertaking, Briscoe was "to see to it that he was put in a state of grace."

"Sure, this was a strange assignment for me," Briscoe, a Jew, remembered, "but it was typical of the devout and devoted leaders of the Irish Revolution. They thought nothing of risking a man's neck; but under no circumstances would they endanger his immortal soul."

Briscoe had met tough men before McGuinness, and he would meet tough men again. But the Derryman, he wrote in the late 1950s, was "the toughest character I have ever met": "He was a short, barrel-chested, wide-shouldered man, who always walked with his elbows out and his hands up ready for a fight. He had a big baldish head, and a fleshy face that was scored and burned by the winds of all the oceans. The tattoo on his hand was nothing. When he was naked he was spectacular. From the soles of his feet to his neck, he was a picture gallery, with everything from mermaids to alligators."

The tattoo on his chest was a fully rigged ship. Those on the soles of his feet were Union Jacks.

Briscoe duly found a "sufficiently shady" doctor to work on McGuinness's left hand. The medic not having access to proper anesthetic, the procedure promised to be painful. McGuinness lay on a couch in a horrid little surgery. The only distraction was a pretty nurse, who dabbed his hand with iodine as the doctor began cutting off the skin. The room was hot, and, watching the procedure, Briscoe felt like vomiting. But McGuinness gave no indication of pain. Then, suddenly, he winked and gestured with his head. Briscoe looked over and saw that McGuinness's free hand was caressing the nurse's leg under her skirt and "evidently enjoying this counter-operation."

The doctor finished, pulling the flaps of skin together, sewing them up, leaving a straight, puckered scar, and bandaging the hand. On their way back to their hotel, McGuinness took a notion that the taxi driver was taking them a circuitous route. "We'll not let the —— think we're fools," he said to Briscoe, putting his right fist through the glass partition behind the driver's head. Briscoe took him back to the doctor; he left with both hands bandaged.

Later, in a bar, Briscoe found two Irish Franciscans, one large and robust and the other thin and frail, attached to a seaman's mission—McGuinness dubbed them Brother Mutt and Brother Jeff, an allusion to a popular cartoon strip. After a few introductory drinks in the Triere Café, the would-be penitent agreed to visit their monastery, and there, while Briscoe drank "miserable tea until it was up to my gullet," the fragile looking fellow heard his confession over several hours.

"You will be glad to know that Charley [*sic*] is now in a state of grace," ran Briscoe's dispatch to Mellows. "But for how long—that is another question."[1]

The British secret service had become aware that IRA weapons were being prepared for shipment in Germany, however. During the Treaty negotiations in London, Lloyd George confronted Collins about it. Collins feigned ignorance and sent Seán MacBride to Hamburg to "salvage" the shipment. There, with the help of Karl Spindler, the master of the port, who in 1916 had captained the gunrunning ship the *Aud*, he managed to locate the Derryman. McGuinness, MacBride later recalled, was "an absolutely marvellous man and a very able sailor," but he had one defect: "He used to drink once he got to port; never on a voyage but as soon as he berthed, he used to go off on a batter. More often than not he would end up in a police station. . . . I think I did actually find him in a police station."[2]

That "absolutely marvellous man" was among the IRA's most successful gunrunners in those troubled times: in November 1921 he landed a massive consignment of arms and ammunition in Waterford, and then in March 1922 an even larger one at Helvick.

But those weapons, sourced to fight the British, ended up being used by the opposing sides in the Civil War, a cause of enduring regret to both Briscoe and McGuinness.

From late May through mid-June 1921, a few months before he told all to Brother Jeff, Charlie McGuinness had been the leader of an "active service unit," commonly "flying column," attached to the Third Brigade of the IRA's First Northern Division; the column included three other Volunteers from Derry, with men from companies in the brigade's four battalions—Mountcharles, Carrick, Ardara, and Glenties—completing it.

McGuinness's column was not the only one active in west Donegal in 1921 that had a core group drawn from Derry. On 29 December 1920, nine men recruited by Peadar O'Donnell had left the city on foot for the Rosses, to fight with the First Brigade; they had arrived on 1 January.[3] The Rosses comprises over three hundred square kilometers of bogs and mountains, with houses at that time dispersed on scattered patches of arable; the only village vaguely resembling a town was single-street Dungloe. Then, as now, the district was accessible by three main roads—one that entered at the Gweebarra Bridge in the south, another at Crolly Bridge some twenty-five kilometers to the north, and a third at Doochary in between; and then, but not now, there was the Londonderry and Lough Swilly Railway that entered at Crolly and ran to Burtonport. For a period in early 1921, the IRA had the run of the place, with the column, led by O'Donnell and Derryman Alfie McCallion, ambushing troop trains and striking out of the Rosses to hit barracks in Falcarragh to the north and Glenties to the south. However, on 16 May, a Royal Navy destroyer landed Gordon Highlanders at Burtonport; the Gordons drove into Dungloe and detained key IRA leaders, notably Frank Carney, the officer commanding the First Northern Division. Meanwhile, massive convoys of Dorsets, Northumberland Fusiliers, and the Rifles approached by the three main roads as airplanes scoured the district. Over a thousand troops were involved in this "round up," which lasted almost a week, and involved house-to-house searches and the screening of adult males. Among those arrested and removed by ship to prison were several members of O'Donnell's column.[4]

At this juncture, McGuinness had just returned to Ireland from Glasgow, where he had been on an abortive mission, with other Derry IRA men, to spring Sligo republican Frank Carty from custody. It was McGuinness's second time to be tasked with rescuing Carty. In February, he had broken him out of Derry gaol—"Are you going to leave the fucking place or not?," he had hissed when Carty balked at trusting the sailor's rope ladders[5]—and spirited him to Scotland on his father's steamer, only for the Sligo man to be quickly rearrested. In Glasgow, the city IRA had dismissed McGuinness's plan—to take control of the ship transporting Carty back to Dublin and steer it for Donegal—and, on 4 May, it tried unsuccessfully to break him out of a prison van. McGuinness and his men evaded arrest after the attack in which they had no part, and made their way back to Ireland. Now, on 16 May, he and a party of Derrymen were in the vicinity of Doochary, en route to Dungloe, as the British moved to seal off the Rosses. This group, with McGuinness in charge, broke through a cordon and returned to Derry to sit out the "round up."[6] But before the end of May, McGuinness was back in Donegal as leader of the column attached to the Third Brigade, which operated south of the Gweebarra estuary. Its most immediate objective was the elimination of the now heavily fortified Glenties barracks: convoys supplying it were to be attacked and the barracks shot up with a view to drawing out the enemy.

What caused those city fellows to head for the hills or, indeed, to involve themselves in republican paramilitarism at all? In old age, the man of letters Sean O'Faolain admitted that he was unable to explain what drove the fight for Irish freedom in 1916–1921, in which he himself, in youth, participated. For sure, he argued, in *Vive Moi!* (1963),

> Most historical motivations of the 1916 Rising and the armed fight that followed had by that date become purely emotional impulses. As for the other and far more powerful impulses behind our fight—for, since it took place, they must have existed—I confess that I still am unsure about them, since they have not, even to this day, been investigated by any modern-minded historian; that is, by a man concerned only to identify and record the complex of social and economic pressures on the depressed urbanised surplus of the countryside that really decided the beginning of our last fight for freedom, determined its course, and foreordained its outcome.[7]

Even in 1963, the assumption that historians are male was outmoded. And the contention that all "historical motivations" for revolt had become "emotional impulses" remains open for debate. Still, the "depressed urbanised surplus of the countryside" might describe the milieu of *some* fellows who, in 1920–1921, left Derry for Donegal. In other words, some of them belonged to a class, common in the cities of poor rural countries, which the critic John Berger once characterized as "a mass of static vagrants, unemployed attendants: attendants in the sense that they wait in the shanty towns, cut off from the past, excluded from the benefits of progress, abandoned by tradition, serving nothing."[8] And those men in ceasing to be static, in going back to the type of place their fathers and grandfathers had left behind, to fashion a future different to the one ordained for the urban poor, may have achieved a freedom that they would never know again.

But importantly, not all—in fact, not most—who took to the hills had been "excluded from the benefits of progress." Many had availed of opportunity, and they had good career paths mapped out. The three other Derry Volunteers in the column that McGuinness commanded were an apprentice marine engineer (son of a publican farmer), an apprentice mechanic (son of a laborer), and an engineering student (son of a schoolmaster), and McGuinness—whatever he had been and whatever he became—could always pass himself off as a master mariner. And the group that left in December 1920 to form the first column in the Rosses included a commercial traveler (Frank Martin [1897–1981], son of a laborer) and several shipyard workers (including Alfie McCallion, son of a mason, and Jim Taylor, son of a railway servant). In general, the men in the columns were, like most of the city Volunteers, "artisans and apprentices," upwardly mobile young men, whom the wartime boom in the city's shipyards had enabled to acquire trades; they were fitters and the like, not dock laborers.[9] Yet even for those men, those months, on their keeping in the hills, hunted by Tans and Tommies, were special, a time replete with possibility.

As for the sources of their republicanism, they doubtless involved cultural and political as well as socioeconomic forces. Alfie McCallion wrote a memoir of his own politicization. Central to it is an emphasis on *history*: "I was born in 1900 and soon my boyhood thoughts were imbued by a desire to continue the efforts of my forefathers in protesting the right of any foreign government to rule in Ireland." He attended school in Culmore, where the teacher, Patrick O'Doherty, was enthusiastic about history—his son, John Francis, became professor of ecclesiastical history at Maynooth—and involved in various cultural organizations. "I displayed a youthful concern [for Irish freedom] in my schooldays at Hollybush School," McCallion recalled, "and for some reason my desire to work to free my country became a part of my schooling." Aged twelve, he joined the nationalist Owen Roe Band, and in his memoir he remembered a picture of Robert Emmet hanging in its hall and how he listened "with wonderment" to "tales of gallantry," back to Brian Boru, and with "sorrow and hate" to stories of the Famine, the suppression of the 1798 Rising, and "the deeds perpetrated by Cromwell and Strongbow": "At the age of fifteen I was eager to become affiliated with any group of men who was [*sic*] to fight and work for their freedom." He joined the Irish Republican Brotherhood (IRB) and then, at sixteen, the Irish Volunteers, which rapidly developed into the IRA. But if "schooling," formal and informal, was crucial, the quiet influence of his father, James, a stonemason born in 1856, was a factor too: "Irish freedom meant a lot to him. Although he very seldom discussed history with his family, he would say 'If you boys think you are right, why should I interfere? God bless you and [I] hope you will live through it.'"[10]

"The men and women who made the Irish revolution knew that they were different to their parents," R. F. Foster has argued in a compelling history of "the revolutionary generation."[11] For sure, that argument holds for McCallion and other men in the columns. Yet, it is clear too that their parents—many of them born, like James McCallion, not long after the Famine—had wished that their children would be different to themselves and, in a phrase of Berger's, not have to suffer for being who they were.[12] And, in the wider region, if that wish caused an older generation to deny the young a certain knowledge of who they were—most obviously in rearing their families through English—some of them passed to their children a sharpened awareness of belonging to an Irish "nation" that had too long endured the effects of British rule.[13]

Interviewed in the 1970s, Neil Gillespie (b. 1899), an IRA associate of McCallion and McGuinness in Derry, remembered how, in youth, he had consumed nationalist writings—*Jail Journal*, *Speeches from the Dock*, and *Knocknagow*; "I can recall reading too about the Famine, the breaking of the van in Manchester, and the story of the *Erin's Hope* and the *Catalpa*. I read too about the heroes of an earlier age, Jimmy Hope, Henry Joy and Wolfe Tone." And thinking in old age of his youthful reading, he admitted, much as McCallion had done, to a certain bafflement about his father's apparent lack of interest in history/politics: "I cannot now understand how those books came into my hands because I did not buy them; they were already in the home, all of which makes it hard to understand when I think of how unpolitical my father was."[14]

Altitude gives attitude. Hills, historian Fernand Braudel once wrote, are the last outpost of freedom.[15] And Charlie McGuinness was at home in the hills: "A mountain man," he opined, "is a proud fellow possessing spine and spirit; a fighter who never flinches under heavy fire. I like the mountain lads, too—quick, taciturn, and ever dependable." The mountain women were also heroes: "dark-eyed and dark-haired, more reticent than the blue-eyed, fair girls of the milder counties . . . lithe, strong, and solid, the equal of their men," always ready to surrender their beds to "fagged republican soldiers" and shiver in the barn. He saw their poverty and the petty tyranny of the priests. But he also glimpsed the limits of the priests' control—there was widespread indifference to their strictures on the IRA in 1919–1921—and he saw the persistence of older ways of seeing:

> The spell of St. Patrick never penetrated very deep into the minds of the people around the mountains of Errigal and Bluestack. They are Catholics, of course, with a strong admixture of paganism that no bishop's letter could ever read out of their hearts. . . . My rendezvous, when the trail became too hot, was a dugout near an old hill-woman's cabin. I visited her several times and held long talks with her in Gaelic. She could tell time by the stars, and knew all the constellations and planets. On the flagstones in front of her cabin was a chart in the form of an elaborate sundial marking the path of the sun in its equinoctial variations. Below, in the distance, a jagged line of hills served as indices for the rising stars and planets.[16]

There had been freedom in the hills, then, and a prospect of freedom—below, in the distance, rising stars. Still, for many of the men who left Derry for Donegal in 1920–1921—and, indeed, for many "mountain men" who joined them and "mountain women" who supported them—the after years were a disappointment. They had fought for an Irish republic—and they had failed. IRA veterans everywhere—some who supported the Treaty, some who were "neutral," and some who opposed it—could acknowledge their failure, even if some of them found in the southern state or their political party some consolation. But in northwest Ulster, failure was glaring, with the regional capital, Derry, in a different jurisdiction to the bulk of its natural hinterland, and, from the 1920s, the majority community in the city subject to partisan policing and gross discrimination in housing and employment.[17] The entire region, the bit in the North and the bit in the South, remained mired in poverty—the settlement of 1921 had not checked emigration, which winnowed the population until the 1970s.

Failure caused IRA veterans, at home and abroad, to assume something of the characteristics of a "lost generation," the name given by Gertrude Stein to a European and American cohort left adrift and disillusioned when the second industrial revolution, which had given the world the automobile and airplane, electricity, radio and film, new fabrics, chemicals, and pharmaceuticals, exploded in the industrialized slaughter of 1914–1918. And, in the northwest, whatever pride those veterans might have taken in having done their best in their youth, "five glorious years"—a euphemism, popularized in the 1950s, for the period between the Rising and the Truce—was to many a half-truth and a hollow boast.

Many stories could be told of Charlie McGuinness in a "global history of Irish revolution." Here, stories are told of his involvement in a minor incident in Donegal in June 1921. That incident seems destined to remain beyond the reach of history—there are irreconcilable differences between the stories told of it. But detailing it cautions against taking military memoir at face value. And looking beyond that incident, to the afterlives of those involved in it—in Ireland, England, Australia, South Africa, and, in the case of McGuinness, the Arctic and Antarctica, China, Europe, Latin America, the Soviet Union, and the States—brings into view the condition of the generation that lost.

### On Another Man's Book

Ernie O'Malley's *On Another Man's Wound* is the most critically acclaimed memoir of the Tan War. In 1931–1934, when O'Malley worked on it, in Mexico, New Mexico, and Peru, Charlie McGuinness also wrote a memoir, in which he gave an account of his own IRA activities and much else besides. He began writing it in New York, in an apartment on Riverside Drive, and after an interlude in the Soviet Union, much of it north of the Arctic Circle, he finished it in Dublin.[18] Published as *Nomad* (1934) by Methuen in London and as *Sailor of Fortune* (1935) by Macrae-Smith of Philadelphia, it is subtitled the "adventures" (US) or "memoir" (UK) of "an Irish Sailor, Soldier, Pearl-fisher, Pirate, Gun-runner, Rum-runner, Rebel and Antarctic Explorer."

It is a poor summary of McGuinness's résumé. He was also a bush-fighter, big-game hunter, hobo, jailbreaker, radio broadcaster, set maker in Hollywood, construction worker on Long Island, journalist, and internee. He was "a hard man for the drink" too, one friend admitted, and Seán MacBride confided in that same friend that he was "never behind the door where women are concerned."[19]

As for *Nomad*, it is similar to but different from *On Another Man's Wound*. First, the similarities: they are IRA memoirs written abroad in the early 1930s, and both were the subjects of successful libel actions by politicians not mentioned in them by name. McGuinness was held to have insinuated that John William Nixon had been the police officer responsible for an atrocity in Belfast in 1922, when uniformed men slaughtered five members of a prominent Catholic business family, the McMahons, and an employee, Edward McKinney, from Inishowen. In 1935, a Belfast court awarded Nixon, by then a Unionist MP at Stormont, £1,250. Two years later, Joseph O'Doherty TD (Donegal) received £550 when the High Court in Dublin ruled that a passage in *On Another Man's Wound* implied that cowardice had kept him from participating in an arms raid in Moville in 1919.[20]

And then the differences: if a modernist sensibility shaped O'Malley's memoir, McGuinness's *Nomad* owes something to eighteenth-century picaresque or the adventure stories of Robert Louis Stevenson. "There are some who may criticize my flouting law and order," he announced in the preface to the UK edition:

> I offer no alibis, apologies, or excuses. Anything I have done has been to satisfy curiosity or the urge for change, but mostly for the thrill of doing something unusual. I have been labelled "soldier of fortune" and "adventurer"; the latter is possibly true, but I have yet to fight for remuneration. I quit the service of Britain during the War because she was winning. I fought in Ireland for the reason that there was no earthly hope of winning. I went to China to help the harassed forces of Chiang Kai Shek; when he became War Lord and an ally of the great powers I returned to America.

In that same preface, he explained that he had omitted the rescue of a maiden in distress because most maidens he encountered in distress blamed him for their trouble. And he asked his readers to remember that "this book is written primarily by a sailor. The absence of fine phraseology comes from the fact that I never use any."[21]

In truth, McGuinness had a fondness for big words. He does not go for a drink; he goes "shopping at some of the beverage emporiums." He does not buy underclothes; he purchases "a complete set of under-rigging." His hat is his *chapeau*.[22] His wit is that of a stand-up comedian: a matter-of-fact relation of extraordinary situations, overblown language to describe the ordinary. And that style becomes an issue when he writes of the Tan War, particularly his activities in west Donegal.

There, he adopts the persona of an accomplished military commander, peering through his field glasses as his men "pick off" Tans and Tommies. He even includes the equivalent of "battle honours": "There is no need to catalogue our ambushes, raids, and night attacks on barracks. Lettermacaward, Finntown, Pettigo, Arran, Ardara, and Donegal are names to bring back vivid memories of our guerrilla activities in the years 1920 and 1921."[23] One is loath to downplay the seriousness of any engagement, however small. Still, there was no confirmed fatality in any incident in which McGuinness was involved in Donegal.

Of course, McGuinness's claim to have joined the IRA because it hadn't a chance of winning is the line of a raconteur. It gets a laugh. And accepting that he was a raconteur, a *reader* will conclude that he had told many of his stories before, and give him some latitude. Problematically, some stories had got *too good* with the telling. For instance, in mid-May 1921, when the British swamped the Rosses, McGuinness claims some twenty men under his command ambushed a column of troops; in the "opening fusillade" they achieved twelve "hits," and then, over the next four hours, "picked off the foe until their casualties must have been considerable." He does not explicitly claim his men inflicted fatalities. However, he does mention two IRA men being shot and killed, and he says that they were buried in the mountains, then later disinterred and reburied.[24] Who were they? There is no record of any IRA fatalities in Donegal in mid-May 1921.

But old comrades liked McGuinness's book. Pax Ó Faoláin, a Waterford IRA leader who landed the weapons smuggled from Germany, was perhaps its sternest critic. "It doesn't tell the quarter," he said.[25] And people who took different positions on the Treaty remembered McGuinness fondly in statements to the Bureau of Military History. Excepting, perhaps, Nancy Wyse Power, a Sinn Féin representative in Europe in 1921–1922, who says Collins sent McGuinness ("an interesting type") to Germany "to get him out of the way," the closest one gets to a negative opinion of the man is from Sean Beaumont, a Dublin IRA man who ran into him in Berlin in 1921–1922. And even Beaumont's attitude seems less censure than appalled fascination. "I found McGuinness a most entertaining companion but absolutely without scruple of any kind, financial or moral. On one occasion he invited me to a well-known night club in Berlin and when I demurred on the ground of expense, he tapped his breast pocket which was bulging with Briscoe's money and said 'That's alright, De Valera will pay for it.'"[26]

Yes, Charlie was funny. His humor could be coarse, however. Once, apparently in the late 1920s, his brother, Hugh, a schoolteacher in Buncrana received a picture postcard from Mexico. The picture was a street scene and the message read "Dear Hugh: not much doing here, only two dogs fucking in the street."[27] The verb "to fuck" was one that McGuinness used a lot. He also had a penchant for racial epithets. *Nomad* has its share of "chinks," "niggers," and "kikes" and plenty of ethnic stereotypes, sometimes inflected by lechery: he lusts after "dusky Polynesian maidens" and "exotic Chinese ladies" while, hypocritically, deploring Belgian officers in the Congo who cohabited with "dusky courtesans." Consistency was never McGuinness's strong suit: in Berlin in late 1921, he had beaten up an Irishman for insulting a Jew whose restaurant he frequented, and Klara Zuckerland, his first wife, was herself a Polish Jew, but in the late 1930s, one finds him ascribing all the woes of Russia and Spain to "the evil Jewish Bolsheviks."[28]

Importantly too, McGuinness's fight for Irish freedom, if told in the style of a *Boys' Own* adventure story, had not been morally unambiguous. In *Nomad*, he describes the killing of a female civilian to his men during vicious street fighting in Derry in the latter half of June 1920; that fighting, which left some twenty people dead, involved the IRA attempting to protect nationalist homes, businesses, and amenities, notably St Columb's College, from an onslaught by unionist gunmen abetted by the British army and the Royal Irish Constabulary (RIC):

> One incident in Bishop Street is unforgettable. A Catholic laborer, with whom I was acquainted, tried to cross the street during a lull. Immediately he was picked off by an Orange sniper. His body lay in the middle of the roadway, a stream of blood running from the hole in his chest.
>
> Generally speaking, women-folk were spared from the fire, although some suffered injuries trying to defend their men from murder.
>
> One old hag, who lived close by, repeatedly walked out of her house screaming vile and blasphemous epithets at the Pope and Catholics in general. We paid no attention to her at first—until she hobbled over to the body of the murdered workman. But, dipping handkerchiefs into the pool

of blood which surrounded him, she shrieked with ghoulish glee. Three times she returned for more blood, kicking and abusing the corpse and reviling the Pope. At last we trained our rifles on her, warning her off; but she misjudged her immunity and, cursing the mothers who bore us, insisted that we were the brood of whores and bitches.

"Let's draw lots and shoot her. That isn't a woman—it's a devil!" I said to my companions.

We drew, and the task fell to me. As a warning to her, I fired several rounds of random shot. My companions did likewise. Then, during a lull, she once more strode into the thoroughfare carrying white strips which, apparently, she was distributing amongst her neighbors as souvenirs of papist blood.

Just as she bent down to dip her rags in the red pool I fired—so did the others, forgetting the lottery in their anger. The hag spun round and fell beside the body she was desecrating.

Under a white flag, her friends ventured forth and pulled the corpse out of the street. When the siege ended, however, the walls of the city were plastered with filthy epithets concerning Catholics. Some of these were printed in the blood of the victims.[29]

History, with certainty, can put a name to that woman. She was fifty-five-year-old Eliza Moore (née Shannon), daughter of an RIC sergeant and the wife of James Moore, a shoemaker and boot dealer. Moore received multiple gunshot wounds near her own door, 105 Bishop Street, at about seven thirty on the morning of Thursday, 24 June: a coroner's inquest heard that she had a bullet wound on the left side of the chest, another on the left side of the neck, and another on the left shoulder; her right eye was lacerated and destroyed, the lower lid torn. She died a week later in the Union Infirmary, not, as McGuinness has it in *Nomad*, on the street. However, the number of wounds is consistent with his mention of a volley being fired at her, and, likewise, the shooting of Moore near her own door rhymes with his description of his victim repeatedly coming out of her house to interfere with a corpse. Conversely, the only other woman killed in Derry in that fighting was Margaret Mills, who was shot the previous day, Wednesday, 23 June, but not multiple times and, while she was shot on Ferguson Street, near Bishop Street, she was not near her own house, which was on Orchard Row.[30]

A name can also be put to the fellow lying dead in the street: he was Robert McLaughlin, a barber, of 93 Foyle Road, who, at twenty-eight years, was the same age as McGuinness. He was shot dead on Bishop Street "early" on the morning of Thursday, 24 June. McLaughlin, who had got married only six weeks earlier, on 12 May, to Jane McCallion, had stopped on the Wednesday night with his wife's people at Tillie's Lane, and the following morning he had left, with his brother William, to take food to the latter's family at 99 Bishop Street, "as all was quiet, he thought." He knocked on the door of No. 99, but received no answer, and, while waiting, received a bullet wound in the hand. "We will run for it," he said to William. They ran in the direction of Henrietta Street, and they were turning the corner at the house of William Cooke, a Unionist builder, when a bullet entered the back of Robert's neck and came out below his right eye. His body lay "for some hours" in Bishop Street before being removed to Nailor's Row. When picked up, it was found that his pockets had been rifled, and a watch, chain, razor, hat, and quantity of money were missing. The shot that killed him had come from Unionist snipers on Abercorn Road or Barrack Street.[31] Mention of McLaughlin's pockets having been rifled adds weight to McGuinness's claims about the conduct of Eliza Moore, but it does not confirm them. And either way, such behavior would not justify killing her.

As for *Nomad*, despite all McGuinness's exaggeration and invention, many details of his IRA activities in Ireland, Scotland, England, and Germany can be corroborated. A historian who "picks off" its taller claims may make a contribution to knowledge, but to dismiss the book out of hand would be a mistake. Some holes may be poked in it, many attributable to style, but the fabric holds. And style, being an expression of the man, reveals something not only of McGuinness, but of people who held him in high regard—Collins and Mellows, Briscoe, MacBride, and Ó Faoláin and the men who were with him in Donegal. Perhaps the most considered criticism of *Nomad* is by historian Uinseann Mac Eoin: it "does not do justice to an extraordinary man."[32]

## 2:50 p.m. Thursday, 16 June 1921

From late May 1921, the column commanded by McGuinness was headquartered in the home of the Gildea family, at Straboy, three kilometers north of Glenties, with contingents from other companies in the brigade area billeted in the wider district of Shallogans. In June, it was decided to move to Rosbeg, a peninsula to the west, where it would be based at the home of Patrick Harkin in Kiltoorish. The column moved on the night of 14 June, shooting up the Glenties barracks en route.

Ardara is about ten kilometers from Kiltoorish. There, on 16 June, two days after the move from Straboy, McGuinness accompanied by one or more members of the column, entered the Ulster Bank on the Diamond, where the town's two streets meet, and they either did or did not rob it. And then later that same day, these IRA men, returning by the shore to Rosbeg, were ambushed by two-lorry loads of Tans who had watched them traversing several kilometers of open strand. McGuinness and another Volunteer managed to draw the Tans into a running gun battle on the beach, enabling the others to escape. "The running scrap," he reported in *Nomad*, with a nod to his experience on another continent, "was reminiscent of bush-fighting in East Africa, except that we had neither bush nor twig to help us."[33] Wounded in the hip, he covered the escape of his comrade before being put out of action by a bullet to the hand and, finally, captured. Also taken were two IRA men assigned to the column from the Ardara company, Paddy Reilly and Francie Gallagher, who was a vice-commandant of the Third Battalion, and Patrick Harkin. Aged about seventy, Harkin had tried to save the IRA's weapons; however, the Tans had spotted him coming out of his door carrying two Lee-Enfields, a bandolier, and a bag of ammunition, and fired upon him, forcing him back inside. When he surrendered, they recovered four rifles, 460 rounds of ammunition, five bombs, military uniforms, several haversacks, field glasses, and five bicycles.[34]

The Tans beat the arrested men and then removed them to Glenties in the Crossleys. There, when they were taking them into the barracks, the commotion gathered a crowd of women and children. "You won't hold that fella long!," McGuinness remembered a "spirited old lady" piping up to the officer in charge when she saw him.[35] And she

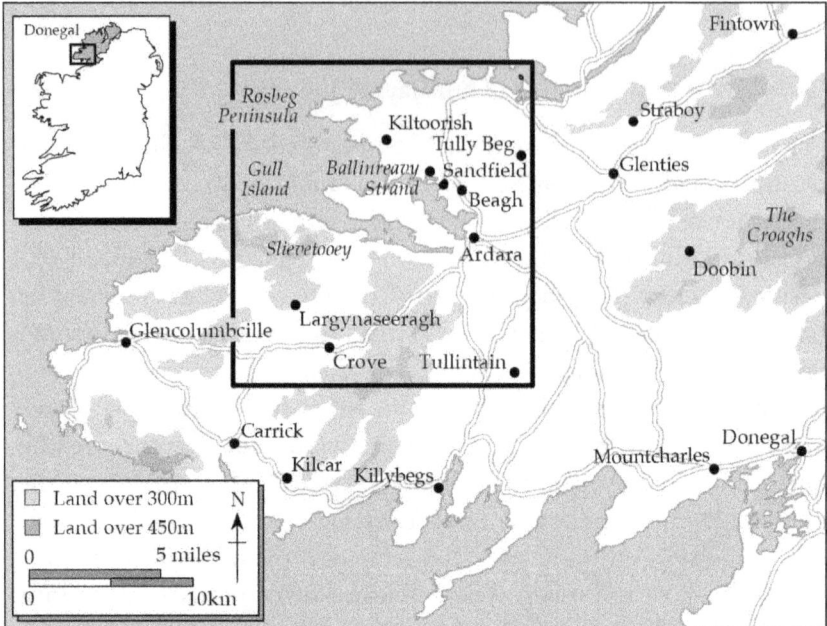

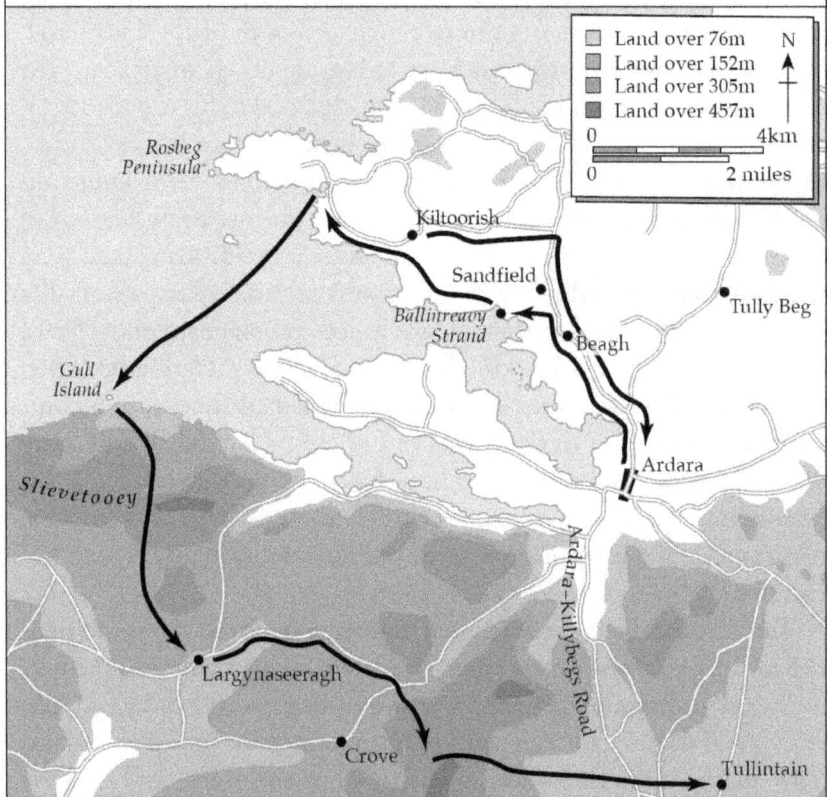

The McGuinness party's route to and from Ardara on 16 June 1921 and the subsequent evacuation of the remnants of the column from Rosbeg. Credit: Courtesy of Matthew Stout.

was right: transferred to Derry, where he was confined in a caged steel hut on the parade ground of Ebrington Barracks, he escaped on 3 July from the hut, the cage, and the barracks and slipped out of Derry disguised as a priest. The British searched in vain for Charlie Hennessey of Drogheda, the name he had given when arrested, and within weeks McGuinness had rejoined the column in Donegal.[36]

There was a sequel to the events of 16 June. The IRA established that the column had been informed upon by Michael J. O'Kane, an engineer belonging to a prominent Derry family, who had been working for the Congested Districts Board (CDB) in southwest Donegal. In Rosbeg for his work, O'Kane had noticed members of the column and left, on his motorbike, for Killybegs or Glenties, where he notified the Tans and brazenly led them to Kiltoorish. Now, on the weekend of 9–10 July, two members of the column extracted him, drunk, from a party in Woodhill, the home of Charles Falvey, the local doctor, outside Ardara. But somehow, he escaped execution. In one telling, by McGuinness, who was not present, O'Kane was shot near Woodhill and a note pinned to him announcing that he had been executed for informing—but in the morning the body was gone: he had been wearing a "steel vest." And, in another, by an IRA man who investigated the incident, the prisoner bolted when one of the two Volunteers tasked with the execution left to fetch the parish priest to hear his confession.[37]

If what happened "out the Wood," allowing O'Kane to escape, is a puzzle, so too is what happened in the bank. McGuinness's account, in *Nomad*, is matter-of-fact: he went up to the town, with five men, to rob the bank and rob it he did.

Two days after the [Glenties] barracks attack I raided a Belfast bank in Ardara. Taking five men with me, I waited under cover until the Black and Tans, thundering through the town in armored cars and exhibiting a load of bristling bayonets as a threat against the inhabitants, made their round of the village.

No sooner had the lorries swept out of sight in a vortex of dust than we came out of our cranny and sauntered into the bank. While I held up the manager, my aide-de-camp covered the cashier. Cramming what we needed into our bag, and with due apologies for our crude method of crimping their standing in the community, we left. But not before I had explained the policy of the Republican war leaders to a raging manager. Whenever I planned a raid I planned also a method of retreat in case of attack. Planting the loot, for further reference, we retired towards our dugouts, not far from the village of Ardara.[38]

Problematically, that account, written in the early 1930s, is at variance with remarks he made later, in 1937, when Department of Defence officials interviewed him in relation to his application for a military service pension. Then, claiming to have "posted up notices for people not to deposit their money in alien banks," he insisted he had not robbed the bank in Ardara:

Q. You stuck it up?
A. Yes. It was to be a warning. I had to give an order that there was nothing to be taken out of it, and there was nothing.[39]

Arising from that interview, in which McGuinness admitted to being "mixed up" about dates, he was asked to clarify his service in a written statement. Here too, he reiterated that he had not robbed the bank: "Late June. To enforce the economic war I made a display of sticking up the Ulster Bank in Ardara. (I gave orders not to touch a penny.) On the way back to our base at Rosbeg, two lorry loads of Tans surprised us. In the ensuing running skirmish I was brought down with a shot to my hip but managed to hold up the enemy until my comrades escaped."[40]

The insistence that no money was taken can be explained. McGuinness had left the IRA in cloudy circumstances: when the Split came, in 1922, he claimed ownership of an IRA boat, sold it, and pocketed the proceeds. Hence, in the tale of derring-do that is *Nomad*, he was eager to talk up what happened in Ardara on 16 June—it would be a poor guerrilla commander who could not get some "loot" from a bank in a small Irish town—but then, later, in his pension application, he had reason to talk it down: the applicant was a man of probity.[41] Complicating matters, both McGuinness's claim, in *Nomad*, to have robbed the bank *and* his subsequent claim not only not to have robbed it but never to have had any intention of robbing it *both* run counter to press reports, based on a communiqué from Dublin Castle, that at 2:50 p.m. *four* IRA men armed with revolvers had tried but failed to rob it: "The bank was searched and the raiders demanded the keys to the safe, but they were refused and the men left without securing any of the bank money."[42] Some later press reports of a failed robbery put the number of IRA men at five not four, probably due to a typographical error; but both figures are close to that given by McGuinness for the number of men who left Rosbeg for the town, six—himself and five others.

And so press reports, *Nomad*, and McGuinness's pension application bring three scenarios into view, all involving *several* IRA men entering the bank: first, the IRA men tried and failed to rob the bank; second, they succeeded in robbing the bank; and third, they never had any intention of robbing the bank and simply made a show of strength to intimidate people from doing business with it.

## On Another Man's Word

The Ulster Bank's archives have no record of any raid (never mind a robbery) at its Ardara branch in June 1921, confirming that, per the newspapers, no money was taken; if money had been taken the bank would have noted it.[43] So at issue here is not whether or not the bank was robbed—it was not. Rather, it is why McGuinness and a number of IRA men entered the bank in the first place.

An account by another member of the column may clarify matters—or it may not. In 1953, Mick Sheerin, then a commandant in the Aer Corps, completed a witness statement for the Bureau of Military History, detailing his IRA activity, in Derry, Donegal, and Glasgow, in 1919–1921. In that statement, he explains how he came to write it. "On the 17th October, 1952," he wrote, "I was introduced by Martin O'Donnell [an Aer Corps commandant] to John McCoy [of the Bureau of Military History] who talked me into doing the job. I am not handy with the English language. I have a plebian taste in Literature, but I seem to remember someone once said 'History is the story of living men.' This may be a good definition. It can be interpreted in at least two ways. I interpret it in one way. The Bureau of Military History will interpret it another way." And he explains something too of his motivation:

I was told the personalities associated in the public mind with the area and for whom the bugles and trumpets sounded in the intervening years were coy when approached and put over the line. Nothing really happened in the area *according to them*. . . . I felt this was most unfair to those who did their duty as they saw it at the time and to their families and descendants. This was the main incitement. I have simple tastes. I harbour no grudges and I have no regrets. As I went along, happy memories came to mind of pleasant places and kindly people who deserved a better fate.[44]

In Sheerin's statement, completed by 13 February 1953, four men left Rosbeg for Ardara—himself, Charlie McGuinness, Owen "Ginger" Callan, and Hughie Martin, the four members of the Derry IRA who had come to Donegal to lead the Third Brigade's column. McGuinness, at twenty-eight years of age, was the eldest. Sheerin, born in 1900 in Legcloghfin in Glenelly, County Tyrone, was not yet twenty-one. He had been intended for the Church, he wrote, and after leaving school, presumably in 1911 or 1912, he had attended Hughes' Academy, a preparatory school, in Derry. He had soon become involved in republican paramilitarism, graduating from Na Fianna to the Irish Volunteers, and, latterly, the IRA. By 1919, the young fellow, who had once been destined for a seminary, was an apprentice marine engine fitter with Swan Hunter; the apprenticeship involved spells in Harland and Wolff's Diesel Works in Glasgow, when he attached himself to the local IRA, and Cammell Laird's in Birkenhead, on Merseyside. Sheerin had been in Derry in 1920 when he was involved in the street fighting there that summer.[45]

Nineteen-year-old Owen Callan (sometimes Eoghan Ó Calláin), nicknamed Ginger, was, in Sheerin's recollection, a "student type." The son of a schoolmaster, in Drummullan, South Derry, he had received training in explosives from Charlie Mawhinney, the engineering teacher in the Derry Tech, and he was forever experimenting with gadgets and bombs. In Donegal, he got his hands on an old six-pounder gun, known locally as the Maas Cannon, that had been recovered from a wreck. He had visions of using this weapon extensively, but it blew itself to bits when Callan fired it and put the would-be artillery man through a wall behind him. He was, Sheerin remembered, "a menace at times."[46]

Hughie Martin, from Union Street, Derry, was the son of a laborer, and at twenty-two going on twenty-three, he was a bit older than

Sheerin and Callan. An apprentice mechanic, he had been wounded in the foot in May 1920, either shooting his way through a Black and Tan cordon, as Sheerin recalled, or "in a scrap with Orangemen," as he himself described it; the injury was to give him trouble in Donegal. He had been arrested in August 1920 and, when a prisoner, treated in Arbour Hill, Dublin, before being released, in error, from Mountjoy in March 1921.[47] "He had poetic aspirations," Sheerin remembered, "and wrote sentimental poems for *Ireland's Own* and publications of that nature. He got inspiration at the most inconvenient times both day and night, and anyone he selected for his audience was in for a bad time. He also possessed a tenor voice that he used on the least encouragement."[48] McGuinness was more appreciative of Martin's talents: "Hughie was a resourceful, courageous fellow who made the war a source of entertainment as well as excitement."[49]

Callan, the schoolmaster's son, belonged to a republican family: he had a younger brother, Robert Emmet.[50] But Martin too had been early exposed to advanced nationalist politics. Although his elder siblings were reared only in English, he and his younger brother, Frank, who would serve in the flying column in the Rosses in 1921, both learned Irish in childhood and, at an early age, involved themselves in cultural organizations; in later years, Hughie would sometimes style himself Aodh Ó Martáin.[51]

Sheerin's account of what happened in Ardara seems straightforward:

On the second day while waiting the arrival of the 1st [Mountcharles] and 2nd [Carrick] Battalion contingents we decided to investigate the possibilities of Ardara, a town which patrols of the enemy passed through regularly from Killybegs to Glenties, as the location of an ambush. I, Martin, Callan and McGuinness proceeded towards Ardara on the morning of the second day, on bicycles. On the way my bicycle got a puncture and I exchanged it with a postman for his bicycle. This was the official Red Bicycle of the period. The postman was not pleased with the exchange.

The remainder of the Column was left distributed in the Assembly area and as far as I remember the O/C, [3rd] Battalion, was left in charge. We arrived in Ardara without further incident.

The main street of the town was then roughly "L" shaped, one "leg" north and south and the other east and west. Martin and I took the former leg, McGuinness and Ginger the latter. Martin and I had examined the buildings on the south of our "leg" and had reached a part about midway up the north side, and were talking to Con Kennedy in his draper's shop when I happened to look out of the window and saw two lorries of Tans preceded by a motor cyclist passing north. We were assured by Kennedy that it was a usual occurrence.[52]

They are unlikely to have gone into the draper's shop solely to buy socks. Kennedy, a "returned Yank" who had been a saloon keeper in Winslow, Arizona, was a prominent supporter of Sinn Féin, and a nephew, also Con Kennedy, was the IRA's intelligence officer in Ardara; or, rather, he was the Third Battalion's intelligence officer; John McConnell, on the Main Street, was intelligence officer of the Ardara company.[53]

Sheerin continues: "A little later McGuinness and Callan came along and told us they had a narrow shave. As they were passing down their 'leg' on the south side opposite the Ulster Bank they spotted the convoy and went into the Bank and shut the door. The occupants of the Bank became alarmed and they had to restrain them until the lorries passed. We finished the job and went by the Strand Road back in the direction of our billeting area."[54]

So, in Sheerin's telling, the bank was not robbed, and the intention of the two (not four or five or six) men who entered the premises had been neither robbery nor the proclamation of a boycott—they had ducked into the bank to hide. Thereafter, Sheerin's narrative is broadly consistent with that in *Nomad*. He too offers a dramatic account of being ambushed; he acknowledges the bravery of Callan and McGuinness in drawing off the Tans, enabling the others to escape; and he details the evacuation of the remnants of the column, by the Third Battalion ferrying them across the bay, whence they marched over Slievatooey to Largynasearagh, where billets had been prepared for them. He describes how the column spent several days in the mountains, dodging Tommies and Tans, before crossing the Ardara–Killybegs road and pushing deep into the Bluestacks and safety.[55] Like McGuinness, he explains that the IRA determined how they had been betrayed, and he gives the informant's actual name; McGuinness gives him a pseudonym. And in detailing the apprehension and escape of O'Kane, he reports that he himself participated in an inquiry that absolved the two Volunteers involved—Callan, who went for the priest, and Martin, who was left guarding the condemned man—of any wrongdoing.[56]

On first perusal, Sheerin's account is more compelling than either of McGuinness's versions of events. His tone is measured, with none of the bravado of *Nomad* nor the transparent self-exculpation of the pension application; and he gives more details, putting named people in specific places at particular times. But tone and detail can deceive. In 1926, over quarter of a century before Sheerin wrote his memoir, Hughie Martin applied for a military service pension. A summary of his IRA activities inserted in his file indicated that he had "raided the Belfast bank in Ardara," flatly contradicting Sheerin's claim that Martin was with him in Kennedy's when McGuinness and Callan entered the premises on the Diamond. That summary was based on an interview with him. Hence, two of the three men identified by Sheerin as having gone to Ardara with him—McGuinness and Martin—remembered a "raid," not an effort to hide from the Tans, and a third, Callan, in supporting Martin's pension claim in 1926, indicated that he took part in "several raids on enemy property" in summer 1921, which could, of course, include the "Belfast Bank." Indeed, Sheerin himself had supported Martin's pension application without contradicting the claim about the bank.[57] And, again, the Castle communiqué put four, not two, IRA men on the premises.

If Sheerin obfuscates, a local history by Liam Briody, a Garda sergeant in Glenties in the 1970s, may explain why. In Sheerin's telling, the column had shifted from Straboy to Kiltoorish because the men were too widely dispersed in the former place while the latter provided better facilities for training. Conversely, the sergeant, drawing on conversations with aging veterans, ventured that the column had moved to Kiltoorish with a view to ambushing Tans who frequently came to bathe in Nairn: when the Tans were in the water, two armed men leading a donkey and cart were to approach sentries left guarding their Crossley (and the bathers' weapons) and disarm them while men in elevated positions would deal with those in the water. This plan had come undone when a member of the column, "on his own initiative," was "involved in a bank robbery in Ardara." Briody reported that "the robbery participant would have been subsequently shot but for the intervention of Charlie Gallagher," meaning the vice-commandant of the Third Battalion.[58]

The reference to a "robbery" can be passed over—again, there was no robbery. The concern is Sheerin's obfuscation. Presumably, the man whom Charlie Gallagher had to dissuade from shooting the "robbery participant" was his own commanding officer, Packie McHugh, the thirty-four-year-old commandant of the Battalion. And well might McHugh have thought to shoot McGuinness. The bank was in his hometown. Moreover, he himself had been in Rosbeg when the Tans arrived; he could have been killed. And his battalion had lost good men, safe houses, and scarce weapons, and it had been put to the pin of its collar to extricate the column from Rosbeg. But if McHugh ever did propose to shoot McGuinness, it was likely only an outburst. After all, it was not only McGuinness's caper in Ardara that drew the Tans to Kiltoorish; O'Kane must have observed IRA men there. According to Sheerin, "In the course of his CDB work [O'Kane] came upon the Column accidentally at Rosbeg. The chaps there paid no heed to him. He mounted his motor bike, proceeded to Killybegs and brought the Tans to the spot where the Column was billeted."[59] But then, as the Tans' first priority when they reached Rosbeg was to lie in ambush rather than to raid houses, they clearly knew that IRA men would be returning to Kiltoorish, so O'Kane must also have observed McGuinness's party leaving for Ardara and/or in the town.

In truth, focus on the bank diverted attention from an imbroglio that reflected poorly on McHugh's battalion. He and the seven other members of the column who had remained in Rosbeg had posted no sentries, paid no heed to O'Kane, and failed to notice the Tans' arrival in two tenders: according to some accounts, several of them were swimming at Tramore, and it was the gunfire that alerted them to the Tans' presence.[60] In other words, nobody had raised an alarm as the Tans deployed. Yet if McGuinness's valor on the strand, his sensational escape from Ebrington, and the Truce diminished the possibility of any disciplinary action, Nancy Wyse Power may have been close to the mark when she surmised that Collins sent him to Germany to get him out of the way. West Donegal was too small a stage for so great a talent.

As for Sheerin's obfuscation, in 1952–1953, could it be that over thirty years after the event, he was embarrassed at having let down McHugh, whom he admired, by participating in an unsanctioned "job," which, to add insult to injury, failed? And why had the IRA men gone into the bank? The hour that they left Rosbeg is not known, but Sheerin indicates that it was in the morning. It does not take an hour to cycle from Kiltoorish to Ardara. Certainly, they were delayed by Sheerin's puncture and the hijacking of the postman's red bicycle. Allowing two hours, then, for the entire journey—the time it would take to walk—if they left midmorning, they would have been there by midday. It would have taken five minutes to walk up and down the Front Street and little more to do the same on the Main Street, if that, in fact, is what they did. On that hot June day, when the rest of column was swimming at Tramore, had four fellows gone "shopping at some of the beverage emporiums" before the incident at the bank at 2:50 p.m.?

Whatever the source of Sheerin's obfuscation, the last word on the events of 16 June can be left to him. Writing a time when, in the South, young people who had never lived under British rule were starting to cock snooks at those who had delivered them from it, he concluded his reflections on the ambush on a wryly indignant note:

> In the intervening years since this incident I have often heard the observation to which I never made any reply, "The IRA were really murderers. They got behind ditches, surprised the unfortunate Tans, opened fire on them without warning and never gave them a chance to surrender. The only bit of luck the poor Tans had was the IRA were notorious bad shots." In this incident and others I can claim to have seen the picture from both sides. In this case the Tans ambushed us in the recognised manner from behind a stone wall. They watched us cycle into them from a distance about a mile on an open strand. They opened fire on us from a range of less than 200 yards without warning, did not call on us to surrender but missed us. The only immediate claim they could make for their efforts was the capture of one bicycle and the recovery of a shot-up postman's bicycle complete with carrier.[61]

Within weeks of being ambushed, Sheerin had again seen "the picture" from the other side: on 29 June, the column—commanded in McGuinness's absence by Hughie Martin and James "Yankee" McGill, a local man who had fought with the Americans in the First World

War—ambushed a Black and Tan convoy at Kilraine, midway between Ardara and Glenties. Several Tans were wounded in the first lorry, and its occupants put their hands up. However, a second lorry having stopped out of range, the column was unable to either accept their surrender or, in Sheerin's phrase, "mow them down." In the confusion, head constable William Duffy (1888–1975), a Monaghan man who had been a sergeant major in the Irish Guards during the war, rallied the Tans, and, pursued for several hours by a detachment of Wiltshires that arrived from Glenties, the column retreated into the Bluestacks.[62]

It was the last major action of the Tan War around Ardara. Word of the Truce came through in the second week of July. "The event," Sheerin recalled, "was celebrated in the fashion of the times." Martin and Callan went into the well-garrisoned port of Killybegs, and they were promptly picked up by the Tans: "The services of liaison officers had to be sought to effect their release."[63]

The Tan most severely wounded at Kilraine on 29 June was thirty-four-year-old Tom Devine; he had been shot in both thighs. A miner, from Lancashire, he had joined the "colours" at the declaration of war in 1914. And after over three years of "distinguished service," during which time he was wounded seven times, he was discharged "unfit for further service" a few months before the armistice. Returning home, he had worked as a shell inspector in a munitions factory and then, in October 1920, had joined the RIC and landed in Ireland.[64]

Evacuated to Lifford Infirmary, Devine died a slow death over two and a half weeks, passing away a few days after the Truce. The matron of the infirmary, Anna Heslin, attended his funeral in Strabane. Years later, E. J. Mullin, a Catholic curate in Glenfin, remembered that, on the day after the funeral, she had remarked to him that the only others present at the graveside had been the dead man's mother, who had come over from England, four policemen, and the chaplain. And, according to Mullin, Heslin had said that when the grave was closed this woman, who was herself English, had addressed the little group, not only forgiving those who had shot her son but wishing them success: "I want the Irish people to know that I did not send my son on this mission to Ireland and that I forgive the people who shot him. I have another son, and if he came on the same mission to Ireland, I should also forgive the people who would shoot him. I have the greatest sympathy with the Irish people and I wish them every success."[65] Mullin's mention of a small group of mourners is at variance with a *Strabane Chronicle* report that puts 150 RIC men at the funeral; that report also has both of his parents (not just his mother) present, and it identifies them as Jane and Thomas Devine, a miner.

But those differences are of no great significance. And consistent with the story ascribed to Heslin, other contemporary accounts noted that Jane Devine made an emotional address at the graveside, with the *Freeman's Journal* reporting that she had asked God to forgive those who shot her son, as she forgave them and that, despite her sorrow, she had sobbed aloud, "God Save Ireland."[66] Therein lies the pity of it all. Thomas Devine Sr. (b. 1868) was a native of Mayo. His wife Jane (b. 1870) had been born in England, but she was the daughter of Irish parents, Mary (b. 1831) and James Manley (b. 1825). Her mother was a native of Cork, as most likely was her father. Part of the human hemorrhage occasioned by the Famine, the Manleys had spent the 1850s and 1860s moving back and forth between Liverpool and Manchester, before settling, by 1871, in Wigan, where men dug coal in the deepest collieries in Britain.[67] And there, surrounded by the dusty faces of the immigrant poor—among them the evicted, the orphaned, and the unwanted of Cork and Mayo—Jane would have early learned the cost of the union of Great Britain and Ireland.

Within a few weeks of Tom Devine's death, his parents applied for £10,000 compensation. Giving evidence "with emotion" at Donegal Quarter Sessions in October, which she attended with her husband, Jane Devine explained that her late son had been sending her £2 10s every fortnight. They were awarded £1,400.[68]

## The Ordinary Volunteer and the Glamour Boys

My grandfather, Néillidh Sweeney, was born and reared in Beagh, three kilometers from Ardara, and seven nearly houseless kilometers from Kiltoorish. McGuinness and friends would have cycled through Beagh en route to Ardara on the morning of 16 June, and it was likely here or in Sandfield, immediately to the north, that they left the road to cut across the strand on the way back to their billets.

In June 1921, my grandfather was a Volunteer in the Kilclooney company of the IRA; its district abutted that of the Rosbeg company to the west and Ardara to the south. Here, the arrival of the column would have been a big deal—now, things were going to get serious. Hitherto, there had been attacks on barracks, including the burning of outposts that the Constabulary had abandoned, and there had been some sniping at convoys and patrols, all of which required scouting and "screening," the posting of sentries, and road cutting. However, a lack of weapons hampered local companies. In August 1920, when twelve IRA men confronted four RIC men on the Main Street in Ardara and called on them to put up their hands, one of the constables took a revolver bullet in the hand but another received over one hundred pellets—he had been blasted by a humble shotgun—and the "ambush" became a fist fight that ended with the constables escaping into Teague Breslin's and John Sweeney's, two pubs.[69] Indeed, the most sensational event in the district, the killing of Major George Hamilton Johnstone, was apparently an accident: on 28 August 1920, when the IRA raided Eden, Johnstone's home in Rosbeg, for weapons, one of their number had supposedly panicked and fired a shot when the popular, hard-living old bluffer, obligingly reached for his gun to hand it over.[70] Now, there would be more and better weapons and more experienced men who knew what to do with them, that is, fellows, like Sheerin and McGuinness, Callan and Martin, in whom, in a phrase of Sheerin's, the "killing instinct" seems to have been awakened by the fighting in Derry the previous summer. Still, if the arrival of the column in mid-June caused a certain frisson, it was all over in the second week of July.

In later years, my grandfather either said little about 1919–1921 or else little of what he said is remembered, and so we say now that he said little. But, for sure, when I was a child, in the 1970s, he pointed to the handlebars of his big black bicycle, saying it was there he had hidden dispatches from the Tans. He had another yarn of how on a night that the barracks in Ardara was to be attacked, only for the plan to be aborted, a man posted as a sentry and ordered to let nobody pass arrested the Volunteer who came with orders to stand down. And he was remembered too, by my late father, as having made mention of carrying supplies to a man named Sheerin, whom he used to meet behind Beagh School.

There is another connection between Mick Sheerin and Néillidh Sweeney—an anecdote about the eerie silence when the gunfire had ceased and the Tans had pulled out of Rosbeg. In Sheerin's telling, "The whole area was deserted, not a human being anywhere. We went into a house. An old woman was saying her rosary and she told us there had been a terrible battle and many people were killed."[71] It is the humor of a man who has had a narrow escape, a talking down of danger, a distancing of himself from death. For all the shooting, there had been no "terrible battle." Nobody had been killed, but four or more young men might have been left for dead on the strand. My grandfather had the anecdote verbatim, albeit prefaced by something like "Some men went into a house. . . ."

It seems now a whisper, carried across time, from behind the School in Beagh, where two young fellows used to meet, in summer 1921, when they thought that they would do great things and unknown was the imminence of failure.

Toward the end of his memoir, Mick Sheerin pays tribute to the "unrecognised and unsung real hero of the period—the ordinary Volunteer in the remote company who never let us down": "He may not have had much conception of aims and objects. He did what he was told to do and did it well. All the chores fell to his lot. He was mainly unarmed and untrained and had to sacrifice himself to capture and ill-treatment by the enemy. The glamour boys of the period—the members of the Column—would have had a short existence without his services."[72]

Such was Néillidh Sweeney—no glamour boy, an ordinary Volunteer in a remote company. His name is not among those listed in IRA records as being under arms in any action around Ardara; indeed, his name is not included in some rolls of company members, although two brothers, Johnny and Joe, the latter of whom had left for the States in 1920 before things got serious, did make the cut. Still, my grandfather got his pension, and in the 1950s when he got John McGill to replace the thatch on the family home with slate, the contractor came on a forgotten stash of dum-dum bullets.

As for the glamour boys—the members of the columns, fellows with rifles and parabellums not shotguns—Sheerin remarks on what became of those men whom he knew best. Here again, there is a concern to refute aspersions then being cast upon the IRA: "The youths of to-day have the impression that all real IRA men were fixed up in some sort of menial State employment, subsequent to the Treaty, where they invariably misbehaved themselves, were fired and ended their days in the South Dublin Union [municipal hospital]. I think I should, therefore, record the subsequent trend in the lives of those I knew."[73]

And so, he tells how Alfie McCallion became waterworks superintendent in Detroit and a "personality in American politics," meaning city politics, and how Ginger Callan emigrated to London, where he became a "constructional engineer of some note" and "supplied a large family to the British services." The details on McCallion are largely correct, but it was in Dearborn not Detroit, Michigan, that he was head of the waterworks. However, the details on Callan are wrong. In May 1929, he had emigrated to America, but returned to Ireland alone, unmarried, in July 1935—too late to have many sons in the British service in 1952—and then, after a period in London, he left for South Africa in February 1938; he returned to Europe in June 1939, lived in Glasgow during the war, and married a miner's daughter in Bathgate High Church in 1942; he and his wife Elizabeth (b. 1916) then moved permanently, with a five-year-old daughter, to South Africa in April 1948.[74]

Hughie Martin, Sheerin continues, became a journalist in America. That is not true—Martin was never in America. But he did have aspirations to be a journalist. Sheerin also reports that the film *Odd Man Out* (1947) "is said to be based" upon Martin's experience fleeing wounded through Derry in 1920: "It reflects the atmosphere very well except the Royal Ulster Constabulary is substituted for the RIC and glamorized. The IRA is, of course, toned down." That claim about *Odd Man Out* being based on an episode in Martin's career is probably untrue, although, intriguingly, his brother Frank lived in Belfast in the 1930s and 1940s when F. L. Green, the author of the novel (1945) on which the movie is based, was also resident there, and he was in London in January 1947, when it received its world premiere.[75]

Finally, Sheerin says that Martin went to Australia where he founded "the Martin Gang of ill fame."[76] That is true. When Hughie Martin quit the Army in 1926, he immediately left his wife and family to go to Australia. The passenger list on the outbound voyage gives his occupation as journalist.[77] And so does his prison record: he was convicted in

Melbourne, in April 1932, of shooting plainclothes constable Charles Derham the previous November. Derham had been escorting a payroll party of G. J. Coles, Australia's largest chain store, when Martin's gang had swooped; Martin had shot him twice in the head, but he survived, saving the shooter from the gallows. He was further convicted, with James Adams and Harold Williams (the latter wrongly), of stealing £980 in that incident, and with robbing £11 10s from a service station, jewelry valued at £500 from a pawnbroker, and £799 from the Commercial Bank of Australia. Martin, who had escaped to Sydney after the "Coles Hold Up," had been captured only when he returned to Melbourne to free arrested associates and, not unlike Johnny McQueen, the central character in *Odd Man Out*, he was informed upon; the press reported that he had published a crime novel in Ireland and notebooks were found in his possession "with notes on poems, [a] novel, and crime stories he was writing."[78]

Martin received fifteen strokes of the lash and did fifteen years in Pentridge Prison.[79] On his release in 1947, he won a legal challenge to his deportation and that, indeed, may explain Sheerin's association of him with *Odd Man Out*: his name was appearing in the Irish press in spring 1947, when the movie was filling theaters.[80] Unknown to Sheerin when he wrote his witness statement, Martin had been again before the courts in 1951 charged with shop breaking and stealing. "It is tragic to see a man of your years going back into gaol," Judge Joseph Francis Mulvany told him, when sentencing him to three years.[81] On release, he settled in Blackwood, an old gold mining town, eighty-nine kilometers northwest of Melbourne, in what is now the Wombat State Forest. There, he worked as a painter and lived alone in a log cabin, drinking occasionally in the local pub. He took ill in 1965 and died in hospital in Ballarat. A memoir of him, by a friend and neighbor, appeared in a local magazine in 2020; it remembered him as "a fine man—a good-looking Irishman . . . [a] taciturn, lonely, gentle-natured man . . . [who] just wanted to be left in peace."[82]

Charlie McGuinness also mentions Hughie Martin's troubles in Australia in *Nomad*, but, from him, there is no hint of reproach. Martin had stood with him against the Tans, and nothing—not taking the wrong side in the Civil War, not shooting a cop in Australia—would ever outweigh it. His own statement of a fact is followed by an emphatic equivocation: "In 1933 he received a severe sentence of penal servitude in Sydney, Australia, for organized banditry and attempted murder. That may be true, but Hughie was a gallant Republican soldier when I knew him, and a most loyal comrade."[83] It is a matter-of-fact way of saying that no facts matter, other than the fact that, when it mattered, Hughie had been true.

And that was Mick Sheerin's attitude to McGuinness, whose "serious mistakes" he glosses over: "Charlie McGuinness established a successful rumrunning business on the Pacific and Atlantic Coasts of America. He had a large fleet of vessels. He wrote several books still in circulation and was in good demand as a radio speaker. He made serious mistakes later and was ultimately lost at sea."[84] With that, Sheerin abruptly wraps up his reminiscences about the later lives of his comrades, emphasizing that, contra the allegations of the "youths of today" about the IRA, none had ever been in the South Dublin Union: "I won't trouble the reader further with the subsequent lives of these men. They were ill-equipped to lead a normal life. Some were broken in health; all were frustrated and easy targets for exploitation; many were absorbed into the American Gangs of the late twenties and thirties, but none of them has entered the portals of the SDU yet." He closes his memoir with no hint of rancor, only regret, and a wish that the young would succeed where his generation had "failed":

> I think it is fitting I should close this narration by paying a tribute to Alfred McCallion, Kathleen McGuinness, Charlie McGuinness, Danny Duggan [sic] and Paddy [sic] McHugh, four very gallant boys and one resourceful girl who, in succession, rescued me from imminent danger and provided me with the borrowed time in which I regret to say I had no opportunity to repay them, [and] to the many families in the city of Derry and the hamlets of the Hills of Donegal who sheltered, fed and assisted us at great personal risk, who were prepared to receive us at all hours day and night, sacrifice their homesteads and children for an ideal, and to assure their descendants it was no fault of theirs we failed. I hope when their effort is made it won't entail so much pain and frustration and that it will be crowned with complete success.[85]

There is magnanimity in that roll call. Alfie McCallion, Charlie McGuinness, and Kathleen McGuinness, all of Derry, had opposed the Treaty. Packie McHugh of Ardara had been neutral; the position, in 1922–1923, of Danny Doogan of Glenties, who had fought with the column at Kilraine, is uncertain, but he was associated with Fianna Fáil in the thirties, suggesting he too had been either neutral or opposed the Treaty.

Sheerin himself accepted it.

## A Lost Generation

> So we beat on, boats against the current, borne back ceaselessly into the past.
> —F. Scott Fitzgerald, *The Great Gatsby*

Mick Sheerin joined the Free State army, aged twenty-one, in February 1922, and he rose through the ranks, becoming an acting commandant in the Aer Corps in 1940 and a commandant in 1947; he was remembered by his juniors more for his proficiency with revolvers than any enthusiasm for flying. He retired in 1957.[86] And of all that he says next to nothing. In his telling, within weeks of the Truce, the column had been disbanded, and, after a course in Glenasmole, he was appointed a paid official in charge of the civil administration in south Donegal. "When the Treaty was signed," he wrote, "I was just one of the many displaced persons of the period. The struggle was over. We were not the victors and the struggle for an existence commenced. In [February] 1922, I joined the Free State Army with the rank of Captain. That is another story."[87]

That story can be told. In his first year in the regular army, when the South slid into Civil War, Sheerin served in Donegal—in Glenties, from February 1922; Donegal Town, from August; and Finner Camp, from November—and then for a few weeks, from January 1923, in Drumkeeran, County Leitrim. On 10 February 1923, he was appointed officer commanding the machine gun company of the Third Infantry Battalion, which was attached to the Donegal Command, and sent to Drumboe Castle, outside Stranorlar.[88] There, the general officer commanding was Joe Sweeney, with whom Sheerin had contact during the Tan War. Among anti-Treaty prisoners in the Castle were eight men belonging to a column captured at Mín na bPoll, in northwest Donegal, the previous November. Sweeney had been friendly with their leader, Charlie Daly, in university in Galway in 1917–1918. Now, his friend's gaoler, he received orders that Daly and three of the men taken with him—Timothy O'Sullivan and Daniel Enright, both, like Daly, from Kerry, and Sean Larkin, from Derry—were to be executed in reprisal for the shooting dead, in contested circumstances, of a Free State soldier in Creeslough. Sweeney questioned the order and investigated claims that the soldier had been shot in a dispute with comrades not by "Irregulars." But the same order came back, and Sweeney complied, picking the firing squad that, on 14 March 1923, dispatched four young fellows, two aged twenty-three and two aged twenty-six.

Sweeney himself was not in Drumboe when the executions took place. Repulsed at the "barbarous system" whereby the provost marshal had to deliver the coup de grâce through the heart to each of the executed men, he had left the Castle and that grisly duty to Mick Sheerin: it was Sheerin, aged twenty-two, who presided as detail officer at the executions.[89]

My grandfather, who took the Republican side in the Civil War, doubtless knew that the man whom he used to meet behind the school in summer 1921 had enlisted, for Sheerin was in Glenties in the spring and summer of 1922. But I do not know, and no one can now tell me, if he knew of the orders that Sheerin followed and, indeed, the orders that he gave in the woods of Drumboe in March 1923. And I cannot but wonder, if told, might he have echoed what Charlie McGuinness said of Hughie Martin: *That may be true, but he was a gallant Republican soldier when I knew him, and a most loyal comrade.*

Mick Sheerin and Néillidh Sweeney, whose paths crossed in the pregnant summer of 1921, had been born within two months of each other in the first year of the twentieth century—Sheerin on 26 September and Sweeney on 11 November. And they died within seven months of each other toward its end—Sheerin in Dublin on 8 August 1985; my grandfather in Donegal on 20 February 1986.

Alfie McCallion, also born in late 1900, died between them, on 11 September 1985, in Michigan; he had lived there for six decades. And many other IRA men died far from the country for which they had fought. From 1935, when there was the prospect of pensions, the surviving staff of IRA battalions commenced compiling rolls of Volunteers active before the Truce: there had been ninety-seven Volunteers attached to A Company (Ardara) in mid-1921; by the late 1930s, twenty-four were in the States, five in England, and two in Scotland.[90] Those figures are far from precise: Francie Kennedy of Tullybeg, listed as being in the States, was in New Zealand and Johnny Sweeney of Beagh was then in the States not at home, as he is listed; they were granduncles of mine.[91] But the loss is clear, about a third were gone. And among that third were some of the most active men—Charles, Andy and Peter McNeilis of Meenavalley, Dan McTeague of Aighe, wounded in Kilraine, and Charles Luke Brennan and Paddy Reilly of the town, the latter captured in Rosbeg with McGuinness. And it was the same in other companies: many, including many of the best, had left.

In later years, when emigrants who had done well abroad returned on holiday or to retire, mention would be made in the local press of their attainments and a nod given to their IRA service. Less ubiquitous were those IRA veterans who, in Sheerin's terms, were "ill-equipped for normal life," "broken in health," "frustrated," and "easy targets for exploitation," who had "drifted" abroad—except, that is, when, like Hughie Martin, they made the news for the wrong reasons.[92] And, of course, some were literally lost. Johnny Sweeney, who left for the States in 1922, lived for periods with his brothers in Oakland, California: but, in time, he "drifted" and they lost track of him.[93] Lost too was Eddie Deane, an IRA man who had trained Mick Sheerin, Alfie McCallion, and the core of the Derry Volunteers in his boxing club: the last thing heard of him in Derry after 1920 was that he was in Perth, Australia.[94]

But there were men "lost" at home too. Doiminic Ó Ceallaigh was the son of a schoolmaster in Doochary. An excellent student—he ranked second in a national examination in 1913—he took a degree in philosophy in Rome, but returned to Ireland in 1918 and joined the IRA. In 1922, he rejected the Treaty and, thereafter, trained as a teacher, taught in good schools, including Belvedere and Blackrock, published on language acquisition in scholarly journals and held positions in cultural organizations, state bodies, and Fianna Fáil. However, his career came undone after a personal crisis in 1939. He returned to teaching in 1943, spending short periods in Lifford, County Donegal; St James Well and Geevagh, both in Sligo; and Claremorris and Ballina, both in Mayo, but he never fulfilled his early promise. In 1960, the year that he retired, a reviewer of a collection of his poetry discerned in it "the profound sadness and frustration of a man who has suffered much." Asked around that time to define "what impact the achievement of our freedom had on him," Ó Ceallaigh replied, "A great disillusionment."[95]

Here, as elsewhere in Ireland, some veterans found an antidote to disillusionment in pride in the southern state or their party, but, in a border-severed, impoverished region, that panacea was never as potent as in other places. In the early 1950s, when Sheerin wrote his memoir, there was a push to get decent pensions for all who had been active in 1916–1921, now represented as "five glorious years." Conspicuous in that campaign, from 1951, was Joe Sweeney. After the Civil War, Sweeney, although a sitting TD, had opted not to contest the general election. He remained in the army, rising to become chief of staff. On leaving the military, in 1940, he took an executive position with an insurance company and then, in retirement, ran the Irish Red Cross. The veterans' campaign, some republicans suspected, was an attempt by "Butcher Sweeney" to "rehabilitate" himself.[96] Through the mid-1950s, he appeared at gatherings around the country, including, in May 1954, as the main speaker at a meeting, for Donegal and Derry veterans, in the Butt Hall, Ballybofey, across the Finn from Drumboe. Inevitably, his presence there summoned the ghosts of 1923. Chairing proceedings, Seán Mac Lochlainn, the county manager, said they were "especially indebted" to Sweeney for attending: "If their meeting did nothing but to help to remove the bitterness of the Civil War it would have been well worthwhile."

The phrase "five glorious years" was much used that night, from the platform and the floor, including by Sweeney; the headline on the *Derry Journal*'s report was "Derry and Donegal Old IRA Men Meet— Better Treatment Sought for 'Five Glorious Years' Veterans." Sweeney's own contribution was to tell those veterans that, if they organized, they could get their pensions increased from five shillings per week to one pound (twenty shillings). He wanted justice, he said, "for the men through whose activities this State was founded, irrespective of what side they fought on in the Civil War—a period that is best forgotten."

The phrasing was practiced, the delivery deliberate: none in attendance had fought in 1916–1921 for the establishment of "this State," and there were men present who had opposed its establishment in arms.[97] But they were in their fifties or older now, and most of those who had rejected the Treaty had come, through Fianna Fáil, to accept "this State," and their party had done, in power, what they had deplored Sweeney for doing during the Civil War: it had allowed the execution of Republicans. They were hard times too, the 1950s: many of them had use for another few shillings a week. Now, for the southern establishment, "the men through whose activities this State was founded" and "five glorious years" were convenient formulae; and if the Civil War was "best forgotten," so was failure, and so too, for all the lip service about reunification, was the North. IRA veterans would receive many plaudits in 1966, the fiftieth anniversary of the Rising, but in 1969, when it was time to mark the Tan War, laid bare again, by events in the North, was the cost of their failure.[98]

Did Joe Sweeney ever forget the Civil War? He admitted that he tried. "It's very hard to describe a war among brothers," he told an interviewer in the 1960s. "It was fierce and it was atrocious. You had family against family and brother against brother, and I've tried to wipe it out of my mind as much as possible because it is not pleasant to think about."[99]

## And One That Got Away?

Charlie McGuinness's sale of a boat, purchased with IRA money, left him in malodor with both sides after the Civil War. The 1920s saw him settle briefly in China and then Long Island, New York, before joining Admiral Richard E. Byrd's expedition to Antarctica. He moved between the States and the Soviet Union and back again, and then, in his forties, in 1937, he decided to go to Spain; he went out a republican and came home to write articles for the *Independent* praising Franco.

Other mistakes followed. On his uppers, his IRA record had got him a pension and, in April 1941, a job training naval cadets in Haulbowline, but in 1942 the Special Criminal Court gave him ten years for attempting to communicate with the German legation in Dublin; he lost his pension. Released in 1945, he came to public attention in May

1947, when he was among two hundred mourners at the funeral of Herman Goertz, a German agent who had been interned with him during the war; a Swastika was draped on the coffin, and some mourners gave the Nazi salute.[100] Then, at the end of that year, McGuinness was lost at sea, when the *Isallt* taking a cargo of manure—and a shady English businessman, Arthur Harris, accompanied by a woman-not-his-wife, Mary Young—from Dublin to Waterford was driven onto rocks off Ballymoney Strand in the early hours of 5 December.

Or was he lost at sea? Harris and Young and two crew members, Thomas Corkish and Patrick Kelly, were drowned, but the body of McGuinness, the skipper, was never recovered. The ship had foundered less than a hundred meters from land, and two young deckhands, Jack Corkish and Joe Whelan, managed to swim ashore—and McGuinness was a strong swimmer.[101]

His first wife had no doubts. "Of course that bastard never went down with the ship," she told a grandchild. And a nephew swore that, in 1955, going down an escalator to the London Underground, he saw Uncle Charlie coming up on the other side. Charlie smiled, he said, and he spoke four words. "You never saw me."[102]

## NOTES

Friends and family members discussed some of the concerns of this essay with me over the past few years. Among them, around Ardara, are Ruth Barton, Francie Dorrian, Gerard Given, Conall Kennedy, Vincent McConnell, Pat McGrath, and Michael Nicholson; and further afield are Éamonn Ó Ciardha, Claire Connolly, Luke Gibbons, Adrian Grant, Laurence Marley, Jim McGill, Kerby A. Miller, Cormac Ó Gráda, Brendan O'Leary, John Ó Néill, Gearóid Ó Tuathaigh, and Jim Smyth. I am grateful to them all. Sadly, three people who commented insightfully on passages assembled here died in 2020–2021 before the essay's completion and cannot now be thanked: Seamus Deane, Tommy Smith, and my father Patsy Sweeney.

1 Robert Briscoe, *For the Life of Me* (London: Longmans, 1959), 96–102. For McGuinness's account of running guns, see Charles John McGuinness, *Nomad: Memoirs of an Irish Sailor, Soldier, Pearl-Fisher, Pirate, Gun-Runner, Rum-Runner, Rebel and Antarctic Explorer* (London: Methuen, 1934), 161–191. Also see John McGuffin and Joseph Mulheron, *Charles "Nomad" McGuinness: Being a True Account of the Amazing Adventures of a Derryman* (Derry: Irish Resistance Books, 2002), chaps. 5–6. And for a wider view of the IRA's efforts to acquire arms, see Brian Hanley, "'Very Dangerous Places': IRA Gunrunning and the Post-war Underworld," in *The Irish Revolution 1919–21: A Global History* (Dublin: History Ireland, 2019), 23–26.

2 Seán MacBride, *That Day's Struggle: A Memoir, 1904–1951* (Blackrock: Currach Press, 2005), 47–48.

3 On these columns, see Adrian Grant, *Derry: The Irish Revolution, 1912–23* (Dublin: Four Courts Press, 2018), chap. 7; Okan Ozseker, *Forging the Border: Donegal and Derry in Times of Revolution* (Dublin: Irish Academic Press, 2019), chap. 6.

4 Joseph Sweeney describes the "round-up" in "Donegal in the War of Independence," *Capuchin Annual* (1970): 425–445, 441–442.

5 Sweeney, in conversation with O'Malley, in 1949, in Síobhra Aiken et al., eds., *Ernie O'Malley's Interviews with the Northern Divisions* (Dublin: Merrion Press, 2018), 31.

6 Neil Gillespie in Uinseann Mac Eoin, *Survivors* (Dublin: Argenta Press, 1980), 162.

7 Sean O'Faolain, *Vive Moi! An Autobiography* (1963; London: Rupert Hart-Davis, 1965), 145.

8 John Berger, *Pig Earth* (1979; New York: Vintage, 1992), xxiv.

9 Mick Sheerin witness statement (WS), Military Archives (MA), Bureau of Military History (BMH), 14. Also see Grant, *Derry*, 6–7.

10 Either the memoir was not completed or only a single chapter survives; Ted Zimbo kindly provided a copy. Also see Ted Zimbo, *McCallions in the IRA* (Michigan: privately published, 2019).

11 R. F. Foster, *Vivid Faces: The Revolutionary Generation in Ireland, 1880–1923* (London: Penguin, 2014), 1.

12 John Berger, *About Looking* (1980; New York: Vintage, 1991), 108.

13 I make this argument in *The End of Outrage: Post-famine Adjustment in Rural Ireland* (Oxford: Oxford University Press, 2017), 245–250, 258–259.

14 Mac Eoin, *Survivors*, 161: "He had no interest in politics; he did not even know what Home Rule was."

15 Fernand Braudel, *The Mediterranean and the Mediterranean World in the Age of Philip II*, 2 vols., trans. Sian Reynolds (1949; New York: Harper & Row, 1972), 1:34.

16 McGuinness, *Nomad*, 142–143.

17 On the region, see Kerby A. Miller and Brian Gurrin, "The Derry Watershed: Its Religious and Political Demography, 1622–1911," *Field Day Review* 9 (2013): 38–53.

18 McGuinness, *Nomad*, v–vi.

19 Pax Ó Faoláin in Mac Eoin, *Survivors*, 141–142.

20 *Northern Whig*, 23 Feb. 1935; *Irish Times*, 27 Nov. 1937.

21 McGuinness, *Nomad*, v–vii.

22 Ibid., 95, 108, 140.

23 Ibid., 123–127, 134.

24 Ibid., 123–127. Later, in 1937, when interviewed by officials about his pension application, McGuinness remarked, "I lost two in the Poison Glen, trying to hit them [the British] up. They were not killed. They were captured." See "Sworn Statement . . . by Charles John McGuinness 31.3.37," 4, in MA, MSP34REF215. They were John "Dip" Kennedy and Dom Doherty, both of Derry.

25 Mac Eoin, *Survivors*, 140.

26  Nancy Wyse Power, BMH, WS 732:16; J. N. Beaumont, BMH, WS 709: 6–7. Wyse Power recalled that McGuinness proposed cutting an oil pipeline in the Persian Gulf to harass the British.

27  McGuffin and Mulheron, *Charles "Nomad" McGuinness*, 99–100.

28  On these inconsistencies, see ibid., 231–234.

29  McGuinness, *Nomad*, 119–120. For analyses of the violence of June 1920, see Grant, *Derry*, 98–101, and Ozseker, *Forging the Border*, 146–154.

30  *Derry Journal*, 2 July 1920. Eliza Shannon had been born in 1865 in England, where her father, John (1830–1895), was serving as a sergeant with the Irish Rifles; he later served as a sergeant in the Constabulary. See the notice of his death at 44 Elmwood Street in *Derry Journal*, 1 Mar. 1895. Her husband, James (m. 1888), was a native of Lismoghry, near Saint Johnston, County Donegal, where they lived into the early 1900s.

31  Details from the inquests on Mills and McLaughlin in *Londonderry Sentinel*, 8 July 1920. McGuffin and Mulheron, *Charles "Nomad" McGuinness*, 63n7, identify the woman shot by McGuinness as Mills; Grant, *Derry*, 101, 164n95, argues that she may have been either Moore or Mills. But confirming that the woman was Moore, a coroner's inquest heard that Mills, from Orchard Row, was shot going down Ferguson Street on the evening of 23 June; also, only two shots were fired at her, and only one hit her. But Moore was shot multiple times at or near the door of her house, 105 Bishop Street, on the same morning, 24 June, that McLaughlin was killed when he failed to get into 99 Bishop Street; see *Derry Journal*, 2 July 1920, for the Moore inquest. Consistent with McGuinness's account, *Derry Journal*, 25 June 1920, reported that, for a period, no one would risk recovering McLaughlin's body as the spot where it lay was covered by "Unionist snipers." Still, in considering McGuinness's account of this incident and other incidents in the Tan War, note that he himself compiled a scrapbook of newspaper clippings, which may well have inflected his own versions of events in *Nomad* and his pension claim. For a reference to the scrapbook, see "Sworn Statement . . . by Charles John McGuinness 31.3.37," 3.

32  Mac Eoin, *Survivors*, 150 n. 5.

33  McGuinness, *Nomad*, chap. 16.

34  *Londonderry Sentinel*, 18 June 1921; *Derry Journal*, 1 Aug. 1921.

35  McGuinness, *Nomad*, 150.

36  Ibid., chap. 17.

37  Ibid., 150–152; Sheerin WS, 25–26.

38  McGuinness, *Nomad*, 146–147.

39  "Sworn Statement . . . by Charles John McGuinness 31.3.37," 3–4.

40  "Statement of Service, 1920–1922," received 3 May 1937, in MA, MSP34REF215.

41  Contra the BMH's witness statements, McGuinness's pension file includes many negative remarks on his character, causing one official to wonder at what point he had gone "crooked": see notes on an interview with Frank Martin (24 Feb. 1939).

42  *Dublin Evening Telegraph*, 17 June 1921.

43  Information supplied by Sally Chowela, Royal Bank of Scotland Archives.

44 Sheerin WS, 33–34. The "men for whom bugles and trumpets had blown" alludes to Joe Sweeney, TD for Donegal West and officer commanding the First Brigade, who became chief of staff of the army.

45 Sheerin WS, 1–5.

46 Ibid., 21; Joe Sweeney in Aiken et al., *Ernie O'Malley's Interviews*, 30.

47 For Martin's IRA activities, see Military Archives (MA), 24/SP/11738; his file includes material supporting his pension application, from, inter alia, Sheerin and Callan.

48 Sheerin WS, 21.

49 McGuinness, *Nomad*, 164.

50 National Archives of Ireland (NAI), Census 1911: 50, Drummullan, Springhill, Londonderry.

51 NAI, Census 1911: 16, Union Street, Londonderry Urban (4).

52 Sheerin WS, 22.

53 MA, MSPC, RO 373.

54 Sheerin WS, 22–23.

55 Ibid., 23–24.

56 Ibid., 25–26.

57 MA, 24/SP/11738.

58 Liam Briody, *Glenties and Innishkeel* (Ballyshannon: Donegal Democrat, 1986), 167.

59 Sheerin WS, 25.

60 P. J. MacGill, *History of the Parish of Ardara* (Ballyshannon: Donegal Democrat, 1970), 111–112.

61 Sheerin WS, 23.

62 Ibid., 26–29.

63 Ibid., 31.

64 *Londonderry Sentinel*, 8 Oct. 1921.

65 Cloghan, 26 June 1948, E. J. Mullen to Secretary, BMH, MA, BMH, WS 133.

66 *Strabane Chronicle*, 23 July 1921; *Derry People*, 23 July 1923; *Freeman's Journal*, 23 July 1921.

67 The places of birth of the Manleys' children are in the family's 1871 census return. The 1901 census entry for Mary Manley, when she was living with Jane Devine, her daughter, gives Cork as her place of birth; it gives Tom Devine Sr.'s birthplace as Mayo.

68 *Belfast Newsletter*, 4 Aug. 1921; *Londonderry Sentinel*, 8 Oct. 1921.

69 MA, MSPC/A/42 (1).

70 *Derry Journal*, 1 Sept. 1920; *Irish Times*, 4 Sept. 1920. The incident is noted but not detailed in "brigade reports" compiled in the late 1930s: MA, MSPC/A/42 (1).

71 Sheerin WS, 23.

72 Ibid., 29.

73 Ibid., 31.

74 Ibid., 32.

75 On Frank Martin having been in London in January 1947, see his application for a medal in December 1946, in MA, 24D8.

76  Sheerin WS, 32.

77  Passenger list of SS *Barradine*, leaving London for Sydney, 30 Sept. 1926.

78  *Melbourne Herald*, 26 Apr. 1932. *Truth*, 5 June 1932, gives details of his literary work.

79  Public Record Office, Victoria, Prison Register: Central Register of Male Prisoners, VPRS 515: Hugh Martin 42,001.

80  *Melbourne Herald*, 21 June 1947.

81  *Melbourne Age*, 4 Apr. 1951.

82  [Reg Bradley], "Hughie Martin," *Blackwood Times* 12, no. 13:2 (2020): 13.

83  McGuinness, *Nomad*, 152.

84  Sheerin WS, 32–33.

85  Ibid., 33.

86  Michael C. O'Malley, *Military Aviation in Ireland* (Dublin: UCD Press, 2010), 257–258.

87  Sheerin WS, 31.

88  Details supplied by the Military Archives.

89  J. J. Silke, "The Drumboe Martyrs," *Donegal Annual* 60 (2008): 167–174, 173.

90  MA, MSPC, RO 373: List of Members of A. Company as on 11 July 1921.

91  Kennedy, aged thirty-six, left Southampton for New Zealand at the end of April 1929. On Sweeney, see Mac Suibhne, *End of Outrage*, 258–259, 261–262.

92  Sheerin WS, 33: "At the outbreak of the Civil War [IRA men] joined the contestants in approximately equal numbers. The victors got rid of their adherents when it was over as easily and quickly as possible. The vanquished could do nothing about theirs. They left the scene of their endeavours in the traditional way. They drifted to America, mainly through Canada."

     In 1949, Hughie Martin's Australian lawyer, lobbying for the restoration of his pension, wrote, "Martin is now unfit for hard work. He has no skill at any trade, his only qualification being that of an ex-soldier of Éire. I am very anxious that he should not *drift* as he did when caught by the depression of 1930/32." See *Melbourne*, 30 Sept. 1949, J. M. Cullity to Seán Mac Eoin, in 24SP11738, emphasis added. Interestingly, Sheerin, writing in support of Martin's pension application in late 1925, had worried that there could be trouble ahead: "Through his Volunteer activities & injuries he received, applicant will have difficulty finding suitable employment when he returns to civic life." See R5/24SP11738.

93  Mac Suibhne, *End of Outrage*, 261–262.

94  "Uncle Eddie" figures in Seamus Deane's *Reading in the Dark* (New York: Knopf, 1996).

95  *Donegal Democrat*, 13 May 1960.

96  Moss Donegan to Florence O'Donoghue, 16 Sept. 1952, quoted in Ozseker, *Forging the Border*, 192.

97  *Derry Journal*, 26 May 1954.

98  For the perspective, in 1981, of one Derry veteran of the Tan War and Civil War on the later conflict, see Breandán Mac Suibhne, "Resolve, 7 July 1922," in *Ireland 1922: Independence, Partition, Civil War*, ed. Darragh Gannon and Fearghal McGarry

(Dublin: Royal Irish Academy, forthcoming); the veteran is George McCallion, a brother of Alfie who features in the present essay.

99 Kenneth Griffith and Timothy E. O'Grady, *Curious Journey: An Oral History of Ireland's Unfinished Revolution* (London: Hutchinson, 1982), 305–306.

100 *Irish Times*, 27 May 1947.

101 *Irish Times*, 6 Dec. 1947.

102 McGuffin and Mulheron, *Charles "Nomad" McGuinness*, 214–215, add that his son Patrick claimed to have met his father about 1950; Patrick would have been about twenty-seven at the time.

# PART THREE

# Imperial Perspectives

# 8

# British Imperial Intelligence and Anticolonial Revolutionaries during and after the Great War

## MICHAEL SILVESTRI

The decade surrounding the Great War was a formative period for British intelligence agencies such as MI5 and SIS (MI6).[1] The British Empire faced an array of threats and perceived threats not only from Imperial Germany but from diverse nationalist and anticolonial groups. To assess and counter these challenges, Britain's nascent intelligence apparatus drew upon a cadre of colonial police, military, and civil service officers. This chapter examines how officers with experience in intelligence work against Indian revolutionaries sought to apply their experience in combatting anticolonial resistance in both North America during the Great War and Ireland during the War of Independence.

The particular focus is on intelligence officers and their agents who were Irish or had Irish connections. Interaction and interchange between Irish and Indian nationalists during the Great War and in the interwar period formed an important dimension of the Irish imperial experience.[2] Ireland's engagement with the British Empire took a variety of forms, however, and the multifaceted Irish imperial experience cannot be reduced to simply "Irish anti-imperialism" (or, for that matter, Irish imperialism).[3] The imperial careers of Indian Civil Service officer Robert Nathan, the brother of Matthew Nathan, undersecretary for Ireland at the time of the Easter Rising, and the Protestant Irishman Charles Tegart, Indian police officer and expert on "Indian terrorism," illustrate aspects of Ireland's engagement with empire. The intelligence work of officers such as Nathan, Tegart, and others demonstrates how issues of colonial governance within the British Empire did not simply emanate from the imperial center, as well as the complexity of imperial networks during Ireland's revolutionary decade.

Prior to the Great War, British intelligence operations in North America against Indian revolutionaries were both small in scale and ad hoc, centered around the former Calcutta police inspector William Hopkinson, who styled himself as an expert in Indian revolutionary matters.[4] Hopkinson's efforts at investigation and surveillance were directed primarily against the Indian revolutionary group known as Ghadar. Established in 1913 among Indian migrants, chiefly Punjabi Sikhs and Indian students on the West Coast of North America, the Ghadar Party sought to achieve Indian independence through armed revolution.[5] Hopkinson first reported to the governor-general of Canada, and after a time advising US immigration officials in San Francisco became an agent for the newly established office of Indian Political Intelligence (IPI) in London.[6] Hopkinson, whose reports were shot through with racist tropes depicting Indian migrants as deviant and degenerate, emerged as "the Ghadarites' nemesis."[7] His zeal in investigating Indian revolutionaries ultimately led to his demise: Hopkinson was fatally shot by a member of the Sikh community in British Columbia on 21 October 1914.

Anglo-American intelligence collaboration on Indian radical activity intensified during the Great War, as the Ghadar Party collaborated with German government representatives to import arms via Southeast Asia in support of an insurrection in India. Following US entry into the war in 1917, a total of thirty-five Indian subjects and German and US citizens were brought to trial for the violation of US neutrality laws in what became known as the Hindu Conspiracy Case. British officials played an important role in the case, supplying intelligence, interrogating suspects and potential witnesses, and even guarding suspected revolutionaries.

Over the course of the war, the British intelligence presence in North American expanded, particularly after Sir William Wiseman arrived in New York in early 1916 with the brief of establishing a new North American section of MI1c (later MI6 or SIS).[8] Indian police and Indian Civil Service (ICS) officers played a prominent role in MI1c's investigation into wartime revolutionary activity, notably a former ICS officer from a prominent Anglo-Jewish family named Robert Nathan. Although the Nathan family had no prior tradition of imperial service, Robert, along with five of his six brothers, established careers in diverse parts of the British Empire in the late nineteenth and early twentieth centuries.[9] The most well known of the Nathan siblings was Matthew Nathan, who served in succession as governor of the Gold Coast, Hong Kong, and Natal and later as undersecretary of state for Ireland at the time of the Easter Rising.[10]

The Cambridge-educated Robert Nathan, who for a time served as private secretary to Lord Curzon, was in many ways a typical member of the Oxbridge-educated late Victorian elite of British India. In 1914 he was appointed vice-chancellor of Calcutta University but was forced to retire from the ICS because of poor health in the following year.[11] Nathan's career in India also included substantial investigations into nationalist and revolutionary groups in the newly created province of Eastern Bengal and Assam. A significant part of Nathan's duties there involved the collection and analysis of intelligence against the Swadeshi movement, formed to protest the 1905 Partition of Bengal, and clandestine revolutionary organizations. Nathan recommended the formation of "secret service police" in the province to counter the "secret meetings and other secret means" of anticolonial activists.[12]

Following his retirement from the ICS, Nathan served as an interpreter for Indian troops on the Western Front and was subsequently placed on "special duty" for the War Office, where his work with Indian troops almost certainly involved intelligence work of some type, presumably through IPI.[13] Nathan moved to MI5 in 1915 and worked in its A2 Section, which dealt with suspected cases of "Espionage, Sedition and Treachery" in Britain.[14] He became MI5 director Vernon Kell's "main Indian expert" and served along with Kell on the wartime interdepartmental committee on Indian revolutionary activity.[15]

In the following year, Nathan arrived in Vancouver, Canada, as a representative of the India Office and by the end of the year had relocated to New York, where he focused on the surveillance of Indian and, increasingly, Irish revolutionaries in the United States and Canada.[16] Nathan's social background, particularly his Cambridge education (which likely aided in the bond he formed with Wiseman, a baronet who had earned a boxing Blue at Cambridge) and his contacts with the highest levels of Indian colonial administration, was an important factor in his rise in SIS.[17] Nathan's experience with Indian revolutionaries was also undoubtedly a significant factor in his entrée into intelligence work in

North America, where he arrived, in the intelligence historian Richard Spence's words, with "a reputation as a plot smasher in Bengal."[18]

Although historians have reconstructed some of the early activities of the SIS in the United States, Nathan was very discreet about his wartime espionage activities and other facets of his intelligence work. Fellow intelligence officer Norman Thwaites recalled the importance of Nathan preserving "a strict incognito, not only for his own sake, but for the sake of preserving his usefulness. He had a great reputation in India, and had it been known to the seditionists that he was working on the case our quarry would have scuttled to cover."[19] A US Justice Department official wrote in 1920 that "no one seems to have been able to learn his true status or mission. He appeared, however, to be an experienced diplomat, highly educated, a world traveler, and holding a rather important place with the British Government."[20]

Networks of informants formed one of the most important elements in SIS's US organization during and after the Great War, and one of Nathan's main responsibilities was the handling of agents and informers who provided information on anticolonial and later Bolshevik movements.[21] According to the financial records of MI1c's New York office, Indian intelligence work constituted about 10 percent of the work of British intelligence officers there during the latter half of the war. Another thousand dollars was paid for "Western Organization Expenses," which dealt in large part with Indian anticolonial activity on the West Coast. One of Nathan's assistants supervised the work of two regular agents, "M," who was paid seventy-five dollars per month, and "K," who received one hundred.[22] Following Nathan's return to London in 1918, two other officers were subsequently delegated to interview what Wiseman's assistant, the former Mexican diplomat Manuel Del Campo, referred to as "N's [Nathan's] dusky friends."[23]

Nathan also played an important role in another of British intelligence's key functions in the United States in this period: collaboration with US intelligence officials regarding anticolonial and radical activity. While European and North American police often considered one of their prime difficulties in anticolonial surveillance to be the "reading" of "inscrutable" natives, the presence of intelligence officers with colonial experience such as Nathan held out the promise of making the "inscrutable" ways of Indians legible.[24] Norman Thwaites recalled that Nathan "worked hard at knitting up the fragments of information which came to us from all parts of the world."[25] According to Wiseman, Nathan was the first British official to grasp fully the scope of Indo-German wartime collaboration. After reviewing papers seized in a police raid on the home of a German agent, Dr. Chandra K. Chakravarty, Nathan found "that they disclose such an interesting connection with the Germans that . . . the case may become much wider and involve the whole question of plots against the Indian Government in the United States."[26]

Nathan's wartime intelligence duties included surveillance and reporting on Irish as well as Indian nationalists. Nathan had a family connection to the Irish administration through his brother Matthew.[27] The degree to which Matthew's experience as undersecretary of state at Dublin Castle impacted Robert's approach to Irish separatist activity in the United States is unclear. Nathan, as we have seen, disclosed little about his intelligence activities; no correspondence between Robert and Matthew appears in the Matthew Nathan Archive in the Bodleian Libraries.[28] In addition, while both brothers had extensive imperial experience prior to the Great War, the degree to which they applied cross-colonial comparisons varied markedly. Robert Nathan drew extensively on his experience with revolutionary groups in India in his investigative work in North America. In contrast, Matthew Nathan made no effort after the Rising to convey to military authorities his experiences with rebellions among the Ashanti and Zulu in British colonial Africa, information that might have led to greater consideration of clemency for the rebel leadership. In Graham Dominy's judgment, Matthew Nathan's response to the Rising was characterized not by cross-colonial analogies but by "excessive bureaucrat-ism," with disastrous consequences for British authority in Ireland.[29]

Nonetheless, Matthew Nathan's experience of the Easter Rising, which led to his resignation as undersecretary on 3 May 1916, likely made his brother regard Irish revolutionary activity as an even more potent threat. Nathan would also have become familiar with Irish separatists in the United States through his investigative work on Ghadar. During the Great War, Irish separatists in the United States offered legal assistance to the Ghadar revolutionaries on the West Coast and helped to facilitate connections to German diplomatic officials.[30] In early 1917, Nathan detailed the role of Clan na Gael member Larry de Lacey to an agent of the Bureau of Investigation (BOI), the precursor to the FBI. De Lacey had ties to the former Fenian and publisher of the *Gaelic American* John Devoy and the prominent Irish American republican Joseph McGarrity and was involved in Irish arms smuggling efforts. He also attended meetings between Ghadar leaders and German agents discussing plans to ship arms to Indian revolutionaries through Southeast Asia. Nathan described de Lacey as the "Irish brain" of the Indo-German conspiracy and noted that "the entire [Ghadar] movement is so co-related and connected with the German and Irish question that it cannot be considered separately and apart."[31]

Around the same time, Nathan authored a report titled "Some Notes on the Constitution and Activities of the Irish Revolutionary Party in America," which discussed the organization of Clan na Gael and republican publications such as the *Gaelic American*. Nathan included brief biographies of Clan na Gael's executive and other prominent Irish republicans in the United States such as Liam Mellows and Patrick McCartan, noting the role that Irish sailors and stewards played in conveying messages between Clan na Gael and Sinn Féin leaders in Ireland. The analysis of captured papers from German agents demonstrated that Clan na Gael and German representatives met as early as September 1914, though Nathan cautioned that it was still necessary "to collect the evidence showing the part played by the German-Irish conspirators in America in the German directed rising of Easter 1916."[32] Nathan shared a number of his analyses of Irish and Indian revolutionary activity with BOI officers, including the above-referenced report.[33]

While British officials treated with concern at times bordering on alarm the real and imagined collaboration between Irish republicans, German agents, and anticolonial activists, they also attempted to utilize Irish networks and the presumption of Irish sympathy for anticolonial endeavors to their advantage. At Wiseman's request, Basil Thomson, the assistant commissioner of the Metropolitan Police, who worked closely with MI5 and SIS during the Great War, in October 1916 sent the Irish-born Scotland Yard officer John Gillian to New York. In the United States, Gillian supervised the private detective agencies responsible for the protection of British shipping and stores and carried out a security analysis of the British embassy in Washington, D.C.[34]

One of the key collaborators with Robert Nathan and other British intelligence officers in New York was another Irishman, New York police inspector Thomas J. Tunney. Born around 1874, Tunney emigrated from Ireland at the age of fifteen and joined the New York Police Department a few years later. He rose to the rank of captain and headed the detective bureaus of a number of New York City precincts. In August 1914, he was tapped to head the newly created Bomb Squad of the NYPD, formed to combat the use of explosives by the Mafia as well as anarchists.[35] In the judgment of intelligence historian Richard J. Popplewell, the Bomb Squad—renamed the Bomb and Neutrality Squad after the outbreak of war—was "the most efficient undercover agency at the disposal of the American authorities during the First World War."[36] Prior to US entry into the war, Tunney led investigations into German espionage efforts in the New York region, which culminated in the arrest of a number of German agents and the thwarting of plans to blow up key elements of infrastructure such as the Welland Canal between Lake Erie and Lake Ontario.[37]

The Irish-born Tunney had family connections to the Royal Irish Constabulary, and whatever nationalist sentiments he might have held, he clearly had no sympathy with Irish separatism.[38] His memoir of the Bomb Squad's wartime operations, *Throttled!*, contains only one disparaging reference to "the Easter Day affair in Dublin which cost several Sinn Feiners their lives."[39] Indeed, during the war Tunney worked closely with British officers, notably Nathan and Thwaites, in the investigation and interrogation of Indian revolutionary suspects. When German agent Chandra Chakravarty was arrested and interrogated in Manhattan, Nathan passed notes to Tunney that indicated "the line of enquiry to take." Nathan conveyed quotations from intercepted letters and "occasionally a few words of Hindustani" for Tunney to use in his examination, which "shook" the doctor and gave the impression that fellow conspirators had betrayed him.[40] In *Throttled!*, Tunney, at the request of Thwaites, omitted all references to his collaboration with Nathan in his discussion of Indo-German conspiracy.[41] Nonetheless, Tunney made clear his debt to British officers in his analysis of the activities of Indian revolutionaries. Seeing a picture of a revolutionary dressed in a fez, he wrote, "I knew [this] was not an orthodox head-dress for a

Bengalese [*sic*]."[42] While Tunney reported that the Bomb Squad "knew certain East Indians who could be depended upon, and told them to call upon" a suspected revolutionary at his apartment, the informants were more likely to have been the "dusky friends" of Nathan referred to by Del Campo.[43]

At the end of the war, Norman Thwaites praised Tunney as one of the Americans deserving recognition for their substantial assistance to the British intelligence efforts: "It was due to this gentleman's extremely clever cross-examination and untiring energy in the Chakravarty-Secuna case that the San Francisco Hindu conspiracy was exposed, and the conviction of the accused made possible. In a number of other cases Inspector Tunney has been of great service to the British Authorities here."[44]

British intelligence networks also sought to take advantage of the extensive collaboration between Irish and Indian nationalists in this era. British intelligence officers at times posed as Irishmen in order to win the confidence of revolutionaries. In 1907, for example, Indian revolutionary Shyamji Krishnavarma met a man "under the name of O'Brien, posing as a member of the *Gaelic American* staff—trying to gain Varma's trust by declaring his solidarity with a member of this other nation oppressed by British Imperialism."[45] Robert Nathan assumed the identity of an Irish-born informant named "Charles Lamb" in his meetings with a US BOI official on the West Coast, something that both concealed Nathan's identity and provided a plausible source for the information about anticolonial conspiracy that he disclosed.[46] During investigations into Indian and Irish revolutionary activity, a "host of agents and informants working in New York and across the country" supplied British intelligence officers with information.[47] Several prominent agents and informants were Irishmen.

One of these was the Irish American lawyer and art collector John Quinn. The son of Famine-era Irish migrants, Quinn was born and lived his early life in rural Ohio. After attending Harvard Law School, he rose rapidly in the world of corporate law in New York City, at the same time developing a prominent reputation as a patron of the arts. Quinn became an early and influential promotor of modernism in the fields of art and literature, purchasing works by Van Gogh and manuscripts by James Joyce. While he deplored the parochialism of Irish and Irish American society, he also became an enthusiastic supporter of the revived Home Rule movement prior to the Great War. Quinn was consistently moderate in his nationalist politics, supporting "a united, self-governing Ireland that maintained its tie to Great Britain."[48]

Although Quinn initially condemned the Easter Rising, which he termed a "horrible fiasco," his friendship with Roger Casement led him to campaign unsuccessfully for clemency for the Anglo-Irish separatist.[49] At the same time, Quinn strongly supported the Allied cause and was particularly disturbed by republicans' overtures to Germany. In his defense of the Irish Home Rule Convention in 1917, Quinn stressed the need to quash German militarism and criticized how "the Sinn Feiners" had "put the home rule and other Irish questions above the winning of the war."[50] It is thus not surprising that Quinn lent his support to British wartime intelligence gathering against Irish revolutionary activities in the United States.

Quinn was a regular visitor to the British consulate in New York at 44 Whitehall Street, where Wiseman's intelligence section was based. He provided Wiseman and his deputy Thwaites with information from his own political circle and from associates of Casement's, with whom he was in still in contact.[51] In June 1916, Quinn dictated a lengthy memo in Thwaites's presence in which he defended Roger Casement against charges of taking German funds and made an impassioned plea for clemency.[52] The statement, clearly intended for circulation to the British Foreign Office, described Casement as "a fine man but a zealot, exceedingly intense and excitable and reckless to the last degree" and argued that his execution would repeat the "colossal blunder" of the execution of the leaders of the Rising in Dublin, one that would alienate both Irish American and broader American public opinion.[53]

Quinn claimed knowledge of both the perspective of political leaders in Washington and "representative American opinion" regarding the executions of "those misguided young men" who led the Easter Rising. He regarded the impact of the executions on the prospects of American entry into the war as nothing less than disastrous: "I am looking at this question solely from the pro-Ally point of view. . . . It is unthinkable now that this country should in this war go in on the side of Great Britain. And that change has been largely brought about by Great Britain's dull, stupid and unimaginative act in shooting those men. I believe that this is a fair reflection of American public opinion."[54] Quinn also claimed an understanding of the counsels of Irish separatists in America. Clearly dismayed at the blow that shifting Irish nationalist opinion augured for the future of Home Rule, Quinn contended that Irish Party leader John Redmond's refusal to press vigorously for clemency for the Rising's leadership had made him "the most unpopular Irishman living" for Americans. Even worse, Quinn argued, the executions had "given new life to the extremist Irish agitation in this country." He reported friends' conversations with John Devoy and Joseph McGarrity. Quinn argued that separatist "irreconcilables" such as Devoy and McGarrity in fact hoped for Casement's execution and martyrdom. Devoy, according to a friend of Quinn's, had stated "that it would be 'better for Ireland if he were executed now.'" "They do not say in terms that they want Casement executed," Quinn added, "but that feeling is background in all their expressions."[55]

In addition to developing contacts with Irish revolutionaries through his friendship with Casement, Quinn also formed relationships with Indian nationalists in New York City during and after the Great War.[56] The most prominent of these was Lala Lajpat Rai, the Punjabi nationalist and founder of the Indian Home Rule League. Rai's vision for Indian self-government within the British Empire, to be achieved by public protest, strikes, and boycotts, though not armed revolution, would have accorded with Quinn's moderate nationalism and affinity for self-rule within the empire. When Rai rented an apartment in New York City in April 1917, he listed Quinn as one of his references.[57] The apartment also served as the base of a somewhat mysterious revolutionary known alternately as Hugo Espinoza and Abdur Raschid. The Latvian-born, naturalized American citizen embraced communism and later Islam and was detained for almost four years in India for his alleged involvement in efforts to smuggle arms to revolutionaries in Bengal during the 1920s before being released and deported to the United States.[58] During the First World War Quinn also employed a Bengali student named Porendra Narayan Sinha as a clerk. British intelligence noted that Sinha was in contact with the leaders of the Indo-German Conspiracy and suspected that he had received German funds at some point. Perhaps introduced into Irish nationalist circles through his relationship with Quinn, Sinha also served as "a link between Irish and

Indian revolutionaries."[59] Here also Quinn may have been a source for British intelligence.

Quinn's wartime work for British intelligence extended to one of the more unusual secret agents of this era: Aleister Crowley, the occultist and self-proclaimed "Great Beast 666."[60] Crowley arrived in the United States via the *Lusitania* shortly after the beginning of the war and represented himself as an enthusiastic supporter of Irish separatism. Although Quinn found the Beast to be rather boring, he entertained him at his apartment several times during the last months of 1914, including an invitation to Christmas dinner. He also purchased seven thousand dollars' worth of books from Crowley, which Quinn's clerk described as "both erotic and blasphemous."[61]

Quinn's book purchase served as an important means of support for Crowley, and according to Richard Spence, Quinn functioned as an unofficial case officer for Crowley through the early part of 1915, presumably while the Australian-born Captain Guy Reginald Gaunt, British naval attaché and at the time ranking British intelligence officer in the United States, was away on tour in the Caribbean.[62] From Quinn, Crowley learned of Roger Casement's departure from the United States, though the relationship did not seem to be a satisfactory one from either man's perspective. As Spence observes, the urbane and literary-minded Quinn "clearly was not cut out to be a spymaster."[63]

Other Irish agents came from social and political milieus with much greater direct connection to Irish and Indian revolutionary circles. These included Ed Gammons, a "Dublin-born saloon-keeper and sometime Fenian activist" who first circulated within Irish separatist circles in New York City after emigrating to the United States around 1910. Gammons moved to San Francisco in 1914, where he became a part of the city's multiethnic and multiracial anarchist movement.[64] After the Great War, Gammons served as secretary to the Pacific Coast Branch of the Friends of Freedom for India and also frequently contributed to Ghadar Party publications. Gammons may have helped to orchestrate the meeting between Irish republican leader Éamon de Valera and representatives of the Ghadar Party in San Francisco on 21 July 1919 at which Ghadar leaders Gopal Singh and Jagat Singh presented de Valera with an Irish tricolor and a ceremonial silver sword. On this occasion Gammons gave a speech stating that Ireland and India "have a common cause and a common enemy. Both of our nations have indisputable claims to nationhood." Speaking for the Ghadarites, he also emphasized that Irish people in America had "joined the labor movements of the world in protesting against the barbarities recently practiced against our people [in India] by Britain." Gammons's account of the ceremony appeared in the Ghadar pamphlet he authored titled *India in Revolt*.[65]

Although Gammons's role in the summit between de Valera and Ghadarites demonstrated the potent potential for collaboration between revolutionary nationalists, by the following year he may have been supplying information to British intelligence. In October 1920 a US BOI official in San Francisco arranged a meeting between Gammons and Malcolm R. J. Reid, one of Robert Nathan's operatives who as a "Special Immigration Officer" in Vancouver handled a number of informants on the West Coast. Gammons "had recently fallen out of favor with the Ghadar movement," apparently resentful that he had been replaced by an "English-speaking Hindo [*sic*]" as the writer of English-language propaganda.[66] In return for a salary of fifty dollars per week, Gammons agreed to inform Reid of developments relating to "Hindu and Irish questions."[67]

As the meeting between de Valera and the Ghadarites shows, despite British imperial authorities' satisfaction with the successful prosecution of the members of the Ghadar Party in San Francisco, the threat that anticolonial activism posed to the British Empire seemed to only escalate after the Great War. Imperial intelligence officers had to confront new threats, which expanded dramatically following the "Wilsonian moment."[68] Irish and Irish Americans played an important role in the establishment of a new Indian nationalist organization known as the Friends of Freedom for India in New York City.[69] Bolshevism was added to the array of revolutionary movements that sought the downfall of the empire. While imperial panics and anxieties did not originate in the aftermath of the Great War, they were given new intensity, as fears of anticolonial collaboration, often tied to communist ideals, escalated.[70]

In the United States, the focus of postwar British intelligence accordingly broadened beyond the activities of Irish republicans and Indian anticolonialists, and officers such as Robert Nathan took an increasing interest in other forms of radical politics. A US Department of Justice officer summed up the wide range of British interests as "Sinn Fein activities, Hindu activities, Negro activities (especially as they affect and became part of the activities of all darker peoples), International radical organizations and individuals, and radical affairs of all kinds in the United States." The author of the report, titled "British Espionage in the United States," added that "to the embarrassment of this Department, the English were, at that time, much better informed in radical circles than was the US Government, at least in New York."[71]

Nathan continued his close collaboration with his American counterparts. Beginning in the spring of 1918, Nathan made regular contact with the head of the BOI office in New York, and the two began a regular exchange of information. A State Department official explained how Nathan was permitted to read BOI

> reports bearing more or less directly upon activities in British possessions, principally among revolutionists. At times, in reciprocity, he would follow these cases out and furnish a report upon the foreign angle of the matter. . . . Within a short time Mr. Nathan voluntarily started bringing, on each trip, half a dozen or more reports on various international phases of the radical situation. These gradually broadened into complete and exceptionally intelligent reports upon radical activities right in New York City. . . . While Mr. Nathan did not so state, it was a simple matter to observe that his data was coming from a regularly employed force of under-cover informants in New York.[72]

In January 1919, Nathan took charge of British secret service operations in the United States.[73] While continuing to supervise the surveillance of Indian revolutionaries, he began to take an increasing interest in communist activities and focused his attention on the Lusk Committee, formed to report on left-wing activity in New York during the Red Scare. Wiseman observed that "Mr. Nathan knows more about the Bolshevist organizations in this country than any other man."[74]

Nathan's knowledge of both Irish nationalism and Bolshevism was brought to bear on one of the more outlandish intelligence rumors of the era. At the beginning of 1921, Mansfield Cumming of SIS believed that he had discovered an agent, codenamed B.P.11, who claimed to have obtained access to the codes of Soviet telegrams sent from the Estonian capital of Reval (now Tallinn), Moscow, and the Soviet Trade Delegation in London. The most sensational of these alleged telegrams concerned two Sinn Féin "germ cells" in Ireland to which communist funds were channeled. While Foreign Secretary Lord Curzon was riveted by this seemingly dangerous Bolshevik intrigue in Ireland, Nathan was "unable to discover anything more about these two germ cells," and the mysterious B.P.11 was discredited as a source.[75]

As US intelligence agencies became increasingly uncomfortable with the continuing operations of British intelligence, overt collaboration seems to have ceased by the summer of 1919, although discreet British intelligence work continued to be tolerated.[76] While SIS maintained a small presence in the interwar United States under the cover of Passport Control, Nathan "hurriedly" departed for Britain in July or August 1919 to take charge of Political Section V of SIS.[77] From the time of his appointment in 1919 as head of Political Section V until his death in 1921 at the age of fifty-four, Nathan was, in the assessment of Keith Jeffery, "the second most important officer in SIS."[78]

This extensive cross-colonial movement of police and intelligence officers also had an impact on Ireland during the War of Independence, although Ireland represented an example primarily of the limits of how intelligence expertise gained in one imperial arena could be applied elsewhere. While the idea that an elite cadre of intelligence officers, the so-called Cairo Gang, was deployed in Ireland seems to have been a later invention, officers with imperial police and intelligence experience against Indian revolutionaries were undoubtedly assigned to Irish intelligence during the War of Independence.[79] These included two of the most prominent officers of the Bengal Police Intelligence Branch, Godfrey Denham and the Irishman Charles Tegart.[80] Denham had led investigations into Indian revolutionaries' assassination attempt on the Viceroy of India in 1912 and during the Great War had worked closely with Robert Nathan in the investigation and prosecution of Ghadar Party revolutionaries, supplying Indian intelligence reports and carrying out numerous investigative duties in collaboration with agents of the BOI. After searching immigration records in San Francisco in order to track "the arrivals and departures of certain Hindus," Denham produced an analysis of the movements of revolutionaries that was utilized by the prosecuting attorney in the 1917 "Hindu conspiracy" trial. At the trial itself, Nathan and Denham sat with the prosecution and offered information and advice, a fact acknowledged by Indian revolutionaries as well as US government officials.[81] By 1918, Denham, assisted by a stenographer, worked full-time on matters related to Indian "seditionists."[82]

After working for SIS in East Asia, Denham was recalled to the United Kingdom for an intelligence mission in Ireland. He was joined by his former police colleague Charles Tegart, who had also been employed on imperial intelligence matters. After serving as director of the Intelligence Branch of the Bengal Police and an advisor to the Sedition Committee, appointed to investigate Indian revolutionary activity at the end of the Great War, Tegart was deputed to IPI in London, where he served until 1923.

The Irish War of Independence, as Paul McMahon has contended, was for both republican insurgents and Crown forces in large part an intelligence war, one in which access to information was crucial to the outcome.[83] Tegart and Denham arrived in Ireland at a time when the civil, military, and intelligence administration had been overhauled and when the Irish Republican Army's campaign against the police and military had escalated significantly. Their appointment came at the request of Prime Minister David Lloyd George, who had requested the loan of Indian officers from Secretary of State for India Edwin Montagu.[84]

The Bengal police officers served under another officer with Indian experience, the chief of Irish intelligence and deputy police chief Colonel Ormonde de L'Épée Winter. Winter, one of the most flamboyant figures of the War of Independence, was a career military officer and an enthusiastic pigsticker; a combat veteran of the Great War, he had virtually no previous police or intelligence experience.[85] Tasked with coordinating army and police intelligence in Ireland, Winter also sought to create a new London secret service bureau that was to recruit Irishmen in Britain and send them to Ireland as agents, equipped with secret ink with which to send their reports back to London.[86]

Tegart and Denham were recruited to head this new London bureau. Many of the features of the War of Independence with which they were confronted would have appeared familiar to them from their experience in Bengal: the difficulty of obtaining accurate intelligence against revolutionaries, the extensive reliance on agents and informers in order to penetrate revolutionary groups, and the insurgents' ruthless campaign against those who provided information to imperial forces. Indeed, Tegart's main suggestion for combatting Irish republicans was to replicate the approach of the Bengal Police Intelligence Branch in order to set up what he considered to be a durable and comprehensive system of intelligence. He cautioned that he had no magical solution to British intelligence dilemmas in Ireland or that because of "my previous experience in India that I possess some 'open sesame,' some quick and ready method of establishing an intelligence system in Ireland which will help the authorities to deal with the situation." Rather, Tegart emphasized how intelligence successes in Bengal were based upon years of patient police work that enabled officers to build up an intimate understanding of revolutionary networks: "The intelligence system established to deal with the Indian Revolutionary movement with which I was associated, and the history of the growth, development and ultimate failure of the conspiracy, was the result of five years plodding and patient investigation assisted by a large and highly trained office in which all information was carefully and systematically indexed, collated and pieced together."

Tegart argued that there would be a need to duplicate the same type of painstaking police work in Ireland. The first task would be to assemble, collate, and analyze information in much the same way that the Bengal Police Intelligence Branch had done. Tegart observed that "in my view the first essential is to collect all papers bearing on the situation from whatever quarter available,—Dublin Castle, D.M.P. R.I.C. Scot. Yard M.I.5. etc.—and to study them carefully, compiling History sheets, card indices etc." He admitted that such an approach would be time-consuming and possibly at odds with the desire for someone who would "strike immediately" against Irish republicans but added that "I know of no short cuts which are likely to succeed, the only way I can suggest is so thorough a sifting of the material which it is hoped already exists and which will be collected in the future, as to afford a sufficiently detailed knowledge of the enemy organization to suggest the lines for attacking it."[87]

This "plodding and patient" approach that sought to create an Irish version of the Bengal police archive on revolutionary terrorism clashed with Winter's desire for agents who would immediately send reports on the republican movement. Tegart and Denham in turn found Winter's approach to intelligence amateurish, and their tenure in the Irish administration lasted only four months.[88] While the effort to import intelligence practices from Bengal to Ireland made little impact (Tegart's successor as head of the London Bureau quickly sent agents who produced very little useful intelligence), the arguments about the difficulty of compiling and acting on political intelligence in a short period of time seemed to have been absorbed by Winter. In his report on Irish intelligence, written in late 1921 or early 1922, Winter observed that "to build up an Intelligence organisation for the investigation of political crime in a few months is, practically, an impossibility. The Criminal Investigation Department of India was in being seven years before it commenced to yield any appreciable results."[89]

British intelligence could claim a number of successes in North America during the Great War. German efforts at sabotage of war materiel amounted to little, and ambitious Indo-German plans for an armed revolution in India also were thwarted. British investigations into Irish separatism, however, yielded less of value. The much larger Irish republican network in North America proved more difficult to manage. While late nineteenth-century Irish American revolutionary separatist organizations had been "riddled with secret agents," the rise of a new generation of revolutionary leadership rendered British inside knowledge of separatists' plans and activities on both sides of the Atlantic more difficult to come by.[90] The networks of Irish informants that the British relied upon were mostly those with ties to Home Rule politics and Anglo-Irish society, not the new "Rising generation." While John Quinn was an urbane and cosmopolitan figure, and a willing collaborator with British imperial authorities, his Irish ties extended to Home Rule networks and the older Clan na Gael revolutionary leadership, not to the new generation of Irish separatists.

Further, while British intelligence efforts thwarted Indo-German plots for revolution, they did not by any means bring an end to Indian revolutionary activity. Indo-Irish revolutionary collaboration reached its peak during the War of Independence in Ireland. The Ghadar Party continued its anti-imperial activity throughout the interwar period and increasingly featured a socialist focus.[91] Within

India, revolutionary groups reorganized in the aftermath of a 1919 royal amnesty, and new organizations in north India such as the Hindustan Socialist Republican Association mounted renewed challenges to colonial authority.[92]

British intelligence, though greatly diminished in size followed the Great War, had developed greater experience and professionalism during the war. Imperial intelligence agencies, particularly in India, expanded dramatically, even as MI5 and SIS became much smaller.[93] While the partition of Ireland and the creation of the Irish Free State altered the United Kingdom and the Anglo-Irish relationship, it did not by any means end Irish imperial involvement. This was most certainly true of policing and intelligence work. Anglo-Irish officers such as Charles Tegart continued to serve in the British Empire through the Second World War. One of the most substantial contributions of the Royal Irish Constabulary to the British Empire took place after 1922, as former members of the "regular" RIC and Black and Tans and Auxiliaries alike migrated to the police force of Palestine.[94] In multiple ways, Ireland continued to resonate within the anticolonial conflicts of the British Empire.

## NOTES

1   Christopher Andrew, *The Defence of the Realm: The Authorized History of MI5* (London: Allen Lane, 2009); and Keith Jeffery, *MI6: The History of the Secret Intelligence Service* (London: Bloomsbury, 2010).

2   Kate O'Malley, *Ireland, India and Empire: Indo-Irish Radical Connections, 1919–1964* (Manchester: Manchester University Press, 2008); Matthew Erin Plowman, "Sinn Féin and the Gadar Party in the Indo-German Conspiracy of the First World War," in *Ireland and India: Colonies, Culture and Empire*, ed. Tadhg Foley and Maureen O'Connor (Dublin: Irish Academic Press, 2006), 233–243; and Michael Silvestri, *Ireland and India: Nationalism, Empire and Memory* (Basingstoke: Palgrave Macmillan, 2009), 13–45. O'Malley and Silvestri also explore the ways Ireland impacted the perspective of imperial intelligence officers.

3   Jill Bender, "Ireland and Empire," in *The Princeton History of Modern Ireland*, ed. Richard Bourke and Ian McBride (Princeton: Princeton University Press, 2016), 351.

4   For Hopkinson's career as an imperial intelligence officer, see Richard J. Popplewell, *Intelligence and Imperial Defence: British Intelligence and the Defence of the Indian Empire 1904–1924* (London: Frank Cass, 1995), 150–161; and Michael Silvestri, *Policing "Bengali Terrorism" in India and the World: Imperial Intelligence and Revolutionary Nationalism, 1905–1939* (London: Palgrave Macmillan, 2019), 288–291.

5  Maia Ramnath, *Haj to Utopia: How the Ghadar Movement Charted Global Radicalism and Attempted to Overthrow the British Empire* (Berkeley: University of California Press, 2011).

6  Kate O'Malley, "Indian Political Intelligence (IPI): The Monitoring of Real and Possible Danger?," in *Intelligence, Statecraft and International Power: Historical Studies XXV*, ed. Eunan O'Halpin, Robert Armstrong, and Jane Ohlmeyer (Dublin: Irish Academic Press, 2006), 175–185.

7  Maia Ramnath, *Decolonizing Anarchism: An Antiauthoritarian History of India's Liberation* (Oakland, CA: AK Press, 2011), 99.

8  Richard Spence, "Englishmen in New York: The SIS American Station, 1915–21," *Intelligence and National Security* 19, no. 3 (2004): 511–537.

9  One brother served in the Indian Public Works Department, three others attended the Royal Military Academy, and one half-brother served as attorney general of Trinidad.

10  Silvestri, *Policing "Bengali Terrorism,"* 292–293.

11  Popplewell, *Intelligence and Imperial Defence*, 219–220.

12  Memo by R. Nathan, 12 June 1907 (British Library, Asia, Pacific and Africa Collections [BL, APAC], GOI Home [Deposit] July 1907, No. 67, IOR NEG 10608).

13  Spence, "Englishmen in New York," 517.

14  Ibid., 518–519.

15  Andrew, *Defence of the Realm*, 91.

16  Jeffery, *MI6*, 112; and Spence, "Englishmen in New York," 517.

17  Jeffery, *MI6*, 113.

18  Spence, "Englishmen in New York," 517.

19  Norman Thwaites, *Velvet and Vinegar* (London: Grayson and Grayson, 1932), 145.

20  M. J. Davis, "British Espionage in the United States: An Internal Memorandum of the United States Dept. of Justice, February 15, 1921" (Early American Marxism, n.d.), 3, http://marxisthistory.org. Nathan's obituary also noted that "he could be as silent as the grave; his intimate friends thought he was doing little more than keeping the War Office informed on Indian conspiracies." "Secret Service in the War. Sir R. Nathan's Work," *The Times*, 28 June 1921.

21  Spence, "Englishmen in New York," 519.

22  "List of Salaries Paid Monthly and Other Monthly Expenditures," 29 Jan. 1918 (Yale University Library, Manuscripts and Archives, Sir William Wiseman Papers, MS 666, Box 6, Folder 177).

23  Del Campo to Wiseman, 21 Nov. 1918 (Sir William Wiseman Papers, MS 666, Box 1, Folder 17).

24  Daniel Brückenhaus, "Every Stranger Must Be Suspected: Trust Relationships and the Surveillance of Anti-colonialists in Early Twentieth-Century Western Europe," *Geschichte und Gesellschaft* 36, no. 4 (2010): 534.

25  Thwaites, *Velvet and Vinegar*, 145.

26  William Wiseman to Cecil Spring-Rice, 7 Mar. 1917 (Sir William Wiseman Papers, MS 666, Box 6, Folder 164).

27  For Matthew Nathan's imperial career, see Anthony P. Hayden, *Sir Matthew Nathan: British Colonial Governor and Civil Servant* (St. Lucia: University of Queensland Press, 1976).

28  Oxford, Bodleian Libraries, Catalogues of the Archive of Sir Matthew Nathan, MSS Nathan 1–671.

29  Graham Dominy, "'Not a Position for a Gentleman': Sir Matthew Nathan as Colonial Administrator: From Cape Coast Castle to Dublin Castle via Natal," *Journal of Imperial and Commonwealth History* 46, no. 1 (2018): 93–120, 95.

30  Plowman, "Sinn Féin and the Gadar Party."

31  Cited in Matthew Erin Plowman, "The British Intelligence Station in San Francisco during the First World War," *Journal of Intelligence History* 12, no. 1 (2013): 8.

32  "Some Notes on the Constitution and Activities of the Irish Revolutionary Party in America," 1917 (Sir William Wiseman Papers, MS 666, Box 5, Folder 140).

33  A number of Nathan's reports are contained in the archives of the Military Intelligence Department in the US National Archives. Popplewell, *Intelligence and Imperial Defence*, 329.

34  Spence, "Englishmen in New York," 516.

35  Thomas J. Tunney, *Throttled! The Detection of the German and Anarchist Bomb Plotters* (Boston: Small, Maynard, 1919), 1–7.

36  Popplewell, *Intelligence and Imperial Defence*, 243.

37  Howard Blum, *Dark Invasion: 1915: Germany's Secret War and the Hunt for the First Terrorist Cell in America* (New York: Harper, 2014).

38  A British intelligence officer who worked with Tunney reported that he had a brother in the RIC, while a later analysis states that his uncle had served in the RIC for two decades. Norman Thwaites, "Suggestions as to Recognition of War Services Rendered by Persons in America," 22 Nov. 1918 (Sir William Wiseman Papers, MS 666, Box 3, Folder 84); and Blum, *Dark Invasion*, 18.

39  Tunney, *Throttled!*, 258.

40  Thwaites, *Velvet and Vinegar*, 147.

41  Popplewell, *Intelligence and Imperial Defence*, 254.

42  Tunney, *Throttled!*, 75.

43  Ibid., 71.

44  Thwaites, "Suggestions as to Recognition of War Services Rendered."

45  Cited in Brückenhaus, "Every Stranger Must Be Suspected," 539.

46  Plowman, "British Intelligence Station," 8.

47  Spence, "Englishmen in New York," 519.

48  The information in this paragraph draws upon Peter Quinn, "John Quinn: The Forgotten Irish American Nationalist," *Irish America*, Dec./Jan. 2017, https://irishamerica.com; and B. L. Reid, *The Man from New York: John Quinn and His Friends* (New York: Oxford University Press, 1968) (quotation from Quinn).

49  Quinn, "John Quinn."

50  *The Irish Home Rule Convention* (New York: Macmillan, 1917), 19.

51  Spence, "Englishmen in New York," 520.

52 "In the Matter of Sir Roger Casement and the Irish Situation in America," 2 June 1916 (Sir William Wiseman Papers, MS 666, Box 5, Folder 140).

53 Ibid., 14, 23.

54 Ibid., 15, 23.

55 Ibid., 16–17, 19.

56 Quinn's relationships with Indian nationalists and Irish separatists were known as well to American intelligence officers, who believed him to be closely connected with "elements that are manipulating the Sinn Fein intrigues and activities" as well as Indian revolutionaries. R. Sharp, Special Agent in Charge, New York Division, Department of State, to R. C. Bannerman, Chief Special Agent, Washington, DC, 3 Feb. 1925. Reproduced in Prithwindra Mukherjee, *Les origines intellectuelles du movement d'indépéndence de l'Inde (1893–1918)* (Paris: Éditions Codex, 2010), 209–211.

57 Sharp to Bannerman, 3 Feb. 1925, reproduced in Mukherjee, *Les origines intellectuelles*, 209–211.

58 Silvestri, *Policing "Bengali Terrorism,"* 210–214.

59 *M.I.5 Black List. Vol. XXI (Indian Volume)* (Nos. 13357–13524), rev. ed. March, 1921, 67 (BL, APAC, IOR L/P&J/12/667).

60 Richard B. Spence, *Secret Agent 666: Aleister Crowley, British Intelligence and the Occult* (Port Townsend, WA: Feral House, 2008).

61 Reid, *Man from New York*, 194.

62 Spence, *Secret Agent 666*, 54–57.

63 Ibid., 57.

64 Davis, "British Espionage in the United States," 6; and Kenyon Zimmer, "A Golden Gate of Anarchy: Local and Transnational Dimensions of Anarchism in San Francisco 1880–1930," in *Reassessing the Transnational Turn: Scales of Analysis in Anarchist and Syndicalist Studies*, ed. Constance Bantman and Bert Altena (New York: Routledge, 2014), 108.

65 Ed Gammons, *India in Revolt* (1919) (South Asian American Digital Archive, n.d.), www.saada.org.

66 Zimmer, "Golden Gate of Anarchism," 111; and National Archives and Records Management, College Park, MD (NARA), Record Group (RG) 65, Records of the Bureau of Investigation, Old German Files, M1085, No. 337716.

67 NARA, Old German Files, M1085, No. 337716; Spence, "Englishmen in New York," 519.

68 Erez Manela, *The Wilsonian Moment: Self-Determination and the International Origins of Anticolonial Nationalism* (Oxford: Oxford University Press, 2007).

69 Silvestri, *Ireland and India*, 13–45.

70 For the fundamental place of anxiety and panics in modern empires, see Harald Fischer-Tiné and Christina Whyte, "Introduction: Empires and Emotions," in *Anxieties, Fear and Panic in Colonial Settings: Empires on the Verge of a Nervous Breakdown*, ed. Harald Fischer-Tiné (Basingstoke: Palgrave Macmillan, 2016), 1–23.

71 Davis, "British Espionage in the United States."

72  Ibid. Davis also reported that Nathan had periodic contact with the US Department of Military Intelligence office in New York.

73  Popplewell, *Intelligence and Imperial Defence*, 323.

74  Wiseman to House, 22 July 1919 (Yale University Library, Manuscripts and Archives, Edward Mandell House Papers, MS 466, Box 123, Folder 4332).

75  Christopher Andrew, *Her Majesty's Secret Service: The Making of the British Intelligence Community* (New York: Viking, 1986), 277–279.

76  Jeffery, *MI6*, 250.

77  Ibid., 248–255; and Davis, "British Espionage in the United States."

78  Jeffery, *MI6*, 167.

79  While Cairo was a center of British intelligence operations during the Great War, the name "Cairo Gang" may well have come from the Cairo Café, a popular venue on Dublin's Grafton Street where these officers reputedly gathered. Although some of those killed in the IRA's targeted attacks on Bloody Sunday, 21 Nov. 1920, had intelligence backgrounds, the republican claim that "the British secret service was wiped out" in Ireland on that day was a considerable exaggeration. Charles Townshend, *The Republic: The Fight for Irish Independence* (London: Penguin, 2014), 201–209.

80  For Denham's and Tegart's careers in imperial intelligence, see Silvestri, *Policing "Bengali Terrorism,"* 296–312, 333–335. Another Bengal police officer named Brian Wardle served in Ireland from April 1921 to June 1922 during the latter stage of the War of Independence and the early months of the Irish Free State (see BL, APAC, IOR L/P&J/6/1790).

81  Plowman, "British Intelligence Station," 10–12.

82  "Miscellaneous Functions of New York Office of British Military Attaché," 28 Mar. 1918 (Sir William Wiseman Papers, MS 666, Box 6, Folder 173).

83  Paul McMahon, *British Spies and Irish Rebels: British Intelligence and Ireland, 1916–1945* (Woodbridge: Boydell Press, 2008), 26.

84  Eunan O'Halpin, "British Intelligence in Ireland, 1914–1921," in *The Missing Dimension: Intelligence Communities in the Twentieth Century*, ed. Christopher Andrew and David Dilks (Urbana: University of Illinois Press, 1984), 74 and 260.

85  Peter Hart, "Introduction," in *British Intelligence in Ireland, 1920–21: The Final Reports*, ed. Peter Hart (Cork: Cork University Press, 2002), 7.

86  McMahon, *British Spies and Irish Rebels*, 38–39.

87  Charles Tegart to Sir Malcolm Seton, 1 July 1920 (National Archives, United Kingdom, Records of the Home Office, HO 317/59).

88  McMahon, *British Spies and Irish Rebels*, 38–39.

89  Ormonde Winter, *A Report on the Intelligence Branch of the Chief of Police, Dublin Castle from May 1920 to July 1921*, in Hart, *British Intelligence in Ireland*, 74.

90  Niall Whelehan, *The Dynamiters: Irish Nationalism and Political Violence in the Wider World, 1867–1900* (Cambridge: Cambridge University Press, 2012), 136. Whelehan also cautions, however, that the influence of police spies within Clan-na-Gael can be exaggerated and that British officers were not simply the "puppetmasters" of Irish separatist organizations and their bombing campaigns.

91  Ramnath, *Haj to Utopia.*

92  Durba Ghosh, *Gentlemanly Terrorists: Political Violence and the Colonial State in India, 1919–1947* (Cambridge: Cambridge University Press, 2017); and Kama Maclean, *A Revolutionary History of Interwar India: Violence, Image, Voice and Text* (Oxford: Oxford University Press, 2015).

93  Silvestri, *Policing "Bengali Terrorism,"* 78.

94  Seán William Gannon, *The Irish Imperial Service: Policing Palestine and Administering the Empire, 1922–1966* (London: Palgrave Macmillan, 2018).

# 9

# Wars, Dominions, and Monarchy

## *The Transnational Imperial Context of Ireland's Revolution, 1916–1922*

HEATHER JONES

A key component of the Irish Revolution was anti-monarchism. It drew upon internal Irish history, particularly Fenianism, but also upon broader global trends emerging from the First World War that dramatically revised popular attitudes to monarchy across continental Europe. It set in motion one of the most pivotal "culture wars" of the Irish revolutionary period, pitting those who continued to view loyalty to the British monarchy as a fundamental element of their identity against those who viewed this as incompatible with Irishness. This division was a major factor in the partition of Ireland and also in the anti-Treaty side's opposition to the 1921 Anglo-Irish Treaty: they rejected its delineation of the relationship between the Free State and the British monarchy. Yet this culture war over monarchism has received little historical attention. Instead the focus of academic historians has been almost entirely upon republicanism, with little discussion of the monarchist cultural and legal frameworks against which republicanism was operating or the anti-monarchist sentiments that republicans drew upon to win some of their popular support. There has been study of the British monarchy's policies toward Ireland, but the wider culture wars over monarchy between 1912 and 1923 remain neglected.[1]

Moreover, this is a subject where a transnational approach can be particularly valuable. If, as Fearghal McGarry and Enda Delaney have argued, our understanding of the Irish Revolution can gain from exploring transnational contexts, then one of the key contexts—the collapse of European monarchism in the final years of the First World War and its immediate aftermath—needs to be examined, particularly as how it impacted upon British views of empire had direct implications for British policies toward Ireland.[2] This question has been largely neglected in the new wave of global history approaches to the Irish Revolution.[3]

This chapter makes three points by way of encouraging more discussion. First, it emphasizes the transnational context for Irish anti-monarchism in the First World War. It also highlights the degree to which Irish anti-monarchism represented a direct and existential challenge to the very fundamentals of British identity and imperial and state structures. Second, it highlights how the Anglo-Irish Treaty settlement put forward for Ireland was central to a wider transnational postwar reconfiguration of the relationship between monarchy and empire—the concept of imperial monarchy was being redefined from 1917 into a form of transnational British monarchism in direct response to the challenges that the war had generated. Examining how the British monarchy's imperial identity was utilized in the Irish settlement north and south reveals the extent to which British imperial identity was effectively being restructured into looser forms of transnational royal allegiance. The chapter also provides greater insight into the contemporary cultural meanings of imperial terminology by situating the monarchist term "dominion status" in the transnational context of the evolving British Empire in 1916–1922. Finally, this chapter examines the Anglo-Irish Treaty debates around the oath of allegiance as a way of illustrating how the relationship to the monarchy was at the core of clashing imagined post-independence identities and what the implications of this were for Irish society.

## The Transnational Context

The First World War brought dramatic challenges for British imperial power relations and monarchist cultural beliefs that ultimately affected Irish republican and unionist agency and attitudes. Revolution was one of the most transnational phenomena of the global conflagration. The same year as the Easter Rising in Dublin, the tsarist Russian Empire crushed the Central Asian uprising.[4] By 1917 Russia would see not one but two revolutions, while 1918 saw revolution in Germany and the various component parts of the Austro-Hungarian Empire and 1919 saw revolution in Egypt. To this extent, the Irish case appears not as an outlier but as the first in a chain of revolutionary insurgencies against imperial and monarchist power dynamics that the war triggered or accelerated, which was one way that it was seen in Britain.

The transnational continental European context matters because most of the revolutions that occurred in Europe between 1916 and 1923 revolved around the rejection of a pre-1914 monarchical, dynastic state structure. It is often forgotten how radical a change this was: before 1914 France was Europe's only major republic, while the Swiss confederation offered a smaller exception to the domination of monarchy. European monarchism, moreover, was underpinned by popular monarchist cultures—clearly visible in Britain, Belgium, and Italy, among other examples, during the war.[5] The Irish Republican Brotherhood ideologues who led the 1916 rebellion were thus innovative in their combination of ideas about republicanism, stemming largely from Fenianism in America, with structural tensions toward monarchy that were emerging out of the Great War itself.[6] Irish Home Rule aspirations for limited self-determination looked increasingly obsolete against the backdrop of 1918's much more radical transnational variants, triggered by President Woodrow Wilson's Fourteen Points speech. Wilson's promotion of self-determination and his Fourteen Points speech openly suggested imperialism was a global enemy of national destiny in a way that Home Rule with its accommodation of devolution within the United Kingdom and British Empire never had.[7] Moreover, such ideas were picked up not only in Ireland but across the Irish diaspora throughout the British world.[8] In sum, monarchism was now being globally contested.

Thus by the British general election of December 1918 the situation in Ireland was subject to a series of rapidly coalescing transnational influences—American and, to a lesser degree, French concepts of republicanism, continental revolutionary nationalisms that were overthrowing monarchical systems, and Woodrow Wilson's radicalization of the concept of national self-determination, which was rapidly taken up by colonized populations, even though his original intent was to apply it only to continental Europe.[9] From Egypt to South Africa, across the British Empire subordinated indigenous populations began mobilizing Wilsonian rhetoric of self-determination to demand imperial reforms. However, this process was largely about demanding greater rights and freedoms *within* the empire; advanced Irish separatism combined it with the anti-monarchical nationalisms seen on the continent to demand not only imperial reform but imperial exit and a new republican Irish nation-state.

European continental nationalisms also legitimized nationalist "purificatory" revolutionary violence to a far wider degree than had happened before in European history; utopian visions of the perfect, ethnically homogenous, "pure" nation-state abounded. Central and eastern Europe were swept up by such violence, which was often justified by its perpetrators as necessary to create new nation-states from 1918 to 1923. Advanced Irish separatists, from 1919, could draw upon these broader continental nationalist revolutionary scripts. The Irish Easter Rising Proclamation's revolutionary declaration that sovereignty rested with the Irish people, and thus not with a British sovereign, originated in the ideas of 1776 in America and 1789 and 1848 in Europe, but it proved prescient as from 1918 to 1923 numerous states, including Poland, the Baltic States, and Turkey, all adopted the nation-state republic model. Aside from the radical, small, Irish Republican Brotherhood (IRB) component, who, as part of the Fenian tradition, advocated republicanism, many Irish separatists had been somewhat ambivalent about what nature a future independent Irish state might take. The increasing collective determination to go for a full republic, which emerged around January 1919 with the establishment of the First Dáil, and to reject any compromise format, was clearly connected to the fact that obtaining a republic had simply become far more realistic by this year, as monarchies tumbled across Europe. As McGarry and Delaney point out, "Many of the reasons why the aspiration to achieve an Irish republic, if necessary through violent means, became credible by January 1919 lay in political and ideological changes occurring beyond the island."[10] The startling success of wartime and postwar transnational anti-monarchism was one of these, yet we still know too little about how it influenced Irish views or indeed about the influence of revolution in continental Europe more generally upon the Irish Revolution.[11]

Seen within this context, radicalization in Ireland from 1919 to 1922 is deeply revealing of the ways that the United Kingdom as a polity was riven by the advent of the Great War's combined transnational challenges to monarchy discussed above. The United Kingdom that entered the First World War was structured entirely around kingship: its armies were the king's armies, with each soldier taking an oath of allegiance to the monarch, and its population was legally defined as subjects of the Crown, not citizens. The monarchy retained significant constitutional powers in the form of royal prerogatives, and the entire state structure, from the courts to Parliament, revolved around a monarchist framework. Irish republicanism, with its espousal of radical forms of anti-monarchism, directly challenged the very meaning of "Britishness" by contesting the monarchist ideas upon which it was based. The Irish Revolution thus not only challenged British rule in Ireland but launched new conceptual questions about power and monarchist identity in the United Kingdom as a whole that threatened the entire edifice of the state and British identity.

This threat was all the more real because it fitted with broader revolutionary European anti-monarchist trends. Irish republicans aimed to form an Irish nation-state out of a multinational dynastic polity—the United Kingdom. Across Europe, the First World War triggered the collapse of such multinational dynastic states that were based entirely upon loyalty to a king-emperor and were dramatically challenged by the way that the war spread nationalism. Jonathan Gumz has shown how prewar Austria-Hungary was an antinationalist state, built upon an imperial ideal of loyalty to the emperor by multiple different nationalities, which by the end of the war could no longer be sustained.[12] Its dynastic state collapsed into nation-state components. Likewise, the United Kingdom, based on the dynastic principle—not a single, uniform nation-state nationalism—was vulnerable to any internal national group challenging its core tenet of British identity, which was based not on nationality but on loyalty to the Crown. The United Kingdom was emphatically *not* a nation-state: a wide variety of national groups—Scots, Welsh, Irish, and English—were all purportedly united into the UK polity by being subjects of the British Crown, and a broader version of this dynastic principle also underpinned the empire with wide-ranging nationalities integrated politically as subjects within an imperial monarchy structure. The violent secession of twenty-six counties of Ireland from the United Kingdom, led by republicans, thus directly challenged this, and this explains why any settlement that the British could accept had to incorporate a monarchist component. This also mattered for Irish unionists, for whom monarchism was often a central tenet of identity.

In fact, what to do with minorities was a transnational problem across Europe in the wake of the collapse of multinational and/or multiethnic states that had been built around a dynastic principle. Basing statehood on loyalty to a king-emperor had often provided protection from a majority nationality's rule for a minority; stripping this structure away left a vacuum. There were numerous cases, from 1916 on, of European national groups toppling or seceding from multiethnic dynastic states to form a nation-state variant and struggling with what to do with their minority populations which differed from their new hegemonic nationality. The League of Nations developed its "Minority Treaties" as one solution.[13] Partitioning most of the "loyal" monarchist unionist minority so as to keep it within the United Kingdom, which was the solution that the British government and northern Irish unionists ultimately adopted, was but one approach to a widespread transnational problem.[14] Britain hoped partition would be temporary, as did the Germans of Silesia who found themselves in the new Poland following the postwar Versailles Treaty settlement. Their future was largely decided by a borderland plebiscite. But partition in Ireland only served to create new religious and political minorities—northern Irish Catholics, southern Protestants, northern nationalists, southern unionists—who ultimately were mainly left to work out the fallout of the revolutionary years by themselves.

Yet partition was never meant to be a standalone policy from the British perspective in 1919–1922. It was meant to operate within an all-island monarchist context, whereby the British monarch remained the head of state of both the Irish Free State and Northern Ireland. Thus, the whole Irish population would remain connected as common subjects of the monarch with legal rights to appeal to the Privy Council, which remained after the Anglo-Irish Treaty. A shared dynastic allegiance would, the British believed, mitigate against divergence between the two parts of the island, which, it was hoped at this point in Britain, would reunite within a relatively short time frame, and the retention of the shared monarchist umbrella would act against the mistreatment of minorities in the new Irelands. King George V, in particular, had marked a new era for the monarchy in proactively opposing ill treatment of Irish Roman Catholics. On Catholicism he was far more open-minded than much of the British establishment, getting the "Protestant Declaration," which was profoundly anti-Catholic in sentiment, dropped from his first parliamentary speech and the anti-Catholic clause annulled from his coronation oath. During discussions in 1913 on the possible exclusion of Ulster from Home Rule, the king had presciently asked "if Ulster were left out" whether the "Protestants would give a promise not to molest the Roman Catholic minority," and he requested assurances about this again privately, after partition, from prominent Northern Irish unionists in 1921.[15] At the height of the War of Independence, an American newspaper reported that the king was at odds with Prime Minister David Lloyd George's policies of repression in Ireland and had even said, "This thing cannot go on. I cannot have my people killed in this manner."[16] The Crown was furious at the leak and never publicly acknowledged that the king had made such a statement—but the quotation according to historian James Loughlin "has the ring of authenticity"; in fact, the king's private secretary, Lord Stamfordham, privately admitted to Lloyd George that he had met the journalist concerned to promote the royal view on peace in Ireland.[17] Stamfordham also wrote in May 1921 to the chief secretary of Ireland, Sir Hamar Greenwood, on behalf of the king to question the government's policy of using violent reprisals.[18] The monarchy—presented as above politics—was thus seen by some British politicians as a counterweight to Irish internal political sectarianism. A settlement that retained an overarching role for the monarch also ensured that the threat to the monarchist-based concept of British identity that Irish republicanism represented was countered.

However, the vision of monarchism being applied here was, in many ways, profoundly experimental. The Irish Free State's establishment marked its exit from the United Kingdom's *internal* dynastic monarchist structure, within which Northern Ireland—albeit with a home rule parliamentary structure—fully remained. For the Free State, membership of the internal UK dynastic state structure was replaced with a dominion-style position within the imperial monarchy, which was itself in full transition at this point. Before 1914, the parliament and civil service in London had considerable direct political and governance power over imperial Crown possessions, carried out in the monarch's name. After 1918 these imperial monarchist structures of empire radically changed. A new language of monarchy as existing only by consent of the people emerged in 1918. Dominions, in particular, gained virtually complete political independence from London, coupled with a new role for the Crown, now seen as directly connected to each individual independent state within the empire separately, operating parallel to—and distinct from—British government and civil service relations with each Commonwealth government, while uniting all British subjects across the world in a common transnational monarchist identity. This was to be the new model of empire for the postwar world, increasingly grounded in the monarchist structural connection to the throne, rather than politically to Westminster or Whitehall. Of course, for many of the peoples of the empire, particularly those who faced discrimination on racial grounds, this purported shift to transnational monarchism by consent was farcical. But it was central to how British commentators understood how their empire was changing from 1919 to 1922 and how they attempted to handle the situation in Ireland, where the establishment of Northern Ireland and the Irish Free State marked a trial of this new "transnational monarchism" as the Free State exited the United Kingdom's existing dynastic state structure.

### From Imperial Monarchy to Transnational British Monarchism

The British input into the Anglo-Irish Treaty was inherently driven by these broader transnational developments and fears. Indeed, we cannot understand it without grasping this. From 1917, the year when the dominion prime ministers forced the establishment of the Imperial War Cabinet to represent their populations' interests in the war effort and gain greater foreign policy independence, there was a growing realization within the British government and elites that for the British Empire to survive it would need to reform in the postwar world. It would need to react to the combined challenges of the collapse of European monarchism, the rise of America, with its republican promise, and the demands for greater independence and increased rights by a wide variety of populations within the empire, as well as the spread of Bolshevism. Only the last of these was considered less relevant to Ireland due to its devout religiosity, which spanned the sectarian divide.

In sum, the First World War had a profoundly radicalizing effect upon the British Empire and imperial identities, as shown in the work of Erez Manela and Jennifer Wellington, among others.[19]

The British by 1919 increasingly saw imperial reform as the way to respond to all of these challenges simultaneously.[20] With the collapse of European monarchism it was important to bolster the status of the British monarchy at home, in ways that gave it a function and purpose, now that its prewar role of liaising and intermarrying with continental monarchies was largely redundant. This was to be done through empire. The dominions could be cut loose completely from any connection to the British Parliament at Westminster as long as their constitutional connection with the British monarchy remained, as this monarchical link was believed in the British cultural mentalities of the time to be the core of "Britishness." This would simultaneously highlight the importance of the monarchy and allow the increasingly skittish dominions full political independence while keeping the empire intact. For Lloyd George, for example, who rather ironically was often not considered by the royal court as a particularly committed monarchist, allegiance to the king was the principle "upon which the whole fabric of the Empire and every constitution within it are based."[21] If, under the Treaty, part of Ireland had gained independence, it still remained part of the monarchist sphere, one of the monarchy's dominions, if the British king remained head of state. In a Britain in which monarchism was the dominant culture, this mattered far more to British decision makers than whether or not all of Ireland remained under direct British governance by Westminster, even for an anti-IRA hard-liner like Lloyd George. This is why the role of the king dominated the debates on the Treaty in the Houses of Parliament at Westminster.[22]

The postwar reformist approach to empire was virtually entirely grounded in monarchism. Hence the idea of including a republican state structure within the Anglo-Irish Treaty was utterly impossible for British negotiators trying to find a solution to the Irish situation. A republic would also, in their eyes, preclude any later reunification with the North—which remained within the UK dynastic monarchist state framework. By bolstering the empire, Britain could continue its great power status into the new interwar era as a victor of the First World War, which had expanded its global territorial reach, allowing it to recover from the war's negative economic and demographic impact and rival the rising global power of the United States with its republican ethos and booming economy. The new language of this re-defined imperialism—mandates, territories held in trust to be granted independence at a later date—emphasized a new discourse of empire by consent, which became central to British interwar imperial propaganda and hid the true degree of violent coercion used in areas such as Britain's Middle Eastern mandates, for example. This explains why the fact-finding missions by Americans to Ireland during the War of Independence to investigate atrocities by British paramilitary police forces in the country caused such consternation in London. They directly contradicted this new imperial image that reformers wished to promote.

The shift in British imperial ideas that was occurring in Ireland—but also *through* Ireland—thus reflected tensions in postwar imperial identities more broadly. The new languages in evidence highlight this. The British Treaty negotiators accepted the dilution of the term "empire" for the more collaborative one "Commonwealth" in the Treaty, and in discussions about it, as a response to the demands of the Irish delegates, but this also reflected changes in thinking about empire more broadly in the new League of Nations era of "mandates" and independent dominions. Michael Collins argued that "we have got rid of the word 'Empire,'" but this actually aligned with a broader British imperial reform trend.[23]

Crucially, the Treaty talks were not just between the United Kingdom and Ireland but also between Ireland *and the empire*: this imperial context mattered hugely. Collins believed Commonwealth membership would protect the Irish Free State's independence as the other dominions would have an interest in guarding it, becoming "guarantors of our freedom."[24] It was certainly true that they followed the changes being piloted in Ireland very closely and in some cases were directly involved. For example, Jan Smuts helped draft King George V's Belfast speech—highlighting transnational exchange between the South African and Irish contexts. Thus, the Treaty offered Ireland a British imperial reform template for independence that was seen as applicable to other fault lines in the empire. This imperial dimension and application of experimental dominion status to Ireland was very clear to contemporaries. Trinity College Dublin provost and Church of Ireland archbishop John Bernard wrote in December 1921, in response to the Treaty terms, "I confess that I don't like to think of myself as a 'Colonial'! Yet that is what it has come to."[25] The discussion in the press and among republicans about "dominion status" being applied to Ireland was not political sloganeering but a very real reflection of the actual legal meaning of, and British vision for, the Anglo-Irish Treaty. This also explains the choice of name of the new state—"Free State," an attempt to rebrand this.

From the British perspective, Ireland had to be solved in a way that fit the postwar imperial reform agenda in response to the transnational challenges Britain faced. But the role that the changing meaning of the British Empire, during and immediately after the First World War, played in the Irish Revolution has often been overlooked. The image presented is of a static British state, one that remained the same from 1914 to 1922. In reality, this was a dynamic period of change for the British state and empire—Irish separatist rebels faced the real problem of this proteanism during these years when they tried to understand what solutions might be acceptable to the British government. When the United Kingdom entered the First World War, every part of the empire automatically entered with it, having no independent control over foreign policy; by the end of the war, following a concerted effort by dominion premiers, the dominions' foreign policies were now increasingly in their own hands as the 1922 Chanak Crisis illustrated. In addition, by 1917 the United Kingdom was a far less liberal state than it had been in 1914, now operating through the Defence of the Realm Act, passing wartime legislation not only through Parliament but also through the royal prerogative in the Privy Council, and considering using force to apply conscription to the Irish population if necessary; this set the frame for martial law in Ireland and state coercion in the War of Independence. By 1920, Britain had devolved its control of Northern Ireland in the Government of Ireland Act. Thus, by the time the Anglo-Irish Treaty talks began, the British view was that the minorities question in Ireland had already been partially solved through partition; what was left was to apply the new imperial dominion reforms to the rest of Ireland as a solution that would allow it independence while keeping the empire intact.

### The Oath of Allegiance and Post-independence Identities

The stumbling block in this plan, of course, was monarchism. The British completely underestimated the degree of anti-monarchism that had gained strength within the Irish independence movement from Easter 1916. This anti-monarchism had long roots, of course, but it had surged after the Rising and the Proclamation's radical declaration of Irish sovereignty as resting with the Irish people, a direct rejection of the actual sovereign, King George V, who in the British state model "embodied" sovereignty. Ireland had a particular—and arguably unique within the British Empire—folk culture of opposition to the British monarchy, dating back to at least the 1798 rebellion, with its republican ideological leadership, and exacerbated by the Great Famine.[26] In 1867, it was clearly in evidence in the Irish Republican Brotherhood's declaration on the eve of its failed uprising, which referred to the "curse of Monarchical Government."[27] The extent of its reach is debated by historians, with James Murphy suggesting that by 1900 there was also significant Catholic monarchism within the population, which had come to a cultural accommodation with the British monarchy.[28] James McConnel paints a different picture of the situation, depicting the Home Rule movement as very divided over the issue of the British monarchy—with even those who accepted the idea of an Irish future within the British Empire under Home Rule reluctant to embrace it.[29] Fearghal McGarry, in turn, suggests that while Irish separatists sought full independence from Britain there was no consensus between 1916 and 1918 on what form an independent Irish state should take.[30] What is clear is that the Irish republican tradition—a minority within nationalism on the eve of the First World War—was vitriolic in its animosity toward the British monarchy, as shown in its protests against Queen Victoria's visit to Ireland in 1900 and King George V's 1911 one.

This contrasted with the then mainstream Home Rule nationalism, which by 1914 had seen a softening of Irish anti-monarchism. The Buckingham Palace Conference of July 1914, where the British press cast the monarchy in a new role of neutral arbiter toward Ireland, as the island polarized between home rule supporters and unionists and their respective armed militias, led to a rapprochement between the Irish Parliamentary Party and the monarchy. This was consolidated by the outbreak of the First World War when John Redmond and the majority of the pro–home rule militia, the Irish Volunteers, supported the British war effort, becoming known as the National Volunteers. The mantle of Irish anti-monarchist agitation now fell entirely to the Irish Republican Brotherhood and the minority of Irish Volunteers who had split from the Redmondites in rejection of the war. This they fully exploited, in particular in antiwar propaganda and in increasingly radical anti-monarchist stances and languages during the Easter Rising and the War of Independence.[31] For example, Kevin Barry's mother refused to appeal to George V to intervene to stop his execution as she believed that would amount to recognizing the monarchy.[32]

From a British perspective, however, distracted by the First World War, there was little understanding of the extent to which anti-monarchism had spread within Irish nationalism by 1921. Sir Edward Grigg, Lloyd George's private secretary, advised the prime minister in a note on 14 June 1921 that "Ireland is very sentimental, and, like India, monarchist to the core."[33] Moreover, anti-monarchism had not emerged in dominions like Canada or Australia as part of their trajectories toward greater independence; Ireland's situation, closer to the anti-monarchist revolutions sweeping Europe, as well as its own history of local opposition to the British monarchy, was unique. The view persisted, for the British, that King George V had established the monarchy as a neutral arbiter in Ireland, a role that the king himself also personally believed in. This explains his decision to accept an invitation to open the new Northern Irish Parliament in person in June 1921 with a speech at Belfast City Hall, a role he also offered to carry out for the opening of the first Irish Free State Dáil, a proposal flatly rejected.[34] The king opted, with the help and advice of Jan Smuts, to make the Belfast speech into a deeply personal appeal for peace and reconciliation on the island of Ireland. His decision to embark on what was a risky personal voyage to Ireland was illustrative of his profoundly held belief that monarchism—and he as an individual—still held traction with Irish nationalists. Here he again underestimated the degree to which radical anti-monarchism had spread within Irish nationalism. A troop train of soldiers and horses was blown up on their way back south after the event, killing three soldiers and a railway guard.[35] His speech, however, was also a clever undermining of the hawks in London, who were calling for increased military repression to defeat the IRA. Above all, by invoking a royal appeal for subjects to honor his request to work toward peace, the king ensured a shift in policy from London. In this deeply monarchist culture, it was impossible to ignore a direct plea from the monarch. Peace talks opened within weeks. The king's personal intervention, which was generally well received by unionists and moderate nationalists, also tested the water for some kind of monarchist solution to the problem of the divided island, and the British conclusion—however misplaced—was that it could work.

Although both sides at the 1921 Anglo-Irish Treaty talks recognized that the peace treaty they were negotiating was officially between Irish separatists and the British monarch, Irish negotiators never fully grasped the emotional complexity of the British attachment to the Crown.[36] Precisely because of the cultural weight of the monarchy, it remained the one aspect of Britishness that Lloyd George and the British delegation could not renege upon: Lloyd George informed Éamon de Valera that "we cannot consent to any abandonment, however informal of the principle of allegiance to the King."[37] He rejected any form of recognition of the Irish delegation that would suggest "Irelands [sic] severance from the King's domains."[38] Hence the long, and torturous, talks over the insistence that members of the Dáil in a new dominion status Irish Free State would have to take an oath of allegiance to the British monarch. The clash was a profoundly ideological one between monarchists and republicans: the British side even researched the American oath of allegiance to the US Constitution to try to find a wording that might fit better with their republican-minded interlocutors.[39] This came to nothing—one minute recording wryly that they had realized what was at issue was not the oath's "form" but the "substance."[40]

On 1 December 1921 Arthur Griffith and Michael Collins, on behalf of the Irish delegation, proposed changing the wording of the oath to "I . . . do solemnly swear to bear true faith and allegiance to the Constitution of the Irish Free state as by Law established and that I will be faithful to His Majesty King George in acknowledgement of the Association of Ireland in a common citizenship with Great Britain and the group of nations known as the British Commonwealth."[41] Needless to say, this version, which is only slightly different from that which the British proposed, was unacceptable to the British side, which viewed the monarchy in almost mystical terms, because the Irish version removed any reference to loyalty to the king's heirs and set up a model whereby Ireland was only "associated" with the Commonwealth in international affairs. The monarch, moreover, would have no internal role in Ireland, which, the Irish delegation argued, could then be an "internal" republic. Griffith's exact wording was that "for external affairs . . . Ireland would recognise the British Crown as proposed, while for internal retaining the Republic."[42] Griffith told those present at the talks that "Ireland is not a Colony but a parent race and a separate entity, and that the Dominions would support them."[43]

The British side was obsessed with loyalty to the Crown as the foundation of the status of all dominions in the British Empire, as each purportedly had an equal relationship to their unifying monarch. As Lord Birkenhead told the Irish delegation, "The British people attached the greatest importance to the symbol of the Crown."[44] Griffith for the Irish delegation rejected this way of thinking. He submitted to the talks that for the other dominions

> the Crown to them is a symbol of the external unity of equal states, not of the internal repression of subordinate states. Ireland, on the contrary lies beside the shores of Great Britain, which has been accustomed for generations to interfere, in the name of the Crown, in every detail of Ireland's life. The desire and temptation to continue interference will remain if the Crown remains, as it cannot be the symbolic Crown that the Dominions know, but will continue to possess the real power of repression and veto which Ireland knows. . . . Propinquity imposes on us a necessity for safeguarding our independence which does not arise in the case of the Dominions. The Crown . . . will never menace the Dominions with its powers.[45]

Griffith pointed out that his side's wording of the oath would associate Ireland with Great Britain and the dominions under the Crown and that "it must be recognised that for Ireland freely to accept the Crown in any capacity is a momentous step on her part in view of history."[46] For the Irish delegate George Gavan Duffy, the Crown "symbolised a unity based on something real, the tie of blood," and this was why it worked for the other dominions—and Ireland recognized this, he claimed, with its concession that it would associate with the Crown for international issues.[47]

Griffith also pointed out that, under the old Home Rule Bills, the Crown—and through it the British government—would have retained supremacy, and the right of veto, over the Home Rule parliament. This, he correctly asserted, was not compatible with full independence. In contrast, it was pointed out by the British delegation that dominion status meant that, as with the other dominions, the king would act with regard to Ireland on the advice of his Irish government ministers only, and not his British government at Westminster. The monarch by 1919 related to each dominion government separately. Indeed, on the British side the belief was that linking Ireland into dominion status modeled on Canada would mean that "the royal prerogatives of appointing ministers, summoning and dissolving parliament etc. would be maintained in the Irish Free State. However, the subsequent Irish Free State Constitution completely ignored the royal prerogatives."[48] For Gavan Duffy of the Irish delegation, the issue went beyond the dangers of political interference: "We cannot agree to use the word allegiance. It is out of date. Loyalty is now due not to Governments but to Nations."[49]

This ultimately became the core of the row that developed over what wording would be acceptable for the oath of allegiance to the sovereign that Irish parliamentarians would take in the new Irish Free State. The British held the view that "there were the gravest objections to any proposal to limit or subtract from allegiance. Irishmen could not be both aliens and citizens. . . . The British representatives were willing that the position of the Crown should be the same as the position of the Crown in Canada and in Australia. They could not accede to anything else. They regarded that as fundamental, the real test of common citizenship."[50] In other words, in this period, the populations of the British Empire, or Commonwealth as it was increasingly referred to at the talks in light of Irish sensibilities, held a *common* universal British nationality by virtue of being a subject of the king; it was not until decades later that the dominions, led by Canada, would successfully establish their own different, separate, legal nationality statuses.[51] Being a subject of the British monarch and being a British national were inseparable within the empire in 1922 and in how it was defined; everyone who was not a royal subject was legally an alien. This was one reason why, after 1922, the British left in place the right to British nationality for the Irish Free State population. In gaining dominion status within the empire, the Irish Free State could not be exempt from the wider imperial norms—if it was to have dominion status, then its population remained royal subjects in British eyes, and they continued to have all the rights of British subjects should they choose to exercise them. Thus, the very fundamentals of the empire's structure were clearly problematic for Irish republicans who wanted an independent Irish nationality, separate from Britishness.

The Irish delegation struggled to find a way around the centrality of the monarchy to dominion status. Griffith told those at the talks that "we are to have a reciprocal citizenship combined only for certain purposes for which we recognise the Crown as head."[52] This was a nonstarter for the British side given their obsession with the Crown as the root of citizenship, which they saw as inseparable from subject status: "The Crown is the symbol of a common citizenship which makes all subjects of the King one in international law. No man can be a subject of two States. He must either be a subject of the King or an alien, and the question no more admits of an equivocal answer than whether he is alive or dead," noted a British memo.[53] "Allegiance to His Majesty the King" was regarded as "vital" for the British delegates.[54] As one memo noted, "The Crown is the symbol of all that keeps the nations of the Empire together. It is the keystone of the arch in law as well as in sentiment. All the Governments of the Empire are His Majesty's Governments."[55]

Ultimately the British wording for the oath would win out: "I do solemnly swear true faith and allegiance to the Constitution of the Irish Free State as by law established, and that I will be faithful to His Majesty King George V, his heirs and successors by law, in virtue of the common citizenship of Ireland with Great Britain, and her adherence to and membership of the group of nations forming the British Commonwealth of nations."[56] Yet even this wording was the source of controversy in the House of Commons, where, during debates on the Treaty on 14 December 1921, die-hard Tories demanded an "unambiguous expression of allegiance to the Crown" and talked of "the surrender of the rights of the crown in Ireland."[57] Indeed the Irish oath was weaker than that which parliamentary members in other dominions had to swear, which referred to being "faithful" *and* bearing "true allegiance" to the monarch, sometimes with the words "so help me God" added.[58] The Irish oath swore "true faith and allegiance to the Constitution of the Irish Free State" first, and only to be "faithful" to the monarch and his heirs and successors.[59] Effectively what has gone down in Irish history as a much maligned "oath of allegiance" was in reality an "oath of fidelity," a subtle difference of wording that highlights how Ireland was a test run for experimentations in new ways of operating for the monarchy within the empire.

The Irish delegation ironically accepted the point that the Irish Free State would make an annual contribution to the king's personal revenue without much fuss. What mattered was the oath. For de Valera, the oath to a British monarch would "disenfranchise every honest Republican like the Test Acts against Catholics and dissenters in the past," a reference to the acts that were part of the Penal Laws, whereby any man serving in public office had to "recognise the king as head of his church as well as head of his state."[60] De Valera put forward his own alternative to the treaty, "Document No. 2," which revised the oath wording as follows: "I do swear to bear true faith and allegiance to the Constitution of Ireland and to the Treaty of Association of Ireland with the British Commonwealth of Nations, and to recognise the King of Great Britain as head of the Associated States."[61] Such a wording was completely unrealistic for the British side as it effectively removed the monarchy from any role in the Irish Free State, thus negating "dominion status," as to be a dominion was by definition to belong, in some form, to the monarchist sphere of the Crown.

The polarizing result of these discussions was obvious—the oath dominated the Treaty debates in the Dáil and ultimately was a key factor in the Irish Civil War. Republican TD (parliamentary deputy) Seán T. O'Kelly's comments on the oath during the Dáil Treaty debates in December 1921 were typical: "I am opposed to this declaration of fidelity to an alien King because it is an outrage on the memory of our martyred comrades . . . and an open insult to the heroic relatives they have left behind."[62] For TD Ada English the oath meant "they were asked to accept the King of England as head of the Irish State and to accept the status of British subjects," which would be "a complete spiritual surrender."[63] Other anti-Treaty figures, including Margaret Pearse, likened the oath of fidelity to the British monarch to "perjury," as it "contradicted the oath they had already taken to the Irish Republic."[64] For Margaret Pearse, "an oath to me is a most sacred vow made in the presence of Almighty God."[65] Anti-Treaty republicans feared that taking the oath would mark Ireland, for the first time, as "voluntarily accepting the sovereignty over them of the British king."[66]

Ultimately the strength of opposition to the oath of allegiance was a major factor in why many TDs and IRA members and a significant minority of the nationalist population refused to accept the Anglo-Irish Treaty and took up arms against the Free State government in the subsequent Irish Civil War. As Liam Weeks and Micheál Ó Fathartaigh have argued, it was the "concessions made in the Treaty on Sinn Féin's Irish republican agenda . . . specifically, the oath of fidelity to the British monarch and the dominion status of the state" that "ruptured the Sinn Féin party in a very arbitrary way," directly leading to the Civil War.[67] Typical was a Civil War "Address from the Soldiers of the Republic to their former comrades in the Free State Army" in December 1922, which referred to how the Treaty "makes England's King Ireland's King."[68] Thus Ireland's monarchism/anti-monarchism dynamic fueled a bitter successor conflict, which, although the radicals opposing the oath lost, ensured through its propaganda vitriol that their arguments on the oath of allegiance prevailed. The Treaty's fudge on monarchism—which allowed a space for northern and southern unionism's monarchist culture on the island—was, after the Civil War, untenable. It was later rapidly dismantled once Éamon de Valera came to power in 1932.

All of this had profound implications for Irish society. On the one hand, the Treaty's retention of the connection with the British monarchy provided a cultural space for southern unionism to adapt and accept the Irish Free State. Ian d'Alton has argued that "an emotional attachment to the crown, representing connectivity with a residual sense of British values . . . took the place of substance" as "political unionism rebranded itself as cultural royalism."[69] Here transnational monarchism to some extent did work, helping soften the transitions from United Kingdom through Free State and into the later Irish Republic for many of the Protestant minority. However, in other ways, the role of monarchism in the Irish settlement highlighted the direct, intractable clash of values that was at the core of the Irish Revolution, the "culture wars" that helped fuel the conflict. Monarchism was foundational to the idea of Britishness, and thus its retention was vital to unionist identity; just as clearly, the radicalization of Irish republicanism from 1916 around extreme anti-monarchist tropes against the British monarchy meant that any settlement around Irish independence that involved the monarchy would provoke a violent reaction. In the Free State, it triggered Civil War.

In Northern Ireland, it fueled a unionist siege mentality: if even dominion status was unworkable for the Free State because of its connections with the monarchy, what space was left for nationalist conciliation with unionism with its strong monarchist belief systems? For northern Catholic nationalists, the radical anti-monarchism that Irish nationalism increasingly demanded from 1916 on as proof of adherence to it meant that they were further alienated from the UK state structure within which they had to live, which was interwoven with monarchist oaths, rhetoric, and practices. Republican anti-monarchism also accentuated unionist suspicion and facilitated the use of emotive monarchist accusatory languages of "treason," "sedition," and "disloyalty" that were employed by extremists to mobilize unionists to exclude the northern Catholic minority.

Finally, in Britain itself, the Irish Free State as a test case of a looser form of dominion status that trialed new kinds of transnational relationships with the monarchy failed. Free State Ireland did not evolve into a new kind of dominion where radical nationalism could exist within a broader global British identity. Instead, its lesson was that any weakening of the monarchy's ties to a dominion would result, inexorably, in a republic and a complete break with Britishness. This was interpreted as a warning for Canada, Australia, New Zealand, and others and helps explain how doggedly the British state sought to maintain ties between its former imperial possessions and the British monarchy throughout the first half of the twentieth century.

## Conclusion

The concept of monarchy as the "arch" that held a changed postwar empire together—and how this was understood—was at the core of the oath of allegiance's meaning both in Ireland and in Britain and helps explain how it could have paid such a key contributory role in triggering the Irish Civil War. Ultimately, only by recontextualizing these imperial meanings and their transnational resonances can we fully understand the Irish Revolution. Shifting the relationships between the peoples of Ireland and Britain from being structured within a common United Kingdom dynastic state to a looser "transnational monarchism" framework was the British solution put forward in 1921–22. However, it was modeled on broader changes within the empire where a transnational British monarchism was being used to resolve imperial demands for greater self-governance or independence from Westminster. Ultimately this formula underestimated the prevalence and intensity of anti-monarchism among Irish nationalists after Easter 1916. The older Home Rule model had been a broader nationalist church, containing radical anti-monarchists alongside those who tolerated the monarchy. For British political decision makers, shifting the language from empire to Commonwealth was possible, but contemplating the idea of a republic as part of the Commonwealth was not. It would not be until after the Second World War, and Indian independence, that India would become the first republic in the Commonwealth, as attitudes toward accommodating republics became more flexible. In sum, the clash between monarchists and anti-monarchists was at the heart of the Irish Revolution. It was central to the shifting definitions of British, Irish, nationalist, unionist, and republican identities between 1912 and 1923 and one of the major constraints on historical agency.

NOTES

1  The best study is James Loughlin's *The British Monarchy and Ireland: 1800 to the Present* (Cambridge: Cambridge University Press, 2007) which covers two centuries. Mary Kenny's *Crown and Shamrock: Love and Hate between Ireland and the British Monarchy* (Dublin: New Ireland, 2009) offers a broad overview. Thomas Hennessey, "Ulster Unionism and Loyalty to the Crown of the United Kingdom 1912–74," in *Unionism in Modern Ireland: New Perspectives on Politics and Culture*, ed. Richard English and Graham Walker (Basingstoke: Macmillan, 1996), 115–129, offers another broad overview. The recent study by Conor Morrissey and Brian Hughes, eds., *Southern Irish Loyalism, 1912–1949* (Liverpool: Liverpool University Press, 2020), is a welcome contribution to filling the current historiographical gap.

2  Enda Delaney and Fearghal McGarry, "Introduction: A Global History of the Irish Revolution," *Irish Historical Studies* 44, no. 165 (2020): 1–10. For another argument

for a transnational approach, see Niall Whelehan, ed., *Transnational Perspectives on Modern Irish History* (London: Routledge, 2015).

3　For global approaches, see Fearghal McGarry and Enda Delaney, eds., *The Irish Revolution, 1919–1921: A Global History* (Dublin: Wordwell, 2019); Maurice Walsh, *Bitter Freedom: Ireland in a Revolutionary World, 1918–1923* (London: Faber & Faber, 2015); Keith Jeffery, *1916: A Global History* (London: Bloomsbury, 2015). On the Irish Revolution and empire, see Enrico Dal Lago, Róisín Healy, and Gearóid Barry, eds., *1916 in Global Context: An Anti-imperial Moment* (London: Routledge, 2018); Kevin Kenny, ed., *Ireland and the British Empire* (Oxford: Oxford University Press, 2004); Timothy G. McMahon, Michael de Nie, and Paul Townend, eds., *Ireland in an Imperial World: Citizenship, Opportunism and Subversion* (London: Palgrave Macmillan, 2017).

4　On the central Asian uprising, see Joshua Sanborn, *Imperial Apocalypse: The Great War and the Destruction of the Russian Empire* (Oxford: Oxford University Press, 2014).

5　See Heather Jones, *For King and Country: The British Monarchy and the First World War* (Cambridge: Cambridge University Press, 2021); Laurence van Ypersele, *Le Roi Albert. Histoire d'un mythe* (Ottignies: Quorum, 1995); Matthew Glencross and Judith Rowbotham, eds., *Monarchies and the Great War* (London: Palgrave Macmillan, 2018).

6　On the origins of Irish republicanism, see Lee Ward, "Republican Political Theory and Irish Nationalism," *The European Legacy, Toward New Paradigms* 21, no. 1 (2016): 19–37, and Fearghal McGarry and James McConnel, eds., *The Black Hand of Republicanism: Fenianism in Modern Ireland* (Dublin: Irish Academic Press, 2009). On transnational Fenian violence, see Niall Whelehan, *The Dynamiters: Irish Nationalism and Political Violence in the Wider World, 1867–1900* (Cambridge: Cambridge University Press, 2012).

7　On Home Rule's accommodations, see James McConnel, "John Redmond and Irish Catholic Loyalism," *English Historical Review* 125, no. 512 (2010): 83–111.

8　Enda Delaney, "The Irish Diaspora," *Irish Economic and Social History* 33 (2006): 35–45; Malcolm Campbell, "Emigrant Responses to War and Revolution, 1914–21: Irish Opinion in the United States and Australia," *Irish Historical Studies* 32, no. 125 (2000): 75–92; Benjamin Grob-Fitzgibbon, "The Curious Case of the Vanishing Debate over Irish Home Rule: The Dominion of Canada, Irish Home Rule, and Canadian Historiography," *American Review of Canadian Studies* 45, no. 1 (2015): 113–128.

9　Erez Manela, *The Wilsonian Moment: Self-Determination and the International Origins of Anticolonial Nationalism* (Oxford: Oxford University Press, 2007).

10　Delaney and McGarry, "Introduction," 5.

11　Ibid., 7. Also see Lili Zách, "'The First of the Small Nations': The Significance of Central European Small States in Irish Nationalist Political Rhetoric, 1918–22," *Irish Historical Studies* 44, no. 165 (2020): 25–40.

12　Jonathan Gumz, *The Resurrection and Collapse of Empire in Habsburg Serbia, 1914–1918* (Cambridge: Cambridge University Press, 2009).

13　On the interwar league and its minorities policies, see Matthew Frank, *Making Minorities History: Population Transfer in Twentieth Century Europe* (Oxford: Oxford University Press, 2017).

14　Tim Wilson, *Frontiers of Violence: Conflict and Identity in Ulster and Upper Silesia, 1918–1922* (Oxford: Oxford University Press, 2010).

15　Kenny, *Crown and Shamrock*, 138, 160.

16　Loughlin, *British Monarchy and Ireland*, 312; Kenneth Rose, *King George V* (London: Weidenfeld and Nicolson, 1983), 240–241.

17　Loughlin, *British Monarchy and Ireland*, 312; Stamfordham to Edward Grigg, 29 July 1921 (Parliamentary Archives, London [PA], LG/F/29/4/63); Memo, 29 July 1921 (PA, LG/F/29/4/62).

18　Kenny, *Crown and Shamrock*, 156.

19　Manela, *Wilsonian Moment*; Jennifer Wellington, *Exhibiting War: The Great War, Museums and Memory in Britain, Canada and Australia* (Cambridge: Cambridge University Press, 2017).

20　John Darwin, "A Third British Empire? The Dominion Idea in Imperial Politics," in *The Oxford History of the British Empire*, vol. 4: *The Twentieth Century*, ed. Judith M. Brown and William Roger Louis (Oxford: Oxford University Press, 1999), 64–87.

21　Copy sent to Stamfordham of Lloyd George reply to Éamon de Valera, n.d. [summer 1921] (PA, LG/F/29/4/77). See also Lloyd George reply to letter from Éamon de Valera, 1921 (National Archives, United Kingdom [NAUK], CAB 24/128).

22　Mel Farrell, "'Stepping Stones to Freedom': Pro-treaty Rhetoric and Strategy during the Dáil Treaty Debates," in *The Treaty: Debating and Establishing the Irish State*, ed. Liam Weeks and Micheál Ó Fathartaigh (Newbridge, Co. Kildare: Irish Academic Press, 2018), 17.

23　Ibid., 29.

24　Ibid., 29.

25　Ian d'Alton, "No Country? Protestant 'Belongings' in Independent Ireland, 1922–49," in *Protestant and Irish: The Minority's Search for Place in Independent Ireland*, ed. Ian d'Alton and Ida Milne (Cork: Cork University Press, 2019), 28.

26　Guy Beiner, *Forgetful Remembrance: Social Forgetting and Vernacular Historiography of a Rebellion in Ulster* (Oxford: Oxford University Press, 2018).

27　John Dorney, "Republican Representations of the Treaty: 'A Usurpation Pure and Simple,'" in Weeks and Ó Fathartaigh, *The Treaty*, 73–74.

28　James Murphy, *Abject Loyalty: Nationalism and Monarchy in the Reign of Queen Victoria* (Cork: Cork University Press, 2001).

29　McConnel, "John Redmond and Irish Catholic Loyalism."

30　Fearghal McGarry, "1916 and Irish Republicanism: Between Myth and History," in *Towards Commemoration: Ireland in War and Revolution*, ed. John Horne and Edward Madigan (Dublin: Royal Irish Academy, 2013), 46–53.

31　See Ben Novick, *Conceiving Revolution: Irish Nationalist Propaganda during the First World War* (Dublin: Four Courts Press, 2001), for anti-monarchist republican propaganda.

32  Jones, *For King and Country*, 266.

33  Note from Sir Edward Grigg to David Lloyd George, 14 June 1921, p. 3 (PA, LG/F/86/1/5).

34  Kenny, *Crown and Shamrock*, 117.

35  Loughlin, *British Monarchy and Ireland*, 318.

36  Copy sent to Stamfordham of Lloyd George reply to Éamon de Valera, n.d. [summer 1921] (PA, LG/F/29/4/77).

37  Ibid.

38  Ibid.

39  Suggestion by Mr. Tom Jones merging the draft oath of allegiance with the oath administered to representatives and delegates to Congress (NAUK, CAB 21/247).

40  Undated, unsigned minute (NAUK, CAB 21/247).

41  Oath proposed by Mr. Griffith and Mr. Collins, 1 Dec. 1921 (NAUK, CAB 21/247).

42  Conference on Ireland, Meeting of Sub-Conference at the House of Lords [Minutes], p. 3, 24 Nov. 1921 (NAUK, CAB 21/247).

43  Notes of a Meeting of the Conference on Ireland held at the House of Lords, 24 Nov. 1921 (NAUK, CAB 21/247).

44  Minutes of Conference on Ireland, Meeting of Sub-Conference at the House of Lords [Minutes], p. 2, 24 Nov. 1921 (NAUK, CAB 21/247).

45  Memorandum by the Irish delegates on their proposal for the association of Ireland with the British Commonwealth, signed Arthur Griffith, 28 Nov. 1921 (NAUK, CAB 21/247).

46  Ibid.

47  Conference on Ireland, Meeting of Sub-Conference at the House of Lords [Minutes], p. 2, 24 Nov. 1921 (NAUK, CAB 21/247).

48  Laura Cahillane and Paul Murray, "The Treaty: An Historical and Legal Interpretation," in Weeks and Ó Fathartaigh, *The Treaty*, 244.

49  Notes of a Meeting of the Conference on Ireland held at the House of Lords, 24 Nov. 1921 (NAUK, CAB 21/247).

50  Aide Memoire by the Attorney General, Conference on Ireland, 25 Nov. 1921 (NAUK, CAB 21/247).

51  The only exception to this norm was the populations of Crown Protectorates. On British nationality rules in this period, see Kathleen Paul, *Whitewashing Britain: Race and Citizenship in the Postwar Era* (Ithaca, NY: Cornell University Press, 1997), 13, 26.

52  Notes of a meeting of the Conference on Ireland held at the House of Lords on 24 Nov. 1921 (NAUK, CAB 21/247).

53  Conference on Ireland, Memo by His Majesty's Government, 27 Oct. 1921 (NAUK CAB 21/247).

54  Note in file, titled "incorporated in S.F.C. 17," n.d. (NAUK, CAB 21/247).

55  Conference on Ireland, Memo by His Majesty's Government, 27 Oct. 1921 (NAUK, CAB 21/247).

56  Kenny, *Crown and Shamrock*, 163.

57 Farrell, "Stepping Stones to Freedom," 17.

58 Cahillane and Murray, "The Treaty," 246–247.

59 Ibid., 246–247.

60 Dorney, "Republican Representations of the Treaty," 74–75.

61 Cahillane and Murray, "The Treaty," 247.

62 Kenny, *Crown and Shamrock*, 163.

63 Sinéad McCoole, "Debating Not Negotiating: The Female TDs of the Second Dáil," in Weeks and Ó Fathartaigh, *The Treaty*, 150.

64 Dorney, "Republican Representations of the Treaty," 72, 74.

65 Ibid., 72.

66 Ibid., 67.

67 Liam Weeks and Micheál Ó Fathartaigh, "Conclusion: Judging the Treaty," in Weeks and Ó Fathartaigh, *The Treaty*, 226–227.

68 Dorney, "Republican Representations of the Treaty," 75.

69 D'Alton, "No Country?," 27–28.

# PART FOUR

# Radical Lives, Global Networks

# Neither Lenin nor Wilson

## *The Evolving Anti-imperialism of Three Women of the Transatlantic Irish Left, 1916–1923*

ELIZABETH McKILLEN

The domestic roots of the nationalist and anti-imperialist thought that guided the Easter Rebels and subsequent Irish revolutionary leaders have been well established by a rich historiography on the Irish Revolution. Yet, as transnational historians have recently emphasized, many revolutionary movements of the period were also influenced by the global contest between Leninist and Wilsonian visions of national self-determination, and the question of which colonial peoples were entitled to political freedom. Particularly engaged by this debate were Irish and Irish American women lecturers from social reform backgrounds, or of leftist political persuasions, who toured the United States to win American financial and political support for Irish independence. Such women often found it beneficial to frame Irish nationalist appeals to mainstream American audiences or to Irish American organizations using Wilsonian rhetoric. Yet these women also gravitated to events sponsored by American labor, feminist, socialist, and left-leaning immigrant organizations and imbibed Bolshevik and other radical ideologies that enjoyed more favor in these circles. As Irish and Irish American women lectured throughout the United States and contributed articles to diverse publications, they reformulated ideas about Ireland's right to nationhood to suit their audiences. In the process, they contributed in important ways both to evolving Irish nationalist thought and to an ongoing debate within American society about the changing US role in the world.[1]

This chapter focuses on three women of the transatlantic Irish Left: Irish émigré Kathleen O'Brennan, Irish feminist Hanna Sheehy Skeffington, and Irish American labor leader Leonora O'Reilly. Recent studies of Sheehy Skeffington and O'Brennan have emphasized the way they developed American identities and used American ideas to raise funds for the Irish nationalist cause in the United States.[2] These three women, however, are perhaps better understood as "organic intellectuals." Their ideas grew from their active involvement in both social movements and the transnational Irish nationalist struggle, and their anti-imperialist visions were syncretic and constantly evolving.[3] Influenced by their American audiences and colleagues, they, in turn, contributed in important ways to ongoing debates over US foreign policy, and to the political mobilization of American women during a critical period when they won suffrage.

## Kathleen O'Brennan

Kathleen O'Brennan was the first of the three to agitate systematically on behalf of Irish independence in the United States. Born into a politically active family in Dublin in 1876, she became involved in the Gaelic League at an early age and, as a young adult, began to write and lecture on Irish themes. Little more is known of her early life.[4] In 1914 she traveled to the United States, planning to stay only briefly to pursue some journalistic projects. The outbreak of the First World War, however, made it difficult for her to return home. Instead she chose to stay in the United States and support herself through lecturing and writing. O'Brennan initially had difficulty landing any writing or even secretarial jobs, but she managed to earn a living lecturing for American women's clubs and Irish American organizations in the American West on themes such as Gaelic customs and the Irish arts. During these engagements, according to one newspaper, she "charmed the hearts of America's smart set."[5] The Irish Easter Rising of 1916, however, further politicized O'Brennan, and she increasingly interspersed her lectures on Irish culture with information on the rebellion and subsequent events in Ireland. Both of Kathleen's sisters participated in the Easter Rising and paid a heavy price for their activism. Her sister Lily was imprisoned at Kilmainham jail for her role in military support work on behalf of the Irish rebels, while her sister Áine was married to Éamonn Ceannt, who was executed for his leadership role in the Easter Rising. Kathleen used information and photos sent by her sisters to emphasize the brutality with which the British suppressed the rebellion and imposed martial law. She also documented the growing support for Sinn Féin, characterizing it as filled with a "pure, beautiful idealism," and arguing that it was "the only democratic party in Ireland." O'Brennan often compared the Irish independence struggle to that of the American Revolution and emphasized that the United States should follow the lead of the French in 1778 by assisting the Irish in achieving their freedom.[6]

O'Brennan's expertise on the Irish rebellion led to invitations to lecture from a broader range of groups, including labor and feminist organizations. Some labor activists initially viewed her as too politically conservative. A Portland, Oregon, trade unionist, for example, criticized one of her talks as insufficiently "anti-capitalist" and too supportive of the Catholic Church. But after O'Brennan befriended, and perhaps became romantically involved with, radical physician, feminist, and labor activist Dr. Marie Equi, she became further radicalized. Equi was deeply engaged in activities on behalf of the syndicalist Industrial Workers of the World (IWW) and introduced O'Brennan to IWW audiences and ideas.[7] O'Brennan's writings and lecture notes for the period after the United States entered the war drew on a class analysis of American society popular among contemporary labor radicals. She continued to praise America's founding revolutionary and anti-imperialist ideals. Yet she also emphasized that, after the US Civil War, "profiteers" had forgotten the American "ideal of liberty" and replaced it with the "worship of material success." US involvement in the First World War had made the material class even more dominant. The consequence was that even as "boys were sent to the front to die for ideals of freedom of small nations, freedom of seas, [and] freedom generally . . . those who sent them were looting the country and extending imperialism." She characterized the American press as "an engine of imperialistic and English propaganda."[8]

Following the passage of the Espionage Act in 1917, both Equi and O'Brennan became targets of government surveillance and prosecution. The Wilson administration used the act, which outlawed the obstruction of military operations during wartime, not only to prevent sabotage but also to prosecute antiwar speech and to censor publications critical of the war effort. Equi was arrested and charged with sedition under the terms of the act even before she met O'Brennan but was released pending trial. In the autumn of 1918, the Portland Bureau of Investigation hired undercover informant Margaret Lowell Paul to befriend Equi and O'Brennan and report on their activities. O'Brennan developed a close friendship with Lowell Paul and unwittingly confided in her. According to the informant, O'Brennan took an increasing interest in labor issues because of Equi and spoke on an almost daily basis to union audiences to raise funds for Equi's defense. This work convinced O'Brennan that the war was fomenting class revolution. O'Brennan also told Lowell Paul that "nearly all 'the Irish' here [were] furious at her for associating with the notorious Dr. Equi." She further reported that O'Brennan was becoming increasingly critical of the Wilson administration and spoke in disparaging terms about the preliminary peace terms and Wilson's intervention in Russia.[9]

Equi's trial began in November, and according to intelligence reports, O'Brennan convinced labor officials from the Oregon State Federation of Labor to testify on her behalf.[10] Equi was nonetheless found guilty in late December and sentenced to three years in prison. A series of legal appeals temporarily kept her out of jail. O'Brennan, meanwhile, was issued a warrant of deportation in early January 1919 at the hotel room she was sharing with Equi. Agents specifically reported on how a "disrobed Equi" chased them from the room.[11] Despite the warrant and her own upcoming deportation hearing, O'Brennan managed the public campaign to raise money for Equi's appeal cases and published a pamphlet urging all workers to unite behind her cause. She wrote a resolution, unanimously passed by the Oregon State Federation of Labor, calling for a reassessment of the intelligence used in Equi's case. Local unions additionally rallied to oppose O'Brennan's deportation and the efforts to "defame" her.[12] Intelligence reports on labor unrest in the Northwest lamented that local AFL and IWW unionists, influenced by O'Brennan and other Irish agitators, participated in parades that simultaneously supported Sinn Féin and Irish freedom, an end to the blockade of Russia, and the release of all war prisoners. Some agents noted that while respectable Irish groups now refused to support O'Brennan, "idiotic Sinn Féiners" wanted to make a "hero" of her and continued to "give her money."[13]

Equi's and O'Brennan's legal problems occurred at a propitious time as President Wilson was negotiating the peace treaty ending the First World War. Equi urged O'Brennan to focus on Irish issues and not attack Wilson because it would get her "nowhere but out of the country."[14] But as Wilson continued to ignore the issue of Irish independence at the peace conference, O'Brennan found it difficult to remain silent. When Wilson first announced his support for self-determination and democracy for oppressed nationalities in early 1918, O'Brennan praised the president and argued that Ireland had supported these same ideals since the twelfth century. His failure to speak about Ireland's fate during the war, however, alarmed her, as did his intervention in Russia. After his silence on the issue during the early months of 1919, O'Brennan warned that if America failed to support the Irish Republic at the peace conference, Irish leaders would "tear the mask of hypocrisy" from all those nations that betrayed their wartime promises. At a large meeting in San Francisco she emphasized that the Allies needed to demonstrate that their "slogans" were not "empty phrases" and argued that "Ireland will be the test of world democracy."[15]

Since so few Irish agencies now supported her lectures, O'Brennan created a new organization, the Women's Irish Educational League, devoted to spreading the facts about Irish independence and related issues. This organization developed branches throughout the Northwest and sponsored debates on critical issues like the League of Nations. Some Friends of Irish Freedom chapters also continued to support O'Brennan, and she went on another lecture tour in the Pacific Northwest highlighting British atrocities during the Irish War of Independence and detailing the democratic government created by Sinn Féin. Her tour included mining camps in Nevada, where she helped to found three Friends of Irish Freedom chapters. One was named after her executed brother-in-law Éamonn Ceannt. Indicative of her growing disillusionment with Wilsonian internationalism, she also attacked plans for the League of Nations, arguing that it would commit the United States to more imperialist wars.[16]

When Equi lost her appeals and was sent to jail, O'Brennan moved east and became one of the leaders of the American Women Pickets for the Enforcement of America's War Aims. This group aggressively picketed the British embassy and insisted that the United States and Britain needed to honor the pledge of self-determination for oppressed nation-alities. To do otherwise, they argued, "would be an insult to American men of Irish blood who fought in the war effort." Historian Catherine Burns has persuasively argued that, during these campaigns, Kathleen O'Brennan engaged in the "deliberate construction of an American identity for both herself and the American Women Pickets" to prevent critics from attacking the campaigns as un-American or radical. She also likely sought to protect herself from further harassment by the Bureau of Investigation and from being further ostracized by Irish American groups. O'Brennan sometimes even used aliases when sending reports of the group's activities to the media. To further highlight the American identity of the group, O'Brennan stressed that its membership included many Protestants with old-stock lineages.[17]

Yet building an American identity for the pickets did not mean that O'Brennan abandoned her radicalism. Following her management of the picket campaign, she became an important speaker for the James Larkin Defense Fund. Larkin, an Irish labor leader, came to the United States in the wake of the Dublin Lock-Out and remained for the du-ration of the war. In 1919 he became a communist and was soon con-victed on charges of criminal syndicalism. O'Brennan did not follow him down the communist path but nonetheless emphasized in her speeches that Larkin was a hero of the working people in both Ireland and the United States. On behalf of Irish workers, she demanded that Larkin be given a "Square Deal." Clearly viewing the issues as interre-lated, her appeals on behalf of Larkin also demanded that Ireland, per-haps the "smallest nation" in the world, be given a "square deal" by the "biggest nation," the United States. She noted that one currently heard a lot about the League of Nations for 100 percent Americanism, but it would be the growing international labor movement that guaranteed liberty for both individuals and small nations. Indeed, "the intellectual and the laborers" were the "only hope of the world today."[18]

Around the same time, O'Brennan attempted to create a branch of the Irish White Cross, without much success. This was due largely to a decision on the part of leaders from major Irish groups in New York to shun her. O'Brennan nonetheless remained influential, publishing two articles in the *New York Times* on the innovative and highly democratic

Sinn Féin government in Ireland. She also published an article in the *San Francisco Chronicle* highlighting the neglected subject of Ireland's labor situation. The Irish Transport and General Workers' Union, she argued, now controlled large swaths of the country and might well determine Ireland's future. O'Brennan opposed the Anglo-Irish Treaty of 1921 on the grounds that it did not give genuine independence to Ireland and partitioned the country by excluding Northern Ireland from the Irish Free State. She attended the Lausanne Conference to formally accuse the Free State government of violating international law and of war crimes under the terms of the Geneva Convention. From her perspective, the British were the puppeteers controlling the Irish Free State's actions. Subsequently, O'Brennan became active in the Women's Prisoners Defense Association, a development that won significant news coverage in American newspapers. O'Brennan also submitted a resolution to Congress from the "Women of Ireland" asking it to denounce Britain for plunging Ireland into civil war and committing war crimes against Irish women and children.[19]

O'Brennan returned to Ireland sometime in 1922 and, after the Irish Civil War, resumed her career as a writer of fiction and poetry. Perhaps this career shift, in combination with the political marginalization of anti-Treaty women in both postrevolutionary Ireland and Irish America, explains why she has been largely overlooked by historians.[20] From 1914 to 1923, however, O'Brennan played a significant role in Irish nationalist politics in the United States and in contributing to American debates about the First World War and the postwar peace settlement. She evolved from a relatively apolitical lecturer on Irish culture to a radical but noncommunist critic of imperialism and US foreign policy. Her thinking was influenced in part by her family's experiences in Ireland. Yet her relationship with Equi and their immersion in the culture of the IWW also proved important, leading her to develop an emphasis on the linkages between the class struggle and imperialism. Although O'Brennan encountered both Wilsonian and Leninist ideas in the varied political landscape of the United States, she ultimately embraced neither and instead hewed her own radical path. Her ideas proved popular in many labor and feminist circles in the United States even as the leaders of Irish America ostracized her.

## Hanna Sheehy Skeffington

Hanna Sheehy was born in 1877 in County Cork, the oldest of six children. Her family owned several small, local businesses but moved to Dublin when Hanna was eight after her father, David Sheehy, won an Irish Parliamentary Party seat at Westminster. In Dublin, Hanna and her sisters attended convent schools, and Hanna chose to pursue university training at St. Mary's University and High School. Recent educational reforms allowed women to sit for university exams, although not to attend classes with men. Hanna took her bachelor's exams in 1899, receiving second-class honors in modern languages, and in 1902 she earned a master's degree with first-class honors. Her unusually high levels of education for a woman of this period proved an asset in her future teaching career and political activities.[21]

Hanna became active in the woman's suffrage movement in Dublin as a young woman and in 1903 married fellow suffragist and pacifist Francis Skeffington. The two took the name Sheehy Skeffington to symbolize their equal partnership with each other and their commitment to feminist ideals. The Sheehy Skeffingtons quickly became leaders in the Dublin suffrage movement. In addition to their suffrage work, Hanna and Francis also supported the activities of the Irish Women Workers' Union because they believed economic independence was critical to women's equality. Although Hanna and Francis also viewed themselves as Irish nationalists, they clashed with Home Rule advocates over their failure to include a clause on women's suffrage in Home Rule bills. Subsequently, the two refused to work on behalf of the Home Rule cause in Ireland. Other Irish nationalists who favored full independence for Ireland, ranging from those who advocated physical force to remove the British from Ireland to the Sinn Féin party that emphasized passive resistance, argued that women had been equal citizens in Irish society before the British colonized Ireland. Most separatists insisted that women's rights would be fully restored once the British left Ireland. Hanna, however, expressed skepticism about this claim, warning women not to be misled by the "thriftless Irish habit of relying on the reputation of its ancestors . . . when one is faced with the problems of today." Although Hanna and Francis both knew people involved in planning the Easter Rising, they did not participate in their efforts.[22]

Yet when the Easter Rising commenced, Hanna took food and supplies to the rebels occupying the General Post Office in Dublin. While
there, she was favorably impressed by their decision to include "equal
citizenship for women" in their proclamation of independence. Francis,
for his part, took to the streets to offer first aid and to prevent looting.
Despite the pacifist nature of his activities during Easter Week, Francis
was arrested by British troops. That night he was taken from his cell,
executed without trial, and buried without notification of the family.
When Hanna discovered the truth about her husband's death two days
later, she used her political connections to demand a court-martial of
the officer who had ordered Francis's execution. Dissatisfied with the
results of the court-martial, she soon "made up [her] mind . . . to go to
America and to tell [the] story of British militarism to every audience
in the States that I could reach." Her decision suggested that she at least
temporarily gave greater priority to the Irish nationalist rather than the
suffragist cause.[23]

In retrospect, Sheehy Skeffington's Irish nationalist work in the
United States can be divided into three stages. During the first stage of
her lecture tour, from late 1916 to March 1917, the United States had
not yet entered the First World War. Sheehy Skeffington's work during
this period was mostly funded by the newly formed American umbrella
group the Friends of Irish Freedom. Her lectures focused primarily on
the brutal and unprovoked murder of her husband and ended with
the vague request that the United States ensure that any future peace
conference consider the cause of Irish independence. During a second
stage, from the time the United States entered the war in early April
1917 until she returned to Ireland in May 1918, she reconceptualized her
lectures to assert Irish claims to independence on the basis of Wilson's
statement of war aims. She did this even as she grew more wary of the
president due to her increased ties to US labor and feminist groups. A
third stage of Sheehy Skeffington's work commenced during the Irish
Civil War in 1922, when she briefly returned to the United States to
raise money for the families of Irish Republican political prisoners and
also began writing weekly front-page stories for the *Irish World and
American Industrial Liberator*, an influential Irish American newspaper.

During the first stage of her lecture tour, Sheehy Skeffington's focused lectures on her husband's murder by the British helped to es-

tablish her reputation as an excellent and popular orator. Newspapers across the country marveled at the large, diverse crowds she attracted, noting that her audiences were often filled not just with Irish American activists but also with representatives from labor and feminist groups. Many also commented on the remarkable poise she demonstrated during her lectures, a quality that she had likely cultivated during her teaching career. Several news accounts noted that while Sheehy Skeffington remained calm, her audiences often responded emotionally to her lectures, yelling "swine" when she detailed Francis's secret execution at the hands of British troops and "sobbing" at other points in the lecture. Whether intended or not, her lectures seemed to reinforce already strong anti-British and antiwar sentiment within Irish America and among some American leftist activists. Her talks depicted British imperialism as barbaric and undemocratic at a time when President Wilson was increasingly tilting toward entering the war on the side of Britain. Letters to Sheehy Skeffington from American feminists, socialists, and labor activists expressed horror at the British actions she described during Easter week and invited her to speak at their events.[24]

During his speech asking Congress to declare war against Germany in early April 1917, Wilson emphasized that the primary wartime goal of the United States would be to defeat German autocracy and make the world "safe for democracy." Such rhetoric provided a natural rallying cry for oppressed nations seeking independence from colonial powers. Ireland was no exception. Yet while the Wilson administration emphasized promoting democracy abroad as a wartime goal, it limited democratic rights within the United States by using the Espionage Act to prohibit nearly all speech and publications critical of the president and the war effort. The Bureau of Investigation initiated widespread surveillance of all speakers it believed might be encouraging disloyalty, including Kathleen O'Brennan. Influenced by both Wilson's democratic war aims and his crackdown on democracy in the United States, Sheehy Skeffington shifted the tone and focus of her lectures following US entry into the war.

The first sign of this shift came in Los Angeles in late April, when she spoke to an audience of over four thousand people. Sheehy Skeffington lauded the president's noble war aims but urged "America not to stop short at Ireland in this splendid move on behalf of the democracies of the world." She asked that Ireland be accorded the same rights to independence as "Belgium, Switzerland, and Holland" at war's end. Subsequently, she made several more highly publicized speeches in the West, including one in the mining town of Butte, Montana, that was followed by anti-draft protests staged by the IWW and the left-leaning Pearse-Connolly Irish Independence Club. When Sheehy Skeffington traveled to San Francisco following her Butte tour, intelligence agents filed the first official surveillance report on her with the Bureau of Investigation, inaccurately noting that she was a wife of an "Irish Revolutionist" executed for his role in the Easter Rising and seemed to be an agent of "German Propaganda."[25]

Sheehy Skeffington further developed her ideas when she returned to the East and lectured to diverse groups, including suffragists, labor unions, socialists, students, and, perhaps most importantly, the Congress of Small and Subject Nationalities held at the Hotel McAlpin in New York. The *Irish World and American Industrial Liberator* signaled the importance of her speech at the last event, publishing it in full under the subheading, "Hanna Sheehy Skeffington, in Brilliant Address Before Congress of Small Nations, States Ireland's Case." She opened her talk by congratulating the congress for "doing the obvious" in a way avoided by the major powers and asking "representatives of the oppressed nations and subject races to state their own case before the tribunal of public opinion." She suggested that the final determination of whether a nation deserved its independence should be decided not on the basis of whether the imperial power had enough guns to continue to hold such countries in subjection but on the basis of a referendum or plebiscite, presumably after a public hearing of their case. The age of big empires, she suggested, was passing because empires were a "foe to progress" and a "menace to world peace, to culture, [and] to civilization." In the meantime, colonized people should come together to create a "trades union for small nations against our exploiters."

Sheehy Skeffington then made her specific case for Ireland. She noted that while some assumed Ireland had always been a possession of Britain's, nothing could be further from the truth. "When the British were painted savages," she suggested, "the Irish were already a civilized people." After the British invaded Ireland in 1172, they pursued a pattern similar to other foreign rulers: they attempted "the extermination of the native, his language, his culture (and later his religion)," with "uprising after uprising quelled by superior might." Even as Britain extended democracy domestically, it failed to export democratic rights to Ireland, depriving it of its own parliament. Instead the British imposed an "inefficient Prussianism" on Ireland and heavily taxed the Irish people to pay the salaries of British administrators and military personnel. Incompetent British rule in Ireland led to the decimation of its population during the potato famine of the 1840s. Once Ireland received its independence, she insisted, it would not only create more democratic political institutions but also "Hooverize [government] administration" by making it more efficient and less costly "to the great benefit of our people." The economy would flourish as Ireland pursued trade with other nations, was relieved of its heavy tax burden, and was no longer forced to help pay Britain's crushing war debts.

Finally, Sheehy Skeffington argued that she, like the other representatives at the meeting, looked to the United States to make her homeland "safe for democracy." Ireland had a "claim upon" America to ensure it received a fair hearing at the peace conference and achieved full independence at war's end. If Belgium, she warned again, became fully independent while Ireland remained a protectorate under British dominion, this would not be either "democratic or impartial." She concluded that "Ireland geographically, racially, historically, and ethically, has as strong a claim as any small nation in the world" to independence.[26]

To help advance Ireland's cause in the United States, Sheehy Skeffington joined with leading Irish American women activists to launch the left-leaning Irish Progressive League and the Irish National Bureau during the autumn of 1917. The former group was distinctive because women enjoyed leadership positions in the organization, in contrast to most Irish American organizations, and pledged itself to promoting a variety of progressive causes. The latter organization was Sheehy Skeffington's brainchild and was designed to coordinate the distribution of propaganda on Irish issues to government representatives in Washington at key times. Likely due to her growing prominence, the Cumann na mBan, a women's auxiliary to the Irish Volunteers that played an important role in the Easter Rising, asked her to present a petition to President Wilson requesting US assistance in promoting independence for all of Britain's colonies, including Ireland, India, and

Egypt. Bainbridge Colby, head of the US Shipping Department and an Irish sympathizer who had introduced Sheehy Skeffington at one of her lectures, helped arrange a meeting for her with the president on 11 January 1918. She found Wilson to be quite "gracious," but doubted he would lead "pioneer-like" on the issue of Irish independence. On the other hand, she believed he could be influenced by political pressure. With this goal in mind, she not only continued her extensive lecturing activities but also began to lobby congressmen on various resolutions demanding Irish independence.[27]

In the spring of 1918, Sheehy Skeffington returned to the West Coast and spoke at a labor meeting in San Francisco on behalf of Irish American labor activist Tom Mooney, who had been arrested and imprisoned for allegedly throwing a bomb at a preparedness parade in 1916. This activity brought her renewed attention from intelligence agents in the West, and at a subsequent meeting she was arrested for making "extremely anti-British speeches" that were "calculated [to] discourage enlistments and particularly encourage women not [to] support war measures and to oppose enlistment and the operation [of] selective draft." The charges were dismissed, but her continued harassment by intelligence agents, in combination with increasing press censorship, made Sheehy Skeffington more wary of the Wilson administration. Although Wilson appropriated the term "self-determination" from the Bolsheviks in the winter of 1918 and began using it to describe his own agenda for small nations, Sheehy Skeffington increasingly doubted that Wilson would intervene to support the struggle of British colonies for independence at war's end. Shortly before returning to Ireland in the spring of 1918, she spoke at a socialist meeting where she warned that unless the president acted to support independence for British as well as German colonies, he would become known as the "greatest hypocrite in history."[28]

In assessing her first lecture tour, Irish labor leader James Larkin dismissed Sheehy Skeffington as an "apologist for the Sinn Féin crowd" whose lectures were largely devoid of radical or labor content.[29] Yet intelligence agents, although often exaggerating her radicalism, may have better understood the subversive potential of her first lecture tour among both Irish Americans, a majority of whom were working class during this period, and the American left. Sheehy Skeffington's initial lectures on her husband's murder by British troops undermined Wilson's efforts to portray the British as more democratic and civilized than the Germans. By using Wilsonian rhetoric about democracy to make a case for Irish independence after the United States entered the war, she made it more difficult for the president to ignore the Irish issue without being accused of hypocrisy. In her talks for audiences like the Congress of Small Nations and labor, socialist, and feminist groups, she developed a broader critique of imperialism and a far more extensive agenda for making small nations "safe for democracy" than either President Wilson or many Sinn Féin leaders presented. Indeed, although Sheehy Skeffington never systematically analyzed Wilson's attitudes and policies with respect to imperialism, her thinking evolved in quite different directions from the president's during the war years. As scholars have emphasized, Wilson was not opposed to all forms of imperialism. He believed that some subject nationalities were not yet ready for independence and needed to first be "tutored" in the ways of democracy by a mature democratic polity. This helped him to justify the continued US military occupations of small Caribbean countries as well as colonization of the Philippines and interventionism in Mexico. It also enabled him to rationalize continued British imperialism. He assumed that democracies like Britain and the United States were helping underdeveloped societies mature to a stage where they would be ready for independent democratic government.[30]

Sheehy Skeffington, sensitized to the dangers of paternalistic thinking by her feminist politics, clearly objected to this kind of condescending reasoning and insisted that the people of subject nations were the ones best qualified to decide whether they were ready to be independent. She also highlighted the innumerable ways in which British imperialism had hindered rather than helped the Irish to achieve political and economic democracy. Her ideas, although not anti-capitalist like Larkin's, proved popular among workers and women and helped inspire new forms of political mobilization, as was evident in the activities of the Irish Progressive League and Irish Nationalist Bureau, and in the anti-draft activities of labor groups in the aftermath of some of Sheehy Skeffington's lectures. Sheehy Skeffington continued to aid some of the left-leaning groups she helped to create even after returning to Ireland and assuming roles in the republican Dáil government.[31]

Sheehy Skeffington returned to a direct role on the American scene during the Irish Civil War, when she briefly traveled to the United States on a fundraising tour for Republican political prisoners and became a regular front-page reporter for the *Irish World and American Industrial Liberator*. During her fundraising campaigns on behalf of anti-Treaty Republican prisoners, Sheehy Skeffington spoke to much smaller groups than she had during her first tour. By contrast, her weekly front-page stories for the *Irish World* circulated widely throughout the United States and proved significant because she was one of the few journalists consistently reporting on the Irish Civil War from an anti-Treaty perspective in either the Irish American or mainstream American press. Equally important, the *Irish World* was smuggled into Ireland during this period and sometimes afforded Republican forces and sympathizers more detailed news coverage of the atrocities committed by Free State forces than they would otherwise have had.[32]

One important theme emphasized by Sheehy Skeffington in her early *Irish World* articles was that neither the vote on the Treaty in the Dáil nor the subsequent general election that led to a pro-Treaty majority in the new Irish Free State government constituted a legitimate referendum of the Irish people on the question of independence. She insisted that both the Dáil and Irish citizens during the general election voted under duress: if they refused to accept the Treaty they were threatened by British authorities with total war. Second, she argued that the general election was based on an old and "bogus register" established under British law that excluded more than one-third of the qualified voters, including women between the ages of twenty-one and thirty and many young men who had recently come of age, while giving "plural votes to property owners." Third, the new British-imposed constitution had been published only on the day of the election, preventing most voters from fully understanding the ways in which democracy would be undermined by new government institutions. Clearly, this process failed to meet the criteria Sheehy Skeffington had established in her 1917 speech before the Congress of Subject Nations for a democratic and impartial plebiscite on independence.[33]

In subsequent articles, Sheehy Skeffington objected to the partition of Ireland and elaborated on her belief that the new government created for southern Ireland, far from constituting a "Free State" as its promoters claimed, was instead a "Freak State" that was far less democratic and independent than the government that had evolved under the direction of the Dáil during the Irish War for Independence. The unicameral Dáil was replaced by a bicameral structure that included an elected lower body but also a senate whose members were nominated by government leaders, other constituencies, and the lower house. The senate, according to Sheehy Skeffington, would give disproportionate representation to "titled nobodies" and big business interests and act as a "gilded brake on democracy" comparable to the House of Lords. Labor, meanwhile, was underrepresented. Further undermining the democratic nature of the government was the power given to the king to summon and dismiss the Irish Parliament as well as the supremacy given to the king over the Irish courts. Also galling to Sheehy Skeffington, like many opponents of the Treaty, was the requirement that governmental leaders take an oath of fidelity to the king. Although the new government gave the vote to women between the ages of twenty-one and thirty who had previously been excluded under British law, Sheehy Skeffington argued that it otherwise maintained "all the legal and juristic disabilities under which women still suffer in the British code."[34]

During her coverage of the Irish Civil War (1922–1923), Sheehy Skeffington regularly and exhaustively detailed atrocities perpetrated by Free State military forces against their Republican counterparts, including the continued torture and execution without trial of Republican prisoners. She also alleged that the Free State was waging a war against women—some of whom were combatants and others of whom were entirely innocent. She detailed innumerable episodes in which women were beaten, strip-searched, detained without cause, imprisoned without trial, and held in atrocious conditions at Kilmainham and Mountjoy jails. The cruelty of Irish Free State tactics, she argued, violated long-established rules of warfare and "aped" British methods. Cartoons published alongside Sheehy Skeffington's articles emphasized that Free State leaders had become the puppets of British imperialists.[35]

Sheehy Skeffington's coverage of the Irish Free State during the Civil War and its immediate aftermath marked another milestone in her evolution as an anti-imperialist. At one time convinced that women's suffrage must take priority over the pursuit of independence, she now believed that neither Irish men nor women could be entirely free without full independence from British political and economic domination. Influenced by Wilsonian rhetoric about making the world "safe for democracy" during her first trip to the United States, Sheehy Skeffington quickly became skeptical of the president and developed an interest in broader theories of imperialism circulating within the American left and in other immigrant communities.

Sheehy Skeffington's lectures and writings, while focused on Ireland, became important to broader debates about imperialism in the United States and internationally. Most immediately, editors of the *Irish World* used her civil war writings to attack the domestic and foreign policies of the US Republican presidents of the 1920s who, they argued, were creating their own "Freak State." In 1924, disillusioned by the imperialist policies of both the Democrats and the Republicans, the editors endorsed the third-party presidential candidacy of Robert LaFollette, whom they had long viewed as a champion of the rights of oppressed nationalities.[36] Joining the *Irish World* in its support of LaFollette were many feminists and labor activists who had been influenced by the lectures of Hanna Sheehy Skeffington and other Irish nationalists. Some of these activists raised critical questions about new forms of informal and economic imperialism practiced by the United States in Latin America and Asia. Other feminist activists, such as Jane Addams, with whom Sheehy Skeffington had cultivated a close personal relationship, joined her in the 1920s in promoting the rights of oppressed nationalities in the International League for Women's Peace and Freedom. At a congress of this organization held in Dublin in 1926, Sheehy Skeffington insisted in a keynote address that Ireland had become the "worst example in the world today of a victim of imperialistic capitalism, or of economic imperialism."[37] Such arguments likely resonated with Irish American women activists of more limited resources, such as Leonora O'Reilly, who played an important role in bringing anti-imperialist concerns more directly into US social movements and the lives of Irish American women.

## Leonora O'Reilly

In contrast to Sheehy Skeffington and O'Brennan, O'Reilly traveled relatively little during her short life. Yet as a lifelong labor and suffrage activist ensconced in her New York community, she planned Irish nationalist activities that reached working-class Irish American women and men in a way that other Irish nationalist campaigns did not. As Tara McCarthy has demonstrated, these types of ethnic activities helped politicize Irish American working and middle-class women during the critical decade in which US women won the right to vote.[38]

O'Reilly was born in 1870 to parents who had both immigrated to the United States as children. Her father died when she was quite young, and her mother took a job in a textile factory to support herself and Leonora, who was an only child. Leonora dropped out of elementary school to work in a textile factory herself at age eleven. She became active even as a child in trade union activity, organizing a Working Women's Society at the age of sixteen and working with Rose Schneiderman to form a women's local of the United Garment Workers of America. O'Reilly soon gained a reputation as an able and compelling speaker and was increasingly invited to give lectures for women's reform organizations. Perhaps most importantly, she frequently lectured for, and eventually became a member of, the Women's Trade Union League (WTUL), a group that brought working- and middle-class women together to fight on behalf of better conditions for women in industry. In 1909, she received a lifetime annuity from a member of the WTUL so that she could become a full-time staff member.[39]

The WTUL served as a pathway through which O'Reilly became involved in the suffrage and pacifist movements. From O'Reilly's perspective, the best way to achieve industrial democracy was through government intervention. The votes of working women could bring into government socialists and other sympathetic politicians who would advance the rights of workers on the job and guarantee them a voice in the management of companies. Yet O'Reilly often complained that middle-class and college-educated women dominated the suffrage movement and treated working-class women in a condescending manner.[40]

O'Reilly joined other suffrage women in trying to prevent US involvement in the First World War and was invited to give a speech at the International Women's Peace Congress at the Hague in 1915. Her journey there was likely the only time she ever left the United States. She distinguished herself at the meeting by criticizing organizers for not inviting more women labor activists and for failing to cultivate ties with the international labor movement that had "done more for international peace than all the capitalist peace movements put together." Following Wilson's declaration of war, O'Reilly chose not to align behind those peace activists who argued that the war should now be supported because of Wilson's noble goal of making the world "safe for democracy." She instead supported the efforts of socialists and anarchists calling for a general strike to stop US intervention. In contrast to O'Brennan and Sheehy Skeffington, O'Reilly never went through a phase when she trusted that Wilson would be a champion of small, oppressed nationalities.[41]

Irish activities provided a refreshing new outlet for O'Reilly, enabling her to assert a cultural as well as class identity distinct from that of the Anglo-Saxon Protestant women who dominated suffrage and reform organizations. Deeply moved by the Easter Rebellion, O'Reilly began lecturing on Irish themes in its aftermath. In 1918, she joyously proclaimed that "we of the Irish race are surely coming into our kingdom." In the past, she argued, the Irish had been "ordered to Connaught or to hell," but the time had finally come to "raise [hell]"—a comment that drew wild applause from the audience. Alluding to her past work for the feminist peace cause, she suggested that "women are now asking for slaughter to stop in all lands, but we are wise enough to know that it cannot cease anywhere while there is injustice on the earth—politically, economically, socially." This comment suggested that she now believed that anti-imperialist wars, in contrast to those fought to protect imperial strongholds and economic investments, were justified. She joined a diverse array of Irish nationalist organizations, most importantly Cumann na mBan, the Irish Progressive League, and the American Women Pickets for the Enforcement of America's War Aims. As one of the leading American Women Pickets, she sometimes toured with Kathleen O'Brennan; as a frequent speaker for the Irish Progressive League, she likely rubbed elbows with Hanna Sheehy Skeffington and leading Irish American women such as Gertrude Kelly and Helen Golden. Her diary suggests that the bulk of her time in 1920 was devoted to Irish rather than labor issues.[42]

Particularly important in O'Reilly's development as a distinct voice within the Irish nationalist movement in the United States was the time she spent urging dockworkers not to unload British ships during a demonstration staged by the American Women Pickets for the Enforcement of America's War Aims in 1920. Initially, the group hoped to encourage a short-term boycott of British ships on the New York docks to bring attention to the British imprisonment of Terrence MacSwiney, the Sinn Féin lord mayor of Cork. MacSwiney began a hunger strike while in custody to protest his imprisonment and was in poor health by the autumn of 1920. The American Women Pickets demanded his release from jail. The boycott unexpectedly grew into a strike of more than three thousand dockworkers that spread up and down the East Coast of the United States and included other demands, among them that British troops leave Ireland. For a time, the strike even brought interracial solidarity to the docks, as some African American dockworkers also walked off the job in support of the Irish cause. O'Reilly emerged as one of the foremost speakers on the New York docks and encouraged the early walkouts. In her messages to the strikers, she emphasized that England was a "parasite nation" that tried to use workers from "one subject nation" to "shoot down [those] of another subject nation." She argued, however, that if dockworkers remained on strike "they can no longer divide us on religious lines or on lines of nationality." English ships would not be loaded and English soldiers would leave Ireland because "labor is labor the world over." The strike lasted some three and a half weeks, despite the opposition of the International Longshoremen's Association leadership, and greatly alarmed intelligence agents.[43]

Although strike leaders were forced to call off the strike when replacement workers were hired, it garnered much positive public attention and may have helped inspire the American Commission on Irish Independence's decision to create a Labor Bureau in the autumn of 1920 to help "centralize the tremendous power and influence of the men and women of organized labor in the great struggle of the Irish people for the maintenance of their duly established Republic." John Fitzpatrick, president of the powerful Chicago Federation of Labor, became its chair and soon announced plans for a nationwide labor boycott of British goods. He failed to win the support of the American Federation of Labor (AFL) for this campaign due to the unwavering opposition of AFL president Samuel Gompers. But he independently implemented a boycott through over two hundred cooperating city labor councils and trade unions. O'Reilly, determined to aid the effort, created the Irish

Women's Purchasing League to convince labor women as well as the wives of trade unionists to support the boycott. Since women were typically in charge of shopping, O'Reilly believed that gaining their support was particularly important. She expressed strong optimism about the boycott to a friend, explaining that Britain had the "disease" of commercial empire and would "listen when we show her we mean to have no commercial relations with her." O'Reilly supplied the boycott campaign with lists of goods to be boycotted and arranged for the sale of alternative products, with the proceeds to go to the Irish rebel leaders. At one point O'Reilly boasted over fifty women volunteers working for her on the campaign and claimed to have sold six hundred pounds of alternative tea and sent seven thousand dollars to Ireland.[44]

The economic success of the boycott initiated by the American Women's Purchasing League and the Labor Bureau is difficult to determine. The campaign, however, received widespread publicity and helped to link the cause of Irish independence with the labor struggle in important ways. By linking questions of imperialism to the daily shopping habits of working-class women, O'Reilly encouraged them to think about the connections between the struggles of workers in the United States and the struggles of those in Ireland in new ways. The *Irish World* further emphasized these themes, arguing that, by boycotting British goods, supporters were helping to create new jobs for the American unemployed as well as aiding the Irish nationalist cause. Among those who took note of the boycott campaign and tried to encourage Irish American fraternal organizations and the Irish government to support it was Hanna Sheehy Skeffington. O'Reilly's friendships with Fitzpatrick and Frank P. Walsh, meanwhile, deepened during this period, and she developed an interest in the Labor Party movement launched by the Chicago Federation of Labor in 1919. This party promoted an extensive anti-imperialist platform that included US recognition of the revolutionary governments that had emerged in Ireland, Mexico, and Russia as well as US withdrawal from the "imperialistic enterprises on which we have already embarked in the Phillipines [*sic*], Hawaii, Cuba, Samoa and Guam." The platform also rejected the League of Nations as a tool of imperialism and instead demanded a "league of free peoples, organized and pledged to the destruction of autocracy, militarism and economic imperialism throughout the world." For a short period, Irish American politics seemed, through the figures of O'Reilly and Fitzpatrick, to dovetail with a strongly anti-imperialist labor party movement.[45]

Like O'Brennan and Sheehy Skeffington, O'Reilly's ideas about imperialism thus evolved in a syncretic fashion from 1916 to 1923. The Irish nationalist struggle encouraged O'Reilly, focused on labor and suffrage issues for most of her life, to add another dimension to her understanding of the class struggle. Always distrustful of Wilsonian rhetoric about self-determination, she seemed equally unimpressed by Bolshevism during the Red Scare and its aftermath. Yet, through her work for the Irish cause, she became convinced that the fight against imperialism was critical to guaranteeing the future welfare of workers and achievement of industrial democracy in both industrial creditor and colonized societies. The best means to defeat imperialism, in turn, was through international labor solidarity in conjunction with the political empowerment of women.

Taken collectively, the examples of O'Brennan, Sheehy Skeffington, and O'Reilly suggest the importance of women of the transatlantic Irish left as organic intellectuals within the Irish nationalist movement who helped to enrich the discourse that swirled around the issues of both Irish independence and how the United States should align on questions of imperialism in the twentieth century. Influenced by Irish nationalists as well as by US debates over Wilsonianism, Leninism, and international labor solidarity, they each nonetheless developed their own unique visions. Through their organizational activities, lectures, and writings, they helped to politicize women and workers previously neglected by Irish American fraternal and nationalist groups and provided important ammunition for American reformers and left activists already committed to anti-imperialist agendas. They also played a significant role in raising funds for the Irish Revolution, and Sheehy Skeffington directly shaped early Sinn Féin policy upon her return to Ireland. Although this kind of nationalist work by women at first inspired gratitude from male revolutionaries, in the bitter aftermath of civil war it led to recriminations against anti-Treaty Irish and Irish American women who were accused of becoming unwomanly "Furies" and "viragos" as a result of their involvement in politics. Such arguments provided a convenient rationale to marginalize women in the new Irish Free State and to reemphasize women's role in domestic life.[46]

Sadly, the political voices of Kathleen O'Brennan and Leonora O'Reilly fell largely silent in the aftermath of the Irish Civil War. O'Reilly suffered deteriorating health and died in 1927 at the relatively young age of fifty-seven, while O'Brennan continued to devote her energies on fiction and poetry. Sheehy Skeffington, however, remained an important figure in left-wing Irish, American, and international politics for decades despite her increasing disillusionment with the conservative governments that prevailed in Ireland during the interwar years and with international capitalism. In 1930 she traveled to the Soviet Union and commented favorably on its achievements for women and workers, suggesting that it had lessons to teach the Irish government. When the Great Depression struck Ireland and the world in the 1930s, she grew critical even of her former anti-Treaty comrade, Éamon de Valera, accusing the president of the Executive Council of becoming a hypocritical "professor-type like Wilson" who was enamored of "phrases and abstractions" even as he sought to create a "Catholic statelet under Rome's grip" in Ireland. Despite her disappointments with the fruits of the Irish Revolution, she nonetheless insisted that she remained dedicated to the revolutionary principles of James Connolly and continued to immerse herself in the activities of labor, feminist, and international organizations until her death in 1946, thereby helping to bequeath Connolly's legacy, as well as that of a remarkable group of female rebels, to future generations.[47]

## NOTES

1 See particularly Erez Manela, *The Wilsonian Moment: Self-Determination and the International Origins of Anticolonial Nationalism* (Oxford: Oxford University Press, 2007), 7–9.

2 Catherine Burns, "Kathleen O'Brennan and American Identity in the Transatlantic Irish Republican Movement," in *The Irish in the Atlantic World*, ed. David Gleeson (Columbia: University of South Carolina Press, 2010), 170–194; Catherine Burns, "American Identity and the Transatlantic Irish Nationalist Movement, 1912–1925" (PhD diss., University of Wisconsin, 2011).

3 Antonio Gramsci, *Selections from the Prison Notebooks of Antonio Gramsci*, ed. Quintin Hoare and Geoffrey Nowell Smith (New York: International, 1971), 5–14.

4 Bridget Hourican, "O'Brennan, Lily," in *Dictionary of Irish Biography*, ed. James McGuire and James Quinn (Cambridge: Cambridge University Press, 2010), http://dib.cambridge.org; Burns, "Kathleen O'Brennan and American Identity," 177–178.

5 "Visitor Leaving," *San Francisco Chronicle*, 12 Nov. 1916, 16; "Kathleen O'Brennan—Brilliant Dublin Woman at West End Catholic Women's Club," *Oak Leaves*, 30 Oct. 1915, 26.

6 Helen Dare, "Tis a Little Bit of Young Ireland That Is Here," *San Francisco Chronicle*, 4 Nov. 1916, 7; "Work of Sinn Féin Group Is Subject of Talk," *San Francisco Chronicle*, 11 Nov. 1916, 7; Kathleen M. O'Brennan, "Sinn Féin and Ulster" (Letter to the Editor), *New York Times* [*NYT*], 8 June 1917, 26; O'Brennan Notes on the Irish Republic and the domination of the seas and roads by a few powers, undated (National Library of Ireland, Ceannt and O'Brennan Collection [hereafter OC], MS, 41, 511/1/21); Burns, "Kathleen O'Brennan and American Identity," 177–180.

7 Adam Hodges, "At War over the Espionage Act in Portland: Dueling Perspectives from Kathleen O'Brennan and Agent William Bryon," *Oregon Historical Quarterly* 108, no. 3 (2007): 475–476. See also Report of Agent Bryon on "U.S. vs. Kathleen O'Brennan, IWW Anarchist," 5–19 Mar. 1919, Case 209551, 41–43 and Report of (Informant) #53, on "Kathleen O'Brennan, Alleged Sinn Fein Propagandist," Oct. 1918, 64, both in Investigative Case Files of the Bureau of Investigation (ICFBI) Case (C) 209551, Case Title (CT): Various, Series (S) Old German Files, 1909–1921 (OGF), Roll number (RN) 619, accessed at Fold 3, http://ancestry.com, www.fold3.com (available by subscription / also available in hardcopy at National Archives and Record Administration, College Park, MD, M1085). Please note that all subsequent cited Investigative Case Files of the Bureau of Investigation (ICFBI), the precursor to the Federal Bureau of Investigation, were also accessed at Fold 3, http://ancestry.com.

8 Kathleen O'Brennan undated draft about "American Attitudes" (OC, MS 41,511/1/14).

9 Agent Bryon Report on "Kathleen O'Brennan, Alien Agitator and IWW," 6 Sept. 1919 (ICFBI, C 209551, 294–303); Informant #53, Report on Kathleen O'Brennan, Oct. 1918 (ICFBI, C 209551, 51–64); A. E. McMahon, "Re: Kathleen O'Brennan," Jan. 1919 (ICFBI, C 209551, 42).

10 Agent Bryon Report, "Kathleen O'Brennan," 6 Sept. 1919 (ICFBI, C 209551, 300–302).

11 Ibid., 304; "Miss O'Brennan Arrested," *Portland Oregonian*, 16 Jan. 1919, 12.

12 Hodges, "At War over the Espionage Act," 475–485; *Morning Oregonian*, 24 Jan. 1919, 3.

13 Agent Bryon, "Report on Radical Situation in the Northwest," 3 Sept. 1919 (ICFBI, C 287856, S OGF, RN 705, 5–7), and Letter from Edward Bell to Lanier (Confidential), 24 Feb. 1919, detailing a comment of an individual in Chicago about O'Brennan in Agent Report of J.J. Fergus, 16 Mar. 1919 (ICFBI, C 504, CT Sinn Féin Activities, S Bureau Section Files [BSF], RN 930, 25).

14 Marie Equi to Kathleen O'Brennan, 20 Mar. 1919 (OC, MS 41,509/1/11, 3).

15 "Irish Lecturer Praises Position of America," *Anaconda Standard*, 29 Apr. 1918, 2; "Plea for Erin made by Dublin Woman," *San Francisco Chronicle*, 24 Feb. 1919, 7; "Miss O'Brennan Talks on Ireland," *San Francisco Chronicle*, 9 Mar. 1919, 4; "Women in the Irish Republic," *San Francisco Chronicle*, 23 May 1919, 6.

16  Burns, "Kathleen O'Brennan and American Identity," 179–180; "San Francisco Girl Finishes Irish Lecture Tour," *San Francisco Chronicle*, 5 July 1919, 13; *Hutchinson News*, 23 Apr. 1919, 9; *Nevada State Journal*, 19 June 1919, 7; *Corona Independent*, 23 July 1919; *San Francisco Chronicle*, 23 Jan. 1919; Kathleen O'Brennan, "Who's Who in Irish Parley," *NYT*, 24 July 1921, 72; and Kathleen O'Brennan, "Sinn Fein's Extremist Woman," in *NYT*, 1 Jan. 1922, 78.

17  Letter from the American Women Pickets for Carrying out of America's War Aims, to the Honorable Stephen Porter, 18 May 1920 (OC, MS, 41,511/1/6); Burns, "Kathleen O'Brennan and American Identity," 177, 184.

18  Report of W. W. West, 16 and 20 June 1920 (ICFBI, C 209551, 278–294).

19  Kathleen O'Brennan, "Who's Who in Irish Parley," *NYT*, 24 July 1921, 78; Kathleen O'Brennan, "Sinn Fein's Extremist Woman Leader," *NYT*, 1 Jan. 1922, 78; Kathleen O'Brennan, "Girl Writer Says Ireland Waits for Big Man to Head Economic Struggle in Ireland," *San Francisco Chronicle*, 17 Feb. 1922, 11; *Anaconda Standard*, 2 Feb. 1923; *Norwhich Bulletin*, Dec. 1922; Statement of the Women of Ireland to the Senate and Congress of the United States (OC, MS 41,511, 131).

20  R. F. Foster, *Vivid Faces: The Revolutionary Generation in Ireland, 1890–1923* (New York: Norton, 2014), 297, 315–319.

21  Margaret Ward, *Hanna Sheehy Skeffington: A Life* (Cork: Cork University Press, 1997), 19–67; Hanna Sheehy Skeffington, "Memoirs," in *Hanna Sheehy Skeffington: Suffragette and Sinn Féiner: Her Memoirs and Political Writings*, ed. Margaret Ward (Dublin: University College Dublin Press, 2017), 1–18.

22  Elizabeth McKillen, "Irish Feminism and Nationalist Separatism: 1914–1923," *Éire-Ireland* 17, no. 3 (Fall 1982): 52–67, 55–56; Senia Pašeta, *Irish Nationalist Women: 1900–1918* (Cambridge: Cambridge University Press, 2013), 68–91, 128–194.

23  Hanna Sheehy Skeffington, "British Militarism as I Have Known It," in Ward, *Hanna Sheehy Skeffington*, 126–131; Hanna Sheehy Skeffington, *Impressions of Sinn Féin in America* (Dublin: Davis, 1919), 5.

24  For more on Sheehy Skeffington's lectures, see Elizabeth McKillen, "Reverse Currents: Irish Feminist and Nationalist Hanna Sheehy Skeffington and U.S. Anti-imperialism, 1916–1924," *Éire-Ireland* 53, nos. 3–4 (2018): 157–170. For a few examples of press coverage, see *Irish World and American Industrial Liberator* (*IW*), 13 and 29 Jan. 1917; *Gaelic World*, 13 Jan. 1917; *NYT*, 7 Jan. 1917. For letters during this period, see Lillian Wald to Hanna Sheehy Skeffington, 9 Jan. 1917 (National Library of Ireland [NLI], Hanna Sheehy Skeffington Papers [hereafter HSS], MS 33,605 (9)); Marie Equi to Hanna Sheehy Skeffington, 23 Dec. 1917 (NLI, HSS, MS 33,605 (16)); Alice Park to Hanna Sheehy Skeffington, 26 Aug. 1917 (NLI, HSS, MS 33,605 (16)).

25  Joanne Mooney Eichacker, *Irish Republican Women in America: Lecture Tours, 1915–1925* (Dublin: Irish Academic Press, 2003), 72–74; Dan Rathbun, "Intelligence Report," 3 July 1917 (ICFBI, C 8000–10,082, CT, Various, S OGF, 5).

26  "Ireland as a Small Nation," *IW*, 17 Nov. 1917, 12.

27  Skeffington, *Impressions of Sinn Féin in America*, 27–29; *Gaelic American*, 12 and 19 Jan. 1918; Mooney Eichacker, *Irish Republican Women*, 80–81; David Brundage, *Irish*

*Nationalists in America: The Politics of Exile, 1798–1998* (Oxford: Oxford University Press, 2016), 152–154.

28 Memo from Alfred Bettman to Mr. Bielaski, enclosing telegram from the San Francisco Office, 8 May 1918 (ICFBI, 8000–10,082, 35); *San Francisco Chronicle*, 17 Apr. 1918; Mooney Eichacker, *Irish Republican Women*, 89.

29 Emmet Larkin, *James Larkin: Irish Labour Leader* (London: Routledge and Kegan, 1965), 221–222.

30 Tyrgve Throntveit, "The Fable of the Fourteen Points: Woodrow Wilson and National Self-determination," *Diplomatic History* 35 (June 2011): 445–481; and Manela, *Wilsonian Moment*, chap. 1.

31 "Mrs. Skeffington a Judge," *NYT*, 27 Aug. 1920, 3; McKillen, "Reverse Currents," 174.

32 Brundage, *Irish Nationalists in America*, 165–180; Mooney Eichacker, *Irish Republican Women*, 168–180; McKillen, "Reverse Currents," 178.

33 Hanna Sheehy Skeffington, "Light Turned on Irish Election," *IW*, 8 July 1922; McKillen, "Reverse Currents," 178–182.

34 Hanna Sheehy Skeffington, "Freak State House of Lords," *IW*, 6 Jan. 1923; Hanna Sheehy Skeffington, "Provisional Parliament's Mad Career," *IW*, 21 Oct. 1922.

35 Hanna Sheehy Skeffington, "Freak State Apes British Methods," *IW*, 3 Mar. 1923 and her articles in *IW*, Oct. 1922–July 1923. See cartoon, *IW*, 7 Oct. 1922.

36 Editorials, *IW*, 16 Sept. 1922, 12 May 1923, 15 Sept. 1923, 4 Oct. 1924, 1 Nov. 1924.

37 Hanna Sheehy Skeffington, "Congress of Women's International League for Peace and Freedom," July 1926 and *IW*, 7 Aug. 1926 in Ward, *Hanna Sheehy Skeffington*, 119–122.

38 Tara McCarthy, *Respectability and Reform: Irish American Women's Activism, 1880–1920* (Syracuse: Syracuse University Press, 2018), esp. chap. 4.

39 Elizabeth McKillen, "Divided Loyalties: Irish American Women Labor Leaders and the Irish Revolution, 1916–23," *Éire-Ireland* 52, nos. 3–4 (2016): 167–170.

40 "Suffragists Elect Hanna H. Shaw Again," *NYT*, 26 Nov. 1912, 11; "Suffrage Demanded by Working Women," *NYT*, 23 Apr. 1912, 24.

41 Elizabeth McKillen, *Making the World Safe for Workers: Labor, the Left and Wilsonian Internationalism* (Champaign: University of Illinois Press, 2013), 112–113; "Anarchists Demand Strike to End War," *NYT*, 19 May 1917, 14.

42 O'Reilly speech published in "New York Irish Meet to Demand the Independence of Ireland," *Irish Press*, 28 Sept. 1918 (Schlesinger Library, Radcliffe Institute, Cambridge MA, O'Reilly Papers [hereafter OP], Microfilm ed., Reel [R] 9); Notes on Speech on "Internationalism," 15 July 1919 (OP, R9); Mary Hickey (Cumann na mBan) to O'Reilly, 1 June 1920 (OP, R7); Peter Golden to O'Reilly, 21 Sept. 1918, and Irish Progressive League to O'Reilly, 24 Aug. 1918 (OP, R7); McCarthy, *Respectability and Reform*, 124–133; O'Reilly Diary for 1919–1920 (OP, R2).

43 "Three Thousand Strike Here," *NYT*, 3 Sept. 1920, 1. This article identifies the speaker as Helen O'Reilly but this is clearly a mistake, as historian Tara McCarthy has convincingly demonstrated. See McCarthy, *Respectability and Reform*, 258, n159; "Resent MacSwiney's Fate," *NYT*, 9 Sept. 1920, 4; Joe Doyle, "Striking for Ireland

on the New York Docks," in *The New York Irish*, ed. Timothy Meagher and Ronald Bayor (Baltimore: Johns Hopkins University Press, 1996), 327–353; Joseph G. Tucker, Intelligence Reports, 4 Sept. 1920–2 Oct. 1920 (ICFBI, CT, Various, CF 8000–208369, S OGF, 533–579, 759–760).

44  Letter from the Labor Bureau of the American Commission on Irish Independence, n.d. (Chicago History Museum, Fitzpatrick Papers [hereafter FP], Box 9, File 67), and "Report of the Labor Bureau of the American Commission on Irish Independence" (FP, Box 11, File 78); Coupon from Irish Women's Purchasing League, 1921 (FP, Box 10, File 72); *New Majority* (paper of the Chicago Federation of Labor), 20 Nov. 1920, 3; 15 Jan. 1921, 1–2; O'Reilly to Arthur Brisbane, 23 Nov. 1920 (OP, R8); O'Reilly to Frank Walsh, 19 Jan. 1921, Walsh to Miss Leonora O'Reilly, 27 Jan. 1921, Walsh to O'Reilly, 23 May 1921, O'Reilly to Walsh, 28 May 1921 (all in New York Public Library, Frank Walsh Papers, Box 29); O'Reilly to Irish Women's Educational League, 1 Dec. 1920 (OP, R8); McCarthy, *Respectability and Reform*, 149–150; Elizabeth McKillen, "American Labor, the Irish Revolution and the Campaign for a Boycott of British Goods: 1916–1924," *Radical History Review* 61 (1995): 35–61; Michael Chapman, "How to Smash the British Empire," *Éire-Ireland* 43, nos. 3–4 (2008): 217–252.

45  Elizabeth McKillen, *Chicago Labor and the Quest for a Democratic Diplomacy: 1914–1924* (Ithaca, NY: Cornell University Press, 1995), 153–154; Elizabeth McKillen, "The Irish Sinn Féin Movement and Radical Labor and Feminist Dissent in America, 1916–1921," *Labor: Studies in Working-Class History* 16, no. 3 (2019): 11–37; Fitzpatrick to O'Reilly, 17 Dec. 1918 (OP, R7), Fitzpatrick to O'Reilly, 7 Aug. 1920 (OP, R8); Walsh to O'Reilly, 11 Oct. 1920 (OP, R8). For a boycott cartoon, see *IW*, 16 July 1921.

46  Brundage, *Irish Nationalists in America*, 168; Foster, *Vivid Faces*, 297.

47  Foster, *Vivid Faces*, 315–317; Ward, *Hanna Sheehy Skeffington*, 371–394.

# W. E. B. Du Bois and the Irish Revolution

## *Anticolonial Activism in New York, 1916–1921*

DAVID BRUNDAGE

In September 1916, noted African American activist and intellectual William Edward Burghardt Du Bois lamented the execution of Irish revolutionary Roger Casement in the pages of *The Crisis*, the monthly journal of the National Association for the Advancement of Colored People (NAACP). Du Bois's purpose, however, was not to praise Casement's courage or honor his martyrdom (as his great rival, the Jamaican-born Black nationalist Marcus Garvey, would regularly do over the next few years) but rather to criticize what he saw as a major political misstep by Britain, a nation whose war effort he firmly supported. By March 1921, Du Bois's outlook had undergone a sea change: he was now an angry critic of British imperialism and utterly committed to "the ultimate freedom of Ireland—which God speedily grant!"[1]

This chapter explores Du Bois's political evolution over these four and a half eventful years to illuminate a larger theme: the way that the Irish Revolution helped focus and stimulate anticolonial thought and activism in a number of places around the world. US president Woodrow Wilson's well-known articulation of the principle of self-determination had an important influence on the development of global anticolonialism, to be sure. But also important was the Irish War of Independence, a remarkable example of a small nation's confrontation with, and partial victory over, the most powerful empire in the world.[2] My approach is biographical, focusing on Du Bois's evolving ideas about Ireland, Irish nationalism, and the Irish diaspora in America over a long period of time—in fact, going back to his childhood. It can thus be seen as part of what some have called a "biographical turn" in recent historical scholarship, an effort to use biography to make sense of larger and seemingly impersonal historical processes. As historian Alice Kessler-Harris has put it, a deep understanding of "an individual life might help us to see not only into particular events but into the larger cultural and social and even political processes of a moment in time."[3]

But, of course, individual lives unfold in continuous interaction with the lives of others. Du Bois's entire biography is an illustration of this truism, but in the pages that follow I mainly emphasize the role of such interactions in shaping the radical shift in his understanding of the Irish Revolution. In particular, I attend to his relationship with Irish republicans or their sympathizers in two New York anticolonial organizations and to his participation in a broad-based effort to investigate conditions in Ireland during its War of Independence. In these settings, Du Bois collaborated with and came to share much of the outlook of political activists who were working for a fully independent Irish republic. It was at least in part these personal interactions that caused his point of view to change.

W. E. B. Du Bois occupies a central place in African American, US, and global twentieth-century political and intellectual history. From exceedingly humble origins in a small New England town, he rose to become an accomplished and world-renowned scholar, beginning his higher education at Fisk, the Black Congregational college in Nashville, and going on to further studies at Harvard (only the seventh Black American to be admitted to the college) and the University of Berlin. By age thirty-five he had published a pioneering sociological study, *The Philadelphia Negro* (1899), and *The Souls of Black Folk* (1903), destined to become a landmark of American letters. Du Bois was also an engaged social and political activist, a founder in 1905 of the Niagara Movement, which opposed the growing segregation, disenfranchisement, and violence directed against Black Americans and, in 1909, of the NAACP, becoming the founding editor of its monthly magazine, *The Crisis*, in 1910. Though decades of both achievement (a series of groundbreaking works of history, sociology, and memoir) and controversy (a bitter break with his former NAACP colleagues and later membership in the Communist Party) were to follow before his death as an expatriate in Ghana in 1963, Du Bois was already by 1916 one of the most well-known public figures in America.[4]

But what role did Ireland play in Du Bois's intellectual and political work in the years before then? Little in the first half century of his long life encouraged any kind of sympathy with Irish nationalism or Irish people. Du Bois spent his first seventeen years in the western Massachusetts mill town of Great Barrington, where he was born in February 1868. Almost everything that we know about those years comes from his own autobiographical writings, which were shaped by the vagaries of memory as well as by his literary reconstruction of events and emotions to fit his later views and agendas. Nonetheless Du Bois's biographers agree that those years were decisive in shaping much of his later outlook. As David Levering Lewis puts it, "The importance of the Great Barrington period, its imprint upon all that Willie Du Bois grew to be, was deep, and certainly singular."[5]

Great Barrington had a population of about four thousand at the time of Du Bois's birth. Like most of the other approximately thirty Black families in the region, members of Du Bois's extended family labored as domestic workers in homes or the summer resorts that grew up in the area in the second half of the nineteenth century. They also farmed several small plots of land between Great Barrington and nearby Sheffield. They were poor—but not as poor as the immigrant Irish, German, and Czech mill workers of the town. These immigrants began arriving in Great Barrington in the late 1840s, when a combination of railroad building, industrialization, and famine in Ireland brought newcomers to work in the paper and woolen mills of the region. Over the next few decades, Irish families began to slowly accumulate a bit of property, often accomplished by sending their children into the workforce at an early age. But opportunities for occupational mobility remained extremely limited and poverty a fact of life for many.[6]

As Du Bois admitted in *Darkwater*, the powerful collection of essays, spirituals, and poems that he published in 1921, he grew up "cordially [despising] the poor Irish and South Germans, who slaved in the mills," adding ruefully that "such is the kingdom of snobs."[7] Du Bois's "snobbishness" was probably based partly on his deep roots in region: his mother's family, the Burghardts, had lived in western Massachusetts since the eighteenth century. As he recounted in his posthumously published *Autobiography*, the newly arrived Irish "became the basis of jokes in town and throughout New England." Such anti-Irish humor was integral to the region's cultural atmosphere. Returning north after his first three years of higher education in Nashville, Du Bois was struck to find that the anti-Black jokes he had encountered in Tennessee "were replaced at Harvard by tales of the 'two Irishmen' and songs like 'mush-mush-mush turaliady.'"[8]

The Great Barrington years marked the beginning of Du Bois's extraordinary intellectual journey. Encouraged in his academic ambitions by his mother Mary and mentored by his high school principal Frank Hosmer, he also spent considerable time in the small bookshop owned by a Welshman named Johnny Morgan, who let the teenager pore through the popular New York comic weeklies *Puck* and *Judge*. "I looked them over each week," Du Bois later recalled, not mentioning that in perusing these two magazines he would have been digesting weekly servings of overwhelmingly negative images of the Irish.[9] Though long-suffering Ireland was sometimes represented by the artists who worked for these magazines as a sad and beautiful angel, actual Irish *people* (in Ireland or America) were invariably caricatured with simian features and behaving like ignorant apes, blindly following unscrupulous politicians, for example, or—worse—handing over their wages to Fenian agitators who employed dynamite in the name of "Irish freedom." As L. Perry Curtis concludes in his study of Victorian-era visual representations of the Irish, in *Puck* and *Judge* "the politicized apes far outnumbered the apolitical angels."[10]

Negative views of Irish national aspirations were reinforced for Du Bois by his first book purchase, in the fall of 1882: "a gorgeous edition of [Thomas] Macaulay's *History of England* in five volumes [that] I wanted fiercely." The teenager jumped at Morgan's suggestion that he buy it on "installments" of twenty-five cents a week. "At Christmas time I took my precious purchase home and it still stands in my library," he recalled—at the age of nearly ninety.[11] A foundational text of the Whig interpretation of history, *The History of England* was a far cry from the crude caricatures of *Puck* and *Judge*; but Macaulay had drawn a sharp line between people like the Scots, who might someday be incorporated into English civilization, and the Irish, who could not. The Irish required imperial repression, not beneficent assimilation.[12]

There was one influential figure who might have given Du Bois a more positive view of Irish nationalism in these years: Timothy Thomas

Fortune, the brilliant if troubled editor of the *New York Globe*, who looked for a while like he might inherit Frederick Douglass's mantle as the dominant voice of Black America. Fortune believed that the Irish Home Rule struggle could serve as an inspiration for African Americans and even proposed the creation of an "Afro-American National League" modeled on Parnell's Irish National League. Du Bois began writing local dispatches for the *Globe* in April 1883—when he was just fifteen—and four years later penned an admiring assessment of Fortune for his college paper, the *Fisk Herald*. But he made no mention of Fortune's high regard for Irish nationalism. Nor did Du Bois's 1884 high school graduation speech on the recently deceased abolitionist Wendell Phillips mention Phillips's vigorous support for Michael Davitt and the Irish Land League.[13]

It was not just snobbishness or the influence of Macaulay that shaped Du Bois's view of the Irish growing up, however; it was also fear. "I was afraid of the Irish and kept away from their part of town as much as possible," he recalled decades later. "Sometimes they called me 'nigger' or tried to attack me." The Irish in western Massachusetts, not surprisingly, shared the fierce anti-Black racism that historians have found among the American Irish generally in this period. Du Bois did have some positive experiences: at the house of a wealthy white playmate, for example, "the Irish servants were kind." But even as he neared the end of his life, these early memories of Irish American racism remained strong.[14]

Du Bois's understanding of Irish American racism was based on more than personal experience. He was also a student of American history, and among the historical themes that he often returned to was the fraught relationship of European immigrants (including the Irish) and African Americans. His 1899 book *The Philadelphia Negro* is recognized today as a groundbreaking work in the discipline of sociology, combing rich ethnographic detail with sophisticated statistical analysis of the city's Black community, then the largest in the northern states. But it was also marked by deep study of the racial dynamics embedded in the history of immigration to the United States. Du Bois described in great detail the rivalry between white working-class European immigrants and African Americans in Philadelphia over the course of the nineteenth century, placing particular emphasis on what he called "the intense race antipathy of the Irish." He showed how the introduction of the streetcar around 1850 both destroyed the coach trade that Black men had prospered in and led to the growing influence of the Irish, who laid the tracks, enforced a color bar in their trade unions, and exercised a virtual monopoly as conductors. As their population grew, moreover, enfranchised Irish men became "the tool of the Democrats," adding their votes to that party's white supremacist ideology.[15] Du Bois's 1902 study of *The Negro Artisan*, one of the eighteen sociological monographs that he published after taking up a faculty position at Atlanta University, echoed these themes in its explanation of why so few of New York City's African American workers were employed in the skilled trades. Noting that the Irish-dominated (and anti-Black) 1863 Draft Riots "had an economic as well as a political cause," Du Bois went on to show how "the ensuing enmity between Irish and Negroes and the absorption of the Irish into the industries kept the Negroes out."[16]

Du Bois's thinking about Ireland, Irish nationalism, and Irish racism, however, was shaped by more than his understanding of conditions in the United States. As the nineteenth century wound down, he emerged as a trenchant commenter on world history and politics as well, prefiguring the broad anticolonial perspective that would be one of the main concerns of his life. In July 1900, he participated in the historic Pan-African Conference, called by Henry Sylvester Williams, a young Black Trinidadian barrister practicing in London. Held at Westminster Town Hall and attended by about thirty delegates, mostly from Britain and the West Indies, the conference was welcomed by the bishop of London and concluded with a promise from Queen Victoria "not to overlook the welfare and interests of the native races." The conference issued no radical call for national determination or the dismantling of empires, and as Du Bois himself later noted, because "the meeting had no deep roots in Africa itself," the Pan-African ideal "died for a generation."[17]

But for Du Bois personally, the conference was a breakthrough, marking his own increasingly global perspective on American racism. In a closing address titled "To the Nations of the World," he jolted his audience by predicting that "the problem of the twentieth century is the problem of the colour line." His was a global vision, referencing "the millions of black men in Africa, America, and the Islands of the

Sea, not to speak of the brown and yellow myriads elsewhere [who] are bound to have great influence upon the world in the future." Du Bois was predicting the worldwide emergence of people of color, rather than of ethnic or political nationalism, but his leading biographer is surely correct that the Pan-Africanism introduced at this small and eminently moderate conference was "another movement exploding into the twentieth century like a stick of dynamite . . . with the Irish, Afrikaners, Armenians, Serbians, and other historic 'races' already lighting fuses for the new century."[18]

Du Bois's international interests continued to grow in subsequent years. He repeated his prediction about the global color line in *The Souls of Black Folk*, and in the first magazine that he edited, *The Moon Illustrated Weekly* (1905–1906), stories on domestic issues (Ohio race riots, Alabama disenfranchisement) sat next to those on events in locales as distant as Liberia and India. *The Horizon: A Journal of the Color Line* (1907–1910), his next foray into magazine editing, went further, denouncing architects of imperialism from King Leopold in the Congo to the United States in Cuba, Puerto Rico, and the Philippines. His global (and increasingly anticolonial) remit was strengthened further when, in July 1910, he resigned his Atlanta University professorship and moved to New York City, to edit the NAACP's new magazine, *The Crisis: A Record of the Darker Races*. True to its name, the monthly journal placed the struggles of Black Americans within a framework of anticolonial activism in Asia, Africa, and the African diaspora. The summer of 1911 took him to London again, this time for an event called the Universal Races Congress, where he heard the theosophist—and advocate of Irish and Indian Home Rule—Annie Besant (among other luminaries) give a speech denouncing British imperialism. She was, Du Bois reported to readers of *The Crisis*, "among the most forceful speakers" at the meeting.[19]

Such experiences and ideas might have pushed Du Bois to reevaluate his highly negative view of the Irish, but that did not occur. In fact, the outbreak of the First World War in August 1914 put him on a direct collision course with Irish nationalism—or at least its American variant. Though Irish Party leader John Redmond gave support to the British war effort as a guarantee of Home Rule, most Irish nationalists in the United States adamantly did not. This led, almost overnight, to the rise of a revolutionary wing of the movement that angrily denounced sending Irish boys off to die in the trenches of France and Belgium. In New York, the erstwhile Home Ruler Dr. Gertrude B. Kelly, a well-known physician and women's suffrage advocate, emerged as an important figure in this transformation, accusing Redmond and his supporters of encouraging national "suicide" in an imperialist war fought "for commercial supremacy." As she rhetorically asked a mass meeting in October 1914, "Is Home Rule to be to be secured for the cattle and the sheep when the young men of Ireland are slaughtered?"[20]

One might suppose that Du Bois would have been sympathetic to this view: after all, in his famous "Credo," published in the liberal magazine *The Independent* in 1904, he had declared simply, "I believe in the Prince of Peace. I believe that War is Murder. I believe that armies and navies are at bottom the tinsel and braggadocio of oppression and wrong."[21] And in "The African Roots of the War," published in the *Atlantic Monthly* in May 1915, he put forward an analysis of the conflict that reflected an even more expansive critique than Kelly's. In a tour de force of just eight pages, Du Bois swept over centuries of African and European history before shifting gears to examine the roles of post-1880 economic imperialism and racism in shaping the modern world and then, finally, showing how competition for Africa's mineral wealth had culminated in global warfare between the great European powers.[22]

But by 1916, Du Bois's position on the war had changed. It was now shaped by his expectation that Britain and the allies would win the war and that such a victory was to be welcomed. Britain was not without faults, he readily admitted, but its long traditions of liberalism and parliamentary democracy were enviable. Most significantly, Du Bois maintained, Britain was "the best administrator of colored peoples," while German power "spells death to the aspirations of Negroes and all the darker nations." "Compared with Germany," he wrote the following year, England was an "Angel of light."[23] Du Bois doubled down on these ideas after America's entry into the war in April 1917, expressing the hope that through service in the armed forces abroad, African Americans could advance the cause of racial equality at home. Their valor, he wrote, would "show the world again what the loyalty and bravery of black men means."[24]

These are some of the factors that affected Du Bois's interpretation of the Easter Rising and its aftermath as he presented it in two editorials in *The Crisis* in 1916. Given that the magazine's circulation was now forty-five thousand, with an ever-growing number of both African American and white readers, his interpretation mattered. While noting in August that the history of Irish American racism had "given the Irish cause little or no sympathy as far as Negroes are concerned," it remained true that "Ireland has suffered at the hands of England" and that "where human oppression exists there the sympathy of all black hearts must go." Still, while the Rising was in some respects admirable, it was also "foolish."[25]

Equally foolish, however, was Britain's response. In September's "Sir Roger Casement—Patriot, Martyr," Du Bois argued that while Britain had an indisputable right to execute Casement for treason, it had made a huge political mistake by doing so: "England has muddled into one more blunder in her stupid list of blunders in dealing with Ireland." Far from a ringing endorsement of the rebellion, or of Casement's heroism, this position was not substantially different from that of the conservative and pro-British *New York Times*, which had characterized the executions that followed the Easter Rising as "incredibly stupid."[26]

What, then, caused Du Bois to alter his views so profoundly in the following four and a half years? First, there was the explosion of anti-colonial activism that emerged in many places around the globe as the First World War drew to a close. Du Bois believed that the tremendous disruptions caused by the war offered colonized peoples around the world an opportunity to benefit from the ideals of democracy and national self-determination that Wilson had expressed in his Fourteen Points speech of January 1918. "This war is the End, and also, a Beginning," Du Bois wrote in *The Crisis* that June. "Out of this war will rise, soon or late, an independent China; a self-governing India, and Egypt with representative institutions; and Africa for the Africans, and not merely for business exploitation."[27]

It was this expansive and hopeful view that had led Du Bois, a year earlier, to accept a position on the Executive Board of an organization called the League of Small and Subject Nationalities, which had been founded in New York in May 1917 by the well-known progressive reformer Frederic Howe, as a "a permanent congress of the small, subject and oppressed nationalities of the world."[28] By November 1918, Howe's organization boasted representatives from no fewer that twenty-two national groups, ranging from Poland and Denmark to Korea and India. Du Bois served as the representative for sub-Saharan Africa. But because this organization was based in New York City—aptly described by the historian Dennis Clark as "the overseas capital of Irish nationalist agitation and mobilization"—it was dominated by revolutionary Irish nationalists from the outset.[29] The Irish republican and feminist Hanna Sheehy Skeffington, for example, was the main speaker at its first public meeting in October 1917, and a year later Frank P. Walsh, the Irish American labor lawyer and political reformer, gave a rousing speech in favor of Irish independence as well. "Ireland" was represented on the league's Executive Board by Irish republican activist Gertrude Kelly, with whom Du Bois eventually developed a friendship. This was the milieu into which he now plunged.[30]

If New York was one site of interaction between Du Bois and Irish republicans, Paris was another. In December 1918 he sailed for Europe to attend the Pan-African Congress that he had persuaded the NAACP to sponsor. Black and white delegates from the United States, the Caribbean, and several African colonies passed a series of what were, from today's perspective, extremely moderate resolutions, simply asking the Paris Peace Conference, then in session, to establish regulations for good colonial governance in Africa. But as Du Bois noted in his report on the congress, the most "inspired" speech at the event—a sweeping denunciation of racism everywhere in the world—was given by a white NAACP founder and muckraking journalist named Charles Edward Russell. Russell, who had been an ardent supporter of Du Bois for a decade, had by this time also become an equally ardent supporter of complete Irish independence.[31]

Du Bois stayed on in Paris after the Pan-African Congress ended, in an effort to present its resolutions to the Peace Conference. He met with several of President Wilson's advisors but received no response to the resolutions. By April he was back in New York. But as Du Bois was returning, a three-person group calling itself the American Commission on Irish Independence was sailing across the Atlantic in the opposite direction. Led by Frank Walsh, the commission attempted to bring the Irish case for national self-determination before the Peace Conference.

They were no more successful than Du Bois had been, and Du Bois himself must have recognized the parallel objectives and disappointing outcomes of their missions. He would certainly have paid attention to the role of Walsh, who had been a longtime supporter of African American civil rights going back to his time in Democratic Party reform politics in Kansas City. In February 1919, just as the Pan-African Congress was ending, Walsh had endorsed the NAACP's call for a National Anti-Lynching Conference to be held in New York.[32]

After his own return to New York in July, Walsh helped found a new anticolonial organization, the League of Oppressed Peoples, designed to fill the vacuum left by the collapse of Frederic Howe's organization earlier that year. Not surprisingly given this lineage—and also given the growing visibility of the Irish independence struggle as 1919 wore on—this new body was even more thoroughly dominated by revolutionary Irish nationalists than Howe's organization had been. The chairperson of the league was a well-known New York Irish American lawyer and radical named Dudley Field Malone, and numerous other Irish republicans also gravitated to the organization. John Fitzpatrick, the president of the Chicago Federation of Labor, served as an officer of the league, and Peter Golden, leader of the left-wing Irish Progressive League, worked to distribute its informational materials to sympathetic New York newspapers such as the *Jewish Daily Forward* and the socialist *New York Call*. Meanwhile, three of the revolutionary Dáil's envoys in New York, Harry Boland, Liam Mellows, and Patrick McCartan, served as the official representatives of Ireland on the league's central committee. At Malone's invitation, Du Bois agreed to join the committee as well, again representing sub-Saharan Africa.[33]

The individual working in both of these New York anticolonial organizations that Du Bois probably had the closest personal relationship with, however, was neither Irish nor Irish American, but Indian. The lawyer, intellectual, and longtime Indian National Congress leader Lala Lajpat Rai had arrived in New York in November 1914. It is not clear precisely when he first met Du Bois, but it must have been shortly thereafter; by June 1915 Lajpat Rai was thanking Du Bois for his help on a "study of the conditions and problems of the coloured people in the United States" that he included in his book, *The United States of America: A Hindu's Impression and Study*.[34] When Lajpat Rai died after a police beating he received during an independence demonstration back in India in 1928, Du Bois agreed to write a short remembrance of him for a newspaper in Lahore. "It was my good fortune to know Lala Lajpat Rai while he was in exile in America during the great War," he wrote to the paper's editor. "He was at my home and at my office and we were members of the same club. I especially admired his restraint and sweet temper."[35] Over his time in New York, which lasted until February 1920, Lajpat Rai had moved steadily from initial support of Irish Home Rule to a full embrace of Irish revolutionary republicanism; by 1919 he was a featured speaker at the Irish Race Convention in Philadelphia and met with Éamon de Valera, president of the Dáil, in New York.[36] Gertrude B. Kelly, Charles Edward Russell, Frank P. Walsh, and Lala Lajpat Rai were all well known to and respected by Du Bois, and all were integral to an Irish republican network in New York that was beginning to transform his view of the Irish Revolution.

An important step in this transformation occurred when Du Bois was invited to join a distinguished body of prominent Americans, the so-called Committee of One Hundred, to sponsor hearings on the subject of British atrocities in Ireland in the fall of 1920. Du Bois readily assented. Both the committee and the eight-member Commission on Conditions in Ireland that it selected were ostensibly neutral bodies, invoking the spirit of "social investigation" that was characteristic of the era. But in private conversation and internal memoranda Dr. William J. M. A. Maloney, who originally proposed the initiative, was candid about its goal: "to enlist the moral forces of the world to the end that the murder of Irish citizens may cease and public opinion may compel Britain to evacuate Ireland." Its neutrality, he readily admitted, was "merely a mask."[37]

In signing on with the Committee of One Hundred, Du Bois was joining an array of well-known public figures, including settlement house pioneer Jane Addams, Nebraska senator George W. Norris, and Protestant minister of the social gospel Norman Thomas. Some of those involved were already his close associates or friends: Addams, for instance, had contributed a chapter to Du Bois's monograph *The Negro American Family* and had attended a 1908 conference that he organized at Atlanta University. She was a strong supporter of the NAACP and had fought (unsuccessfully) for a plank espousing racial equality that

Du Bois had drafted for the 1912 Progressive Party convention that nominated Theodore Roosevelt for president.[38] L. Hollingsworth Wood, who chaired the commission and guided its hearings, was also an acquaintance of Du Bois. In 1910 Wood, a white real estate lawyer and Quaker reformer, had helped found the National Urban League, an organization devoted to Black "uplift" that sometimes worked in partnership with the NAACP.[39]

A much more complicated acquaintance for Du Bois was the individual who, after Maloney himself, played the most important role in bringing the American Commission on Conditions in Ireland to life: Oswald Garrison Villard, the publisher of both the *New York Evening Post* and the liberal weekly magazine *The Nation* who was related to Maloney by marriage. Grandson of abolitionist William Lloyd Garrison and son of one of the wealthiest men in America, the imperious Villard did not have an easy relationship with Du Bois. Villard had written a glowing review of *The Souls of Black Folk* but had panned Du Bois's 1909 biography of abolitionist John Brown, possibly—at least this is what Du Bois believed—because he getting ready to publish his own biography of Brown. Though the two men had worked closely in the NAACP from the outset (Du Bois's first New York office space was provided by Villard at the *Evening Post*), they were often on opposite sides of internal debates. In early 1918, Du Bois had effectively blocked the "unpleasant candidate" Villard from assuming chairmanship of the organization.[40]

An undercurrent of racism troubled their relationship. "To a white philanthropist like Villard," Du Bois wrote decades later, "a Negro was quite naturally expected to be humble and thankful, or certainly not assertive and aggressive; this Villard resented."[41] Still, the two men developed what David Levering Lewis calls "a grudging mutual respect," one based on "labor in a common cause and the discipline of intellect." Du Bois and Villard were "kindred egos."[42] Thus when Villard, who threw himself and the weight of his important periodicals into the Irish cause in 1920, Du Bois was prepared to follow.

Much less complicated was an Irish American ex-newspaperman by the name of John Edgar Milholland, a key figure in the NAACP and a founder of the Constitution League, a forerunner of the American Civil Liberties Union, whom Du Bois recalled fondly in his autobiography as one of the "extraordinary helpers" in the struggle against "prejudice and reaction."[43] According to Lewis, the two men "had liked each other instantly, which was unusual for Du Bois." Prior to the founding of *The Crisis*, the two had discussed putting out a magazine together, and it had been at Milholland's urging that Du Bois had traveled to the London Universal Races Congress.[44] Like Du Bois, Milholland was a member of Maloney's Committee of One Hundred, but his Irish republican activism went far deeper than that. When Harry Boland lobbied members of Congress to endorse "the right of the people of Ireland to the principle of national self-determination" in early 1920, he had relied heavily on the experienced Milholland for political advice.[45]

The shared perspective on the Irish Revolution among many of Du Bois's closest friends or associates had a significant impact on his own. When Terence MacSwiney, the republican lord mayor of Cork, died in Brixton Prison in October 1920 after a wrenching seventy-four days on hunger strike, Du Bois's response was very different from his response to Casement's death back in 1916. Not only did he devote a laudatory editorial to MacSwiney ("No cause with such martyrs can ever die"), but he was soon quoting a version of MacSwiney's famous dictum ("Not those who inflict most, but those who suffer most are the conquerors") in reference to the Black American struggle for the franchise.[46]

Still, it is important to be absolutely clear about where Du Bois was—and was not—at this end of this intellectual and political journey. In an editorial titled "Bleeding Ireland" in the March 1921 issue of *The Crisis*, he focused on contradictions. Du Bois was forthright in his support for Irish independence: "The Irish resist, as they have resisted hundreds of years, various and exacting forms of English oppression." But with his now characteristically global perspective, he also referenced the multiple generations of Irish men who had served as British soldiers throughout the empire, often violently suppressing those who *also* sought to resist colonial oppression. "No people in the world have in the past gone with blither spirit to kill 'the niggers' from Kingston to Delhi and from Kumassi [*sic*] to Fiji." The fact that Ireland was *itself* the victim of British domination rendered the actions (and the racism) of Irish men in British uniform tragically ironic, a powerful illustration of "how in this world it is the Oppressed who have continually been used to cow and kill the Oppressed in the interest of the Universal Oppressor."[47]

Shortly after his editorial appeared, Du Bois received a letter from Reverend D. J. Bustin, an assistant priest at the New York headquarters of the Catholic Board for Mission Work among the Colored People, who strongly objected to the picture of Irish and Irish American racism that he had drawn in "Bleeding Ireland." In his response, Du Bois could not have been more forceful or clear about where he stood. "I regret to say that there can be no doubt of the hostility of a large proportion of Irish Americans toward Negroes," Du Bois wrote. "I have been in personal contact with Irish Americans from my childhood up until the present. I have found very few of them who have expressed the slightest sympathy for the Negro." However, he continued, "this fact does not for a moment invalidate the justice of the Irish cause and I shall at all times defend the right of Ireland to absolute independence."[48]

## NOTES

I would like to thank Carl Fan for his research assistance and participants at the 2019 national meeting of the American Conference for Irish Studies for their helpful comments on an earlier version of this chapter.

1   W. E. B. Du Bois, "Sir Roger Casement–Patriot, Martyr," *The Crisis*, Sept. 1916, 215–216; "Bleeding Ireland," *The Crisis*, Mar. 1921, 200. For Garvey's view of Casement, see "Dedication of UNIA Liberty Hall [27 July 1919]," in *The Marcus Garvey and Universal Negro Improvement Association Papers*, 10 vols., ed. Robert A. Hill (Berkeley: University of California Press, 1983–2011), 1:471–473, and, for Garvey's support for Irish republicanism more generally, see David Brundage, *Irish Nationalists in America: The Politics of Exile, 1798–1998* (Oxford: Oxford University Press, 2016), 153–159. See also Miriam Nyhan Grey, "'Ireland Should Be Free, Even as Africa Shall Be Free': Marcus Garvey's Irish Influences," in this volume. For an insightful analysis of the impact of the Irish Revolution on "the black nationalist imagination," which includes a brief discussion of Du Bois, see Bruce Nelson, *Irish Nationalists and the Making of the Irish Race* (Princeton: Princeton University Press, 2012), 181–211.

2   For Wilson's impact on anticolonialism, see Erez Manela, *The Wilsonian Moment: Self-Determination and the International Origins of Anticolonial Nationalism* (Oxford: Oxford University Press, 2007). For a sampling of new work on the global impact of the Irish Revolution, see Enda Delaney and Fearghal McGarry, eds., *The Irish Revolution, 1919–21: A Global History* (Dublin: Wordwell, 2019) and Delaney and McGarry, eds., "A Global History of the Irish Revolution," *Irish Historical Studies* 44, no. 165 (May 2020).

3   Alice Kessler-Harris, "Why Biography?," *American Historical Review* 114, no. 3 (June 2009): 626. See also David Nasaw et al., "AHR Roundtable: Historians and Biography," *American Historical Review* 114, no. 3 (June 2009): 573–661, which in-

cludes Kessler-Harris's essay, and Barbara Caine, *Biography and History* (Basingstoke: Palgrave Macmillan, 2010).

4 The quality and depth of writing on Du Bois, capped by David Levering Lewis's prize-winning biography, is stunning. See Lewis, *W. E. B. Du Bois*, 2 vols. (New York: Henry Holt, 1993–2000). For a short recent study, see Shawn Leigh Alexander, *W. E. B. Du Bois: An American Intellectual and Activist* (Lanham, MD: Rowman & Littlefield, 2015).

5 Lewis, *Du Bois*, 1:12.

6 For a concise overview of Irish migration in this era, with a particularly insightful discussion of the harshness of the Irish experience in New England, see Timothy J. Meagher, *The Columbia Guide to Irish American History* (New York: Columbia University Press, 2005), 60–94.

7 Du Bois, *Darkwater: Voices from within the Veil* (New York: Harcourt, Brace, 1921), 10.

8 Du Bois, *The Autobiography of W. E. B. Du Bois: A Soliloquy on Viewing My Life from the Last Decade of Its First Century* (New York: International, 1968), 82.

9 Du Bois, *Autobiography*, 87.

10 L. Perry Curtis, *Apes and Angels: The Irishman in Victorian Caricature*, rev. ed. (Washington, DC: Smithsonian Institution Press, 1996), 65.

11 Du Bois, *Autobiography*, 87–88.

12 For an illuminating analysis, see Catherine Hall, *Macaulay and Son: Architects of Imperial Britain* (New Haven, CT: Yale University Press, 2012), esp. 317–319.

13 Herbert Aptheker, *Annotated Bibliography of the Published Writings of W. E. B. Du Bois* (Millwood, NY: Kraus-Thomson, 1973), 1, 6; Shawn Leigh Alexander, *An Army of Lions: The Civil Rights Struggle Before the NAACP* (Philadelphia: University of Pennsylvania Press, 2013), 9–11; Eric Foner, *Politics and Ideology in the Age of the Civil War* (New York: Oxford University Press, 1980), 150–151, 181.

14 Du Bois, *Autobiography*, 82, 89. For good summaries of the research on Irish American racism and the embrace of "whiteness" in this era, see Kevin Kenny, *The American Irish: A History* (Harlow, UK: Longman, 2000), 66–71, and Meagher, *Columbia Guide*, 214–233.

15 Du Bois, *The Philadelphia Negro: A Social Study* (Philadelphia: University of Pennsylvania Press, 1899), 10, 373. See also Lewis, *Du Bois*, 1:155–161, 182, 186–187, 204–205, and Michael B. Katz and Thomas J. Sugrue, eds., *W. E. B. Du Bois, Race, and the City: The Philadelphia Negro and Its Legacy* (Philadelphia: University of Pennsylvania Press, 1998).

16 Du Bois, *The Negro Artisan: Report of a Social Study Made under the Direction of Atlanta University* (Atlanta: Atlanta University Press, 1902), 134–135.

17 Du Bois, "The Pan-African Movement," in *Writings by W. E. B. Du Bois in Non-periodical Literature Edited by Others*, 4 vols., ed. Herbert Aptheker (Millwood, NY: Kraus-Thomson, 1982), 4:242. For a full discussion of the conference, see Jonathan Schneer, *London 1900: The Imperial Metropolis* (New Haven, CT: Yale University Press, 1999), 213–225.

18  "Report of the Pan-African Conference, ca. 1900" (typescript), 12–13 (Special Collections & University Archives, University of Massachusetts Amherst, W. E. B. Du Bois Papers [hereafter Du Bois Papers]), https://credo.library.umass.edu; Lewis, *Du Bois*, 1:248.

19  Lewis, *Du Bois*, 1:326, 338, 441–442; Du Bois, "The Races Congress," *The Crisis*, Sept. 1911, 202.

20  Kelly, quoted in Brundage, *Irish Nationalists in America*, 143–144. See also Francis M. Carroll, *American Opinion and the Irish Question, 1910–23: A Study in Opinion and Policy* (New York: St. Martin's, 1978), 36–46, for an excellent discussion of the crisis of the American Home Rule movement in these years.

21  Du Bois, "Credo," *The Independent*, 6 Oct. 1904, 787. The "Credo" was both a political manifesto and a kind of catechism of racial pride. It had a huge influence among African American readers and could be found on the walls of many African American homes in the form of a "hanging card." See Lewis, *Du Bois*, 1:312–313.

22  Du Bois, "The African Roots of War," *Atlantic Monthly*, May 1915, 707–714.

23  Du Bois, quoted in Lewis, *Du Bois*, 1:515–516, 556, who provides a persuasive analysis of Du Bois's attitudes toward Britain and the war. See also Mark Ellis, "'Closing Ranks' and 'Seeking Honors': W. E. B. Du Bois in World War I," *Journal of American History* 79, no. 1 (June 1992): 96–124.

24  Du Bois, "The Greater Crisis," *The Crisis*, Aug. 1918, 165.

25  Du Bois, "Ireland," *The Crisis*, Aug. 1916, 166–167.

26  Du Bois, "Sir Roger Casement," 215–216; *New York Times*, 3 May 1916. For an excellent survey of US press opinion, see Robert Schmuhl, *Ireland's Exiled Children: America and the Easter Rising* (Oxford: Oxford University Press, 2016). Lewis overstates Du Bois's position as one of championing "Irish liberation" in these 1916 editorials. As Bruce Nelson observes, Du Bois was not endorsing "the right of an oppressed nation to full self-determination." Such an endorsement was still a few years in the future. See Lewis, *Du Bois*, 1:516, and Nelson, *Irish Nationalists*, 210.

27  Du Bois, "The Black Soldier," *The Crisis*, June 1918, 60. See also Manela, *Wilsonian Moment*, 7–8, who argues that Wilson's lofty rhetoric about democracy and national self-determination was adopted by some African American activists like Du Bois and William Monroe Trotter, as well as by anticolonial activists outside the United States.

28  "Small Nations Leagued Together," *The Survey*, 5 May 1917.

29  Dennis Clark, *Hibernia America: The Irish and Regional Cultures* (Westport, CT: Greenwood, 1986), 58.

30  For a discussion of both this organization and the League of Oppressed Peoples that succeeded it, see David Brundage, "The Easter Rising and New York's Anticolonial Nationalists," in *Ireland's Allies: America and the 1916 Easter Rising*, ed. Miriam Nyhan Grey (Dublin: University College Dublin Press, 2016), 347–360. For Du Bois's friendship with Kelly, see, in the same volume, Miriam Nyhan Grey, "Dr. Gertrude B. Kelly and the Founding of New York's Cumann na mBan," 87.

31  Du Bois, "The Pan-African Congress," *The Crisis*, Apr. 1919, 273. For the Pan-African Congress's combination of "complicity and resistance," see Tyler Stovall, "Black Modernism and the Making of the Twentieth Century: Paris, 1919," in *Afromodernisms: Paris, Harlem and the Avant-Garde*, ed. Fionnghuala Sweeney and Kate Marsh (Edinburgh: Edinburgh University Press, 2013), 20. For the close relationship between Russell and Du Bois at this point, see Lewis, *Du Bois*, 1:389, and for Russell's deep engagement with Irish republicanism, see Brundage, *Irish Nationalists in America*, 170–172.

32  Moorfield Storey to Frank Walsh, 5 Mar. 1919 (New York Public Library Archives and Manuscripts, Frank P. Walsh Papers, Box 7). For the American Commission on Irish Independence, see Carroll, *American Opinion*, 131–139.

33  Arthur Upham Pope to Du Bois, 10 Nov. 1919 (Du Bois Papers), https://credo.library.umass.edu.

34  Lala Lajpat Rai, *The Collected Works of Lala Lajpat Rai*, 15 vols., ed. B. R. Nanda (New Delhi: Manohar, 2004), 5:96.

35  Du Bois to the Editor of *The People* [Lahore], 10 Jan. 1929 (Du Bois Papers), https://credo.library.umass.edu. The New York Civic Club, to which Du Bois referred, was one of the few interracial clubs in the city.

36  See David Brundage, "Lala Lajpat Rai, Indian Nationalism, and the Irish Revolution: The View from New York, 1914–1920," in *1916 in Global Context: An Antiimperial Moment*, ed. Enrico Dal Lago, Róisín Healy and Gearóid Barry (Abingdon, UK: Routledge, 2019), 62–75.

37  "Maloney's Memorandum on Washington Commission on British Atrocities," Appendix IV, in Patrick McCartan, *With De Valera in America* (New York: Brentano, 1932), 259. For an analysis of the American Commission on Conditions in Ireland, see Carroll, *American Opinion*, 162–165.

38  Lewis, *Du Bois*, 1:377–378, 422. Du Bois had insisted that Addams stay on the campus of the Black university rather than face the possible hostility of Atlanta's white residents. This was not their first meeting: the previous year, Du Bois had given a well-attended lecture on Abraham Lincoln at Hull House, the pioneering settlement house that Addams had founded in Chicago.

39  See L. Hollingsworth Wood to Du Bois, ca. 8 Aug. 1917, praising him for the "prompt and efficient way" that he and other NAACP leaders had responded to the East St. Louis anti-Black race riot: organizing a silent parade of over eight thousand African American men, women, and children down Fifth Avenue, a demonstration unlike anything seen before in the history of Black protest (Du Bois Papers), https://credo.library.umass.edu.

40  Du Bois's long-running feud with Villard is a major theme in Lewis's biography. See Lewis, *Du Bois*, 1:295–296, 360–361, 400, 544.

41  Du Bois, *Autobiography*, 256–257.

42  Lewis, *Du Bois*, 1:361, 471.

43  Du Bois, *Autobiography*, 226–227.

44  Lewis, *Du Bois*, 1:348–349, 382–383, 439.

45  David Fitzpatrick, *Harry Boland's Irish Revolution* (Cork: Cork University Press, 2004), 137–138.

46  Du Bois, "McSwiney [*sic*]," *The Crisis*, Dec. 1920, 57; "Reduced Representation in Congress," *The Crisis*, Feb. 1921, 149.

47  Du Bois, "Bleeding Ireland," *The Crisis*, Mar. 1921, 200. See also Lewis, *Du Bois*, 2:61. Kumasi, in what is now Ghana, was burned to the ground by British soldiers in 1874, during the Third Anglo-Ashanti War.

48  Du Bois to Rev. D. J. Bustin, 30 Mar. 1921 (Du Bois Papers), https://credo.library. umass.edu.

# "Ireland Should Be Free, Even as Africa Shall Be Free"

## *Marcus Garvey's Irish Influences*

MIRIAM NYHAN GREY

Far more than any other nationalist struggle, the Irish revolutionary struggle assisted in focusing Garvey's political perspective.
—Robert A. Hill, *Marcus Garvey and Universal Negro Improvement Association Papers*[1]

Even into the twenty-first century, Ireland's pathway to independence from Britain features in the discourse on Caribbean nationalism. On 1 August 2020, at an event to mark the centenary of Marcus Garvey's achievement of the first convention of the United Negro Improvement Association and the African Communities League (UNIA), the former prime minister of Jamaica, P. J. Patterson, contextualized Garvey and his impact. Garveyism, as his movement became known, evolved as the "largest mass movement in the history of the African diaspora." No less than it had done in an Irish setting, the crisis of the Great War exposed the "vulnerability of empire" and propelled the ferment in which British Caribbeans and African Americans would seek to ameliorate their status in their respective societies. The period would see the collapse of several empires, Russian, Austro-Hungarian, Ottoman, and German, and significant weakening of their British and French counterparts. Noting that the era of the Great War saw the emergence of "upheaval and revolt against Britain," Patterson cited Ireland as his sole example. Exactly a century earlier to the day, Marcus Garvey had invoked the Irish at the first UNIA convention in Liberty Hall in Harlem, New York.[2]

Marcus Garvey was born into modest circumstances in Saint Ann's, Jamaica, in 1887. At the age of fourteen he began training as a printer in the apprenticeship system that was a feature of Jamaican society after emancipation. An autodidact, he would become a dominant player in Black nationalism in the United States and the Caribbean from 1917 into the mid-1920s, and an internationally known figure until he died in 1940. Garvey and the UNIA, as Robert Hill puts it, would come to symbolize "the historic encounter between two highly developed socioeconomic and political traditions: the social consciousness and drive for self-government of the Caribbean peasantry and the racial consciousness and search for justice of the Afro-American community." Garvey's name features prominently in the American pantheon of Black leaders, including Frederick Douglass, Booker T. Washington, W. E. B. Du Bois, Martin Luther King Jr., and Malcolm X.

Radical and enigmatic, dubbed the "Black Moses," Garvey was posthumously reinterred from England and bestowed the honor of being Jamaica's first national hero after independence was secured eventually in the 1960s. His international strategy, drawing on his experience of British imperialism, marked Garvey apart from others, gave him a common cause with the Irish, and drew the ire of many. As Tony Martin observes, "The United States government was against him because they considered all black radicals subversive; European governments were against him because he was a threat to the stability of their colonies; the communists were against him because he successfully kept black workers out of their grasp." At the same time, "the National Association for the Advancement of Colored People and other integrationist organizations were against him because he argued that white segregationists were the true spokesmen for white America and because he in turn advocated black separatism."[3]

In March 1916, one month before Dublin's Easter Rising and the same month as the historic Irish Race Convention in New York's Hotel Astor, twenty-nine-year-old Garvey arrived in New York from Jamaica "unheralded and unestablished." He came in hopes of meeting Booker T. Washington, who, although his critics condemned his conservativism, preached a message of racial pride and uplift that had a decisive influence on the Jamaican. By 1919 Garvey was firmly established as "one of Harlem's most important radical figures" and sufficiently influential to encounter a "powerful conglomeration" of hostility. Those four years from March 1916 until the first UNIA convention in August 1920 were foundational for Garvey. This chapter argues that the Irish example, in this formative period, was central to the emergence of Garvey's global approach and his impetus to find, with other groups, a "sense of unity." Through themes of empire, race, and organizational culture, I identify the influence of Ireland on Garveyism, in a type of dialogue framed by what Erez Manela views as "component parts of a single historical moment."[4]

## Imperial Ties That Bound

Marcus Garvey was a Jamaican man who bore an Irish surname. That one of the twentieth century's most radical political movements was led by a Black man with an Irish name seems all the more fitting when it is noted that the name, Ó Gairbhi, anglicized under English domination of Ireland, roughly translates as "rough peace." As a British imperial subject, Garvey knew that the Irish were both subjects and agents of empire. He carried the Garvey surname as a colonial subject who was born at the zenith of Britain's imperial century. His forefather had been most likely given the appellation by a slave owner, though not by way of ancestry. Ireland marked Garvey from the moment of his birth literally and metaphorically.[5]

Garvey's exposure to the Irish question probably began early, most definitely during his early Kingston years (1906–1910) but perhaps even earlier back home in Saint Ann's. What is clear is that the young Marcus Garvey was framing from an early age "a picture of himself that was bigger than his surroundings." His father, Malchus Mosiah, a stonemason who was just a generation removed from slavery, was a "self-educated man who had amassed an impressive collection of precious books" and dispensed advice like "a local lawyer." The son was known to "steal into his father's library and luxuriate in the knowledge contained therein" and later acknowledged that this reading had inspired him to want to become a "personality of the world." It is not clear what exactly Malchus, and therefore possibly Marcus, read, but Malchus is reported to have had an interest in anticolonial activists like Paul Bogle and George William Gordon, and the Jamaican thinker Dr. T. E. S. Scholes. A lawsuit that later ruined the elder Garvey suggests that he read *Galls News Letter*, published by a Scottish-born newspaper man who reported out of Kingston in a manner that "ran counter to the Establishment" and "championed the cause of Black Jamaicans." The Garveys probably also read the "aggressive nationalist newspaper," the *Jamaica Advocate*, published by Dr. Robert J. Love, whom Marcus Garvey would later seek out when he moved to the Jamaican capital.[6]

Garvey certainly had Irish activity on his radar by 1910, when he became involved in the National Club in Kingston, "the first attempt by Jamaicans to create a nationalist political platform." By then a printer of some experience, he was charged with publishing the organ's journal, titled *Our Own*—a nod, perhaps, to the influence the Sinn Féin movement had on the founder of the party, S. A. G. Cox. Dr. Love, the publisher of the nationalist *Jamaica Advocate*, was a radical activist with an interest in Irish Home Rule, and his mentorship of the young Garvey has been viewed as critical to the evolution of Garvey's political ideology. And there are other, broader and more speculative, ways in which the Irish example might have resonated with Garvey. Both Jamaica and Ireland were dominated by a small colonial elite. Both were heavily rural, but their capital cities, Kingston and Dublin, were marked by severe poverty and class conflict. And Jamaica and Ireland were, and remain, countries of extraordinary high emigration. Garvey knew what it was to grow up in a place he would probably leave. And leave he did.[7]

In the late spring of 1912 Garvey traveled to England from Jamaica having recently returned from a stint in Central America. There, he became engaged to a "Spanish Irish" heiress and later claimed to have visited Ireland, during his own version of a grand tour. During this sojourn, he devoured "political tracts, theories of social engineering, African history and Western Enlightenment" and claimed to have studied at Birkbeck College. There is no doubt that he saw his time in England as an opportunity to "complete his informal education." As he wrote back to Jamaica in January 1914, "I have seen wonders. I have learnt wonders and I hope to teach wonders." It was in this period that Garvey had his first sustained encounters with the Irish question and anti-imperialism more broadly. He frequented Hyde Park's Speaker's Corner, where he had a chance to listen to "Sinn Feiners, stalwarts of anti-imperialism." As he had done in Kingston by gravitating to individuals who were challenging British imperialism, in London he worked for Duse Mohamad Ali, publisher of the *African Times and Orient Review*. Ali was campaigning for Egyptian independence and was connected to W. B. Yeats through Sarojini Naidu. But perhaps most importantly, Garvey's time in England coincided with a period of "uninterrupted crisis in both England and Ireland" over Irish Home Rule.[8]

Contrary to what one might expect, especially with the benefit of hindsight, Garvey at this time was not a radical. At any rate, he certainly did not present himself as one. On the contrary, until 1917 Garvey went to great lengths to present himself as a loyal British subject. He was at pains to describe the fledgling UNIA as a nonpolitical organization, emphasizing education and culture as the tenets of the organization, and as a "tool for liberation." He also described the UNIA as a vehicle of "social improvement" intended to alleviate "the condition of the masses of the island." Like the Irish nationalist leader John Redmond, Garvey urged Jamaicans to fight for the empire in the First World War. Throughout the early months of the conflict, clearly trying to raise his own visibility and assert the representativeness of the UNIA, he attempted to ingratiate himself, mainly through the Colonial Office, with the highest levels of British power: Asquith, Lloyd George, Bonar Law, and newspaper titans like Sir Harry Lawson and Lord Northcliffe. Garvey cast his native island as an integral part of the British Empire, one that could serve as "a guide to the world on the reorganization of racial exclusiveness." In 1915 he wrote that "the flag of England . . . afforded them liberty, and they should esteem it an honor to die for it." He also asserted "the duty of every true son of the Empire to rally to the cause of the Motherland." Garvey's ambition suggests that his protestations of loyalty were partly strategic, yet they stand in marked contrast to his later anti-imperialism.[9]

American entry into the war in 1917, under Wilson's slogan of "Make the World Safe for Democracy," presented African Americans and Irish Americans with somewhat of a dilemma. Would Black military service abroad alleviate discrimination at home? Should Irish Americans join an American war in which the British were allies, especially in the aftermath of Easter 1916? Both groups enlisted in significant numbers in the American military. Garvey continued to support Caribbean and African American participation in the Allied cause. He enlisted himself in the summer of 1917 but was quickly granted a medical exemption. But in 1918 he asked bluntly, "What is the Negro to get out of the war?" And by this time Ireland was beginning to feature more prominently in Garvey's discourse, as he kept an eye on international developments. "The Irish, the Jews, the East Indians and all other oppressed people . . . are getting together to demand from their oppressors Liberty, Justice and Equality," he declared in a UNIA poster in December 1918, "and we now call [u]pon the four hundred million Negros of the world to do likewise."[10]

## Becoming More of a "Race" and an "Irish" Man

In the period 1918–1920, Garvey's thinking shifted from empire to the related theme of race. His goal, rhetorically, was the establishment of an alternative type of empire defined by the racial solidarity of Blackness, and in that sense the first theme directly feeds into the second, which had lingered in the shadows during Garvey's wartime strategy of Blacks being seen to be well-behaved colonials. In refining its message of African redemption, the UNIA was influenced by both the changing international scene and the postwar wave of violence against African Americans. Between the summer of 1918 and the 1920 convention, Garvey established his plan for establishing an African republic, and it was precisely in this period that references to Ireland increased in his rhetoric, as Ireland and the Irish diaspora emerged as a roadmap for Garveyism.

There are two ironies at play here. The first is that Garvey embarked on an empire-building agenda when other empires were collapsing or being significantly eroded. The second is that even as Garvey was emphasizing Black solidarity, the Irish became his model for how to challenge an existing empire from within and supplant its authority with another type of empire. "Race" at this time was often used conterminously with people or nation. Contemporary sources refer repeatedly to the Irish "race." The convention called in Hotel Astor the month before the Easter Rising, for example, was an Irish "race" convention. A popular book of the era was *The Story of the Irish Race*. The Irish "race," often presented in typologies as Celts/Celtic, was presented as being inferior to Anglo-Protestant Americans. But the Irish in the United States were not barred from citizenship, could vote, and did not face segregation or vigilante violence. In these respects, there was no comparison with the ordeal of African Americans. Indeed, as African Americans moved to northern cities, it was often the Irish who greeted them with the most hostility. The American Irish, moreover, wielded considerable political power, not only in cities but nationally. The elevation of the recognition of the Irish Republic in the American Senate was just one example. Garvey, as the third section of this chapter demonstrates, was acutely aware of Irish American power and organizational prowess.[11]

Just as Garvey had traveled to Europe to see the imperial metropole at work firsthand, when he wanted to learn about race in the United States he adopted a comparable strategy by embarking, in the summer of 1916, on a six-month "sweep across thirty-eight states," including the American South, "conducting his one-man survey of African-American life." The plight of African Americans, as Colin Grant notes, stirred him into starting to "detach himself from an outlook formed through the prism of a Jamaican colonial world, governed firstly through class privilege and secondly by racial prejudices. On American soil that order was reversed: race came first." The segregation and terror Garvey witnessed on his trip marked him deeply and inspired his vision of international Black solidarity. "We are here tonight to renew our pledges," as he put it in 1918, "to stand more firmly on the platform of this great organization that takes in all the negroes, whether he be a French negro, a Spanish negro, an Italian negro, a German negro (laughter), or an Irish negro (great laughter)." Language pertaining to a global "negro" community occurred increasingly, as Garvey saw "the negro question as no longer a local one, but of the Negroes of the World, joining hands and fighting for one common cause." The word "global" appeared in Garvey's language with increasing frequency.[12]

Yet Garvey still anticipated a reward for the wartime loyalty of people of African descent. The headline of the *Negro World* of 20 November 1918, "NEGROES AT VERSAILLES," conveyed this hope. He was clear that African American participation in the war effort meant diverting energies from the battle for equity and justice back home in the United States: "The man who lost arms and legs in France could have lost them in a better cause in America." The "Wilsonian moment," as Erez Manela notes, was one when "peoples from the periphery who had made significant contributions to the Allied effort felt it entitled them to a great voice in their own government and in the international arena. If they could die alongside Europeans, why could they not govern alongside them?" Just as Garvey saw the imperial powers as owing peoples of African descent a debt for their loyalty, the Irish in the United States saw Wilson's administration, in particular, as being in "the position to repay the debt it owes the Irish race" by advancing the cause of independence from Britain. Irish American activists were not shy in calling out what failure of American support of the Irish in Paris could mean: "If [the Democratic Party] fails us there," said a Friends of Irish Freedom member, "we shall fail the Democratic Party." Garvey, like his Irish counterpart, had made vigorous attempts to get the status of peoples of African descent on the table in France. Indeed, Wilson realized only retrospectively how much he had elevated expectations with his public statements, which is almost never a good strategy for a politician. As the American journalist Ray Stannard Baker observed, Greek, Albanian, Lithuanian, Egyptian, Jewish, and Irish representatives attended the peace conference, and "a group of Negroes were there to lead the cause of the black man before the tribunal of the world." But Wilson "had become convinced that Ireland was a domestic concern of the British Empire and that no foreign leader had a right to interfere." This position is telling. If Wilson would not interject on the Irish question, then who in Paris could justify addressing the African American question in the United States when that too could be classified as "domestic"? What is clear is that support for Black America did not count for as much as the loss of Irish America, which likely cost the Democrats the 1920 presidential election.[13]

If 1916 and the heavy-handed executions of the leaders by the British were a galvanizing moment in terms of public opinion in the Irish case, then the East St. Louis "riots" of 1917 were critical for Garveyism. One biographer goes as far as identifying East St. Louis as a "turning point" in Garvey's life. His American tour the previous year had taught him a lot about the plight of Black Americans, and it clearly politicized him. The earlier orthodoxy of the UNIA gave way to a commitment to a much more assertive and increasingly radical ideology, especially with the realization that wartime loyalty meant nothing in terms of alleviating the status of Black peoples. The deteriorating conditions for African Americans were underscored by a sharp increase in lynching. Even returning servicemen in military uniform were lynched, while the horrific lynching of Mary Turner in May 1918 showed that even a pregnant woman and her unborn child were deemed fair game for racist America.[14]

As Garvey was reacting to the disappointing outcome of the Peace Conference, some of the worst race "riots" in American history were occurring. Between April and November 1919, twenty-six cities saw racial unrest with deaths and loss impacting most heavily on African Americans. Garvey's remarks from that summer hint at his rage and convey a sense of unity of purpose with others in similar predicaments, even if few groups suffered as much as African Americans at this time: "My appeal is to every member of the race in every part of the world," Garvey wrote. "The Universal Negro Improvement Association realizes that the war of 1914–1918 is over, but all Negroes must prepare for the next world war." Garvey felt certain that more wars would follow because "stronger nations and races are still robbing and exploiting the weaker ones. So long as the Negro is oppressed all over the world there can be no abiding peace." With four hundred million Negroes "suffering from the injustices of the white man," he concluded, "we cannot entertain any idea of peace that does not mean equality for all peoples. Negroes must now combine with China, India, Egypt, Ireland and Russia, to free themselves in the future." But Garvey knew that his was not the only group that had been let down by the British. In 1919, he noted, "the Premier of England during the election of 1912, made great promises to the Irish people. Home rule for Ireland was practically written on the statutes of England, and up to now those people have not gained their freedom." How could the Irish "continue to have confidence in English professions"?[15]

Garvey's observations here imply something that informs the final part of this chapter: how the Irish felt they could place "confidence" in somewhere beyond Britain to amplify their cause. For Garvey, as of June 1919, there was no one country or group of people to support those of African descent. "As far as Negroes are concerned," he wrote, "there is absolutely no one, no nation, or no race that they can place their confidence in." American disdain and inaction on recent racial violence spoke volumes. The African colonies had been carved up between the allied victors. Ireland was in a much stronger position, and the team that had presented the Irish case in Paris knew that the strategy needed to adapt to the new landscape. Adapt they did. The fight for recognition of the Irish Republic would be taken across the Atlantic from Paris to New York and would serve as a model for Garvey's African republic.[16]

## New York: Statecraft in Exile

By the spring of 1919 two anticolonial activists were preoccupied with similar concerns on opposite sides of the Atlantic Ocean. One man was phenotypically Caucasian and saw himself as being Irish, despite being born in Manhattan decades earlier. He bore a surname of Spanish origin: de Valera. The other activist, self-identified as a "Jamaican of full African blood," bore the Irish surname of Garvey. Both were products of the British Empire and at just five years apart in age were born when the imperial reach was at its zenith. The months of late 1918 and early 1919 were decisive for both men. In Ireland, the success of Sinn Féin in the general election of December 1918 had refuted the naysayers who had seen the 1916 Easter Rising as an evanescent moment spearheaded by a small number of unrepresentative hard-liners. This electoral result meant that Irish republicanism had a mandate.[17]

For Marcus Garvey the period from 1918 to 1919 had marked a shift in emphasis too, especially with the emergence of race as a complementary theme to empire. More and more, Garveyism was influenced by the Irish case, in part no doubt because it was becoming more visible on the world stage. But Garvey's drawing on Ireland was partly strategic, as his speeches and editorials amply reflect. Aligning with the Irish would not have been in his interests earlier. Now, however, the news from Dublin buoyed Garvey, and he saw his followers, like the Irish, as having entered an "age of struggle for liberty." For both de Valera and Garvey, the peace conference had yielded disappointing results. Garvey concluded that "small powers . . . were invited to the [Peace] conference only as pure camouflage." Both men decided that it was in North America that the battles for Irish and African self-determination needed to be fought. Efforts to gain recognition on the American stage, along with fundraising initiatives, became central to their activities.[18]

By June of 1919, Garvey and de Valera found themselves in New York City, although there is no evidence to suggest they ever met. Garvey was three years into his term in the United States by then. De Valera had taken a more circuitous route since 1916, which had involved fighting in the Dublin rebellion, arrest and an ensuing death sentence, commutation of this sentence, election to the British Parliament in 1917, being broken out of an English jail, and a clandestine sailing across the Atlantic. Their introductions to postwar America serve as a metaphor for the standing of their respective groups at that time. Garvey, an archetypal impoverished Black immigrant, barely stayed afloat at first. His accommodation and access to food left a lot to be desired. The summer of 1916 was unusually hot even for New York, and the asthmatic Jamaican was often unwell. By 1919 his personal situation had improved. In contrast, and despite an unorthodox transatlantic passage marred by severe sea sickness, de Valera found himself lodged in one of the most luxurious and famous hotels in the world, the Waldorf Astoria. His American handlers knew the power of public relations, and the Irish leader settled into a protracted stay in this iconic location for the periods when he was in New York City in between his transcontinental trips. His arrival was feted by the American press. But de Valera and Garvey encountered very different diasporic communities. The Irish still faced religious prejudice but not the type of racial discrimination directed at Black Americans. New York at this time was a very Irish city. It had a sizeable Irish immigrant population as well as a second and third generation of American-born Irish who "had not only figured out how the nation's premier metropolis worked but had given it an indelible imprint of their own and begun to enjoy the success that comes with commanding a city's affairs." Garvey, by contrast, endured the minority status of Blackness; bigotry and de facto segregation touched almost all aspects of daily life.[19]

While they had some features in common, de Valera's and Garvey's American trips were correspondingly different. De Valera was in the United States to seek recognition for the Irish Republic and to fundraise, initially through the Friends of Irish Freedom, which was founded at the first Irish Race Convention in 1916 just as Garvey was setting sail from Jamaica for New York. The ethnic base that de Valera's campaign drew on was robust and well established, and its social, cultural, and political capital was immense. Garvey, by contrast, witnessed segregation and discrimination that politicized him on the issue of civil rights for African Americans. On this basis, he became focused on organizing in the North American setting. "Whether it is the Irish people, the

Polish people, the Jews, or the Hindoos, everybody is looking out to protect himself," Garvey wrote. "Organization is the force that rules the world. All peoples have gained their freedom through organized force. All nations all empires have grown into greatness through organized methods." It was in this context that the first American branch of UNIA was formed and incorporated, the *Negro World* newspaper was established, and New York supplanted Kingston as the world headquarters of the movement. With these organizational structures in place, Garvey looked eastward, but his gaze was no longer primarily on Europe as a source of inspiration. Garvey now looked toward his new "motherland" of Africa, and he began to devote his energies to founding a physical means for people of African descent to "go back" to Africa to "create empires of their own." To accomplish this "they needed ships," and Garvey founded the Black Star Line in 1919. An informer would claim that Irish America's Friends of Irish Freedom had aided in establishing the line.[20]

Garvey knew that for an event of the magnitude of publicly announcing the Black Star Shipping Line, he needed a space that was iconic. Carnegie Hall fit the bill. He knew the symbolism involved in using a location that had been used by other groups, most especially the Irish, who frequently held significant events there throughout the 1910s. "America helped the Irish," Garvey noted. "America helped the Jew. America helped the people of Eastern states of Russia to air their grievance to the world, and for those principles I love America—and for those principles only. (Applause)." The words "Ireland" and "Irish" appeared no fewer than one dozen times that night. Garvey described the wartime era as a "period of reconstruction" for African Americans and applied that same term, "reconstruction," to the Irish "striking homewards towards Ireland." "The Irish," he declared, "have been fighting for over 700 years to free Ireland. From the time when Robert Emmet, when he lost his head, to the time of Roger Casement, Ireland has been fighting, agitating and offering up her sons as martyrs." And just as Emmet "bled and died for Ireland, we who are leading the Universal Negro Improvement Association, are prepared at any time to free Africa and free the negroes of the world. (Applause)."[21]

A few weeks after de Valera landed in New York, Garvey's UNIA moved into a new phase with its relocation to its own dedicated building, Liberty Hall, on the site of what was once a Baptist Church at 138th Street and Lenox Avenue in Harlem. The naming of the New York headquarters has been interpreted as a nod to the Dublin location of the same name. While Garvey did not mention the 1916 rebellion in his speech at the dedication, he did take the opportunity to invoke some Irish historical heroes: "The time had come for the Negro race to offer up its martyrs upon the altar of liberty even as the Irish had given a long list from Robert Emmet to Roger Casement." Emmet crops up again in an October 1919 meeting in Chicago, when Garvey referred to his own personal persecution by the authorities. "If necessary," Garvey said, "I will spend 20 years in the same jail for the Universal Negro Improvement Ass'n. When I think of [Eugene V.] Debs, of Robert Emmet, the sacrifices they have made, there is no sacrifice that I will not make for four hundred million negroes."[22]

For Garvey 1920 would become a banner year. In late February 1919, somewhere between five and six thousand Irish Americans congregated in Philadelphia for the third Irish Race Convention. Garvey must have watched these proceedings closely, for by then he was a seasoned student of the "symbols and stages of the quest for Irish independence." He would have seen how the Irish were bringing others into their cause by having a Presbyterian Socialist, an outspoken Episcopalian minister, and a high-profile Jewish rabbi on the dais. But even more significantly, he would have seen how a fundraising drive was launched, with a million and a half dollars pledged within thirty minutes. Writing in the 1 March edition of the *Negro World* within days of the close of the Irish gathering, Garvey paid the Irish the ultimate compliment by publishing a call for a UNIA "International Convention" to start on 1 August 1920. This development marked an important moment for Garvey. He was aware that he had made significant inroads in organizing his movement and that his activities were inspired by those around him, not least by the anti-imperialist efforts of the Irish. Garvey recalled how, for many months, he spoke on the corners of Lennox Avenue, "and when I started to talk about the larger matters of the race they said I was a crazy man. They called me all kinds of names." He decided "to see the matter through because just at that time other races were engaged in seeing their cause through—the Jews through the Zionist movement and the Irish through their movement. . . . And thank God, after two years of campaigning and agitation, we are three million strong tonight." In June 1920, Garvey announced his own two-million-dollar convention fund, invoking the Irish counterpart: "If Germany is to follow the Kaiser, if England is to follow George V, if Italy is to follow Emanuel, if France if to follow its President, and Ireland is to follow De Valera, then the time has come for four hundred million Negroes to follow a Negro elected by themselves."[23]

The much-anticipated UNIA convention opened on 1 August 1920 "amid great pomp in Madison Square Garden." The convention commenced with a dramatic announcement from Garvey, who held in his hand a telegram to be sent to Éamon de Valera. The text read, "25,000 Negro delegates assembled in Madison Square Garden in mass convention, representing 400,000,000 Negroes of the world, send you greetings as President of the Irish Republic. Please accept sympathy of Negroes of the world for your cause." The telegram continued, "We believe Ireland should be free even as Africa shall be free for the Negroes of the world. (loud applause) Keep up the fight for a free Ireland. Marcus Garvey, President-General of the Universal Negro Improvement Association. (applause)." Increasingly, de Valera was being referred to as the provisional president of Ireland. On 30 August, Garvey was elected "provisional president of Africa," while a banner during the closing ceremony was emblazoned, "A President for Ireland, Why not One for Africa?"[24]

## Conclusion

Marcus Garvey was not the first Black leader inspired by Ireland. Frederick Douglass's 1845 sojourn in Ireland shaped his abolitionist ideology and activism around abolitionism. Many of Garvey's contemporaries, including (as explored in the preceding chapter) W. E. B. Du Bois, Hubert Harrison, and Claude McKay, also had an eye on Ireland. Garvey's encounters and interest in Ireland were galvanized by the dual and interrelated reach of empire and diaspora. For Garvey, Ireland, Jamaica, and Africa were connected to one another as components of the British Empire and as exponents of a diaspora nationalism espoused most visibly in New York City. An appreciation of how Ireland influenced Garvey, whose rhetoric and activism made the example of Ireland resonate throughout the Caribbean, Black America, and Africa, enriches the global dimensions of Irish history, while an Irish reading of Garvey also complements recent scholarship that has sought to place the impact of Garveyism in a more global framework, thereby counterbalancing Garvey's marginalization within American historiographical debates.[25]

To be sure, Ireland was not the only place that provided a roadmap for Garvey, as Hill's research on the influence of Jews and Palestine shows. But Hill's own observation, which serves as the epigraph to this chapter, reminds us of the significance of the Irish to this famous Jamaican. Garvey truly saw his work as a struggle akin to that of the Irish. One of his confidants compared him to Ireland's national icon: "The same courage which St. Patrick showed in defying the pagan gods of Ireland Marcus Garvey shows in defying Anglo-Saxon caste prejudice." And it is clear that there is much more research to be done, as is implied by Caribbean scholar Clem Sheechran during a lecture on Garvey's mentor Dr. Robert Love: "We haven't quite understood the extent to which the Irish nationalist struggle influenced, not only what happened [here] in the Caribbean, but [also] what happened in India and what happened later on in the African continent." Garvey is a dynamic case study in this vein.[26]

In the summer of 2020, in the aftermath of the brutal police killing of George Floyd, the Black Lives Matter movement became a worldwide phenomenon. The Pan-African flag, a horizontal tricolor of red, black, and green, experienced a resurgence at many of the protest marches. It had also been a symbol during the Black Liberation era of the 1960s. The flag was first adopted during the August 1920 UNIA convention, and while Garvey often asserted that the green color alluded to the abundance of Africa, he also presented the color choice as a nod to Ireland. That the American Irish continued to play a prominent role in policing the protests was not the least of the ironies in 2020. A Black Jamaican with an Irish name, even in death, was still providing symbolism for a wave of activism that divided some Irish Americans from African Americans, while it also brought other members of both groups together in the name of racial justice.

NOTES

I am grateful to Professor Kevin Kenny for reading this chapter in draft form and for making valuable suggestions.

1  Robert A. Hill, ed., *The Marcus Garvey and Universal Negro Improvement Association Papers*, 2 vols. (Berkeley: University of California Press, 1983), 1:lxx.

2  Hon. P. J. Patterson in "Marcus Garvey, a Virtual Forum: 100th Anniversary
   Convention of the Negro Peoples of the World," 1 Aug. 2020, www.youtube.com/
   watch?v=Rq8lEWUZzpI; Ronald J. Stephens and Adam Ewing, eds., *Global Garvey-
   ism* (Gainesville: University Press of Florida, 2019), 1; Erez Manela, *The Wilsonian
   Moment: Self-Determination and the International Origins of Anticolonial Nationalism*
   (Oxford: Oxford University Press, 2007), 4; ibid.; Patterson, Convention; *Gaelic
   American*, 14 Aug. 1920.

3  Tony Martin, *Race First: The Ideological and Organizational Struggles of Marcus Garvey and the Universal Negro Improvement Association* (Baltimore: Black Classic Press,
   1976), 3–4; Hill, *Marcus Garvey*, 1:xxxvi; Colin Grant, *Negro with a Hat: The Rise
   and Fall of Marcus Garvey* (Oxford: Oxford University Press, 2008), 3; ibid.; Martin,
   *Race First*, 13; ibid.

4  Grant, *Negro with a Hat*, 74; E. David Cronon, *Black Moses: The Story of Marcus
   Garvey and the Universal Negro Improvement Association* (1955; Madison: University
   of Wisconsin Press, 1969), 19–20; Martin, *Race First*, 11, ibid., Robert A. Hill, "Black
   Zionism: Marcus Garvey and the Jewish Question," in *African Americans and Jews in
   the Twentieth Century: Studies in Convergence and Conflict*, ed. V. P. Franklin, Nancy
   L. Grant, Harold M. Kletnick, and Genna Rae McNeil (Columbia: University of
   Missouri Press, 1998), 41; Manela, *Wilsonian Moment*, x.

5  "Garbh" means rough in Irish. See Edward MacLysaght, *The Surnames of Ireland*, 6th
   ed. (Newbridge: Irish Academic Press, 1985); Hill, *Marcus Garvey*, 1:12; ibid., 1:40.

6  Grant, *Negro with a Hat*, 13; ibid., 9; Rupert Lewis, *Marcus Garvey* (Jamaica: Univer-
   sity of the West Indies Press, 2018), 2 and 18; Hill, *Marcus Garvey*, 1:xl; Lewis, *Marcus
   Garvey*, 1; Cynthia Wilmott, "James Gall: A Maverick in Journalism," *Jamaica
   Journal* 19, no. 2 (1986): 19, 23; Hill, *Marcus Garvey*, 1:533.

7  Hill, *Marcus Garvey*, 1:lxxi; ibid., 1:lxxi; Lewis, *Marcus Garvey*, 18.

8  Grant, *Negro with a Hat*, 24; Hill, *Marcus Garvey*, 1:35, Martin, *Race First*, 5; Grant,
   *Negro with a Hat*, 54; ibid., 35; Hill, *Marcus Garvey*, 1:35; Grant, *Negro with a Hat*,
   36; ibid., 44; Hill, *Marcus Garvey*, 1:lxxii.

9  Hill, *Marcus Garvey*, 1:68, 75, 152, and 159; Martin, *Race First*, 24; Hill, *Marcus Garvey*, 1:152; ibid., 1:70; ibid., 1:91–92; ibid.; ibid., 1:105; ibid., 1:163.

10 Chad L. Williams, *Torchbearers of Democracy: African American Soldiers in the World
   War 1 Era* (Chapel Hill: University of North Carolina Press, 2010), 6; Grant, *Negro
   with a Hat*, 63; ibid., 97; Hill, *Marcus Garvey*, 1:322; ibid., 1:315.

11 *The Gaelic American*, 11 Mar. 1916; Seumas McManus, *The Story of the Irish Race:
   A Popular History of Ireland* (New York: Devin-Adair Company, 1921); M. Alison
   Kibler, *Censoring Racial Ridicule: Irish, Jewish, and African American Struggles over
   Race and Representation, 1890–1930* (Chapel Hill: University of North Carolina Press,
   2015), 3–5; John B. Duff, "The Versailles Treaty and the Irish-Americans," *Journal of
   American History* 55, no. 3 (1968): 594–595.

12 Grant, *Negro with a Hat*, 83; ibid., 93; Hill, *Marcus Garvey*, 1:499–500; ibid., 1:301.

13 Hill, *Marcus Garvey*, 1:292; ibid., 1:299; ibid., 1:310; Manela, *Wilsonian Moment*,
   12; Duff, "Versailles Treaty," 587; ibid., 597; ibid., 589; Bernadette Whelan, *United*

*States Foreign Policy and Ireland: From Empire to Independence, 1913–29* (Dublin: Four Courts Press, 2006), 242.

14 Michael J. Pfeifer, "Mary Turner and the Memory of Lynching," *Journal of American History* 99, no. 2 (2012): 629–630.

15 Grant, *Negro with a Hat*, 101; Hill, *Marcus Garvey*, 1:303; Grant, *Negro with a Hat*, 86; Hill, *Marcus Garvey*, 1:332; ibid.; see Cameron McWhirter, *Red Summer: The Summer of 1919 and the Awakening of Black America* (New York: Henry Holt, 2011); Hill, *Marcus Garvey*, 1:461; ibid., 1:355.

16 Hill, *Marcus Garvey*, 1:355.

17 Ibid., 1:151.

18 Hill, *Marcus Garvey*, 2:478, ibid., 2:416–417.

19 Ibid., 1:lxxv; see Kevin Kenny, "Éamon de Valera," in *Serendipitous Adventures with Britannia: Personalities, Politics and Culture in Britain*, ed. Wm. Roger Louis (London: I.B. Tauris, 2019), 30–44; Grant, *Negro with a Hat*, 75; David McCullagh, "De Valera in America," 1 Sept. 2020 (Century Ireland), www.rte.ie; Hill, *Marcus Garvey*, 1:lxxiv; Chris McNickle, "When New York Was Irish and After," in *The New York Irish History*, ed. Ronald H. Bayor and Timothy J. Meagher (Baltimore: Johns Hopkins University Press, 1996), 337.

20 *Gaelic American*, 11 Mar. 1916; Hill, *Marcus Garvey*, 1:374; ibid., 1:248, 282; ibid., 1:lxxi, 411; ibid., 1:lxxiii.

21 For example, Dr. Gertrude B. Kelly used Carnegie Hall for a rally of Irish women in March 1914. See Miriam Nyhan Grey, "Dr. Gertrude B. Kelly and the Founding of New York's Cumann na mBan," in *Ireland's Allies: America and the 1916 Easter Rising*, ed. Miriam Nyhan Grey (Dublin: University College Dublin Press, 2016), 78; Hill, *Marcus Garvey*, 1:499; ibid., 1:502.

22 Hill, *Marcus Garvey*, 1:472; ibid., 2:57. Debs was an American socialist leader who was incarcerated in 1918.

23 Duff, "Versailles Treaty," 587; Grant, *Negro with a Hat*, 198; Duff, "Versailles Treaty," 587; ibid.; Hill, *Marcus Garvey*, 1:384; ibid., 2:235–236; ibid., 2:374.

24 Hill, *Marcus Garvey*, 1:lxxiv; ibid., 2:499; ibid., 1:lxxiv, lxxv.

25 Christin Kinealy, *Frederick Douglass and Ireland: In His Own Words* (New York: Routledge, 2018); Mathew Pratt Guterl, "The Irish Rebellion That Resonated in Harlem," 25 Mar. 2016, https://newrepublic.com; Adam Ewing and Ronald J. Stephens, "Introduction," in Stephens and Ewing, *Global Garveyism*, 2.

26 See Hill, "Black Zionism," 40–41; Hill, *Marcus Garvey*, 1:lxx and lxxiii; Clem Sheechran, "Dr. Robert Love: Early West Indian Intellectuals and Their Focus on a Free Press and Civil Liberties, Part 2" (2014), www.youtube.com/watch?v=4vA9Eoy8hWA&t=54s.

# ABOUT THE EDITORS

Patrick Mannion is a historian of the Irish diaspora based in St. John's, Newfoundland, Canada. His most recent academic position was as Research Fellow in Irish History at the University of Edinburgh, and his first book, *A Land of Dreams: Ethnicity, Nationalism, and the Irish in Newfoundland, Nova Scotia, and Maine, 1880–1923*, was published in 2018.

Fearghal McGarry is Professor of Modern Irish History at Queen's University Belfast. A member of the Royal Irish Academy, he is the author of *The Abbey Rebels of 1916: A Lost Revolution* (2015) and *The Rising: Ireland: Easter 1916* (2010). With Darragh Gannon, he edited the recently published interdisciplinary volume *Ireland 1922: Independence, Partition, Civil War*.

# ABOUT THE CONTRIBUTORS

DAVID BRUNDAGE is Professor of History at the University of California, Santa Cruz and the author of *Irish Nationalists in America: The Politics of Exile, 1798–1998* (2016). His current book project is titled *New York against Empire: Challenging British Colonialism in a Time of War and Revolution, 1910–1927*.

MARTYN FRAMPTON is Reader in Modern History at Queen Mary University of London. His initial research focused on Irish Republicanism and "the Troubles" in Northern Ireland and produced three books, including *Legion of the Rearguard: Dissident Irish Republicanism* (2011). Since then his research agenda has evolved to consider histories of empire, Anglo-American foreign policy, and Islamism. His most recent book is *The Muslim Brotherhood and the West: A History of Enmity and Engagement* (2018).

DARRAGH GANNON is Lecturer in Irish Studies at University College Dublin and ICUF Beacon Fellow at the University of Toronto. He has published widely on the global Irish diaspora and the Irish Revolution, including *Proclaiming a Republic: Ireland, 1916 and the National Collection* (2016), *Conflict, Diaspora and Empire: Irish Nationalism in Great Britain, 1912–1922* (2022), and (with Fearghal McGarry) *Ireland 1922: Independence, Partition, Civil War* (2022). He is currently preparing a monograph for publication titled *Worlds of Revolution: Ireland's "Global Moment," 1919–1923*.

MIRIAM NYHAN GREY has been on the faculty at New York University since 2009, teaching an array of classes on Irish history, oral history, and comparative migration history. She has an interest in the intersections of migration, race, and ethnicity, focusing on immigrant and ethnic experiences in comparative frameworks. The founder of the

Black, Brown and Green Voices project, which amplifies the voices of Black and Brown Irish Americans, she is on the board of the African American Irish Diaspora Network.

DÓNAL HASSETT is Lecturer in the French Department in University College Cork, specializing in colonial history. His first book, *Mobilizing Memory: The Great War and the Language of Politics in Colonial Algeria, 1918–1939*, appeared in 2019. His research explores issues of colonial commemoration, memory, and heritage as well as examining veterancy in colonial contexts and, more recently, links between Ireland and Algeria.

HEATHER JONES is Professor of Modern and Contemporary European History in the Department of History at University College London. She is the author of *Violence Against Prisoners of War in the First World War: Britain, France and Germany, 1914–1920* (2011) and *The British Monarchy and the First World War* (2021).

ANNA LIVELY is a history PhD candidate at the University of Edinburgh, funded by the Scottish Graduate School of Arts and Humanities. Her PhD research looks at transnational connections between Russia and Ireland, 1905 to 1923. She has co-authored two articles with Dr. Matthew Rendle on the centenary of the Russian Revolution in *Historical Research* (2017) and *History and Memory* (forthcoming).

BREANDÁN MAC SUIBHNE is Professor at the National University of Ireland, Galway, where he directs Acadamh na hOllscolaíochta Gaeilge. He is a historian of society and culture in modern Ireland, and his publications include *The End of Outrage: Post-Famine Adjustment in Rural Ireland* (2017) and *Subjects Lacking Words? The Grey Zone of the Great Famine* (2017). He was a founding editor, with critic Seamus Deane, of *Field Day Review* (2005–), and with David Dickson, he edited Hugh Dorian's *The Outer Edge of Ulster: A Memoir of Social Life in Nineteenth-Century Donegal* (2000).

ELIZABETH McKILLEN is Bird and Bird Professor of History at the University of Maine. She is author of *Making the World Safe for Workers:*

*Labor, the Left, and Wilsonian Internationalism* (2013), *Chicago Labor and the Quest for a Democratic Diplomacy: 1914–1924* (1995), and many articles in labor, diplomatic, and Irish diaspora history.

MICHAEL SILVESTRI is Professor of History at Clemson University. He is the author of *Ireland and India: Nationalism, Empire and Memory* (2009) and *Policing "Bengali Terrorism" in India and the World: Imperial Intelligence and Revolutionary Nationalism, 1905–1939* (2019) and a co-author of *Britain Since 1688: A Nation in the World* (2014).

# INDEX